THE BOOK OF CHARACTER

The Book of Character

Writings on Character and Virtue from Islamic and Other Sources

Selected and Edited by
Camille Adams Helminski

The Book Foundation
Watsonville, California
Bristol, England

THE BOOK FOUNDATION
www.thebook.org

Publication Design by Threshold Productions.
Cover Design by Kabir Helminski.
Special Thanks to Talal and Nadia Zahid for their support.

First Book Foundation edition published 2004.

British Library Cataloguing in Publication Data
A catalogue record of this book is available from the British Library

Library of Congress Cataloging-in-Publication Data
The Book of Character / Selected and Edited by Camille Adams Helminski
Bath, England: The Book Foundation, 2004.

ISBN 1-904510-09-4
Includes bibliographical references.
I. Islam II. Ethics
I. Camille Adams Helminski II. The Book Foundation

Acknowledgments

The editor wishes to thank Charles Upton for his diligent efforts in beginning the research for the Book of Character and for his many contributions, and Jeremy and Tania Henzell-Thomas for their gracious editorial assistance. We also wish to thank Subhana Ansari for her careful and dedicated assistance with transliteration, copyediting, and indexing of the manuscript; Mahmoud Mostafa for his kind assistance with Arabic terminology; Marjorie Wolfe for her valiantly persistent, careful, and patient help with permissions; Hamida Battla for her continuously gracious support; and the generosity of all the publishers of works that have been excerpted who are noted on the intial pages of the selections quoted. May God forgive us for our mistakes and grant good fruitfulness.

Notes on Translation

In most cases we have attempted to transliterate Arabic words as they are pronounced. In quoted material, the spelling may vary according to the custom of the author. Throughout this book, references to the Qurʾān are in brackets. These refer to the name of the *sūrah,* the *sūrah* number, and verse (*āyah*). The first time the Prophet Muḥammad ﷺ is mentioned in a paragraph, his mention is followed by the calligraphic symbol for *ṣalla Allāhu ʿalayhi wa sallam,* "May the peace and blessings of Allāh be upon him." When Muḥammad's companions are mentioned, they are followed with the symbol for *raḍīallāhu ʿanhu* (may Allāh be pleased with him) or *raḍīallāhu ʿanha* (may Allāh be pleased with her). In material that is being quoted, we have used the symbols to replace these blessings, but have not added them if they were not present in the original text.

When quoting the Qurʾān or referring in the text to God, exalted is He, we have used the masculine pronoun. Please be aware that this is merely a limitation of language and that within the universe and understanding of the Qurʾān, God is without gender and far beyond any words or manner by which we might try to describe Him/Her. *Subḥān Allāhi Rabb il-ʿālamīn!*

Table of Contents

Preface 1

I. Our Essential Nature; Essential Faith; Trustworthiness, Truthfulness, and Sincerity

Our Essential Nature (*Fiṭrah*) 8

The Soul's Longing 10

Muḥammad 15

Essential Faith (*Īmān*) 21

Khadījah 26

Trust, Trustworthiness, Truthfulness, Sincerity (*Tawwakul, Amānah, Ṣidq, Ikhlāṣ*) 30

Abū Bakr 37

The Shield of Trust 42

II. Repentance, Taking account, and Forgiveness

Repentance (*Tawbah*) 46

He Frowned 51

Accountability and Responsibility (*Iḥtisāb* and *Mas*ᶜ*ūliyyah*) 56

Paying our Debts 59

Forgiveness (*Ghufrān*) 61

III. Compassion, Mercy, and Charity

Compassion (*Raḥmāniyyah*) 68

St. Francis and the Wolf of Gubbio 72

Mother Teresa 73

The Shifa Clinic 77

Mercy (*Rahīmiyyah*) 79

The Mercy of the Prophet 84

ᶜAlī 86

Charity (*Tazkiyyah*) 93

Fāṭimah 100

IV. PATIENCE, PERSEVERANCE, AND FORBEARANCE
PATIENCE (*Ṣabr*) 108
The Desert of Waiting 110
PERSEVERANCE (*Thabāt*) 123
It's Not About the Bike 127
FORBEARANCE (*Ḥilm*) 132
Bilāl 136
He Who Seeks the Truth Chooses the Good and Holds it Fast 137

V. MODESTY, DISCRETION, AND HUMILITY
MODESTY (*Ḥayā*ᶜ) 144
Principles for the Musician 147
DISCRETION (*Ḥusn at-Tadbīr*) 150
HUMILITY (*Tawāḍu*ᶜ) 155
ᶜUmar 159
Humility Opens Us to God's Grace 160
The Humility of Muḥammad 162
Muḥammad's Visit to Hilāl 163
Flow Like Water 166

VI. PURITY (*ṬAHĀRAH*): PURIFICATION OF THE HEART, OF THE MIND, AND OF THE BODY (PHYSICAL CLEANLINESS, MODERATION IN EATING, PHYSICAL DISCIPLINE, AND SPORTS)
PURIFICATION OF THE HEART (*Taṭ-hīr ul-Qalb*) 168
Purifying the Heart of a Prophet 174
PURIFICATION OF THE MIND (*Taṭ-hīr ul-ᶜAql*) 177
The Truthful Friend 184
Be Impeccable with Your Word 186
PURIFICATION OF THE BODY (*Taṭ-hīr ul-Badan*) 191
Archery 198
Zen in the Art of Archery 200

VII. CLARITY (*WUḌŪḤ*): INTENTION, DISCERNMENT, AND TRUE KNOWLEDGE
INTENTION (*Niyyah*) 206

The Blossoming Light of the Mind 211
DISCERNMENT OF TRUE AND FALSE (*Furqān*) 217
Surah Tā Hā: "O Humankind" 228
TRUE KNOWLEDGE (*ᶜIlm ul-Ḥaqq*) 235
The Soul is the Perceiver and Revealer of Truth 242
The Journey Towards Full Knowledge of the Self 244

VIII. GRATEFULNESS, GENEROSITY, AND KINDNESS
GRATEFULNESS (*Shukr*) 248
GENEROSITY (*Karam*) 254
Red Brocade 263
Giving of What We Love 264
Truly, with Every Difficulty Comes Ease 267
KINDNESS (*Ṭībah*) 269
Keeping Appointments 274
Visiting Manners 275

IX. RESPONSIVENESS—FAITHFUL AND RIGHT ACTION (*AL-IJĀBA—AL-ĪMĀN WA ᶜAMAL UṢ-ṢĀLIḤĀT*): CREATIVITY AND BEAUTY; STRENGTH, COURAGE, AND VIGILANT AWARENESS; JUSTICE AND CONFLICT RESOLUTION 280
CREATIVITY AND BEAUTY (*Badāᶜah* and *Jamāl*) 282
Truth is Beauty and Beauty is Truth 287
Eternal Beauty 288
Centering Clay 291
COURAGE, STRENGTH, AND VIGILANT AWARENESS (*Shajā'ah, Quwwah,* and *Taqwā*) 295
Wrestling 304
JUSTICE AND CONFLICT RESOLUTION (*ᶜAdl* and *Iṣlāḥ*) 307
The Rebuilding of the Kaᶜbah 319
Seeking a Language of Spirit 320
Using Truth-Force 321

X. CONTENTMENT, LOVE, AND INNER PEACEFULNESS
CONTENTMENT (*Riḍā, Qanāᶜah*) 328
The Guest House 332

Happiness 334
Love (*Ḥubb*) 340
Brotherly Love 350
Inner Peacefulness (*Sakīnah*) 353
Peace as a Triumph of Principles 358

XI. Courtesy, Chivalry, and Noble Character
Courtesy (*Ādāb*) 362
Watch for the Unity 372
Laws of the Khwajagan 374
Chivalry (*Futuwwah*) 376
May Chivalry Endure 381
The True Hero or Heroine 383
Noble Character (*Akhlāq*) 386
Rightful Dignity 388
Muḥammad's Farewell Pilgrimage 392
The Ideal Human Being 392
A Prophet's Qualities 395

Appendix: Supplemental Biographies
ʿĀʾishah 397
ʿUmar 404
Rābiʿa 412
Lady Nafīsa 416
Saladin 422
Al-Ghazālī 424
Jalālu'ddin Rūmī 428
Florence Nightingale 431
Martin Luther King 437
Samiha Ayverdi 444

Bibliography 449

Index 457

Preface

Truly, in the Messenger of God
you have a beautiful standard
for anyone whose hope is in God and the Last Day
and who remembers God unceasingly.
[*Sūrah al-Aḥzāb* 33:21]

And indeed, after the reminding,
We wrote in all the books of wisdom:
"My righteous servants shall inherit the earth."
Truly, in this is a Message
for people who would worship God.
We have sent you as a mercy for all creatures.
Say: "What has come to me by inspiration
is that your God is One God:
will you then surrender yourselves to Him?"
[*Sūrah al-Anbiyāʿ* 21:105-108]

Consider the soul and the order and proportion given to it,
and its enlightenment as to that which is wrong and right:
truly, the one who purifies it shall reach a happy state
and the one who corrupts it shall truly be lost!
[*Sūrah ash-Shams* 91:7-10][1]

The Prophets, peace and blessings be upon them all, are gifted to humanity by our Most Gracious Sustainer and enjoined with a responsibility to convey a Way of Being in response to a need that wells up

[1] The above quotes from the Qurʾān and those that preface each chapter are either excerpted from *The Light of Dawn, A Daybook of Verses from the Holy Qurʿān*, selected and rendered by Camille Adams Helminski, or are based upon the verses from Muhammad Asad's *The Message of the Qurʿān*.

within a community. The *dīn*, the Way, the primordial religion has been repeatedly revealed in new unfoldings in response to the need of humankind. These messengers come to us as human beings like ourselves, yet shining brightly with the Light of Divine inspiration as a grace and a mercy to draw us closer to the Truth.

Fourteen hundred years ago the Prophet Muḥammad ﷺ conveyed the revelation of the Qurʾān renewing the monotheistic religion of Abraham and bringing together the law of the Prophet Moses and the love of Jesus into the manifestation of a harmonious way of life balanced within nature and all realms of human society. Muḥammad is referred to as the "seal of the prophets," the confirmation and completion of prophethood, so we should be able to find in the Book that he conveyed, and the example of his life and ways of being, the keys to being and behavior in our own time as well. As we question what it really means to be a human being and what the finest proportion of character for a human being is, we can look to both the words of the revelation, the Qurʾān, and the example and sayings of Muḥammad for instruction, inspiration, and guidance.

In one of the earliest surahs, God speaks to Muhammad, ﷺ reassuring him, *Truly, you are of the noblest of character!* [*Sūrah al-Qalam* 68:4]

Regarding Muḥammad ﷺ, Umm Maᶜbad al-Khuzāᶜiyya said:

> I saw him to be a man of evident cleanliness, fine in character, his face handsome, slim in form, his head not too small, elegant and good looking, his eyes large and black, his eyebrows long, his voice deep, very intelligent, his eyelids brown, his brows high and arched, his hair in plaits, his neck long and his beard thick. He gave an impression of dignity when silent and of high intelligence when he talked. His logic was impressive, he was decisive, not trivial, not trite, his ideas like pearls moving on their string. He seemed the most splendid and fine-looking man from a distance and the very best of all from close-by, medium in height, the eye not finding him too tall nor too short. A tree-branch, as it were, between two others, but he was the finest-

looking of the three, the best proportioned. He was the centre of his companions' attention. When he spoke, they listened well, and if he ordered, they hurried to obey, a man well helped, well served, never sullen, never refuted."[2]

When ʿĀʾishah was asked what Muḥammad ﷺ was like, she replied that he was the living Qurʾān.

ʿAlī describes the Prophet ﷺ:

God's Messenger was the most generous of people in giving out and the mildest and foremost of them in patience and perseverance. He was the most truthful of people in speech, and the most amiable and congenial in companionship and the noblest of them in family. Whoever sees him first is striken by awe of him but whoever knows him closely is attracted to him deeply, and whoever attempts to describe him says: "I have, either before him or after him, never seen the like of him, upon him be peace and blessings."[3]

[Ibn Kathīr comments] that when first built, the mosque of the Prophet ﷺ had no *minbar*[4] from which to address the congregation. He would speak while leaning against a palm tree trunk in the wall next to the *qibla* near where he prayed. Eventually he began to use a *minbar*. . . . As he moved over towards it to make his address from it and passed by that tree trunk, it

[2] Imām Abū'l-Fidāʾ Ismāʿil ibn Kathīr, *The Life of the Prophet Muḥammad,* translated by Prof. Trevor Le Gassick (Reading, United Kingdom: Garnet Publishing Limited, 1998, 2000), Vol. II, p. 172. This and other excerpts from *The Life of the Prophet Muhammad* included within this volume are reprinted by permission from Garnet Publishing.

[3] M. Fethullah Gulen, *Prophet Muḥammad, the Infinite Light* (London: Truestar London, Ltd., 1996, http://www.fgulen.org), Vol. II, p. 147.

[4] A *minbar* is a pulpit from which the *imām* gives a short sermon, at times such as Friday midday prayers. Usually it is a moveable staircase. The first *minbar* of the prophet had three steps.

moaned like a love-lorne camel because it had always heard his speeches delivered near itself. And so the Prophet ﷺ returned to it and hugged it until it settled down, just like a baby, and became quiet. Details of this will be given hereafter through various lines, from Sahl b. Saᶜd al-Saᶜidi, Jābir, ᶜAbd Allāh b. ᶜUmar, ᶜAbd Allāh b. ᶜAbbās, Anas b. Mālik, and Umm Salama, God be pleased with them.

What more appropriate than the comment made by Al-Ḥasan al-Baṣrī after relating this story, from Anas b. Mālik, "O Muslims! A piece of wood so pining for the Messenger of God ﷺ! Do not men hoping to meet him have even more right to yearn for him?"[5]

The human being can have nothing
but that for which he strives.
[*Sūrah an-Najm* 53:39]

The Prophet was asked what was the best thing a Muslim could be given, and he replied, "Good character."[6]

Aṣ-Ṣādiq relates that a man came to the Prophet saying, "O Messenger of Allāh, which people have the most perfect faith?" "Those of them who have the best character," he replied.[7]

It is related on his [Aṣ-Ṣādiq's] authority that the Messenger of Allāh said, 'Most of my people who gain entry to the Garden will gain entry by having *taqwā* (fearful awareness of Allāh) and good character.'[8]

With the example of the Prophet Muḥammad ﷺ before us and the

---

[5] Ibn Kathīr, *The Life of the Prophet Muḥammad,* Vol. II, p. 205.

[6] Shaykh Fadhlalla Haeri, *Prophetic Traditions of Islam: On the Authority of the Family of the Prophet* (London, United Kingdom: Zahra Publications, 1999), p. 164 (*al-Khisāl*, I, 30). This and other excerpts from *Prophetic Traditions of Islam* included within this volume are reprinted by permission of Zahra Publications.

[7] Ibid., p. 164 (*Mishkāt*, 221-224).

[8] Ibid.

light of the Qur'ān to guide us, may we strive towards the meeting with our Lord. May we find ourselves in the best possible condition when we come to meet our Maker, our most Trusted, Most Compassionate, and Truest Friend.

I.

Our Essential Nature, Essential Faith, Trustworthiness, Truthfulness, and Sincerity

Our Essential Nature
(*Fiṭrah*)

In the Name of God, the Infinitely Compassionate and Most Merciful
Consider the fig and the olive, and Mount Sinai,
and this city of security!
Truly, We have created human beings in the best proportion.
Then We reduce them to the lowest of the low—
except those who have faith and act rightly:
For they shall have an unceasing reward!
What, then, could from now on cause you to deny this moral law?
Is not God the Wisest of Judges?
[*Sūrah at-Tīn*, 95:1-8 complete]

Always remember the blessings
which God has bestowed on you,
and the solemn pledge by which He bound you to Himself
when you said, "We have heard, and we pay heed."[9]
And so, remain conscious of God:
truly, God has full knowledge of what is within hearts.
[*Sūrah al-Māᶜidah*, 5:7]

Witness, the only true religion in the sight of God
is self-surrender to Him.
[*Sūrah Āl ᶜImrān*, 3:19]

Say: "My Sustainer has but urged the doing of what is right;
and He wants you to put your whole being into every act of worship,
and to call Him, sincere in your faith in Him alone.
As it was He who brought you into being in the beginning,
so also to Him will you return."
[*Sūrah al-Aᶜrāf*, 7:29]

---

[9] See also *Sūrah Al-Baqarah* 2:285.

> Imām ᶜAlī has said, "Increase your remembrance of Allāh, for it is the best of remembrances, and desire what has been promised to those who live their lives fearing Him—for His promise is the truest of promises. Model yourselves according to your Prophet, for his is the best guidance."[10]

The word "character" in English originally meant a sign, a brand, or a stamp. "A man of that stamp" means a man of this or that particular character. The letters and image stamped on a coin give it its *character*. According to Al-Ghazālī, "A trait of character . . . is a firmly established condition of the soul, from which actions proceed easily without any need of thinking or forethought."

A thing's character is its essence, its true nature. Yet we talk about building human character, as if character were something that could develop over time. If our character is our true nature, isn't it something we were born with? Why do we have to develop it?

To say that someone "has character" means that he or she has taken some real steps toward becoming a true human being. To have character means to be fully formed; to have no character, or a bad character, is to be undeveloped, or developed in an unbalanced way. Just as a body-builder who builds certain muscle groups but not others is not really well developed, someone who develops his mind but not his feelings, or his will but not his mind, will be unbalanced. He will have flaws and weaknesses in his character.

So character is something we have to work on. But we need to develop it on the basis of who we really are as God made us. God "stamped" us with our true character before we were ever born; our job is to develop, to actualize, what God has stamped us with. Just as to "envelop" means to wrap something up, to "develop" means to unwrap something. Character development, then, is the process of *unpacking* what God has provided us for our journey through this world, and into the next. Various experiences during this life may *stamp* us and mold our character. But since all experiences ultimately come from God, everything we encounter in this life is part of God's knowledge of the character

---

[10] Haeri, *Prophetic Traditions in Islām*, p. 101 (*Nahj*, IV, 712).

He has stamped us with, in eternity, before we came into this world.

In Arabic the word for character, with the connotation of good character, is *khuluq*, which is related to the word *khalq*, creation. Character is the form in which God has created us; our responsibility is to live up to it—to conform ourselves, in time, to the shape in which God has created us, in eternity.[11]

The Soul's Longing

The journeys of spiritual teachers of humanity, prophets, and messengers of God towards Truth are eternal sources of inspiration for all souls who long for meaningfulness on all levels. Their experiences enlighten the way of humanity forever. Deep reflections on their journeys could inspire the modern world with so many meanings that our era lacks. Learning from them does not imply going back to the past; it is an invitation to humanity to refresh its memory of how a human being can fulfill his or her humanity with the hope that we might have a better future. Of course we are not to handle the life of great spiritual teachers with the assumption that we would be able to absorb them fully. This is not possible because the part cannot encompass the whole. Even though a drop of the ocean carries its entire characteristics, it can never be the ocean. So, a soul who longs for truth is a glimmer of the Light of great teachers, and with that quality he or she is qualified to derive some wisdom from his or her journey.

The great teachers longed for a truthful life during times when the majority of people were satisfied by a false one. They longed for knowledge during times when ignorance and superstition were overwhelming. They longed for the spreading of peace during times when conflict was commonplace. They longed for the prevailing of justice during times

---

[11] Charles Upton, contributor.

~ "The Soul's Longing," by Aisha Rafea, is excerpted from *Women of Sufism, A Hidden Treasure*, selected and edited by Camille Helminski (Boston, Massachusetts: Shambhala Publications, 2003), pp. 199-204.

when oppression was legitimized. They longed for spiritual freedom while the majority accepted the constraints of matter.

From that perspective, I share with you some reflections on how the Holy Qur᾿ān presented their stories with the focus that all of them sought surrender to Allāh, and thus they are all termed "Muslim." Namely, the word "Islām" is used in the Holy Qur᾿ān with a deeper dimension than a creed to be compared to other creeds, or a set of social or cultural customs and traditions of certain societies who carry this label. Rather, Islām in the Holy Qur᾿ān points to a living Truth that transcends names, labels, languages, and/or religious affiliations. It is the Law of full surrender to Allāh as existentially experienced and sought by all souls who search for a truthful life infinitely. The Revelation to the Prophet Muḥammad ﷺ clarifies that this potential for surrender to Allāh is embedded in the primordial nature of the soul and stamped on its texture since God breathed of His Spirit into humankind. It is what the Holy Qur᾿ān terms "*fiṭrah,*" asserting that if human beings communicated with their *fiṭrah*, it would lead them to the fulfillment of their souls' longing, to life according to the Law of creation. The Prophet Muḥammad ﷺ said, "Islām is the Religion of the Primordial nature (*fiṭrah*). Every newborn baby is born according to *fiṭrah*, then parents give him a name of a religious affiliation (Christianity, Judaism, Magus . . . etc.).[12]

However, to live according to *fiṭrah*; to surrender to Allāh fully, is not taken for granted, for the human soul is susceptible to being imprisoned in the "vessel of clay" of the body with all its limitations, and to forgetfulness about his or her primordial nature (*fiṭrah*). So, living according to *fiṭrah* is an expression of the highest degree of spiritual awareness. It is an objective to be sought, and a fruit of great spiritual struggle. That is to say, Islām as revealed to the Prophet Muḥammad ﷺ clarifies that even though each human soul has a potentiality to feel his or her longing for submission to Allāh by giving the chance to his or her *fiṭrah* or spiritual origin to be awakened, a human soul needs to be liberated from the constraints of matter to be able to communicate with his or her *fiṭrah*.

---

[12] *Fiṭrah* is not to be confused with "instinct" since instinct is related to the attributes of the physical body, while *fiṭrah* is the primordial nature of the soul that carries the spiritual awareness and quality.

The Holy Qur᾽ān reveals that the pure nature (*fiṭrah*) has led great souls to a common Path that has fulfilled their longing. That common Path is a language of a spirit who longs for full surrender to the Eternal Law of Life.

Primordial Nature (*Fiṭrah*) Leads to a Common Path

Even though great teachers of humanity were living in different times and places, and confronted different challenges, they had something in common: 1) a natural deep inner light that made them feel the existence of the Transcendent Supreme, and pushed them to reject the widespread dogmas and practices of their people; 2) they all sought guidance from within and from a higher source, and they prepared themselves to receive that guidance; 3) the Supreme responded to their striving and revealed to them from within and from the Beyond a path by which to lead a truthful life; a path that made of their whole life a language of spirit. They were guided to present the fruit of their experiences to other searching souls.

Rejection of Dogmas

The Holy Qur᾽ān reveals that Prophets can see that people's projection of physical or mental images towards God reflects a direct deficiency of realization and conceptualization of the Supreme Transcendent. As great souls, they can see that such practices lead human beings to being encased in dense layers of falsity through which they can never reach Truth. Prophets are reluctant to be like those people who commit a fatal mistake by being captured in worshiping images of several kinds, those who put limits to what is limitless, and measure what is eternal, absolute, and perfect with the yardstick of what is transient, relative, or imperfect. These lose their link to the really Divine. To take an idol as Divine is not merely an outward practice; it is also an inner attitude of rigidity and stagnation that blocks the human being's capability to be spiritually free. It is an attitude that captures the soul in illusions created by limited existence. From that perspective, we read in the Holy Qur᾽ān that Noah, Abraham, Moses, Jesus, Muḥammad, and most prophets were not satisfied with the dogmas of their time. Abraham, for instance says to his father,

"Takest thou idols for gods? For I see thee and thy people in manifest error." [*Sūrah al-Anʿām* 6:74]. *"O my father! Why worship that which hears not, and sees not, and can profit thee nothing?"* [*Sūrah Maryam* 19:42]

False deities that great souls reject, the Holy Qurʾān clarifies, are not only stone idols, they are stagnant traditions, labels, and dogmas. Joseph, for instance says, *"If not Him, you worship nothing but names which you have named, you and your fathers, for which Allāh has sent down no authority."* [*Sūrah Yūsuf* 12:40]

The Holy Qurʾān quotes prophets criticizing those who stick to blind imitation and bestow divinity on stagnant traditions. Prophets try to direct their attention to that deficiency, but the common response is: *Nay! they say: "We found our fathers following a certain religion, and we do guide ourselves by their footsteps."* [*Sūrah az-Zukhruf* 43:22]

Another false deity that prophets never have worshiped is what the Holy Qurʾān refers to as *hawā*, which means the lust for something of the material realm that a human is apt to adore or bestow an absolute value to. The Holy Qurʾān says to Prophet Muḥammad ﷺ that one who worships his *hawā* is not qualified to discern the truth. *Then do you see the one who takes as his god his own vain desire? Allāh has, knowing [him as such], left him astray, and sealed his hearing and his heart [and understanding], and veiled his sight: Who, then, will guide him after Allāh [has withdrawn guidance]? Will you not then receive admonition?* [*Sūrah al-Jāthiyah* 45:23].

The Holy Qurʾān relates parables of people who were not ready to receive guidance because they were fully involved in worshiping their *hawā*. It gives the parable of Qārūn who lived at the time of Moses and had such a great lust for money that he could feel no divine dimension in life. The Pharaoh at the time of Moses also lusted for authority so much that he made of himself a god, and consequently could not feel the existence of God. In the time of Muḥammad, some people adored physical existence so much that they could not feel any spiritual depth in life. They were so captured within the constraints of matter that the paramount dogma with which they lived in accordance was denial of a coming life: *And they say: "What is there but our life in this world? We shall die and we live, and nothing but Time can destroy us." But of that they have no knowledge; they merely conjecture* [*Sūrah al-Jāthiyah* 45:24]. *No vision can grasp*

Him. But His grasp is over all vision: He is above all comprehension, yet is acquainted with all things [*Sūrah al-Anᶜām* 6:103]. *Glory to Him! He is high above all that they say! Exalted and Great* [*beyond measure*]*!* [*Sūrah al-Isrā* 17:43]. *Praise and glory be to Him!* [*For He is*] *above what they attribute to Him!* [*Sūrah al-Anᶜām* 6:100]. *Glory to Him, and far is He above having the partners they ascribe unto Him!* [*Sūrah an-Naḥl* 16:1]. *There is nothing whatever like unto Him* [*Sūrah ash-Shūrā* 42:11].

The Holy Qurʾān also clarifies that it is part of the *fiṭrah* that the soul is liberated from dogmas and false deity when he believes in the Unseen, *Al-Ghayb*. To believe in the Unseen in the Holy Qurʾān is an inner certainty within a human that makes him sure that whatever he might come to know, there is always more that is beyond the known and the knowable. When this certainty exists, souls do not become imprisoned in dogmas, nor do they bestow divinity on anything in the transient realm. Rather, they continuously move forward towards greater knowledge and freedom ceaselessly.

But how can a human being be liberated from all dogmas and false deities? This takes us to the second point.

Seeking Guidance from Within and from a Higher Source

Since they were not satisfied with other people's practices and approach to life, the prophets began to search within and beyond. They were guided from within to open to listen to what their hearts would tell them. They naturally wanted to distance themselves from the noise of a corrupt life and the negative energy of the overwhelming darkness. They spent time in seclusion purifying the whole of their existence by controlling the physical body's desires. The vibrant *fiṭrah* guided them to allow the divinity within to come to the surface of consciousness. In the meantime, they would also direct their faces to the Supreme Transcendent, seeking guidance from a higher source. We read in the Holy Qurʾān that Abraham said: *I will go to my Lord! He will surely guide me!* [*Sūrah aṣ-Ṣaffāt* 37:99]. *And I will turn away from you* [*all*] *and from those whom you invoke besides Allah: I will call on my Lord* [*Sūrah Maryam* 19:48].

The Holy Qurʾān gives us an example of the search of a soul longing for a source of guidance in the story of the experience of Abraham. The story reveals his longing for his Lord whom he recognizes first in a star, then in the moon, and then in the sun. The moment Abraham came to be fully certain that Allāh transcends any of His manifestations was the very moment he realized that he was receiving guidance and support from his Lord. Namely, Abraham reached a moment of receiving great divine knowledge in which he could realize with no confusion that Allāh is both Unseen and also Manifest because all aspects of nature sign to Him, and also because He manifests Himself to man from within himself as well as all around him. The guidance was not letters or words; it was a superb power of enlightenment that made Truth in Abraham's heart clearer than the rays of the sun. Abraham could evidently discern his own *fiṭrah*, and God's closeness and guidance.

So also did We show Abraham the power and the laws of the heavens and the earth, that he might [with understanding] have certitude. When the night covered him over, he saw a star. He said: "This is my Lord." But when it set, he said: "I love not those that set." When he saw the moon rising in splendour, he said: "This is my Lord." But when the moon set, he said: "Unless my Lord guide me, I shall surely be among those who go astray." When he saw the sun rising in splendour, he said: "This is my Lord; this is the greatest [of all]." But when the sun set, he said: "O my people! I am indeed free from your [guilt] of giving partners to Allāh. For me, I have set my face, firmly and truly, towards Him Who created the heavens and the earth, and never shall I give partners to Allāh." [*Sūrah al-Anʿām* 6:75-79]

Muḥammad

Since Muḥammad ﷺ is the archetype of sainthood, it is in strict conformity to his *sunna*, and by taking nourishment from his example, that the aspirant manages to restore his original nature of *imago Dei*.

"God created Adam in His own image," says a famous *ḥadīth*. Like-

---

~ This selection on Muḥammad is excerpted by permission of the Islamic Texts Society from their publication *Ibn Arabi: The Voyage of No Return* by Claude Addas. English language translation © The Islamic Texts Society 2000, pp. 23-24.

wise, man has virtually all the Divine Names engraved in the very clay of his being. It is because of this divine similitude that God has called him to be His *khalīfa,* his "vicegerent" on earth. "Vicegerency *(khilāfa)* was assigned to Adam, to the exclusion of the other creatures of the universe, because God created him according to His image. A vicegerent must possess the attributes of the one he represents; otherwise he is not truly a vicegerent."[13] But these two favours granted exclusively to man, his divine form and his governance, simultaneously expose him to the greatest danger of his existence: the illusion of sovereignty. As the Shaykh al-Akbar [Ibn al-ᶜArabī] points out on a number of occasions, being conscious of his original theomorphism leads man to forget that he was created from clay—the most humble of substances and a symbol of his "ontological servitude" (*ᶜubūdiyya*). The power and the authority that his mandate grant him lead him to consider himself autonomous. He appropriates sovereignty, which rightfully belongs only to Him Whom he represents and he betrays the oath of vassalage that he made when he replied to the question "Am I not your Lord?" with "Certainly, we are witnesses!"[14]

When he refuses to assume his status as "servant of God" *(ᶜabd Allāh),* he is henceforth unworthy of being "God's vicegerent" *(khalīfat Allāh).* "The homeland of man is his servitude; he who leaves it is forbidden to take on the Divine Names."[15] To regain his original nobility, he must reactivate the divine characteristics inscribed in his primordial form; characteristics that his pretension and ignorance had covered up. The Prophet ﷺ said, "I have come to complete the 'noble character traits'." He who lives in accordance with the "noble character traits" follows a law of God even if he is not aware of it [...] To perfect one's character means to strip it of all that tends to give it a vile status. Actually, vile characteristics are vile only by accident, while noble characteristics are noble by essence, for what is vile has no foundation in the divine [...], while noble characteristics do have foundation in the divine. The Prophet

---

[13] Muḥyīuddīn Ibn al-ᶜArabī, *Futūḥāt I,* p. 263.

[14] *Sūrah Al-Aᶜrāf* 7:172.

[15] Ibn al-ᶜArabī, *Futūḥāt I,* pp. 362, 367.

perfected the noble character traits to the extent that he established the ways through which a character can maintain a noble status and be exempt from a vile status."[16]

★ ★ ★

Consider the soul and the order and proportion given to it,
and its enlightenment as to that which is wrong and right:
truly, the one who purifies it shall reach a happy state
and the one who corrupts it shall truly be lost!
[*Sūrah ash-Shams* 91:7–10].

Muḥammad ﷺ is the Complete Man, *al-Insān al-Kāmil*. He is the exemplar of our *fiṭrah*, of the human form in its original nature as God created it. The love Muslims feel for the person of the Prophet ﷺ has to do with the fullness of his humanity—not in any sentimental sense, but rather because in him is revealed an unfailing and providential capacity to bring out the full humanity of any and every situation, and then act upon it.

In the Islamic view, humanity is both *ᶜabd*, God's servant, and *khalīfah*, God's fully-empowered representative in this world. This is our *fiṭrah*. And our central example of what it is to be *ᶜabd* and *khalīfah* is Muḥammad ﷺ. His submission to God was perfect, not because, like some of the greatest saints, he intensely desired to submit to God in a passionate and self-sacrificial way, but because he was one with the nature of things. According to the nature of things, in the face of the Absolute Reality of God, the creature is as nothing; whatever reality he has is a pure gift from the Absolute Reality, nor can he ever break out of, or wander away from, the sovereign Will of God. Whether or not he submits *willingly*, he always submits *actually*. Muḥammad knew this, and therefore submitted willingly, and perfectly, thus becoming a perfect representative and messenger.[17]

> Not only does the messenger who is a [servant] subordinate his own will to that of his Lord; there is nothing in his mind or

---

[16] Ibn al-ᶜArabī, *Futūḥāt II*, p. 562. This is the close of the selection by Addas.

[17] Charles Upton, contributor.

> in his memory that could obstruct the free passage of revelation. Muḥammad is *ᶜabd* and *rasūl*; he is also *nabī al-ummi*, the unlettered Prophet; a blank page set before the divine pen. On this page there is no mark made by any other pen, no trace of profane or indirect knowledge. A prophet does not borrow knowledge from the human store, nor is he a man who learns in the slow human way and then transmits his learning. His knowledge derives from a direct intervention of the Divine in the human order, a *tajalli*, or pouring out of the truth upon a being providentially disposed to receive it and strong enough to transmit it. The purity of the stream of revelation remains unsullied in its course from the spring which is its origin to the lake into which it flows; in other words, the Qurʾān exists in written form exactly as it issued from the Divine Presence.[18]

It was out of this perfect submission that Muḥammad ﷺ became the complete *khalīfah* of God. He was like a mirror turned to face all of God's Names and Attributes. The mirror itself does nothing, and (as it were) *is* nothing. It is because of this submission, this *Islām*, that all the forms of life can appear within it. The Prophet was a shepherd, a businessman, a caravan-leader, a contemplative, a warrior, a diplomat, a legislator, a judge, a ruler, a man of his clan and his family, a father . . . but he was not thereby a "Renaissance man," a person who seeks diversity of experience for its own sake, who develops and over-develops many and diverse talents because he is basically in flight from his true nature, and from the God who made him. He never departed from his Center in order to develop this or that side, or fragment, of his character. His character was unified, and beautiful, because it reflected the Unity of God.[19]

> Allāh has created the intellect from a stored-up light which was hidden within His fore-knowledge, and neither emissary,

---

[18] Reprinted by permission from *Islam and the Destiny of Man*, p. 64, by Charles Le Gai Eaton, the State University of New York Press © 1985, State University of New York. All rights reserved.

[19] Charles Upton, contributor.

> prophet, nor high-ranking angel has seen it. Then He has made knowledge its self, understanding its spirit, doing-without (*zuhd*) its head, modesty (*ḥayā*ʾ) its eyes, wisdom its tongue, compassion (*raʿfah*) its purpose, and mercy its heart. Then He filled and strengthened it with ten things: certainty, faith, truthfulness, tranquility (*sakīnah*), sincerity, kindness (*rifq*), generosity (*ʿaṭīyyah*), contentment (*qanūʿ*), submission (*taslām*), and patience. Thereupon He spoke to it saying, "Go back," and it went back; "Come forward," and it came forward; then, 'Speak!' and it replied, "Praise belongs to Allāh, Who has neither enemy nor rival, to Whom there is not likeness and no comparison and no equal, before Whose might everything is submissive and humbled."[20]

We develop character by practicing and realizing the *virtues*. The word "virtue" is related to the word "virility" (similar in meaning to *shahama*, manliness.) We used to talk about the "virtues" of herbs and stones—by which we meant their power to heal us, to make us complete. Virtue is power. It is the power to be who we really are, to attain and maintain the human state God has commanded us to embody. The virtues are what allow us to live up to the Trust God has placed upon us, which we as a race have willingly assumed (*Sūrah al-Aḥzāb* 33:72). They are what allow us to be *ʿabd*, God's servant, and *khalīfah*, God's fully-empowered representative in this world—not only in our essential nature, by which we are *ʿabd* and *khalīfah* from all eternity, but consciously and intentionally. Virtue is the power which allows our intent to match our nature.

According to the Qurʾān [*Sūrah al-Fāṭir* 35:15], "*O men! It is you who stand in need of God, whereas He alone is Self-sufficient, the One to Whom all praise belongs.*" Only God is the Rich (*Al-Ghanī*) because Being itself can be attributed only to Him (*Al-Qayyūm*); we are so poor that we can't even claim Being for ourselves. If our very being is a gift from God, we certainly can't attribute any of the virtues to ourselves. All the virtues, all the powers, belong to God alone; they are His Names and Qualities.

---

[20] Haeri, *Prophetic Traditions in Islam*, p. 143.

When we practice a virtue until we have fully embodied it, then our soul has been qualified with the Divine Name which corresponds to that virtue. We have been *stamped* by God with that Name.

Virtues are the actions we must perform in the greater *jihād*, the struggle against the commanding self;[21] but they are also *truths*, penetrating insights, new ways of looking at things. To practice a virtue is to transform our experience of ourselves, society, and our fellow human beings in very specific ways. To acquire a particular virtue is to train ourselves in how to see the signs of a specific Name of God in the world around us.

The virtues, or constellations of virtues, elucidated in this text are clearly visible in the character of Muḥammad ﷺ. . . . There is no virtue, no Name of God, which is not reflected in the character of the Prophet. All virtues are Muslim, just as all virtues are Hindu or Jewish or Christian or Buddhist. But since every revelation of God is unique, Islamic virtue carries its own particular "fragrance," which is unmistakable.[22]

---

[21] *Nafsi ammārah.*

[22] Charles Upton, contributor.

ESSENTIAL FAITH
(*Īmān*)

Such is God, your Sustainer: there is no god but Hu,[23]
the Creator of everything: then worship Him alone—
for it is He who has everything in His care.
No vision can encompass Him, but He encompasses all human vision:
for He alone is Subtle Beyond Comprehension, All-Aware.
Means of insight have now come to you
from your Sustainer[through this divine Message]
Whoever, then, chooses to see,
does so for the benefit of his own soul;
and whoever chooses to remain blind,
does so to his own harm.
[*Sūrah al-Anᶜām* 6:102-104]

The parable of those who take protectors other than God
is that of the spider who builds itself a house;
but truly, the spider's house is the flimsiest of houses
if they only knew.
Truly, your Sustainer knows what they call upon besides Him
and He is Most Exalted, the All-Wise.
And such are the parables We offer humankind
but only those of inner knowing understand them.
In true proportions God created the heavens and the earth:
truly, in that is a sign for those who have faith.
[*Sūrah al-ᶜAnkabūt* 29:41-44]

---

23 Hū: the pronoun of Divine Presence. All words in Arabic have a gender grammatically ascribed to them as they do in French and Spanish, etc. Although Allāh is referred to with the third person masculine pronoun Hū (Huwa), it is universally understood that Allāh's Essence is beyond gender or indeed any qualification, far beyond all our attempts at definition, limitless in subtle glory.

And know that among you is God's Messenger:
were he in many matters to follow your inclinations,
you would surely fall into misfortune;
but God has caused faith to be dear to you,
and has made it beautiful within your hearts,
and He has made hateful to you lack of faith, wickedness,
and rebellion against that which is good.
Such indeed are those who walk in righteousness—
through God's grace and favor;
and God is All-Knowing, Truly Wise.

[*Sūrah al-Ḥujurāt* 49:7-8]

From an early age it seems that Muḥammad ﷺ had a strong sense of connection with his Creator and sought to know His Source better through the witnessing of creation, solitary retreat, and inner listening and prayer. His earliest years were spent in the desert under the care of his foster mother, Ḥalīma. As he grew older, his grandfather, ʿAbd al-Muṭṭalib, and then his uncle, Abū Ṭālib, took him along on trading journeys where he spent many days and nights encompassed by the wide expanse of the desert and the vast dome of sky and stars.

As a young man, Muḥammad ﷺ began to retreat periodically to a cave in the hills overlooking the town of Mecca. Here he would fast during the month of Ramaḍān and deepen in prayer and contemplation, seeking to know better his Creator and to fathom His creation of humankind and worlds within worlds.

Later, after his marriage to Khadījah ﵂, it was here that the revelation of the Qurʾān began to be conveyed:

> This occurred when he was forty years of age. . . . Al-Bukhārī stated that Yaḥyā b. Bukayr related to him . . . from ʿĀʾishah ﵂ who said, "The first indication of revelation to the Messenger of God ﷺ came in the form of true visions in his sleep. Every vision he had came like the breaking of dawn.
>
> "He then developed a liking for solitude. He would spend time alone in the cave Ḥirāʾ, where he would seek religious pu-

rification through devotions. He would stay there many nights and then return to his family for more provisions to continue doing so; then he would come down to Khadījah and repeat the same.

"Eventually the truth came to him while he was there in that cave Ḥirā'. The angel came and told him, 'Read!' He replied, 'I don't read.' He then said, 'The angel then overpowered me and choked me until I could bear it no more, and then he released me. Again he said, 'Read!' Again I replied, 'I don't read.' Once more he overpowered me and choked me till I could bear it no more, then he released me and said, 'Read!' I replied, 'I don't read.' Again he overpowered me and choked me a third time until I could bear it no more. Then he released me and said, '*Read in the name of your Lord who created; He created man from a clot.*[24] *Read! Your Lord is the most noble, He who taught by the pen. He taught man what he did not know*' [*Sūrat al-ᶜAlaq* 96:1-5].

"The Messenger of God ﷺ returned home with this, his heart palpitating. He went in to Khadījah, daughter of Khuwaylid, and said, 'Wrap me up! Wrap me up!' They did so until the terror left him.

"He then spoke to Khadījah, telling her what had happened, saying, 'I was afraid for myself.'

"Khadījah replied, 'Oh no! I swear by God He would never abuse you. You maintain family ties, you are hospitable to guests, you support the weak, provide for the poor, and help out when tragedy strikes.'

"Khadījah then hurried off with him to Waraqa b. Nawfal b. Asad b. ᶜAbd al-ᶜUzzā, who was her cousin. He had earlier become a Christian, and used to write the Hebrew script, copying out from the Bible in Hebrew whatever God inspired him to write. He was an old man by then, and he was blind.

---

[24] *ᶜAlaq,* often translated as "clot" is rather a clinging, connecting substance or hooked cell; it indicates our innate connection with the Divine and subsistence through God, as well as the first moments of life in the womb.

"Khadījah told him, 'O cousin! Listen to your nephew!' Waraqa then addressed him, 'O nephew, what did you see?' The Messenger of God ﷺ then told him what he had seen. Waraqa commented, 'This was the angel Gabriel who used to come down to Moses. How I wish I were a young man again! I hope I am still alive when your people exile you!' The Messenger of God ﷺ exclaimed, 'Are they to exile me?' 'Yes,' he replied, 'no one has ever received what you have without being treated as an enemy. If I am alive when your time comes, I will give you every help.'"[25]

The faithful are those
whose hearts tremble with awe whenever God is mentioned,
and whose faith is strengthened
whenever His signs are conveyed to them,
and who place their trust in their Sustainer—
those who are constant in prayer
and spend on others out of what We provide for them as sustenance:
In truth, these are the faithful!
They shall have stations of dignity with their Sustainer,
and forgiveness, and a most generous provision.
[*Sūrah al-Anfāl* 8:2-4]

The Fear of God manifested by the Prophet Muḥammad ﷺ was not a fear for the future, but rather an awe and terror in the face of God's Majesty in this present moment.[26] According to Anṣārī, "Daqqāq says: 'Awe is a precondition of knowledge of God. As God says, *God warns you to beware of Him* [*Sūrah Āl ʿImrān* 3:28].' (*Resala-ye qoshayriya*). The fear of the elect resides in their awe of Majesty, not in their fear of chastisement. Fear of chastisement is to worry for oneself and one's welfare, but awe of Majesty is reverence for God and forgetfulness of self."[27]

---

[25] Ibn Kathīr, *The Life of the Prophet Muḥammad*, Vol. I, pp. 278-279.

[26] Charles Upton, contributor.

[27] Javad Nurbakhsh, *Sufism II: Fear and Hope, Contraction and Expansion, Gathering and Dispersion, Intoxication and Sobriety, Annihilation and Subsistence,* translated by

We have noticed that there is a shared Path among all revelations and words of wisdom. Teachings are diverse in their means of expression and each revelation has its distinct character but they all guide man to a kind of life where the evolvement of spirit is the focus. They all teach him how to make of his life on earth a fruitful journey where he gains truthful life. We call that Path, Way, Road the Primordial Religion. In all of them man is guided to be on the Path by being linked to the Origin of all existence within and around. He is also taught how to gain real life by turning all aspects of his earthly life into means for his spiritual growth. In other words, revelations guide man to live according to the Eternal Law of Life. The more he evolves spiritually, the more he gets in harmony with the Law, and the more capable he becomes of making his earthly life a profound expression of the spiritual goals.[28]

God is the Protector of those who have faith,
leading them out of the depths of darkness into the light.
[*Sūrah al-Baqarah* 2:257]

The messenger, and the faithful with him,
have faith in what has been revealed to him by his Sustainer:
they all have faith in God, and His angels,
and His revelations, and His messengers,
making no distinction between any of His messengers;
and they say: "We have heard, and we pay heed.
Grant us Your forgiveness, O our Sustainer,
for with You is all journeys' end!"
[*Sūrah al-Baqarah* 2:285]

In the Old Testament, revelations guide man to go beyond diversities in order to see the underlying unity and order. That is the way to realize the existence of the Transcendent Unseen Supreme Power. This Supreme Power is called God. Even though God manifests Himself in His creation, God remains Transcendent, Unknown, and Unseen. If man is

---

William Chittick (London and New York: Khaniqahi Nimatullahi Publications, 1982), p. 3.

[28] Rafea. *Beyond Diversities: Reflections on Revelation* (2000), p. 11.

not aware of that truth, he is either confused between God and His manifestations or distracted by the manifestations and cannot discern the existence of the One Beyond.

Torah means Law; the guidance of Moses led his people to recognize the Divine Law which governs everything. The Ten Commandments themselves reveal the ethical law that is believed to be universal. Moses reveals to his people the epitome of the Law, to know God: "You will find Him if you look for Him." (The Bible, Deuteronomy 4:29)

Allāh is the Omnipresent, yet cannot be seen; He is everywhere and in no particular place.[29]

No vision can grasp Him. But His grasp is over all vision:
He is above all comprehension, yet is acquainted with all things.
[*Sūrah al-Anᶜām* 6:103]

To Allah belong the East and the West:
wherever you turn, there is the face of God.
For Allah is All-Embracing, All-Knowing.
[*Sūrah al-Baqarah* 2:115]

And if My servants ask you about Me—witness, I am near;
I respond to the call of the one who calls,
whenever he calls Me:
let them, then, respond to Me, and have faith in Me,
so that they may follow the right way.
[*Sūrah al-Baqarah* 2:186]

Khadījah

Khadījah bint Khuwaylid was known in the community of Mecca[30] as *aṭ-Ṭāhira,* "the pure one." A woman of great integrity, intelligence,

---

[29] Ibid., p. 25.

~ This biographical sketch of Khadījah is excerpted from *Women of Sufism, A Hidden Treasure*, pp. 5-7, selected and edited by Camille Helminski.

[30] Mecca is the locale where Muḥammad was raised. It is here that the Kaᶜbah is

and spiritual depth, she became the wife of the Prophet Muḥammad, peace and blessings be upon them both, before the responsibility of Prophethood came to him. Before marrying Muḥammad, she had previously been married and widowed, and had developed and been conducting her own business in caravan trade. She was forty years old, when, being aware of Muḥammad's sincere trustworthiness and skillfulness, she hired him to oversee one of her trading caravans. At the time, Muḥammad was twenty-five and of meager financial means. When her caravan returned from a very successful trading venture under his charge, through her cousin Khadījah proposed marriage to Muḥammad. At first Muḥammad was hesitant to believe such a match was possible for someone of his financial state and limited tribal status—he had been orphaned at an early age and taken under the wing of his uncle.[31] However, he was of the noble tribe of the Banū Hāshim, who held the honorable responsibility of providing water to the pilgrims visiting the Kaᶜbah.

Muḥammad accepted Khadījah's offer, and a very happy marriage unfolded. More independent now that he was supported by Khadījah's love as well as her wealth, Muḥammad would often retire to a nearby cave to meditate and pray for long periods. It was here, during the month of Ramaḍān in 610 A.D., that he received the first revelation of the Qur'ān.[32] Overwhelmed and concerned that perhaps he was losing his mind, he rushed home to Khadījah and told her to cover him with a blanket. She held him close and reassured him that a man such as he did

---

located, the temple which was dedicated to the one God by Abraham, and originally, before him, it is said, built by Adam, which was then later cleansed and rededicated by Muḥammad. Mecca is in Saudi Arabia near the Red Sea and is the direction toward which all Muslims turn in prayer five times a day.

[31] The Prophet was born after the death of his father, ᶜAbdullāh ("the servant of the One God"). When he was six, his mother, Āmina, died, and he became the ward of his grandfather, ᶜAbd al-Muṭṭalib. When he was nine, his grandfather also died, and he was taken in by his father's brother, Abū Ṭālib. Abū Ṭālib loved the Prophet dearly and often took him with him on his trading journeys; his wife, Fāṭimah, gave Muḥammad a mother's love. He grew into manhood alongside their sons, including the young ᶜAlī.

[32] *Sūrah Al-ᶜAlaq* 96:1: *"Recite, in the Name of your Sustainer who created. . . ."*

not suddenly go crazy but that indeed what had taken place was a tremendous spiritual experience. She went to her cousin, Waraqa, a Christian who was well-versed in Jewish and Christian prophecy, and he confirmed for her that indeed Muḥammad must be the messenger whose coming was referred to in the Jewish and Christian scriptures and that this must be the opening of his mission as a Prophet. Khadījah was the first to have faith in his mission as a prophet who had come to renew the message of monotheism of the whole Abrahamic tradition, coming both to the peoples of Arabia and *as a mercy to all the worlds.*[33]

Through the early years of prophecy, Khadījah supported Muḥammad when many in the community were against him. Even though she and her family were eventually ostracized and forced to endure great hardship, she never waivered in her support of Muḥammad and his mission. She was his constant companion and confidant and welcomed and helped to support all who joined with them in the newly awakening faith.

After years of deprivation due to the intensity of the boycott against the emerging Muslim community, Khadījah died at the age of 65 in 619 A.D. just before permission came for the *hijrah.*[34] She and Muḥammad had lived contentedly together for 25 years. Together she and Muḥammad had two sons, Qāsim and ᶜAbd Allāh, who both died in infancy and four daughters, Zaynab, Ruqayyah, Umm Kulthūm, and Fāṭimah, who were the only children of the Prophet Muḥammad ﷺ to live past infancy. She raised them all with a strong sense of Spirit, and reliance upon their Sustainer. She was known for her purity, her wisdom, her generosity, and her kindness. Khadījah was buried in the al-Mala' cemetery in Mecca.

Even after remarrying, Muḥammad long mourned his devoted wife.

---

[33] *Sūrah Al-Anbiyāᶜ* 21:107.

[34] *Hijrah*, the emigration in 622 A.D. of the beleaguered new Muslim community from Mecca 260 miles north to the settlement of Yathrib, subsequently known as Medina, where they were received by Arab and affiliated Jewish tribes who were looking to Muḥammad to help them establish peace among their warring tribal factions. This year of the emigration is the year 0 in the Muslim lunar calendar, i.e., the year of 2001 C.E. is the same year as 1422 A.H.

"Khadījah had been for the Holy Prophet ﷺ more than a wife. She had placed all her wealth, which was considerable, at his disposal. She had given him love. She was the first person to be converted to Islām, and had been a pillar of strength for the Holy Prophet ﷺ as well as the Muslims."[35] When his later wife, ᶜĀʾishah, questioned him about the extent to which he continued to remember and miss her, he said, "She embraced Islām when people disbelieved me, and she helped me in her person and her wealth when there was none else to lend me a helping hand. I had children only from her."[36]

---

[35] *Alīm 6.0: The World's Most Useful Islamic Software* (Silver Spring, MD: ISL Software Corporation, www.alim.org, © 1986-2002).

[36] Musnad Aḥmad 6:117, 118.

Trust and Trustworthiness, Truthfulness, and Sincerity
(*Tawwakul, Amānah, Ṣidq, Ikhlāṣ*)

Truly, We offered the Trust
to the heavens, and to the earth, and to the mountains;
but they refused to undertake it, as they were afraid of it—
but the human being undertook it
though he was indeed unjust and foolish,
so that God must chastise the hypocrites, men and women,
and the deniers, men and women,
yet God turns in mercy to the faithful, men and women:
for God is Ever-ready to Forgive, Infinitely Merciful.

[*Sūrah al-Aḥzāb* 33:72-73]

Put your trust in God if you are of the faithful.

[*Sūrah al-Māʿidah* 5:23].

Whosoever puts his trust in God, He will suffice him.

[*Sūrah al-Māʿidah* 65:3]

Let there be no compulsion in religion;
right wayfaring stands clearly apart from error.
Whoever turns away from the powers of evil and has faith in God
has grasped the most trustworthy handhold
which shall never give way.
And God is All-Hearing, All-Knowing.

[*Sūrah al-Baqarah*, 2:256]

Whoever submits his or her whole self to God and is a doer of good
has indeed grasped the most trustworthy hand-hold:
for with God rests the final outcome of all endeavors.

[*Sūrah Luqmān* 31:22]

And put your trust in God,
for God is sufficient as your Guardian.
[*Sūrah al-Aḥzāb* 33:3]

On the authority of Anas b. Mālik, it is told that a man came riding his camel, and he asked, "O Messenger of God, shall I leave my camel untied and trust [*tawwakul*] in God?" He replied, "Both tie your camel and trust in God."

Ibrāhīm al-Khawwas commented, "Whoever genuinely trusts in God when dealing with himself will also trust in God when dealing with others."[37]

When Hamdun was asked about trust in God, he answered, "This is a degree I have not reached yet, and how can one who has not completed the state of faith speak about trust in God?" It is said, "The one who trusts in God is like an infant. He knows of nothing in which he can seek shelter except his mother's breast. Like that is the one who trusts in God. He is guided only to his Lord Most High."[38]

The most common title of the Prophet Muḥammad ﷺ is *al-Amīn*, "the Trustworthy," based on the uprightness of his behavior as a youth and on his reputation as a merchant and caravan-leader. Frequently people entrusted their affairs to him, confident of his truthfulness and trustworthiness. Continually he trusted in his Sustainer.

O you who have attained to faith!
Remain conscious of God,
and be among those who are true to their word!
[*Sūrah at-Tawbah* 9:119]

---

37 Al-Qushayri, *Principles of Sufism*. Translated from the Arabic by B. R. Von Schlegell. (Oneonta, New York: Mizan Press, 1990), p. 116. This and other excerpts from *Principles of Sufism* included within this volume are reprinted by permission of Mizan Press.

38 Ibid., p. 121.

Follow those who ask no reward from you
and are themselves rightly guided.
[*Sūrah Yā Sīn* 36:21]

Every word of the Qur'ān had to pass through the purified being of Muḥammad ﷺ. It had to be received by him in order to be conveyed.

In the *ḥadīth al-ifk* ['Ā'ishah ﵂] stated, "By God, the Messenger of God ﷺ did not get up, nor did any member of the family leave, until revelation came down to him. He underwent the agony that used to seize him (on such occasions) with sweat emerging like pearls from him, even though it was a winter's day, because of the heavy burden of the revelation that came down upon him."

... "I ['Urwa b. 'Abd ar-Raḥmān b. 'Abd al-Qārī] heard 'Umar b. al-Khaṭṭāb say, 'When revelation came down to the Messenger of God ﷺ, it would be heard like the buzzing of a bee near his face.'"[39]

Ḥussain Abbās comments:

When we understand something from the depth of our being, we sometimes lose control. We burst out. We're happy for days. We are in a daze. We know of poets, who having come up with something really wonderful are then unable to continue ... this joy that bubbles up, the sight that you get into the nature of reality. Consider all this and consider this is the person on whom the Qur'ān came line by line. This is the person on whom it kept coming for twenty three years, ten months and five days. So crushing was this experience that he said that he would burst out in a cold sweat even if it were winter. If he were sitting on a camel, the camel would sit down. Consider the pulverizing nature of the divine revelation. And now consider that he never had a gap in his day to day activities.

---

[39] Ibn Kathīr, *The Life of the Prophet Muḥammad*, Vol. I, p. 306.

This is trustworthiness incarnate and the guardians of trustworthiness are "veracity" and "sincerity." According to Javad Nurbakhsh, Veracity (*ṣidq*) is "being truthful with God and the creation, both outwardly and inwardly, and being what one shows oneself to be"[40]; while Sincerity (*ikhlāṣ*) "is that, without paying attention to any creature or taking into account the gratification of your own self, you think, do, and act for God."[41]

Whoever possesses the virtues of veracity and sincerity will be trustworthy in his dealings with others, keeping his or her promises and fulfilling his or her responsibilities. In Shakespeare's words, "to thine own self be true/And it must follow, as the night the day/Thou canst not then be false to any man." To be true to yourself is not to follow the passions of your commanding *nafs*, but to be true to your *fiṭrah*.[42]

For all those who listen to God and the Messenger
are among those on whom God has bestowed His blessings:
the prophets, and those who never deviated from the truth,
and those who with their lives bore witness to the truth,
and the righteous ones; and what a beautiful friendship this is.
Such is the abundance of God—
and it suffices that God is All-Knowing.
[*Sūrah an-Nisāᶜ* 4:69-70]

Sufyān ibn ᶜAbdullāh al-Thaqafi asked the Messenger of Allāh to teach him so that he need never ask anyone again. The Messenger of Allāh answered, "Say that you believe in Allāh; then always be truthful."[43]

---

[40] *Sufism: A Journal* V:91.

[41] *Sufism: A Journal* IV:105

[42] Charles Upton, contributor.

[43] From *The Way of Sufi Chivalry*, p. 40, by Ibn al-Ḥusayn al-Sulami, Inner Traditions International, Rochester, Vermont 05767 www.InnerTraditions.com; copyright © 1983, 1991 Tosun Bayrak al-Jerrahi. This and other excerpts from

On the Day of Reckoning God will say:
"Today, their truthfulness shall benefit
all who have been true to their word.
Theirs shall be gardens through which running waters flow,
there to dwell beyond the count of time;
well-pleased is God with them,
and well-pleased are they with Him: this is the ultimate success."
[*Sūrah al-Mā^cidah* 5:119]

Is it not to God that sincere devotion is due?
[*Sūrah az-Zumar* 39:3]

An authentic tradition states that the Prophet ﷺ related, on the authority of Gabriel (peace be upon him), who related about God (may He be exalted!) that He said, "Sincerity is a secret taken from My secret. I have placed it as a trust in the hearts of servants I love."[44]

Yūsuf b. al-Ḥusayn commented, "The dearest thing on earth is sincerity. How many times have I struggled to rid my heart of hypocrisy, only to have it reappear in another guise!"[45]

O you who have faith! Why do you say that which you do not do?
It is most displeasing in God's sight
that you say that which you do not do.
[*Sūrah aṣ-Ṣaff* 61:2-3]

If one of you trusts another,
then he who is trusted should deliver his trust.
[*Sūrah al-Baqarah* 2:283]

The Way of Sufi Chivalry included within this volume are reprinted by permission from Inner Traditions.

[44] Al-Qushayri, *Principles of Sufism*, p. 187.

[45] Ibid., p. 189.

Never make a promise while intending not to keep it. This is forbidden as it falls within lying and hypocrisy. Al-Bukhārī and Muslim narrated that the Prophet ﷺ said, "Three traits single out a hypocrite, even if he prays or fasts and claims to be Muslim: If he speaks, he lies. If he makes a promise, he does not keep it. If he is entrusted, he betrays the trust."

Imām Al-Ghazālī in *al-Iḥyā* explains that this *ḥadīth* is applicable to those who promise while intending not to fulfill it, or those who, without an excuse, decide later not to fulfill the promise. Those who promise but could not fulfill their promise due to a proper excuse are not hypocrites. But we should be careful not to present a false excuse, as Allāh knows our inner thoughts and intentions.[46]

The word *ṣadiq* (truthful one) is derived from truthfulness. The word *ṣiddīq* (exceedingly truthful, veracious) is the intensified form of it, being he who is pervaded by truthfulness.... The lowest degree of truthfulness is that one's inner being and outward actions are in harmony. The *ṣadiq* is one who is truthful in word. The *ṣiddīq* is one who is truthful in all his words, deeds, and inward states.

Aḥmad b. Khiḍrūya instructed, "Let one who wishes God to be with him adhere to truthfulness, for God Most High has said, *Surely God is with the truthful ones.*"[47]

Abū Bakr ؓ, the first free man to accept Islām[48] was known for his trustworthy truthfulness. After the *Miʿrāj* of the Prophet ﷺ when others

---

[46] Shaykh ʿAbdul Fattah Abū Ghudda, *Islamic Manners*, translated by Muḥammad Zahid Abū Ghudda and edited by S.M. Ḥasan al-Banna (Swansea, United Kingdom: Awakening Publications, 2001), pp. 37-38.

[47] Al-Qushayri, *Principles of Sufism*, pp. 190-191.

[48] The first person to accept Islām was Khadījah, then her slave Zayd ibn Ḥāritha, and Muḥammad's young nephew ʿAlī ibn Abī Ṭālib, then followed by Abū Bakr.

derided Muḥammad, it was Abū Bakr who immediately acknowledged what must be the truth of the Prophet's experience. Abū Bakr trusted in the truthfulness of Muḥammad. He said, "I believe that he is communicating revelation from God, early in the day or in the evening; so how should I not believe him regarding this?" From then on Abū Bakr was referred to as Abū Bakr aṣ-Ṣiddīqi, the "trusting."

The best livelihood is trust in God. ~ Mevlana Jalālu'ddin Rūmī

Your livelihood is seeking you more than you are seeking it. ~ Imām ᶜAlī

In reply to the question, "What is the best that people can possess, what brings them truest happiness, what is the sweetest of the sweet, and what is the pleasantest way to live?" the Buddha answered: "Trust is the best that people can possess; following the way brings truest happiness; truth is the sweetest of the sweet; and the practice of insight is the pleasantest way to live."[49]

The Originator of the heavens and the earth—
He has made for you pairs from among yourselves
and pairs among cattle:
by this means He multiplies you; there is nothing whatever like Him
and He is the All-hearing, the All-Seeing.
To Him belong the keys of the heavens and the earth;
He grants abundant sustenance
or bestows it in meager measure to whom He wills:
for He knows well all things.
The same clear Path has He established for you
as that which He enjoined on Noah,
that which We have sent by inspiration to you,
and that which We designated for Abraham, Moses, and Jesus:
that you should steadfastly uphold the Faith
and make no divisions within it.

---

[49] Anne Bancroft, editor, *The Pocket Buddha Reader (Sutta Nipata),* (Boston, Massachusetts: Shambhala Publishing, 2001), pp. 23-24.

To those who worship other things than God,
the way to which you call them may appear difficult.
God draws to Himself those who are willing
and guides to Himself everyone who turns to Him.
[*Sūrah ash-Shūrā* 42:11-13]

With reference to numerous verses from the Qurʾān, Aisha Rafea elucidates in her essay on "The Soul's Longing" how all the prophets of the Abrahamic tradition have sought guidance from within and from a higher source, and have prepared themselves to receive that guidance; "the Supreme responded to their striving and revealed to them a path that made of their whole life a language of spirit." She indicates how longing souls have the possibility of becoming accessible to God's graces if they follow the paths of the prophets, and concludes that this journey is of benefit not just for the individual soul, but for the whole community of which He is a part. She proposes that it is the resulting greater spiritual awareness and the dissemination of spiritual knowledge that could lead to increased creativity in solving the problems and challenges of the modern age, and that it is in the development and continued sharing of this essential "Language of Spirit," rather than deified dogmas, that our hope lies.[50]

The greatest trust is that which is between us and our Most Gracious Sustainer. It is that which gives us strength and enables us to be trustworthy according to our *fiṭrah*, our essential nature, and our essential bond with God. May we learn each day to be more truthful and trustworthy and connect ever more deeply with our essential sincerity.

Abū Bakr

When Abū Bakr accepted Islām and announced this fact, he prayed to God the Almighty and Glorious. Abū Bakr was a man

---

[50] Aisha Rafea, "The Soul's Longing," in *Women of Sufism, A Hidden Treasure*, selected and edited by Camille Helminski, pp. 199-214. Excerpted from a talk delivered at the annual Sufism Symposium held by the International Association of Sufism in Fremont, California in 2001. © Aisha Rafea.

admired by his people, a well-liked and easy-going man. He knew more than anyone about the genealogy of Quraysh and of the good and bad in their history. He was a business man of fine character and charity.

His people would come and consult with him on all kinds of matters because of his knowledge, his business experience, and the pleasantness of his company. He soon began inviting those he trusted of his friends and associates to join him in accepting Islām.

I have been told that those who accepted Islām through him were: az-Zubayr b. al-ᶜAwwām, ᶜUthmān b. 'Affān, Ṭalḥa b. ᶜUbayd Allāh, Saᶜd b. Abū Waqqāṣ and ᶜAbd ar-Raḥmān b ᶜAwf, God be pleased with them.

They all went, accompanied by Abū Bakr, to the Messenger of God ﷺ who explained Islām and its correctness to them and recited to them from the Qurʾān; they then believed. These eight men were the earliest to accept Islām. They prayed and believed in the Messenger of God ﷺ and in the mission he had received from God.[51]

Ṭalḥa b. ᶜUbayd Allāh said, "I attended the trade fair at Buṣrā and there, in his cell, was a monk who called out, 'Ask the Meccans at the fair whether any man of them is from the holy quarter.'"

Ṭalḥa stated, "I replied, 'Yes; I am.' The monk then asked, 'Has Aḥmad come forth yet?' I asked, 'Who is Aḥmad?' He responded, 'He is the son of ᶜAbd Allāh b. ᶜAbd al-Muṭṭalib; this is the month during which he will appear. He is the last of the prophets. He will come forth from the holy quarter and go into exile to a place of date-palms, stony tracts, and salty earth. Be sure not to let anyone precede you to him."

Ṭalḥa went on, "His words deeply impressed me. So I left quickly for Mecca. There I asked, 'Is there any news?' People

[51] Ibn Kathīr, *The Life of the Prophet Muḥammad*, Vol. I, p. 317.

replied, 'Yes indeed; Muḥammad son of ʿAbd Allāh, "the trustworthy," has declared himself a prophet. And he has Abū Bakr b. Abū Quḥāfa as a follower."'

Ṭalḥa continued, "So I went off to Abū Bakr and asked him, 'Have you really become a follower of this man? "Yes,' he replied. 'And you should go off to him, see him, and follow him. He is calling to the truth."' Then Ṭalḥa told him what the monk had said.

Abū Bakr then took Ṭalḥa with him and they went in to see the Messenger of God ﷺ. Ṭalḥa then accepted Islām and told the Messenger of God ﷺ what the monk had said; he was delighted to hear this.[52]

After years of persecution, when divine permission was finally received for the Muslims to emigrate to Medina, Abū Bakr رضي الله عنه remained behind until the Prophet Muḥammad ﷺ was ready to depart:

"And, as I have been told, no one knew of the departure of the Messenger of God ﷺ except ʿAlī b. Abū Ṭālib and Abū Bakr, "the Trusting," and his family.

"ʿAlī was ordered to remain behind to return to people the items they had deposited with the Messenger of God ﷺ; anyone in Mecca who had concerns about things they owned would leave them in his care, such was his reputation for honesty and trustworthiness.

"Having decided to leave, the Messenger of God ﷺ went to the house of Abū Bakr b. Abū Quḥāfa and they made their exit via a window at its rear."

Abū Nuʿaym recounted, through Ibrāhīm b. Saʿd from Muḥammad b. Isḥāq, who said, "I have been informed that as he was about to leave Mecca as an emigrant to Medina for God, he said, 'Praise be to God who created me when I had been nothing. O God, protect me from earthly terrors, misfortunes,

[52] Ibid., Vol. I, pp. 317-318.

and mishaps in the nights and days to come. O God, accompany me on my journey and keep my family safe. Bless me in what You have granted me and humble me before Yourself. Raise me to the finest qualities in my character. Endear me to You, O Lord. And do not entrust (my fate) to people.

"'O Lord of the frail, you are my Lord. I take refuge in Your noble visage before which the heavens and the earth rejoice, the dark shadows dissipate, and the troubles of those who are first and those who are last are made right. (I pray) that You spare me your anger and discontent. I appeal to You not to cease your favours and to spare me your sudden wrath, removal of your favour, and all your anger. I will repay as best I can all your favours to me. And there is no power nor strength except in You.'"[53]

The first night of their journey to Medina, the Prophet ﷺ and Abū Bakr ؓ hid themselves in a cave on the outskirts of Mecca. Not long after their entry into the cave, suddenly a spider wove a large web across the opening and a dove nested in the ledge of rock beside the cave door. When the Meccans who were pursuing them approached the cave and witnessed the spider web and the nesting dove they assumed that such settled creatures could not have been disturbed by human beings in flight and so they left the cave and continued their search elsewhere. Truly our protector is God.

Later, after the death of the Prophet Muḥammad ﷺ, Abū Bakr ؓ was chosen as the first caliph, the first leader of the new Muslim state. He presided as head of the community for two years until his death in 634 when ʿUmar ؓ succeeded him.

Al-Bayhaqī stated, "The *ḥāfiẓ* Abū ʿAbd Allāh informed us . . . quoting Muḥammad b. Sīrīn, as follows, 'Some men were talking during the period of the rule of ʿUmar and apparently expressed their preference for ʿUmar over Abū Bakr. This

---

[53] Ibid., Vol. II, p. 155.

reached ʿUmar and he commented, "By God, a single night or a single day of Abū Bakr would be better than the whole clan of ʿUmar! On the night when the Messenger of God ﷺ went to the cave with Abū Bakr, the latter would walk in front for a while, then walk behind. Eventually the Messenger of God ﷺ realized this and asked, 'Abū Bakr, why do you walk behind for a while, then go and walk ahead?' He replied, 'O Messenger of God, I think of pursuit and walk behind you, but then I think of ambush and so walk ahead of you.' The Messenger of God ﷺ then asked, 'You mean if something happened you'd rather it be to you than to me?' 'Yes indeed, by Him who sent you with the truth,' he replied.

"When they reached the cave Abū Bakr said, 'Stay outside, O Messenger of God, until I make sure the cave is safe for you.' He went inside and made sure it was safe, but then remembered he had not checked out the crevice. So he said, 'Stay where you are, O Messenger of God, while I check again.' He then went back in, made sure the crevice was safe and said, 'Come on down, O Messenger of God.' And he did so.

"ʿUmar then commented, 'By Him who holds my soul in His hand, that night was better than the whole clan of ʿUmar!'"[54]

Combining these various accounts we see that Khadījah was the first woman to accept Islām, the leader of the pack, as it were, and also she preceded the men. Among slaves, the first to accept Islām was Zayd b. Ḥāritha. And the first boy to accept Islām was ʿAlī b. Abū Ṭālib; he was young then and had not reached puberty—as generally believed. These were then the family of the Prophet ﷺ. The first free man to accept Islām was Abū Bakr, "the trusting.". . .

Ibn Isḥāq stated that Muḥammad b. ʿAbd ar-Raḥmān b. ʿAbd Allāh b. al-Ḥusayn of Tamīm related to him that the Mes-

[54] Ibid., Vol. II, p. 157.

senger of God ﷺ said, "I never called upon any man to embrace Islam without him expressing reluctance, hesitation, and argument except Abū Bakr. He did not *ᶜakam* ("hold back") from Islam when I told him of it, nor did he hesitate at all."[55]

The Shield of Trust

The Prophet carried a shield . . . whoever puts his hand on the grip of the shield must do so in the way of the Prophetic practice, in order that it may be a refuge and a recompense.

If asked: With whom did the shield originate? Say: With Kayūmarth, the son of Adam. It is also said that he was Adam's grandchild and that Adam made him king of his [descendants]. Kayūmarth loved hunting.

One day when he was hunting, he suddenly came upon an animal said to be a wolf. However much Kayūmarth struck it with his weapon, his blows had no effect. He reflected that the animal's skin would be of good use against instruments of warfare, so he ordered that the animal be taken by means of a charm and killed. He cut the skin into the shape of a shield and hung it up. At times of battle, he carried it in front of his body and head. After him, alterations were made until the shield attained the form it now has.

If asked: How many are the kinds of shields? Say: Four:

1. The shield of caution
2. The shield of destiny
3. The shield of patience
4. The shield of meekness

If asked: What is the explanation of each of these? Say: The shield of

---

[55] Ibid., Vol. I, p. 314.

~ "The Shield of Trust" is excerpted from Ḥusayn Wāᶜiẓ Kāshifī Sabzawārī, *The Royal Book of Spiritual Chivalry* (Chicago, Illinois: Great Books of the Islamic World, Inc., KAZI Publications, 2000), pp. 345-347. This and other excerpts from *The Royal Book of Spiritual Chivalry* included within this volume are reprinted by permission from Kazi Publications.

caution is a shield woven of silk and cord in the customary manner. One carries it to ward off the wounds of arrow and sword.

As for the shield of destiny, it can repel some of the divine decrees; it is prayer and alms, as the Prophet said: "Nothing repels destiny except canonical prayer." Another time he said: "Giving alms repels calamity and increases one's lifespan." This refers to conditional fate, not inescapable fate.

As for the shield of patience, it is to be sewn from the pains of the arrows of misfortune. Whoever makes patience his calling will achieve his desire.

The shield of meekness is that which wards off the blows of the sword of anger, for the meek are safe from the sparks of the fire of wrath.

If asked: What is the truth of the shield? Say: Taking refuge in God and knowing Him to be the (Uncaused) Cause.

If asked: How many are the rules of conduct for taking up the shield? Say: Five.

1. One must trust in God, not the shield; for if God wishes, He will protect His servants even without a shield. Should He not, a shield cannot save him. As Sa[c]di said: "You have put the shield on your shoulder against the arrow of fate; if the arrow strikes your liver, what is its use?"
2. One should not touch the grip of the shield in a state of impurity.
3. Whenever one takes up the shield, he should invoke God.
4. When taking it up, he should kiss the grip and, some say, the covering of the shield.
5. After removing the shield from the neck, it should be stored respectfully.

If asked: What does the shield and its handgrip resemble: Say: A circle.

If asked: What is the significance of the circle and its center? Say: It signifies that whoever holds the shield must remain firmly within the circle of moral reasonableness and compassion, as does the center. Just as the shield protects him, he, too, should protect the poor and the afflicted in order to be worthy of that handgrip.

II.

Repentance
Taking Account
Forgiveness

Repentance
(*Tawbah*)

Our Sustainer!
You embrace all things within Your compassion and knowledge.
Forgive then those who turn in repentance and follow Your Path,
and preserve them from suffering through the blazing fire!
And O our Sustainer! Bring them into the Gardens of Eternity
which You have promised to them and to the righteous
among their parents, their spouses, and their descendants!
For You are Almighty, Truly Wise.
And preserve them from harmful deeds;
and any whom You preserve from harmful deeds,
on that Day, truly, You will have graced with Your Mercy.
And that will be the ultimate success.
[*Sūrah Ghāfir* 40:7-9]

Such as repent and have faith and do good—
these shall enter the garden,
and they shall not be dealt with unjustly in any way.
[*Sūrah Maryam* 19:60]

Except those who repent, and amend their ways, and hold fast to Allah
and purify their religion in God;
these are among the faithful,
and in time, God will grant to the faithful an immense reward.
[*Sūrah an-Nisā*ᶜ 4:146]

But if they repent and are constant in prayer and with charity purify,
they are your brethren in faith.
[*Sūrah at-Tawbah* 9:11]

O You who believe! Turn to God in sincere repentance.
[*Sūrah at-Taḥrīm* 66:8]

O our Sustainer, in You we have placed our trust
and to You we turn in repentance:
for with You is all journeys' end.
O our Sustainer! Do not make us a ploy
for those who deny the Truth,
but forgive us, O our Sustainer!
For You are the Almighty, the Truly-Wise."
(A prayer of Abraham and his followers)
[*Sūrah al-Mumtaḥanah* 60:4-5]

Turn all together toward God in repentance,
O faithful ones, that you may attain bliss.
[*Sūrah an-Nūr* 24:31]

It is reported on the authority of Anas b. Mālik that the Messenger of God (may God's blessing and peace be upon him and his family) said, "The one who repents from sin is like one without sin, and if God loves a servant, sin does not adhere to him." Then he recited, *Verily God loves those who turn unto Him in repentance, and He loves those who purify themselves* [*Sūrah al-Baqarah* 2:222]. It was asked, "O Messenger of God, what is the sign of repentance [*tawbah*]?" He replied, "Remorse."

On the authority of Anas b. Mālik, the Messenger of God (may God's blessing and peace be upon him and his family) is reported to have said, "There is nothing more loved by God than the youth who repents."

Therefore repentance is the first degree among the degrees of the wayfarers and the first station among the stations of the seekers. The inner meaning of repentance in Arabic is "return." It is said, "He repented," meaning, "He returned." So repentance is to return from what is blameworthy in the law of Islam to what is praiseworthy in it.

The Prophet ﷺ said, "Remorse is an act of repentance." Therefore, those well versed in the fundamentals of religion among the people of the *Sunnah* have said, "There are three conditions of repentance [which must be present] in order that it be sound: remorse for the violations that have been committed, immediate abandonment of the lapse, and firm resolve not to return to similar acts of disobedience." One must apply these principles to make repentance effective.

. . . One among the people of realization has said, "Remorse is sufficient in fulfillment of that because it has as its consequence the other two conditions, for it is impossible one should be remorseful for an act in which he persists or the like of which he intends to commit." This is the meaning of repentance by way of summary definition.

By way of elucidation and explanation, we may say that repentance has causes, an order, an arrangement, and divisions. The first cause is the awakening of the heart from the slumber of heedlessness and the servant's becoming aware of his evil state. He attains this by means of the divine favor of attentiveness to the restraints imposed by God (may He be exalted!) that come to his mind. This is by means of the audition of his heart, for it has come in the report, "The warner of God in the heart of every person is a Muslim." The tradition "There is a piece of flesh in the body which, if it be healthy, the whole body is healthy and if it be corrupt, the whole body is corrupt. Truly, it is the heart." also speaks to this matter. If his heart reflects on the evil of his deeds, he perceives the despicable actions he commits, and the desire for repentance comes to his heart, along with refraining from repugnant doings. Then God (may He be exalted!) supports him in correcting his firm intention, in embarking on the path to a goodly return, and in becoming receptive to the means of repentance.

The first of these means is to part company with brothers in evil, for they prompt him to deny this goal and cause him to doubt the correctness of this firm intention. And that is not complete except by perseverance in witnessing, which increases his longing for repentance, and by the presence of motives impelling him to fulfill his resolve, from which he strengthens his fear and hope. Then the despicable actions that form a knot of insistence on his heart are loosened, he ceases the practice of forbidden things, and the rein of his self (*nafs*) is held back from pursuing passions. Then he immediately abandons his sin and concludes a firm resolve not to return to similar sins in the future. If he continues in accordance with his goal and acts in conformity with his firm will, this means that he has been granted true sincerity.

If repentance diminishes once or twice and his desire causes him to renew the lapse—which may happen quite frequently—one should continue to hope for the repentance of such a person, for *Verily, to each period is a decree established* [*Sūrah ar-Ra^cd* 13:38] . . . .

Abū Ḥafṣ al-Ḥaddād remarked, "I abandoned a certain [reprehensible] deed and returned to it. Then the deed abandoned me, and I did not return to it after that."[56]

Repenting to Him is freeing the heart of wrong actions and a returning from a distance to a proximity; in other words, stopping wrong actions immediately and making a resolution to stop them in the future. Moreover, it is striving to understand one's deficiencies in the past.

Turning to Him is obligatory whenever wrong action is committed, and immediately after such an action. One of the conditions is that it be undertaken for the sake of Allāh alone, not only for material reasons, social standing, or out of fear of the ruler; a second condition is that one be full of regret, namely that the heart be pained and saddened at the wrong action. Regret is the essence of turning to Him in repentance, and the key to genuine repentance. . . .

The fruit and excellence of regret is that one realizes the ugliness of one's wrong actions.[57]

Delay in turning to Him is self-deception, and continued

---

[56] Al-Qushayri, *Principles of Sufism*, pp. 1-4.

[57] Haeri, *Prophetic Traditions of Islām*, p. 109 (*Qurrat al-^cUyūn*, 285-286).

procrastination is confusion: seeking an excuse not to turn to Allāh is ruin.[58]

The master Abū ᶜAlī ad-Daqqāq (may God grant him mercy) said, "Repentance is divided into three parts The first is *tawbah* (repentance), the middle is *ināba* (turn to God), and the last is *awba* (return)." He placed *tawbah* at the beginning, *awba* at the end, and *ināba* between the two. Whoever repents out of desire for [divine] reward is in the state of *ināba*. Whoever repents for the sake of obeying the [divine] command, neither for the desire of reward nor for the fear of punishment, is in the state of *awba*.

It is also said, "*Tawbah* is the quality of the Believers." As God Most High says, *Turn* (tūbū) *together toward God in repentance, O Believers* [*Sūrah an-Nūr* 24:31]. *Ināba* is the quality of the saints and those drawn nigh unto God. God Most High says, *And those who brought a heart turned in devotion* (munīb) [*to Him*] [*Sūrah Qāf* 50:33]. *Awba* is the quality of the prophets and messengers. God Most High says, *How excellent a slave. Ever did he* [*Solomon*] *turn* (ᵓawwāb) *to Us* [*Sūrah Ṣād* 38:30].

Al-Junayd stated, "Repentance has three senses. The first is remorse; the second is the resolve to give up reverting to what God has forbidden; and the third is the righting of grievances."[59]

But He turned to them;
surely to them He is Most Kind, Most Merciful.
[*Sūrah at-Tawbah* 9:117]

[58] Ibid., p. 110 (*Qurrat al-ᶜUyūn*, 287-294).
[59] Al-Qushayri, *Principles of Sufism*, pp. 6-7.

He Frowned

In the early days of his mission, the Prophet Muḥammad ﷺ was involved in conversation one day with some of the influential people of pagan Mecca, attempting to convey to them the truth of his message. While he was so engaged, a blind man approached and asked a question of him regarding the Qurʾān. Muḥammad frowned and turned away from him, annoyed by the interruption. Shortly thereafter, Muḥammad was reproved by God with these first verses of the *sūrah* which then took on the title "He frowned."[60]

He frowned and turned away
because the blind man came to him.
But how were you to know whether he might grow in purity,
or whether he might have received counsel
and been helped by this reminder?
And the one who regards himself as self-sufficient,
to him you pay attention;
though if he does not grow in purity you are not to blame.
But as for the one who came eagerly to you

---

[60] "Al-Walīd b. al-Mughīra was standing talking with the Messenger of God ﷺ who was addressing him, wishing to convert him to Islam, when Ibn Umm Maktūm, that is, the son of ʿĀtika, daughter of ʿAbd Allāh b. ʿAnkatha, passed by. Ibn Umm Maktūm, who was blind, addressed the Messenger of God ﷺ and began asking him to recite the Qurʾān. This so upset the Messenger of God ﷺ as to anger him, and this was because he was interfering with his efforts to convert al-Walīd to Islam as he was hoping.

"When the blind man persisted, he turned away from him frowning and ignored him. And so God Almighty sent down, '. . . *and he frowned and turned away when the blind man came to him* . . .' up to the words, '. . . *exalted, purified*' [*Sūrat ʿAbasa* 80:1-14]. It is also said that the person who was talking to the Messenger of God ﷺ when Ibn Umm Maktūm came along was Umayya b. Khalaf. But God knows best." ~ Ibn Kathīr, *The Life of the Prophet Muḥammad,* Vol. II, p. 36.

and with an inner awe,
him you disregarded.
By no means should it be so!
For this is indeed a reminder
for anyone who will remember.
[*Sūrah ᶜAbasa* 80:1-12]

Muḥammad ﷺ immediately felt remorse for having mistakenly rebuffed the sincere seeker, and became ever more watchful over his own behavior that he might respond ever more appropriately in every situation.

> Repent ceaselessly, with the strongest will not to return to the thing of which you repent, for only then is the repentance acceptable. Through Manṣūr ibn ᶜAbdullāh al-Harawi we hear Abūl-Ḥasan al-Muzayyin say, "Three things make repentance real: regretting the past, deciding firmly not to return to the state of which one repents, and having fear in one's heart, One is afraid because one knows perfectly well when one sins, yet does not know if one's repentance is going to be accepted or refused."[61]

Then whoever follows My guidance, no fear shall come upon them, nor shall they grieve [*Sūrah al-Baqarah* 2:38]. Those who fear God's future punishment—who encounter Him in His names *Aḍ-Ḍārr*, the Punisher, and *Al-Muntaqim*, the Avenger—are being called by Him to repent; and so fear is an aspect of Mercy, since God is also *Ar-Raᶜūf*, the All-Pitying, *Al-Ghaffār*, He Who is Full of Forgiveness, and *Al-Ghafūr*, the All-Forgiving. . . . In the words of Ḥaḍrat ᶜAlī ﷺ, "If you are able, increase your fear of Allāh while at the same time having a good opinion of Him; the best of actions is to achieve a balance between fear and hope."[62]

It is related by ᶜAlī ibn Rabīᶜah that: "I saw ᶜAlī ibn Abī Ṭālib ﷺ presented with a horse to ride. When he placed his

---

[61] Al-Sulami, *The Way of Sufi Chivalry*, pp. 43-44.
[62] Charles Upton, contributor.

foot in the stirrup (to mount), he said: '*Bismillāh.*' When he had settled himself in the saddle, he said: '*Al-ḥamdu lillāh*, Glory be to the One who has made all this subservient to our use—since (but for Him) we would not have been able to attain to it. Hence, it is unto our Lord that we must always turn.'

Then he said *Al-ḥamdu lillāh* three times, and *Allāhu Akbar* three times, and then he recited the following: 'Glory to you, O Allāh, I have done wrong, so forgive me. Surely no one can forgive me of my wrongdoing except You.'

Then ᶜAlī ibn Abī Ṭālib laughed. When he was asked what it was that caused him to laugh, he replied: 'Once I saw the Prophet do exactly as I have done just now, and then laugh, so I asked him why he had laughed. He replied, "Your Lord is pleased with His servant when, in the knowledge that there is no one else who can forgive him, he asks the Lord to forgive him his wrongdoing." ' "

When a servant commits a wrong, he does something most unsavoury and unbecoming. In relation to Allāh, that wrongdoing takes on the further aspect of transgression and insolence. He does these things as a result of being overcome by passion, or by distorted thinking. But for how long will he remain under the influence of his passions, or his warped ideas? Undoubtedly Allāh awaits the return of those who stray, and rejoices with the repentance of His servant, and appreciates every step in His direction taken by that servant. . . .

How did he forget in the first place? What caused him to stray? Now he feels his own weakness and depravity, aware that it is Allāh alone who can treat his wounds and restore his health: *And those who, when they commit an indecency or do wrong to themselves, remember Allāh and seek forgiveness for their sins—and who but Allāh can forgive one's sins?—and do not knowingly persist in what they do* [*Sūrah Āl ᶜImrān* 3:135].[63]

---

[63] Muḥammad al-Ghazālī, *Remembrance and Prayer: The Way of the Prophet Muḥammad,* translated by Yusuf Talal De Lorenzo. (Leicester, United Kingdom:

In this life, we are engaged on a journey of return to our Sustainer.

The *ādāb* or code of exemplary conduct of the Prophet ﷺ with regard to travel encourages the traveler to actively seek the protection of Allāh, and to expect to see the workings of His infinite mercy.

Whenever one of his people set out on a journey, ʿAbdullāh ibn ʿUmar would say to him:

"Come close to me so that I may say goodbye to you the way that the Prophet used to say goodbye to us. He used to say: 'I commit your *dīn* (religious conviction) to the keeping of Allāh, and (so also) your responsibilities, and the outcome of your doings.'"[64]

Once when the Prophet Muḥammad ﷺ was returning from battle, he told his companions: "Now we are returning from the lesser *jihād* to the greater *jihād*." "And what is the greater *jihād*?" they asked. The Prophet answered: "The struggle with the self."

Be aware of your states, count each breath and every moment of time allotted to you, and do not waste it. Sahl ibn ʿAbdullāh at-Tustarī said, "Your time is the most valuable thing you have. Give every moment its due." Abū Saʿid ar-Rāzī reports that Junayd said: "All good is gathered in three conditions. If you cannot pass your days with what furthers you, at least do not pass your days with what works against you. If you cannot befriend good people, at least do not keep company with bad people. If you cannot give away what is yours for Allāh's sake, at least do not spend your fortune on things that will anger Him.

The Islamic Foundation, 1986), pp. 78-79. Reprinted by permission of the Islamic Foundation, Marfield Conference Centre, Rathby Lane, Markfield, Leicestershire, LE67 9SY, United Kingdom. Tel:(01530) 244944. Fax: (01530) 244946.

[64] Ibid., p. 77.

Keep continuous repentance. . . ."

Hold on to Truth under any circumstances, . . . and [do not allow your] hearts [to] fall into heedlessness and imagination.[65]

[65] Al-Sulami, *The Way of Sufi Chivalry*, pp. 57-58.

Accountability and Responsibility
(*Iḥtisāb* and *Mas*ᶜ*ūliyyah*)

That you have faith in God and His messenger,
and that you strive in God's cause
with your possessions and your lives:
that is best for you, if only you knew!
[*Sūrah aṣ-Ṣaff* 61:11]

But He will call you to account for what your hearts have conceived,
and Allah is Forgiving, Forbearing.
[*Sūrah al-Baqarah* 2:225]

And be true to every promise—
for, truly, you will be called to account for every promise
which you will have made!
And give full measure whenever you measure,
and weigh with a balance that is true:
this will be for your own good, and best in the end.
And never concern yourself
with anything of which you have no knowledge;
truly, hearing and sight and heart—all of them—
will be called to account for it!
And do not walk upon the earth with proud self-conceit:
for, truly, you can never rend the earth asunder,
nor can you ever grow as tall as the mountains!
The evil of all this is odious in your Sustainer's sight:
this is part of that knowledge of right and wrong
with which your Sustainer has inspired you.
[*Sūrah al-Isrā*ᶜ 17:34-39]

See how God has purchased of the faithful
their lives and their possessions;
in return, theirs is the Garden,
and so they struggle in God's way.
[*Sūrah at-Tawbah* 9:111]

Muḥammad ﷺ established a new assessment of accountability (*iḥtisāb*).

> By establishing law and order in this way, the Prophet ﷺ brought the entire tribal society together into a moral community capable of accepting it, with the result that:
> - Order and discipline replaced tribal customs and conventions and eliminated their barbarity and savagery;
> - All people were now equal before the law, whether weak or strong, poor or rich;
> - There was no longer any place for favoritism or any preferential treatment in this community, where the principle of justice and equity prevailed; and
> - The sanctity of law was duly preserved and zealously guarded within this Islamic community, which abided by Allāh's commandments and thereby maintained its own security and safety.[66]

Not long before his death, Muḥammad ﷺ made the ritual pilgrimage together with his community. On the plain of ᶜArafāt he delivered his farewell sermon, encouraging his community with the best of behavior. He then called out asking if he had indeed fulfilled his mission. The crowd on the plain of ᶜArafāt called out, "Yes." Again he asked, and again they confirmed, and a third time he asked and a third time the people acknowledged the fulfillment of his mission. It was here then that the final verse of revelation of the Qurʾān was received: *This day I have perfected your religion, completed My favor upon you, and have chosen for you submission as your religion.* [*Sūrah al-Māᶜidah* 5:3].

After his return from the pilgrimage, just before his death when he was quite ill, Muḥammad ﷺ visited the mosque beside his home and made a final effort to rectify his accounts. He called out asking if there were anyone whom he had ever hurt who had not received recompense. One man stepped forward and said that the Prophet had once knocked

---

[66] Ḥasan al-ᶜAnani, *Freedom and Responsibility in Qur'anic Perspective.* Translated from the Arabic by M.S. Kayani. (Indianapolis, Indiana: American Trust Publishers, 1990), p. 193.

into him with his elbow when in battle. Muḥammad asked his forgiveness. He called out again asking if there were anyone to whom he owed anything who had not been repaid. A man stepped forward saying that he had once given the Prophet three small coins which he not repaid. Muḥammad repaid him with apologies and stated that it is better to blush in this world than in the next.

The life of the prophets is exemplary in the way that they each were completely devoted to their Sustainer and continually taking account of their actions and attempting to fulfill the purpose of their existence. Within Islām, we are given the five pillars of faith upon which to base our lives: the witnessing of the Unity of God and Muḥammad's messengership, the practice of prayer and devotion to our Sustainer, the support of others through the offering of purifying charity (*zakāt*), the fast of Ramaḍān, and the journey of pilgrimage. Each of us as human beings is continually called to take account of our state before God and to look well to the responsibility of the trust we have undertaken.

> The first practical step for me, then, in acquiring religious efficiency is to make an account of myself, [to keep a journal] of my supply of time and my manner of using it. Remember, time is really the most wonderful of God's gifts, for when it ceases for us, all else ceases with it, that is, in the sense of meriting or gaining anything for heaven. In this all men are equal: no one has more than twenty-four hours a day. Time flows on in a constant stream and cannot be halted in its course. Our day is, in a way, laid out for us by obedience, and our very manner of life suggests a certain routine, but we must go farther and find out if there are not some little "inbetweenities," as someone has aptly styled these spare moments, and we will be surprised and astonished at the number wasted, due either to mismanagement or sheer carelessness.
>
> But records do more than this. "Know thyself." Self-knowledge is the information they give. ~ Sister Mary Cecilia[67]

---

[67] Dorothy Stewart (compiler), *Women of Vision: An Anthology of Spiritual Words from Women Across the Centuries* (Chicago: Loyola Press, 2000), p. 47.

We do not know when the moment of meeting with our Lord may come and we wish our account book to be clean. Continually Muḥammad ﷺ prayed for right guidance from his Lord, and also made every effort to keep rectified his accounts with his fellow human beings, as the following story also illustrates. May we likewise be responsible for and repay our debts, whether material, psychological, or spiritual, with gracious generosity.

Paying our Debts

Abū Nu'aym told in his work, *ad-Dalā'il* (*The Signs*), . . . "ᶜAbd Allāh b. Sallām stated that God having wished good guidance for Zayd b. Saᶜya, Zayd said, 'All marks of the prophethood were there as expected for me to recognize on the face of Muḥammad ﷺ when I looked at him, except that there were two I had not explored in him: that his patient wisdom preceded his ignorance, and that the more ignorance was directed at him, the more his patient wisdom increased.'

"He stated further, 'I used to be nice to him so that I could mix with him and get to know his wisdom and his foolishness.'

"He then told a story of his having made an advance payment to the Prophet ﷺ for profit. He went on, 'And when the time for the loan was due, I went to him and grabbed him by the closure of his cloak and gown, he being then at a funeral with some of his Companions. I also glared at him in an ugly fashion and said, "O Muḥammad, aren't you going to pay me my due? By God, I never knew you of the tribe of ᶜAbd al-Muṭṭalib to be late payers!"

"ᶜUmar stared over at me, his eyes rolled like revolving celestial bodies. Then he said, "You enemy of God! Do you dare say to the Messenger of God ﷺ what I am hearing and do what I am seeing? By Him who sent him with the truth, if I were not wary of his blaming me, I would cut off your head with my sword!"

"Meanwhile, the Messenger of God ﷺ was looking at ᶜUmar, smiling quietly with gentleness. Then he said, "'ᶜUmar, both he and I were in need of something other than that from you; you should have told me to pay up properly, and him to behave better. Take him away, ᶜUmar, and pay him his due. And give him 20 *ṣāᶜs* weight of dates as a bonus!'"

"And so Zayd b Saᶜya, may God be pleased with him, became a Muslim. He was present with the Messenger of God at all the battles, and he died in the year of Tabūk, God bless him."[68]

---

[68] Ibn Kathīr, *The Life of the Prophet Muḥammad*, Vol. I, p. 214.

FORGIVENESS
(*Ghufrān*)

And if you pardon and forbear and forgive,
then surely Allah is forgiving, merciful.
[*Sūrah at-Taghābun* 64:14]

Repel [evil] with what is better, and see!
he between whom and you was enmity
may then be as if he were a close friend.
[*Sūrah Fuṣṣilat* 41:34]

Strive among yourselves to attain your Sustainer's forgiveness
and a paradise as vast as the heavens and the earth,
which has been readied for those who are conscious of God—
who spend [in His way] in times of abundance and in times of hardship,
and restrain their anger,
and pardon their fellow human beings,
because God loves those who do good;
and who, when they have committed a shameful deed
or have otherwise wronged their own souls,
remember God and pray for forgiveness for their mistakes—
for who can forgive sins but God?—
And do not knowingly persist
in doing whatever [wrong] they may have done.
[*Sūrah Āl ʿImrān* 3:133–135]

And so, do not let those of you who have been graced
with God's favor and ease of circumstances
ever be neglectful of helping their near of kin, and the needy,
and those who have turned from the domain of evil for God's sake,
but let them forgive and endure.
Do you not desire that God should forgive you your sins,
seeing that God is Ever Ready to Forgive, and is Most Merciful?
[*Sūrah an-Nūr* 24:22]

Say: "O my Servants who have transgressed against your own selves!
Do not despair of Allah's Compassion:
for Allah forgives all mistakes:
for He is Often-Forgiving, Infinitely Merciful.
Turn to your Sustainer and surrender to Him
before the suffering comes upon you:
after that you will not be helped.
And before the penalty suddenly comes upon you
without your perceiving it,
follow the best of that which your Sustainer has revealed to you!"
[*Sūrah az-Zumar* 39:53-55]

As for those who avoid the grave sins and shameful deeds,
though occasionally they may stumble—
truly, your Sustainer is vast in forgiveness.
He knows you well when He brings you out of the earth
and when you are hidden in your mother's wombs;
so do not claim purity for yourselves—
He knows best who is conscious of Him.
[*Sūrah an-Najm* 53:32]

When those come to you who have faith in Our signs, say:
"Peace be with you.
Your Sustainer, has willed upon Himself the law of compassion—
So that if any of you does harm out of ignorance
but afterwards repents and changes,
your Sustainer is Ever Ready to Forgive, Most Merciful."
[*Sūrah al-Anʿām* 6:54]

When Allāh revealed the verse, *Take to forgiveness, enjoin good, and turn aside from the ignorant* [*Sūrah al-Aʿrāf* 7:199], Gabriel said, "O Muḥammad, it means that you should be forbearing with the man who has insulted you, forgive the man who has wronged you, and give to the man who has denied you something."

A man once asked the Apostle to tell him about nobility of character. He said, "It means that you should forgive him who has wronged you, re-establish ties with him who has broken them off, give to him who has denied you something, and speak the truth even if it is against your own interests."[69]

Al-Bāqir relates that the Jewess who poisoned the sheep's flesh eaten by the Prophet was brought before the Prophet, who asked her, "Why did you do what you did?" She replied, "I told myself that if he is a prophet then it will not harm him, but if he is merely a tyrant, then the people will be free of him." And according to al-Bāqir, the Messenger forgave her.[70]

According to Aṣ-Ṣādiq, the Messenger said: "Be forgiving, for surely forgiveness only increases a servant in nobility; be forgiving to each other, and Allāh will increase you in honour."[71]

Forgiveness is the crown of noble qualities, [while] of all the acts of a powerful man, vengeance is the most odious. ~ Ḥaḍrat ᶜAlī

The more we are able to clearly take account of our own mistakes and seek forgiveness of God for our own mistakes, the more we are able to open also to extend forgiveness to others. In the Bible, Jesus tells people rather than worrying about the mote in someone else's eye, to take care of the beam in our own. It is often blindness to our own mistakes that veils our sight to a more understanding view of someone else's error. When we are able to see our own limitations more clearly, and seek forgiveness for them, our hearts soften and forgiveness flows through us more readily.

There may, however, be instances in life when intense hurt or abuse has been experienced when forgiveness opens, but resumption of rela-

---

[69] Haeri, *Prophetic Traditions in Islām*, p. 165 (*Mishkāt*, 216-218).

[70] Ibid., p. 168 (*Mishkāt*, 228-229).

[71] Ibid.

tionship may not be indicated. Muḥammad's dear uncle Ḥamza ﷺ was killed and terribly mutilated in the Battle of Uḥud. When later Waḥshī, the man who had killed him, converted to Islām and asked to be allowed to return to Mecca, the Prophet ﷺ forgave him and allowed him to return to the community, but asked him not to come near him, rather to stay out of his sight.

Whatever you are given here is for the convenience of this life:
but that which is with God is better and more enduring—
for those who have faith and put their trust in their Sustainer;
those who avoid the greater crimes and shameful deeds
and when they are angry, even then forgive;
those who pay attention to their Instructor and are constant in prayer;
who conduct their affairs by mutual consultation;
and who give out of the sustenance We bestow on them.
[*Sūrah ash-Shūrā* 42:36-38]

Ibn al-Musabib relates, "I entered the presence of Ibn al-Munkadir of Tyre and said quietly '*Istaghfirullah* [May God forgive me].' Ibn al-Munkadir heard me and admonished me, "Beware of hasty repentance for it is the act of liars." I asked him why and he replied, "Sincere repentance requires seven things: the first is to feel remorse in the heart. The second is to do what Allāh has commanded. The third is to desist from what He has forbidden. The fourth is to make up for what you have let lapse. The fifth is to give each person his or her right so that you will free yourself for the Day of Reckoning. The sixth is to melt your ego with acts of obedience. The seventh is to let every member of your body taste the sweetness of obedience the way that you let them taste the sweetness of disobedience. If after all this you say '*Istaghfirullah*,' then your repentance will reverberate in you and rise to the heavens without any veils.[72]

---

[72] C. Helminski, *The Mevlevi Wird* (translation of the *Awrad-i Sharif)*, p. 71.

Margaret Cundiff reminds us: "As I look at my life I see areas of hardness, of shallow 'promises, promises' which never get anywhere, areas of preoccupation with my own life, with what I want to do, what I want to be. I allow these things to put a stranglehold on my effective ministry, but it's often not until I feel the life being squeezed from me that I come to my senses. It is often a very painful process, and could have been avoided if I had taken more care.

The joy is, though, that the sower does not sow once, but over and over again, year in and year out. He never gives up, because He is confident of a harvest. In the book of Isaiah there is a promise which I hold on to, and it is this:

'My word is like the snow and the rain that come down from the sky to water the earth. . . . So also will be the word that I speak—it will not fail to do what I plan for it; it will do everything I send it to do.' (The Bible, Isaiah 55:10-11).

God does not give up on me or you; we get chance after chance. But how sad that we waste those chances so often, when we could have been beautiful and useful if only we had listened and received what he had for us."[73]

The Prophet Muḥammad ﷺ said that the following prayer is among the best of all calls for forgiveness:

> O God! You are my Lord. There is no God but You. You created me. I am Your servant. I shall try to fulfill my pledge with You as well as my power permits. I seek refuge with You from the evil of my deeds. Due to Your favors to me I turn to You and thank You and also confess my mistakes. Forgive me, for there is none to forgive sins but You.[74]

---

[73] Margaret Cundiff in *Women of Vision* by Dorothy Stewart, p. 53. By permission of the Rev'd Margaret Cundiff, Selby, North Yorkshire, England.

[74] This prayer appears in many of the *awrād* (litanies, or daily prayers) of the Islamic world.

The Prophet ﷺ was known to ask forgiveness of God "seventy times a day." He urged his companions to pray as he prayed and to seek forgiveness as he did. When they asked him how he sought forgiveness, he recited the following prayer:

I ask forgiveness of God for all the sins I have committed consciously or accidentally, openly or secretly. I turn to God in repentence for all my errors, those of which I am aware and those of which I am unaware.[75]

Jesus also taught his disciples what has come to be known as "The Lord's Prayer" seeking for forgiveness and alignment with God's will:

Our Father who art in heaven, Hallowed be Thy name.
Thy kingdom come. Thy will be done on earth, as it is in heaven.
Give us this day our daily bread.
And forgive us our trespasses, as we forgive our trespassers.
And lead us not into temptation, but deliver us from evil,
for Thine is the kingdom, and the power, and the glory,
forever. Amen. (The Bible, Matthew 6:9-13)

Forgiveness allows us to re-establish connection with our Lord, our Sustainer. It allows our hearts to find rest as our consciousness focuses on our Sustainer and His Compassion and Mercy rather than with our wounds or even our own error.

Surely in the remembrance of God, hearts find rest.
[*Sūrah ar-Raᶜd* 13:28]

But ask forgiveness of your Sustainer
and turn to Him:
for truly, my Sustainer is infinitely merciful and loving.
(Words of the Prophet Shuᶜayb)
[*Sūrah Hūd* 11:90]

---

[75] Ibid., p. 63.

III.

Compassion
Mercy
Charity

Compassion
(*Raḥmāniyyah*)

In the Name of God, the Infinitely Compassionate, Most Merciful
All praise is God's, the Sustainer of all worlds,
the Infinitely Compassionate, the Most Merciful
Sovereign of the Day of Reckoning!
You alone do we worship, and You alone do we ask for help.
Guide us on the straight path—
the path of those whom You have blessed, not of those who have earned Your wrath, nor of those who have gone astray!
[*Sūrah al-Fātiḥah*, 1:1-7, complete]

And so, do not repulse any of those
who morning and evening call on their Sustainer, seeking His Face.
You are in no way accountable for them—
just as they are in no way accountable for you—
and you have no right to repulse them,
for then you would be among those who do harm.
For it is in this way that we try them through one another—
so that they might ask, "Is it these among us whom God has favored?"
Does God not know best those who are grateful to Him?
And when those who have faith in our signs come to you,
say: "Peace be with you.
Your Sustainer has willed upon Himself the law of Compassion."
[*Sūrah al-Anʿām* 6:52-54]

And your Sustainer says: "Call on Me; I will answer you."
[*Sūrah Ghāfir* 40:60]

It is He Who has sent His Messenger with guidance
and the Way of Truth,
so that it might prevail over all false ways;
and God is sufficient as witness.
Muhammad is the Messenger of God;
and those who are with him stand firm

when facing those who deny the Truth,
and are compassionate with each other.
You can see them bow and prostrate themselves in prayer,
seeking grace from God and His good pleasure.
On their faces are their marks, traced by prostration.
This is their parable in the Torah,
and their parable in the Gospel:
like a seed which sends forth its shoot, which grows strong,
so that it becomes thick, and then stands firm on its stem,
delighting those who sow with wonder.
[*Sūrah al-Fatḥ* 48:28-29]

In the *Qur^cān*, each *sūrah* (chapter) but one of the revelation begins with *Bismillāh ir-Raḥmān ir-Raḥīm* which means "In the Name of God, the Infinitely Compassionate, the Most Merciful." *Raḥmān* speaks to the fundamental compassionate beneficence inherent in the Divine nature; *Raḥīm* to the particular mercy which manifests. Both words come from the same root which is the word for "womb." God's compassion and mercy is always emphasized as being greater than God's wrath; the encompassing generosity and nurturance of the Divine is the milieu in which we live. As we come to recognize the magnificence of the Compassionate Source of Life, we can come to see ourselves in harmony with that Source. We can become a conduit for that compassion.

Muḥammad's message was one of great compassion; he brought a message of integration of spirit and matter, of essence and everyday life, of recognition of the feminine as well as the masculine. Though cultural manifestations may have layered over some of the original purity of intention, the words of the Qur^ɔān convey the equality of women and men before the eyes of God; at a time when the goddess-worshipping Arabian tribes were still quite barbaric, even burying infant girls alive in favor of male offspring, this new voice of the Abrahamic tradition attempted to reestablish the recognition of the Unity of Being. It tried to address the imbalances that had arisen, advising respect and honor for the feminine, for the enslaved, as well as for the graciousness and harmony of nature. The Qur^ɔān enjoins mutual respect and valuation of each human being regardless of sex or social status. And everyone, regardless of gender or social position, is expected to establish his or her own direct connection with the Divine.

> God's Messenger was particularly compassionate towards children. When he saw a child crying, he sat beside him or her and shared his or her feelings. He felt the pain of a mother for her child more than the mother herself. Once he said:
>
> "I stand in prayer and wish to prolong it. However, I hear the cry of a child and cut the prayer short for the anxiety which the mother is feeling."
>
> He took children in his arms and hugged them. He was once hugging his beloved grandsons, Ḥasan and Ḥusayn, when Aqra ibn Habis told him: "I have got ten children. So far, I haven't kissed any of them."
>
> God's Messenger responded: "The one with no pity for others is not pitied."
>
> According to another version, he said: "What can I do for you if God has removed from you the feeling of compassion?"
>
> Once, he said: "Take pity on those on earth so that those in the heavens should have pity on you."[76]

> According to Ḥamād al-Laḥḥām, a man came to Aṣ-Ṣadiq saying, "A certain son of your uncle has been talking about you, mentioning all kinds of scandal and insult." Thereupon Aṣ-Ṣadiq asked his [servant] to bring him water so as to make the ablution. When he had made his ablution he returned, and al-Laḥḥām [thought] to himself that he would make prayers against the man; but he prayed as follows: "O my Lord it is my right—You have granted it to me and You are more generous and magnanimous than I; thus I ask You that you may accord me this right and do not punish him because of me." Then he was seized with compassion and continued to pray, while al-Laḥḥām looked on him in astonishment.[77]

[76] Gulen, *Prophet Muḥammad, the Infinite Light*, Vol. II, pp. 128-129.

[77] Haeri, *Prophetic Traditions in Islām*, p. 167 (aṭ-Ṭabarsī, *Makārim al-Akhlāq* 430).

When Imām ᶜAlī handed over the governorship of Egypt to Muḥammad ibn Abī Bakr, he commanded him to deal justly with the citizens, saying, "Treat them kindly, be gracious to them, extend to them the benefits of your position and be fair in the way you regard different ranks of men, so that the powerful do not desire you to commit injustice in their favour and the weak do not despair of your justice towards them; truly Allāh will ask your servants about the smallest and greatest of your deeds, about the deeds made in public and those hidden from view. Indeed, if He punishes, then you were surely worthy of the punishment, and if He forgives, then He is the most generous."[78]

Muᶜāwiyah ibn Sufyān asked Khālid ibn Muᶜammar why he loved ᶜAlī ibn Abī Ṭālib. He replied, "I love him for three qualities: for his compassion when he becomes angry, for his truthfulness when he speaks, and for his justice when he is generous."[79]

Is it really paradoxical that when we are distressed we turn to the friend who knows what distress can be like? We don't know why, but there doesn't seem much point in going for sympathy, the deep-down, understanding kind, to those other friends whose paths have always been smooth. It is as though human beings lack a whole dimension and cannot come to maturity until they have faced sorrow. There is an old Arab proverb: "Too much sunshine makes a desert" and the human heart is very often a desert. But sorrow irrigates the desert.[80]

On a hot summer day, a man found a thirsty dog at the edge of a well, unable to reach the water. He said to himself, "This dog must be suffering from thirst as I am now." The man went

---

[78] Ibid., p. 19 (al-Ḥākim, *al-Ḥayāt*, II, 198; from *Nahj*, III, 543).

[79] Ibid., p. 19 (al-Ashtarī, II, 75).

[80] Cicely Saunders and Mary Craig in *Women of Vision,* by D. Stewart, p. 104.

into the well, filled his shoe with water and offered it to the dog to drink. God was pleased with him, and granted him forgiveness of his sins.[81] The Prophet ﷺ was asked: "Messenger of God, are we rewarded for kindness to animals?" He said, "There is a reward for kindness to every living thing."[82]

Naṣr ibn Muḥammad reports that Junayd related that there was a sheikh in Damascus called Abū Mūsā al-Qumasi who was a man of *Futuwwah;* everyone praised him. One day, the sheikh's house collapsed on top of him and his wife. When people began to dig in the ruins, they found his wife first. "Leave me," she said. "Go and try to find the sheikh and save him. He was sitting in a corner over there." They left the woman, dug where she had pointed, and found the sheikh. "Leave me," he said. "Go and save my wife." Each wanted the other to be saved. That is the state of those who are together for the sake of Allāh and who are friends and brothers in the name of Allāh. They are in that compassionate state at all times.[83]

St. Francis and the Wolf of Gubbio

One of the most beloved saints of Christianity, St. Francis of Assisi of the thirteenth century, was known for his great compassion. A favorite story about St. Francis is that of the wolf of Gubbio.

The people of Gubbio were in terror of a certain huge wolf that had been devouring not only animals but also human beings. They dared not go beyond the city walls. St. Francis resolved to meet the wolf to try to alleviate the terror and heartache of the people of Gubbio. As the people watched, he went forth to meet the wolf.

---

[81] Ḥassan Hathout, *Reading the Muslim Mind* (Plainfield, Indiana: American Trust Publications, 1995), p. 83.

[82] From the *ḥadīth* collections of Bukhārī, Muslim, Tirmidhī, and Bayhaqī.

[83] Al-Sulami, *The Way of Sufi Chivalry*, p. 61.

The wolf ran towards him as though to devour him, too, but St. Francis called to him as "Brother wolf," commanding him in the name of God to neither harm him nor anyone else. The wolf looked at St. Francis, closed his jaws, and approached him as meekly as a lamb. Francis then spoke to him, calling his awareness to the murderous acts he had committed, but saying to him that as a brother he would make peace between him and the people of Gubbio and call off their dogs if the wolf would agree to no longer hunt the animals and people of Gubbio. The wolf bowed his head in assent. Francis then told him that he would assure him that the people of Gubbio would then feed him every day so that he would no longer be hungry and driven to killing. St. Francis asked of him his promise that he could trust him and the wolf again indicated his assent by bowing his head and shaking his tail. St. Francis then held out his hand and the wolf placed his paw in it in pledge. Then together they returned to the city walls that all the people might see.

Everyone came out to witness this miracle. St. Francis told the people of the wolf's promise and asked if they indeed would agree to feed him. They agreed and again he asked the wolf for his pledge. Again the wolf placed his paw in St. Francis's hand and bowed his head. From then on he went peacefully about Gubbio and was fed by the inhabitants for two years until one day he passed away of old age. The people mourned him greatly because when he went about so gently among them he had been a continual reminder for them of the goodness and compassion of St. Francis calling forth something of that same quality from within themselves.

Mother Teresa

A modern-day saint is Mother Teresa of Calcutta, a Catholic nun who was born in Macedonia in 1910 and who passed away in 1997. With indeed a mother's love and compassion, she witnessed the deep humanity of each person and treated all with equal respect and care. From this witnessing of the essential value of each being's *fiṭrah*, she began work among the poor and needy of Calcutta.

Her first work was as a teacher and it was not long before her enthusiasm and tender compassion endeared her to her students and drew more to come. It was they who first began to call her "ma." She then began to visit the hospitals and slums of Calcutta to help in any way that she could. Yearning to be able to help more, she went to Patna to receive further training in nursing. A number of young women were drawn to her side to work with her in serving the poor.

The need arose to establish a home for the young women and a center of healing and help. At last, it was a Muslim who was moving to Pakistan who sold his large home to Mother Teresa for a low price who enabled the first "Mother house" to be established. The force of her compassion was such that people then came from all over the world to assist Mother Teresa in her efforts, and she herself began to travel to all parts of the globe to speak, and to help the poor and needy. Eventually she was able to establish orphanages and homes for the impoverished, ill, and dying, the lepers and the outcasts. She created *Shanti Nagar* (the City of Peace), where sick and healed lepers are cared for, learn a job, and can find work. Little by little others followed her lead so that she was able to form a society for service of the poor and needy throughout the world.

She would tell people, "I want you to find the poor here, right in your own home first. And begin love there. Be that good news to your own people. And find out about your next-door neighbor. Do you know who they are?"[84]

Even a Smile

> The poor are very wonderful people. One evening we went out and we picked up four people from the street. And one of them was in a most terrible condition. And I told the Sisters: "You take care of the other three; I will take care of this one that looks worse." So I did for her all that my love can do. I put her in bed, and there was such a beautiful smile on her face. She

[84] This quote and the following paragraphs of "Even a Smile" are excerpted from Mother Teresa's Nobel Peace Prize speech in 1979 in Oslo, Norway. Reprinted by permission of the Missionaries of Charity, Calcutta, India.

took hold of my hand, as she said one word only: "thank you"—and she died.

I could not help but examine my conscience before her. And I asked: "What would I say if I was in her place?" And my answer was very simple. I would have tried to draw a little attention to myself. I would have said: "I am hungry, I am dying, I am cold, I am in pain," or something. But she gave me much more—she gave me her grateful love. And she died with a smile on her face—like that man who we picked up from the drain, half eaten with worms, and we brought him to the home —"I have lived like an animal in the street, but I am going to die like an angel, loved and cared for." And it was so wonderful to see the greatness of that man who could speak like that, who could die like that without blaming anybody, without cursing anybody, without comparing anything. Like an angel—this is the greatness of our people.

And that is why we believe what Jesus has said: "I was hungry, I was naked, I was homeless; I was unwanted, unloved, uncared for—and you did it to me."

I believe that we are not really social workers. We may be doing social work in the eyes of the people. But we are really contemplatives in the heart of the world. . . .

There is so much suffering, so much hatred, so much misery, and we with our prayer, with our sacrifice are beginning at home. Love begins at home, and it is not how much we do, but how much love we put in the action that we do. It is to God Almighty—how much we do does not matter, because He is infinite, but how much love we put in that action. How much we do to Him in the person that we are serving.

Some time ago in Calcutta we had great difficulty in getting sugar. And I don't know how the word got around to the children, and a little boy of four years old, a Hindu boy, went home and told his parents: "I will not eat sugar for three days. I will give my sugar to Mother Teresa for her children." After three days his father and mother brought him to our house. I had never met them before, and this little one could scarcely pronounce my name. But he knew exactly what he had come to do. He knew that he wanted to share his love. . . .

I want you to find the poor here, right in your own home first. And begin love there. Be that good news to your own people. And find out about your next-door neighbour. Do you know who they are?

I had the most extraordinary experience with a Hindu family who had eight children. A gentleman came to our house and said: "Mother Teresa, there is a family with eight children; they have not eaten for so long; do something." So I took some rice and I went there immediately. And I saw the children—their eyes shining with hunger. I don't know if you have ever seen hunger. But I have seen it very often. And [the mother] took the rice, she divided the rice, and she went out. When she came back I asked her: "Where did you go, what did you do?" And she gave me a very simple answer: "They are hungry also." What struck me most was that she knew—and who are they? a Muslim family—and she knew. I didn't bring more rice that evening because I wanted them to enjoy the joy of sharing.

But there were those children, radiating joy, sharing the joy with their mother because she had the love to give. And you see this is where love begins—at home. . . .

I believe that love begins at home, and if we can create a home for the poor, I think that more and more love will spread. And we will be able through this understanding love to bring peace, be the good news to the poor. The poor in our own family first, in our country, and in the world.

When I pick up a person from the street, hungry, I give him a plate of rice, a piece of bread, I have satisfied. I have removed that hunger. But a person that is shut out, that feels unwanted, unloved, terrified, the person that has been thrown out from society—that poverty is so hurtful and so much, and I find that very difficult. . . .

You must come to know the poor. Maybe our people here

have material things, everything, but I think that if we all look into our own homes, how difficult we find it sometimes to smile at each other, and that smile is the beginning of love.

And so let us always meet each other with a smile, for the smile is the beginning of love, and once we begin to love each other, naturally we want to do something."

"We are not social workers or social assistants. We want to bring the joy and love of God to the people, we want to bring them God Himself, who gives them His love through us. At the same time we love God and show Him our love by serving Him in these people. There are a lot of institutions caring for the sick. We do not want to be one among them. We are not one or another organization of social service. We have to be more, to give more, we have to give ourselves. We have to bring God's love to the people by our service. And the poor people have taught us what it really means to love and to serve God—although our full understanding will only come after we have died."

The Shifa Clinic

For centuries, in earlier eras Muslims throughout the Middle East established clinics and hospitals for the treatment of the ill and impoverished at little or no cost to the patients. Today, continuing in the West, in Sacramento, California, Muslims have coordinated efforts with the local university and students of medicine there to begin a free clinic for the poor and needy[85] in their area. God willing, more and more of these compassionate efforts may blossom and yield good fruit of service throughout our world.

[85]To learn more about the Shifa Clinic, http://cim.ucdavis.edu/clinics/Shifa/about.shtml.

It may be a drop in the ocean, but the ocean is made up of drops.

~ Mother Teresa of Calcutta[86]

[86] Stewart, *Women of Vision*, p. 131.

MERCY
(*Rahīmiyyah*)

God is the Best Protector and the Most Merciful of those to show Mercy.
[*Sūrah Yūsuf* 12:64]

We sent you not except as a mercy to the worlds.
[*Sūrah al-Anbiyā*ᶜ 21:107]

ᶜĀʾishah asked [Muḥammad ﷺ]: "Does one come to Paradise only by the mercy of Allāh?" He repeated three times over: "No one comes to Paradise except by the mercy of Allāh!" "Not even you, Messenger of Allāh?" she asked. "Not even I, unless Allāh enfolds me in His mercy."

He told his companions: "When Allāh completed the creation He wrote the following, which is with him above His Throne: 'My mercy takes precedence over My wrath,'" and this *ḥadīth* is decisive for the Muslims; it states categorically that all the "names" and attributes by which the Qurʾān indicates various aspects of the divine nature as they relate to humanity are subordinate to this supreme and essential attribute. . . . Speaking in the first person in the Qurʾān, God says: *My mercy embraceth all things* [*Sūrah al-A*ᶜ*rāf* 7:156], and this mercy communicates itself to those who are receptive: *Indeed, those who believe and do good, the Merciful will endow them with loving kindness* (wuddan) [*Sūrah Maryam* 19:96]; and: *Who else but those who have lost their way could despair of the mercy of their Lord?* [*Sūrah al-Ḥijr* 15:56].[87]

According to the *ḥadīth qudsī*, in which God Himself speaks through the mouth of the Prophet ﷺ, "My Mercy takes precedence over My wrath." Without Mercy, nothing would be; it is

---

[87] Reprinted by permission from *Islam and the Destiny of Man*, p. 67, by Charles Le Gai Eaton, the State University of New York Press © 1985, State University of New York. All rights reserved.

> through Mercy alone that God creates the worlds. In the words of another *ḥadīth qudsī*, "I was a hidden treasure and loved to be known, so I created the world that I might be known."[88]

Our very existence is a free gift of God's compassionate generosity. God has also given us prophets and messengers to guide us to Him, helping us to be better able to receive the mercy that is intended for us. The more we respond to the guidance of our Sustainer, the more Mercy is able to reach us and be received by us.

> The path He has laid out for us to return to Him is a Mercy: the word *sharīʿah* literally means "a path that leads to water, to refreshment." Even the dire warnings that appear in the Qurʾān are essentially nothing but the protective words of a Friend who doesn't want to see us lose our way and come to grief. And if our existence is a gift, and God's guidance a further Mercy, what better way to show gratitude for Our existence, and for God's sustenance and protection, than to extend Mercy to all creation?
>
> One of Muḥammad's titles is the 'Key to Mercy.' Perhaps the Prophet's greatest act of Mercy was his clemency to his former enemies, the Quraysh, after his conquest of Mecca.[89]

Rather than returning as a proud victor, he rode into Mecca with head bowed, in humility before his Lord as an instrument of His mercy:

> Mounted on Qaṣwāʾ, Muḥammad rode into his birthplace unopposed and immediately proclaimed a general amnesty. "This," he said, "'is the Day of Mercy, the day upon which Allāh hath exalted Quraysh." He had come, not to destroy, but to rectify, and a noble people had been reborn. The historical consequences of this act of clemency were incalculable. Over the

---

[88] Charles Upton, contributor.

[89] Ibid.

> succeeding centuries no conquering Muslim general could enter a territory or city without knowing himself subject—on pain of damnation—to the obligation of mercy and the necessity to follow the example set that day; and this in turn led to countless conversions among people who learned forebearance from this example.[90]

It is a great mercy from God that He has communicated to us, and told us that He will listen to our call upon Him and respond. *And if My servants ask you about Me—witness, I am near; I respond to the call of the one who calls, whenever he calls Me: let them, then, respond to Me, and have faith in Me, so that they may follow the right way.* [*Sūrah al-Baqarah* 2:186]. Sometimes a response to our prayer may be delayed as sometimes we *pray for things that are harmful as if they were praying for that which is good: for people are inclined to be hasty* [*Sūrah al-Isrā*ᶜ 17:11].

Yet always does He give you something
out of what you may be asking of Him,
and if you tried to count God's blessings,
you could never compute them.
[*Sūrah Ibrāhīm* 14:34].

The supplicant's realization that he stands in constant need of Allāh's help, his confidence in a positive response to his prayers, his trust in Allāh's providential care, and his avoidance of any spite or ill-will, or other attendant negative feelings, all impact directly on a person's practical behavior. For example, the feeling that I am completely dependent on Allāh makes me hope and fear. I look forward hopefully for His mercy, but also fear His displeasure. This psychological state should make me more eager and careful to abide by His will in my practical life.

When a person is in distress, his supplications tend to be more urgent and vehement. This urgency and vehemence, with

[90] Reprinted by permission from *Islam and the Destiny of Man*, p. 127, by Charles Le Gai Eaton, the State University of New York Press © 1985, State University of New York. All rights reserved.

all the repetition involved, forge a sense of commitment on both intellectual and behavioral levels.

My confidence that Allāh does listen to my prayers makes me love Him and adore Him, and commits me in practice to what I beseech of Allāh in my supplications. If I am sure of the answer to my prayers; then I do tend to behave accordingly.

When I pray for forgiveness and feel sure that my prayer will be granted, I become more careful and try not to repeat anything that could blemish my purity and state of innocence attained through supplication for forgiveness. Similarly if I pray for success in life, I must try to mold my approach and conduct in whatever way is essential to achieve a higher degree of excellence in my work. In this way, supplication instills in my mind love of work, mastery and perfection in work, and love for Allāh, which latter is of prime importance as a result of my greater confidence in Him.

Reposing one's trust in Allāh and entrusting one's affairs to His providential care is an effective way to engender enthusiasm and love for one's work, because it strikes a balance between what man cherishes and actually achieves and what he desires but cannot realize in practice.

Successful undertakings and critical situations, such as wars and other emergencies, and momentous events, whether happy or sad, undoubtedly call for fortitude, calm, and forbearance. Perhaps the most important of these undertakings is the struggle to change one's self and the community or society in which one lives for the benefit and betterment of all people.

The injunction that one's supplication must be free of any spite, ill-will, or desire to harm others is conducive to creating a healthy and sound relationship between a man and his fellow men.[91]

---

[91] Al-ᶜAnani. *Freedom and Responsibility in Qur'anic Perspective*, pp. 199-200.

The *sunnah* [example] of the Prophet ﷺ exemplifies a perfect harmony between supplication and its practical manifestations. Once a Companion from among the Anṣār came to the Prophet ﷺ and complained to him about his needs and poverty. Thereupon the Prophet ﷺ mercifully taught him in a practical way how to overcome his difficulties and live up to the higher ideals of supplication wherein a Muslim seeks refuge with Allāh from incapacity and laziness.

"Haven't you got anything in your house?" he asked him. "Yes, I have a piece of old cloth which we use as a dress as well as a floor-cover, besides a pot that we use for drinking water."

The Prophet ﷺ publicly auctioned these articles among his Companions. They were sold for less than two dirhams. He then ordered the Anṣārī companion to buy food for his family with one dirham, and an axe with the other. He then ordered the man not to come to see him for a fortnight, and advised him to spend all this time in cutting wood and selling it. Two weeks later, the Anṣārī companion came to see him. Now he had ten dirhams. Thereupon the Prophet ﷺ said to him, "This is better for you than coming on the Day of Judgment with your face marked (and disfigured) with beggary."[92]

The mercy that Allāh created in human beings prompts us to sympathize with those who fall ill. Al-Bukhārī narrated a *ḥadīth* by Abū Huraira that the Prophet ﷺ emphasized that human mercy is a minute continuation of the mercy of Allāh. The Prophet ﷺ said: "Allāh divided mercy into a hundred portions. He kept ninety-nine portions for Him, and released one portion on the earth. It is from this portion that creatures have mercy [towards each other], that a mare would lift her hoof lest it hit her child."[93]

---

[92] Ibid., p. 205.

[93] Abū Ghudda, *Islamic Manners*, p. 89.

On the authority of Abū Hurayrah ﷺ someone stated, "O Messenger of God, call [the wrath of] God down upon the polytheists!" He replied, "I was sent as a mercy; I was not sent as a punishment."[94]

The Mercy of the Prophet

When the Prophet ﷺ was an infant a bedouin woman by the name of Ḥalīma took him as her foster child to care for him and nurse him in the desert. This was the custom among the noble Meccan tribes. Muḥammad stayed with her for six years, though each year he was brought back to his grandfather and mother for a visit. When he was six Ḥalīma returned him to his mother who cared for him until she died two years later.

Thereupon his grandfather ᶜAbd al-Muṭṭalib took charge of him, but he too died when the Prophet ﷺ was ten. Then his two uncles, his father's two brothers, Az-Zubayr and Abū Ṭālib, took responsibility for him. In his early teens his uncle az-Zubayr took him to Yemen. His account states that on that journey they saw signs (of his prophethood). One of these was that a stallion camel had made its way some distance along a valley through which the party was passing. When the stallion saw the Messenger of God ﷺ it knelt down and rubbed its chest on the ground and so he mounted it. Another sign was that they came to a stream in violent flood but God Almighty dried it up so that they could cross it. Thereafter his uncle az-Zubayr died; at that time he was fourteen and Abū Ṭālib alone took charge of him.

What is implied here is that the blessedness of the Prophet ﷺ came down upon Ḥalīma as-Saᶜdiyya and her family, when he was young and then his virtues reverted to the people of

[94] Al-Qushayri, *Principles of Sufism*, p. 247.

Hawāzin when he took them prisoners after their battle; that occurred a month following the capture of Mecca. They were related to him because of his being suckled among them. He therefore released them, taking pity on them, and treating them with kindness. . . .

Concerning the battle with Hawāzin, Muḥammad b. Isḥāq related . . . "We were with the Messenger of God ﷺ at the battle of Ḥunayn and when he seized their properties and took them prisoners, a delegation from Hawāzin who had accepted Islām came to him at al-Jiʿrāna.[95] They said, 'O Messenger of God, we are one family and tribe. You know well what misfortune has befallen us. Have mercy on us, and may God have mercy on you.' Their spokesman Zuhayr b. Ṣurad then arose and said, 'O Messenger of God, those prisoners you have in the stockades are your aunts and your nurses who looked after you. If we had suckled Ibn Abū Shamar or al-Nuʿmān b. al-Mundhir and then we were to suffer from them what we have from you, we would have hoped for their help and kindness. And yet you are the most honourable of men.' He then recited the verses:

'Have pity on us, O Messenger of God, in kindness; for you are the man we plead with and implore.

Have pity on a tribe ruined by fate, their whole divided, their fortune adversely changed,

Which has left us to cry out in sorrow; a people in whose hearts there is gloom and tragedy,

Unless you ward it off with kindnesses you spread forth, O most superior of men in wisdom when it is tested.

Have pity on women you once sucked, your mouth filled with their pure milk,

Have pity on women you once sucked, for then whatever happens will sustain your reputation.

Do not make us as those who scattered and died; spare us, for we are a tribe of fame.

---

[95] A place between Mecca and aṭ-Ṭaʾif.

We give thanks for kindnesses even if not redeemed, and after this day we will have a store (of good will). . . .

Dress in forgiveness those you used to suck, your mothers; for acts of forgiveness become widely known.

We hope for forgiveness from you; dress these people in it, if forgive you will, and then be triumphant.

So forgive and may God forgive you from whatever you fear on Judgement Day when victory shall be given you.'

"The Messenger of God ﷺ then said, 'Whatever prizes were due myself or the family of ʿAbd al-Muṭṭalib, that goes to God and to you all.' *Al-Anṣār*[96] then said, 'And what was to be for us we give to God and to his Messenger ﷺ.'"

It will be later told how he set them free; they were 6,000, men and women combined. He gave them many camels and people. So that Abū al-Ḥusayn b. Fāris said, "The value of what he gave them that day totalled 500,000 dirhams."[97]

ʿAlī

There is no youth braver than ʿAlī.
I am from ʿAlī and ʿAlī is from me.
The truth circulates with him (ʿAlī) wherever he goes.
I am the City of Knowledge and ʿAlī is its Gate (*bāb*).

~ Ḥadīth of Muḥammad

Amīr al-muʿminīn[98] ʿAlī ؑ was the son of Abū Ṭālib ؑ, the leader of the Banū Hāshim. Abū Ṭālib was the uncle and guardian of the Holy Prophet ﷺ and the person who had brought the young Muḥammad to his house and raised him like his own son after the death of his grandfa-

---

[96] *Al-anṣār* is a term denoting the Muslims of Medina who granted the Prophet refuge following his migration from Mecca.

[97] Ibn Kathīr, *The Life of the Prophet Muḥammad*, Vol. I, pp. 166-168.

[98] The "prince of the faithful."

ther. It was also Abū Ṭālib who shielded Muḥammad from tribal anger during the early days of his prophetic mission.

ʿAlī عليه السلام was born ten years before the commencement of the prophetic mission of the Prophet ﷺ. When ʿAlī was six years old, due to famine in the region of Mecca, Muḥammad took him into his household and guardianship. Now that he was married to the wealthy Khadījah رضي الله عنها, Muḥammad was able to better care for his cousin and relieve some of the burden on his uncle's household. It was here that ʿAlī became one of the first to accept the prophethood of Muhamamd just after he received the first divine revelation.

> ʿAlī was always in the company of the Prophet until the Prophet migrated from Mecca to Medina. On the night of the migration to Medina (*hijrah*) when the [angry Meccans] had surrounded the house of the Prophet and were determined to invade the house at the end of the night and cut him to pieces while he was in bed, ʿAlī slept in place of the Prophet while the Prophet left the house and set out for Medina. After the departure of the Prophet, according to his wish ʿAlī gave back to the people the trusts and charges that they had left with the Prophet. Then he went on to Medina with his mother, the daughter of the Prophet, and two other women. In Medina also ʿAlī was constantly in the company of the Prophet in private and in public. The Prophet gave Fāṭimah, his beloved daughter from Khadījah, to ʿAlī as his wife and when the Prophet was creating bonds of brotherhood among his companions he selected ʿAlī as his brother.
>
> ʿAlī was present in all the wars in which the Prophet participated, except the battle of Tabūk when he was ordered to stay in Medina in place of the Prophet.[42] He did not retreat in any battle nor did he turn his face away from any enemy. He never disobeyed the Prophet, so that the Prophet said, "ʿAlī is never separated from the Truth nor the Truth from ʿAlī."
>
> On the day of the death of the Prophet, ʿAlī was thirty-three years old. . . . ʿAlī was almost completely cut off from

public affairs. He retreated to his house where he began to train competent individuals in the Divine sciences and in this way he passed the twenty-five years of the caliphate of the first three caliphs who succeeded the Prophet. When the third caliph was killed, people gave their allegiance to him and he was chosen as caliph. [He governed] for four years and nine months.[99]

According to the testimony of friend and foe alike, ʿAlī had no shortcomings from the point of view of human perfection. And in the Islamic virtues he was a perfect example of the upbringing and training given by the Prophet. . . . In science and knowledge ʿAlī was the most learned of the companions of the Prophet, and of Muslims in general. In his learned discourses he was the first in Islām to open the door for logical demonstration and proof and to discuss the "divine sciences" or metaphysics (*maʿārif-i ilāhiyah*). He spoke concerning the esoteric aspect of the Qurʾān and devised Arabic grammar in order to preserve the Qurʾān's form of expression. He was the most eloquent Arab in speech. . . .

The courage of ʿAlī was proverbial. In all the wars in which he participated during the lifetime of the Prophet, and also afterward, he never displayed fear or anxiety. Although in many battles such as those of Uḥud, Ḥunayn, Khaybar, and Khandaq the aides to the Prophet and the Muslim army trembled in fear or dispersed and fled, he never turned his back to the enemy. Never did a warrior or soldier engage ʿAlī in battle and come out of it alive. Yet, with full chivalry he would never slay a weak enemy nor pursue those who fled. He would not engage in surprise attacks or in turning streams of water upon the enemy. . . .

ʿAlī was also without equal in religious asceticism and the worship of God. . . . Abū Dardāʾ, one of the companions, one

[99] ʿAllāmah Sayyid Muḥammad Ḥusayn Ṭabāṭabāʾī, *Shīʿite Islam*, translated by Seyyed Hossein Nasr (Albany, New York: SUNY Press, © 1980), pp. 191-192.

> day saw the body of ʿAlī in one of the palm plantations of Medina lying on the ground as stiff as wood. He went to ʿAlī's house to inform his noble wife, the daughter of the Prophet, and to express his condolences. The daughter of the Prophet said, "My cousin (ʿAlī) has not died. Rather, in fear of God he has fainted. This condition overcomes him often."
>
> There are many stories told of ʿAlī's kindness to the lowly, compassion for the needy and the poor, and generosity and munificence toward those in misery and poverty. ʿAlī spent all that he earned to help the poor and the needy, and himself lived in the strictest and simplest manner. ʿAlī loved agriculture and spent much of his time digging wells, planting trees, and cultivating fields. But all the fields that he cultivated or wells that he built he gave in endowment (*waqf*) to the poor. His endowments, known as the "alms of ʿAlī," had the noteworthy income of twenty-four thousand gold dinars toward the end of his life.[100]

He, too, was a mercy to other human beings. The story is told of how an enemy spat in the face of the Prince of the Faithful, ʿAlī ﵁, and how when anger then arose in ʿAlī, he put down his sword:

> Learn how to act sincerely from ʿAlī:
> know that the Lion of God (ʿAlī) was purged of deceit.
> In fighting he got the upper hand of a warrior,
> and quickly drew a sword to slay him.
> That warrior spat on the face of ʿAlī,
> the pride of all the prophets and saints;
> He spat on that countenance before which the moon's face
> bows low in the sanctuary.
> ʿAlī at once threw his sword away
> and stopped fighting.
> That champion was astounded and amazed
> by his showing forgiveness and mercy without need.

---

[100] Ibid., pp. 193-194.

He said, "You lifted your keen sword against me:
 why have you now flung it aside and spared me?
What did you see that was better than combat with me,
 so that you no longer seek to kill me?
What did you see, that from seeing only its reflection
 a flame appeared in my heart and soul?
What did you see, beyond this existence and space,
 that was better than life?—so that you gave me life.
In bravery you are the Lion of the Lord:
 in generosity who indeed knows what you are?
In generosity you are like Moses' cloud in the desert,
 from where did these incomparable dishes of food arrive?"
"O ᶜAlī, you who are all mind and eye,
 relate a little of that which you have seen!
Even without speaking, the moon shows the way,
 With speech it becomes light upon light. . . .
Since you are the gate of the City of Knowledge,
 since you are the beams of the Sun of Clemency,
Be open, O Gate, to him that seeks the gate,
 so that by means of you the husks may reach the core.
Be open unto everlasting, O Gate of Mercy,
 O Entrance-hall to *None is like unto Him.*"
Every air and mote is indeed a place for vision of God,
 but as long as it is unopened, who will say,
 "There is a door"?
Unless the Watcher opens a door,
 this idea never stirs within.
When a door is opened for someone, he becomes amazed,
 grows wings, and flies.[101]

---

[101] Jalālu'ddin Rūmī, *The Mathnawī of Jalālu'ddin Rūmī*, Translation of Books I & II, edited and translated from the Persian by Reynold A. Nicholson (London, Luzac and Company, Ltd., © 1930, reprinted 1982), pp. 202-204 (I:3721-3768); adapted by Camille Helminski.

How the Prince of the Faithful responded:
For God's sake, for Reality
whose slave I am, I wield this sword.
The body does not command me,
nor does the lion of craving
overcome the lion of God.
Like a sword wielded by the sun,
I embody these words in war:
Thou didst not throw when thou threwest.
I've dropped the baggage of self.
That which is not God is nothing.
God is the sun, and I am a shadow.
Jewelled with the pearls of Union,
my sword brings life in battle, not death.
Blood will not dull my shining sword;
nor will the wind blow my sky away.
I am not chaff but a mountain of patience.
What fierce wind could lift a mountain?
What the wind blows away is trash,
and winds blow from every side—
the winds of anger, lust, and greed
carry away those who do not keep
the times of prayer.
I am a mountain, and my being is His building.
If I am tossed like a straw,
it is His wind that moves me.
Only His wind stirs my desires.
My Captain is love of the One.
Anger is a king over kings,
but anger, once bridled, may serve.
A gentle sword struck the neck of anger.
God's anger came on like mercy.
My roof in ruins; I drown in light.
Though called "the father of dust,"
I have grown like a garden.

And so I must put down my sword,
that my name might be *He loves for God's sake,*
that my desire may be *He hates for God's sake,*
that my generosity might be *He gives for God's sake.*
My stinginess is for God, as are my gifts.
I belong to God, not to anyone else;
and what I do is not a show,
not imagined, not thought up, but seen.
Set free from effort and searching,
I have tied my sleeve to the cuff of God—
if I am flying, I see where I fly;
if I am whirling, I know the axis on which I turn;
if I am dragging a burden, I know to where.
I am the moon, and the sun is in front of me.
I cannot tell the people more than this.
Can the river contain the Sea?[102]

---

[102] Jelaluddin Rumi, *Love Is a Stranger,* translated by Kabir Edmund Helminski, (Brattleboro, Vermont: Threshold Books, 1993), pp. 82-83 (*Mathnawī* I:3787-3810).

CHARITY
(*Tazkiyyah*)

And yet, they have been commanded no more than this:
to worship God, sincere in their devoted faith in Him alone;
turning away from all that is false;
and to remain constant in prayer;
and to practice regular charity:
and that is the true and straight Way.
[*Sūrah al-Bayyinah* 98:5]

O you who have faith!
Spend on others out of the good things which you may have acquired,
and out of that which We[103] *bring forth for you out of the earth;*
and do not choose for your spending
anything bad which you yourselves would not accept
without averting your eyes in disdain.
And know that God is the One Who is Rich,
the One Worthy of Praise.
Satan threatens you with the prospect of poverty
and bids you to be stingy,
while God promises you His forgiveness and abundance;
and God is infinite, all knowing,
granting wisdom to whom He wills:
and whoever is granted wisdom
has indeed been granted abundant wealth,
but none bears this in mind
except those who are gifted with insight.
[*Sūrah al-Baqarah* 2:267-269]

---

[103] In the revelation of the Qur'ān, the Divine Source sometimes chooses to speak or refer to Itself from the first person singular, "I" or "Me," sometimes as the third person singular, and sometimes as the first person plural, "We." Some commentators suggest that the usage of "We" refers to the attributes of God.

Establish for us what is good in this world
as well as in the life to come:
see how we have turned to You in repentance!"
God answered: "With My stringency I try whom I will—
but My mercy overspreads everything,
and so I shall confer it upon those who are conscious of Me
and spend in charity, and who have faith in Our signs."
[*Sūrah al-Aʿrāf* 7:156]

Witness that you are those invited to spend freely in the Way of God;
but among you are some who are stingy.
But any who are stingy are so at the expense of their own souls.
But God is free of all wants and it is you who are needy.
[*Sūrah Muḥammad* 47:38]

I call to witness this land
in which you are free to dwell,
and the bond between parent and child:
truly, We have created the human being to labor and struggle.
Does he think that no one has power over him?
He may boast: "I have spent abundant wealth!"
Does he think that no one sees him?
Haven't We made a pair of eyes for him?
And a tongue and a pair of lips?
And shown him the two ways?
But he has not quickened along the path that is steep.
And what will explain to you what the steep path is?—
the freeing of one who is enslaved,
or the giving of food in time of need
to the orphan with claims of relationship,
or to the helpless, lowly one in the dust,
and being of those who have faith and encourage patience,
and who encourage deeds of kindness and compassion.
These are the companions of the right hand.
[*Sūrah al-Balad* 90:2-18]

Truly, those who live in awe of their Sustainer;
those who have faith in the signs of their Sustainer;
those who do not attribute divinity to any but your Sustainer;
and those who distribute their charity
with their hearts trembling with awe
because they will return to their Sustainer—
it is these who quicken in every good work
and these who are at the forefront.
On no soul do We place a burden greater than it can bear;
with Us is a record which clearly shows the truth:
never will they be wronged.
[*Sūrah al-Muʾminūn* 23:57-62]

Those saved from the covetousness of their own souls,
they are the ones who achieve prosperity.
[*Sūrah al-Ḥashr* 59:9]

Let the person of means spend according to his means:
and the one whose resources are restricted,
let him spend according to that which God has given.
God puts no burden on any soul beyond what He bestows.
Surely, after hardship God will bring ease.
[*Sūrah aṭ-Ṭalāq* 65:7]

There are numerous verses in the Qurʾān encouraging human beings to help each other by any means given.

In Islām man, spiritually speaking, does not own anything. He is given everything, even his own life, as a [loan] from God. Almsgiving is a reminder of this fact and it is a kind of purification for every other thing he has. It is also as in the other Revelations an expression of attaching oneself to God through being a channel for His Mercy and support to others who are less fortunate in their worldly life. It is remarkable that whenever prayer is mentioned in the Qurʾān, almsgiving, *zakāh*, follows.

The reason is that both prayer and almsgiving are related. When man is attached to the Higher Source he feels that what he gives is not his. It is the "right" of others. In so doing he attaches himself to the Higher Source. The Qur'ān describes those who have that feeling: *In whose wealth is a recognized right for the [needy] who asks and him who is deprived* [*Sūrah al-Ma'ārij* 70:24-25].

In Islamic teachings, almsgiving, *zakāh*, is the religious practice that gives a person a chance to be purified through a regular divine duty to the whole of society. Islamic teaching [instructs a person to give in charity] 2.5 percent of the amount he has saved in that year to the needy. As for people who earn their living from agriculture, if they depend on rain, they must give one tenth of their harvested crop to the poor; if they irrigate their land, then one twentieth.[104]

For it is He who has brought into being gardens—
both the cultivated ones and those growing wild—
and the date-palm, and fields bearing all manner of produce,
and the olive, and the pomegranate:
all resembling one another and yet so different!
Eat of their fruit when it ripens,
and contribute appropriate portions on harvest day.
And do not be wasteful:
truly, He does not love those who are wasteful!
[*Sūrah al-An'ām* 6:141]

Take heed that you do not do your alms before men,
to be seen of them:
otherwise you have no reward of your Father which is in heaven.
Therefore when you do your alms,
do not sound a trumpet before you, as the hypocrites do
in the synagogues and in the streets,
that they may have glory of men.

---

[104] Rafea, *Beyond Diversities: Reflections on Revelation*, p. 98.

Verily I say unto you, they have their reward.
(The Bible, Matthew 6:1-2)

This leads us to still another consideration. What one wants for oneself, one must also desire for others. Islām induces man to share the good things of life with his fellowmen as his brothers. Islām teaches us that the more general a supplication is, the more likelihood there is of its acceptance. There are many sayings of the Prophet ﷺ that corroborate this. For example, he told us that the prayer of a brother for his brother without his knowledge is always granted; and that the angels also supplicate for the sake of those who supplicate for the sake of others, saying, 'And may you also be granted a similar good."

When a Muslim supplicates for others and wishes for them what he wishes for himself, and continues to do so over a long period, he benefits personally. It brings him nearer to Allāh as well to his fellowmen. And he gradually attains to a state where his likes and dislikes merge and become one with the pleasure and displeasure of Allāh. In addition, he is saved from moral diseases, like malice, envy, spite, and hatred of others. Good and healthy feelings eventually become the hallmark of his social behavior, so he is eager to help others and overlook their faults and is ready to forgive them.

He who helps his brother, will be helped by Allāh. Another *ḥadīth* as narrated by Anas reports that the Prophet ﷺ said, "None of you can be a true believer unless he wishes for his brother what he wishes for himself."[105]

To be a channel of the higher power is not limited to giving money. Every act that emerges out of love, compassion, and sympathy exposes man to God's Blessings.

The Prophet ﷺ said: "A good word is considered a gift. To take away a stone out of a traveler's way is counted as charity."

---

[105] Al-ʿAnani. *Freedom and Responsibility in Qur'anic Perspective*, pp. 200-201.

A kind word with forgiveness is better than almsgiving followed by injury. Allāh is Absolute, the Kind. [*Sūrah al-Baqarah* 2:263]

The teaching puts a minimum regular contribution of man's [portion] to his fellow brethren as a symbol of responsibility, yet almsgiving is unlimited and encouraged.[106]

The parable of those who spend their substance in the Way of Allah
is that of a grain out of which grow seven ears,
and each ear has a hundred grains.
Allah gives manifold increase to whom He pleases,
and Allah is All-Encompassing, All-Knowing.
[*Sūrah al-Baqarah* 2:261]

Imām ᶜAlī has said, "Take care of faith by giving away in charity, protect your wealth by giving the poor-rate, and avert the waves of misfortune by prayer."[107]

The Messenger said, "Do you know the rights of the neighbour? Methinks you know but little. Surely a man does not believe in Allāh and the Last Day if he does not protect his neighbour from harm. If he asks for a loan then he should lend it to him; if something good happens to him he should congratulate him; if something evil, he should console him. He should not construct a high building in such a way as to cut off the wind except with his permission. If he desires fruit, then he should be given it, for if the fruit is taken in secrecy and neither he nor his children are given any of it then they will be vexed. There are three types of neighbour: those who have three rights—the rights of Islām, the right of being a neighbour, and the right of kinship; those who have two rights—the rights of Islām and that of the neighbour; and those who have one right—the unbeliever who has the right of the neighbour."[108]

---

[106] Rafea, *Beyond Diversities: Reflections on Revelation*, p. 99.

[107] Haeri, *Prophetic Traditions in Islām*, p. 127 (*Nahj*, IV, 691).

[108] Ibid., p. 216 (*Mishkāt*, 212-215).

Do good as you would like good to be done to you.[109]

When a child of Adam dies, he is completely cut off (from this world) in the hereafter except for three things (whose blessings shall reach him): a perpetual charity, useful knowledge that others continue to gain from, and a pious child praying for him. (A *ḥadīth* of the Prophet Muḥammad)[110]

A man asked, "O Prophet of God, which is the best part of Islām?" He said, "That you give food [to the hungry] and extend greetings to all whom you know and whom you do not know."

Some poor Muslims complained to the Prophet: "The affluent have made off with (all) the rewards: they pray as we pray, fast as we fast, and they give away in charity from their money (and this we can't match)."

The Prophet said: "Has not God made things for you to give away in charity? Every praise to God of His perfection is a charity. Every thankfulness to God is a charity. Every utterance that there is no God but God is a charity. To enjoin good and forbid evil is charity.[111]

And a smile is also charity:

Know happiness and joy in your relationships with your brethren. ᶜAbdul-ᶜAzīz ibn Jaᶜfar of Baghdad reports that al-Ḥusayn ibn Zayd said to Jaᶜfar ibn Muḥammad, "Tell me, did our beloved Prophet ever joke?" He answered, "Allāh bestowed on him the best manner of joyfulness. Allāh sent other prophets who had suffering and distress, but He sent Muḥammad ﷺ for mercy and compassion. One of the signs of his kindness and love for his people was that he joked with them. He did this so that they would not stay away from him out of

[109] Ibid., p. 171 (*Makārim al-Akhlāq,* 245).

[110] Hathout, *Reading the Muslim Mind,* p. 85.

[111] Ibid., p. 87.

awe. My father, Muḥammad, told me that his father, ᶜAlī, was told by his father, al-Ḥusayn, that he heard the Messenger of Allāh say: "Allāh hates those who make disagreeable and sad faces at their friends."[112]

The Messenger of God ﷺ said, "You will not be able to give happiness by means of your wealth, so do it by means of a cheerful expression and good character."[113]

Fāṭimah

Fāṭimah (c. 608–633 C.E.), may God preserve her secret, was called the "resplendent one" (*az-Zahrā*) because of her luminous face, which seemed to radiate light.[114] It is said that when she stood for prayer, the *mihrab*[115] would reflect the light of her countenance. She was also called *al-Batul* ("the virgin" or "the devoted one") because of her asceticism. She spent a great deal of her time in prayer and worship, in recitation of the Qur'ān, in fasting, and in service to the growing Muslim community. The youngest daughter of Khadījah and Muḥammad, she was born near the time of the opening of his prophethood, and so she grew up under the dynamic influence of the new message that was being conveyed.

---

[112] Al-Sulami, *The Way of Sufi Chivalry*, p. 43.

[113] Al-Qushayri, *Principles of Sufism*, p. 242.

~ This brief biography of Fāṭimah is excerpted from *Women of Sufism, A Hidden Treasure* by Camille Helminski, pp. 8-12. It is interesting to note that one of the most important appearances of the Virgin Mary in recent times is "Our Lady of Fāṭimah." Mary appeared to three young children in Portugal in 1917, near the small village of Fāṭimah, named after the Prophet Muḥammad's daughter, and was subsequently witnessed there by tens of thousands of people. Since that event, numerous Christians worldwide address the Virgin Mary in prayer as "Our Lady of Fāṭimah," further interweaving the strands of the Abrahamic faiths.

[114] *Alīm 6.0*: see "Fāṭimah bint Muḥammad."

[115] The *mihrab* is the prayer niche, which indicates the direction of prayer. It is also the word for "sanctuary"; see *Sūrah Āl ᶜImrān* 3:37.

As his youngest child, she would often accompany Muḥammad as he moved about the Meccan community, handling the family errands, praying at the Kaᶜbah, or visiting Muslim friends and families, continually speaking of the new faith. During these early years of Islām, she witnessed countless episodes of persecution and would staunchly defend her father and care for him. Some years later, after the death of her mother, when she was the only one of his own children still living at home with him, witnessing his sorrow, this loving concern for her father intensified and so earned her the title Umm Abī-ha ("the mother of her father"). Some also refer to this title as being indicative of the fact that his familial line was carried forward through her.

Fāṭimah's fine manners and gentle speech were part of her lovely and endearing personality. She was especially kind to poor and indigent folk and would often give all the food she had to those in need even if she herself remained hungry. She had no craving for the ornaments of this world nor for the luxury and comforts of life.[116]

After enduring extreme hardship during the Meccan boycott, two years after the community emigrated to Medina, and three years after the death of her beloved mother, at the age of approximately sixteen, Fāṭimah married ᶜAlī ibn Abī Ṭālib (the son of Muḥammad's dear uncle Abū Ṭālib), who had been living with the family since the death of his father some years earlier and who had been among the first to become a Muslim. ᶜAlī was known for his courage, virtue, and piety. He and Fāṭimah soon had a hut of their own near the Prophet in Medina. Two sons were born to them, Ḥasan and Ḥusayn, and two daughters, Umm Kulthūm and Zaynab. A third son, Muḥsin, died in infancy. The line of the family of the Prophet traces itself through Fāṭimah, Ḥasan, and Ḥusayn, and their children.

The marriage of Fāṭimah and ᶜAlī, although inspired by the Angel Gabriel,[117] also, like many marriages, had its vicissitudes. One day when

---

[116] *Alīm 6.0*: see "Fāṭimah bint Muḥammad."

[117] See John Pairman Brown and H. A. Rose (editor), *The Darvishes: Or Oriental Spiritualism* (Frank Cass Publishers, 1968), pp. 397-400.

Fāṭimah and ᶜAlī were at odds with each other, Muḥammad came to visit them. It is said that he lay down between them and had each of them place a hand on his belly. He told them to breathe with him and to remain together in that position until peace came to both of them. Sometime later he left their hut, smiling broadly. A companion who witnessed the difference in his countenance from when he had entered questioned him as to why he was now smiling. He responded that he was now smiling because the two people most loved by him were now at peace. [118]

Fāṭimah's life with ᶜAlī was as simple and frugal as it had been in her father's household. To relieve their extreme poverty, ᶜAlī, when he was not called to battle to defend their faith, worked as a drawer and carrier of water and she as a grinder of grain. One day Fāṭimah told ᶜAlī, "I have ground grain until my hands are blistered."

"And I've drawn water until my chest is aching," said ᶜAlī. He suggested to her that she ask her father, whose power and influence had grown since coming to Medina, to give her a servant.

Reluctantly, she did go to the Prophet, but when he inquired what had brought her to him, she could only respond, "I came to give you greetings of peace," and could not bring herself to ask for what she had intended.

When she returned home, she told ᶜAlī she had been ashamed to ask, so they went together to the Prophet and asked him for assistance, but the Prophet felt that others were in greater need, especially the *Ahl aṣ-Ṣuffah*, the "People of the Bench."[119]

ᶜAlī and Fāṭimah returned home somewhat dejected, but then that night, after they had gone to bed, they heard the voice of the Prophet

---

[118] SeeMuḥammad Ibn Saᶜd, *The Women of Madina*, translated by Aisha Bewley (London, United Kingdom: Ta-Ha Publishers, 1995), p. 18.

[119] These were impoverished Muslims who lodged on a bench at the entryway to the mosque in Medina. Fāṭimah and others of the Prophet's family and community did their best to care for them. They were devoted servants of God, purifying their hearts of all but Him. Many among them learned the Qur'ān by heart and the Prophet often stopped to engage in *muḥabbat* (affectionate conversation) with them. The Prophet was known to have said, "Poverty (*faqr*) is my pride."

asking permission to enter. Welcoming him, they both rose to their feet, but he told them: "Stay where you are," and sat down beside them. "Shall I not tell you of something better than that which you asked of me?" he asked and when they said yes, he said: "Words which *Jibrīl* (Gabriel) taught me, that you should say '*Subḥān Allāh*' (Glory be to God) ten times after every Prayer, and ten times '*Al-ḥamdu lillāh*' (Praise be to God), and ten times '*Allāhu Akbar*' (God is Great). And that when you go to bed you should say them thirty-three times each." ᶜAlī used to say in later years: "I have never once failed to say them since the Messenger of God taught them to us."[120]

It was often to the "word of God" that they turned for nourishment and well-being.

It is said that Fāṭimah greatly resembled her father and that her ways of sitting and standing and speaking were quite similar.

She inherited from Muḥammad a persuasive eloquence that was rooted in wisdom. When she spoke, people would often be moved to tears. She had the ability and the sincerity to stir the emotions, move people to tears and fill their hearts with praise and gratitude to God for His grace and His inestimable bounties.[121]

> ᶜĀʾishah, the later wife of the Prophet, said of her: "I have not seen any one of God's creation resemble the Messenger of God more in speech, conversation, and manner of sitting than Fāṭimah, may God be pleased with her. When the Prophet saw her approaching, he would welcome her, stand up and kiss her, take her by the hand and sit her down in the place where he was sitting." She would do the same when the Prophet came to her. She would stand up and welcome him with joy and kiss

---

[120] *Alīm 6.0:* see "Fāṭimah bint Muḥammad." See also Ibn Saᶜd, *The Women of Madina*, pp. 17-18. "ᶜAlī is also reported to have said: 'The Prophet of God has taught me a thousand doors of knowledge, each of which has opened to me a thousand others'." (Brown and Rose, *The Darvishes*, p. 432).

[121] *Alīm 6.0*, see "Fāṭimah bint Muḥammad."

him.[122]

The Prophet had a special love for Fāṭimah. He once said: "Whoever pleases Fāṭimah has indeed pleased God and whoever has caused her to be angry has indeed angered God. Fāṭimah is a part of me. Whatever pleases her pleases me and whatever angers her angers me."[123] When he went on a journey the last person of whom he took leave was Fāṭimah, and when he returned from the journey the first person he would see was Fāṭimah.

The Prophet extolled her as one of the four most exemplary women in history along with Mary, mother of Jesus; her own mother, Khadījah; and the wife of Pharoah, who rescued and raised Moses. These four women are considered the four holiest women of Islām.

One day while the Prophet was ill, he whispered something to Fāṭimah and she cried, and then he whispered again in her ear and she smiled. After the Prophet's death, ᶜĀʾishah asked her what Muḥammad had whispered to her. She answered that at first he had told her of his impending death, but then he had told her that she would be among the first to join him in paradise.

It was Fāṭimah who eloquently delivered her father's eulogy. She deeply mourned the death of the Holy Prophet and is later reported to have said: "It is not surprising that whoever catches the fragrance of Muḥammad's tomb will never know another perfume. Destiny injured me with a bereavement so sorrowful, and so dark, that if it had fallen on the days they would have been turned into eternal nights."[124]

Then, six months after the death of her beloved father, after a prolonged illness, she arose one morning smiling and called for a mat to be placed in the open courtyard of their home. She asked her companion, Salmā, for assistance in washing and perfuming herself, and then with her face turned towards the heavens, she asked for her husband, ᶜAlī.

He was taken aback when he saw her lying in the middle of the

---

[122] Ibid.

[123] Ibid.

[124] Ibid.

courtyard and asked her what was wrong. She smiled and said: "I have an appointment today with the Messenger of God." ʿAlī cried, and she tried to console him. She told him to look after their sons, al-Ḥasan (age seven) and al-Ḥusayn (age six), and advised that she should be buried without ceremony. She gazed upwards again, then closed her eyes and surrendered her soul to the Mighty Creator.[125]

She was twenty-nine years old when she passed from this world in 633 C.E. ʿAlī used to visit the grave of Fāṭimah frequently, and used to write verses to express his grief. On one occasion he wrote:

O thou grave, to thee I resort for paying homage to thee.
O thou, the repository of my beloved, thou answer me not.
O thou beloved tomb, what ails thee—
Thou respondeth not to my supplications.
Art thou out of humor, Because of the love that I bear thee?[126]

Though there is a sepulcher referred to as Fāṭimah's tomb near the Prophet's tomb in Medina, she most probably rests in al-Bāqī cemetery on the outskirts of Medina, and it was probably there that ʿAlī would often go for solace.

---

[125] Ibid.

[126] Ibid.

IV

Patience
Perseverance
Forbearance

Patience
(*Ṣabr*)

O you who have attained to faith!
Seek help through steadfast patience and prayer:
for observe, God is with those who are patient.
[*Sūrah al-Baqarah* 2:153]

And if you are patient in adversity and conscious of Him-
Truly, this is something upon which to set one's heart.
[*Sūrah Āl ʿImrān* 3:186]

And the messengers whom We sent before you were all human beings
who ate food and walked through the streets;
We have made some of you as a test for others.
Will you have patience?
For God is One Who sees.
[*Sūrah al-Furqān* 25:20]

Witness, I have rewarded them this day for their patience;
truly, it is they indeed who have achieved a triumph.
[*Sūrah al-Muʾminūn* 23:111]

Surely, it is We Who have sent down the Qur'an to you step by step.
So be constant in patience with the command of your Sustainer
and do not yield to the one who is in error or is ungrateful.
And mention your Sustainer's Name morning and evening,
and during the night prostrate yourself before Him
and praise Him throughout the long night.
[*Sūrah al-Insān* 76:23-26]

The journey of revelation of the Qurʾān was a long one for Muḥammad ﷺ. The first revelation, the first portion of the Qurʾān that was conveyed, was only a few lines long. It was over a period of twenty-three years that the words of the Qurʾān unfolded. A time came when people challenged Muḥammad, questioning God's power and asking him why he didn't just convey the Qur'ān as a whole. An *āyāt*, a verse or sign, was then revealed explaining that the Qur'ān was conveyed in stages in order to strengthen his heart. The power of God is infinitely great, capable of any feat, but for our sake and our needs, our learning and development is gradual. It takes nine months for a child to mature in the womb before it is ready to be born. If we rush such a process, we can cause harm. Patience with God's measure allows the fruit of our being and our work to mature appropriately.

> Imām ᶜAlī has said, "Bear patiently a task whose reward is indispensable to you, and desist from action whose punishment you are not capable of bearing; withstand the judgment of someone who has nothing but that on which to rely and take refuge in. If trials are met with contentment and patience they are a constant blessing, and if blessings are devoid of gratitude they are an ever-present trial."[127]

> He [ᶜAlī] also said, "There are two kinds of patience: patience in misfortune is a fine and beautiful thing, but better than this is patience when Allāh deprives you of something. Remembrance is of two kinds also: remembrance of Allāh in misfortune, and better than this is remembrance of Allāh when He deprives you of something and impedes you."[128]

> Aṣ-Ṣadiq said, "When the believer enters his grave, prayer is on his right, *zakāt* on his left, righteous actions are spread over him and patience bends down at his side, and if he enters the place of questioning, patience says to prayer, *zakāt,* and righteous actions, 'Take heed of your companion: if you fail him, then I am beneath him'."[129]

---

[127] Haeri, *Prophetic Traditions in Islām* p. 181 (Al-Ashtarī,I , 40-41).

[128] Ibid., p. 181 (*Mishkāt*, 19-26).

[129] Ibid., p. 182 (*Mishkāt*, 19-26).

Aṣ-Ṣadiq said, "Patience has the same relation to faith as the head to the body; if the head is removed the body dies, and if patience is removed faith dies."[130]

ᶜAlī b. Abī Ṭālib ﷺ observed, "Patience is a mount that never stumbles."[131]

It is often said that, "Patience is the key to joy."[132]

The Desert of Waiting

Joyce called a laughing good-bye after them, but, as she stood shading her eyes with her hand to watch them ride away, all the brightness seemed to die out of the mid-afternoon sunshine.

"How much I should have enjoyed it!" she thought. " I could ride as well as Jack if I had his pony, and shoot as well as Lloyd if I had her rifle, and would enjoy the trip to the river as much as either of them if I could only leave the work.

But I'm like that old Camelback Mountain over there. I'll never get away. It will be this way all the rest of my life."

Through the blur of tears that dimmed her sight a moment, the old mountain looked more hopeless than ever. She turned and went into the house to escape the sight of it. Presently, when the loaves were in the oven, and she had nothing to do but watch the baking, she brought her portfolio out to the kitchen and began looking through it for a sketch she had promised to show to Lloyd. It was the first time she had opened the portfolio since she had left Plainsville, and the sight of its contents made

---

[130] Ibid.

[131] Al-Qushayri, *Principles of Sufism*, p. 149.

[132] Rūmī, *The Mathnawī of Jalālu'ddin Rūmī*, translated by Nicholson, p. 9 (I:96).

~ "The Desert of Waiting" is excerpted from *The Little Colonel in Arizona* by Anne Fellows Johnston, published in 2000 by Pelican Publishing Company, Inc., pp. 139-161.

her fingers tingle. While she glanced over the sketches she had taken such pleasure in making, both in water-colours and pen and ink, her mother came into the kitchen.

"Joyce," she said, briskly, "don't you suppose we could afford some cookies while the oven is hot? I haven't baked anything for so long that I believe it would do me good to stir around in the kitchen awhile. I'll make some gingersnaps, and cut them out in fancy shapes, with a boy and girl apiece for the children, as I always used to make. Are there any raisins for the eyes and mouths ?"

It seemed so much like old times that Joyce sprang up to give her mother a squeeze. "That will be lovely!" she cried, heartily. "Here's an apron, and I'll beat the eggs and help you."

"No, I want to do it all myself," Mrs. Ware protested. "And I want you to take your sketching outfit, and go down to the clump of willows where Jack put the rustic bench for me. There are lovely reflections in the irrigating canal now, and the shadows are so soft that you ought to get a very pretty picture. You haven't drawn any since we left home, and I'm afraid your hand will forget its cunning if you never practice."

"What's the use," was on the tip of Joyce's tongue, but she could not dim the smile on her mother's face by her own hopeless mood, and presently she took her box of water-colours and started off to the seat under the willows. Mary and Norman, like two muddy little beavers, were using their Saturday afternoon playtime in building a dam across the lateral that watered the side yard. Joyce stood watching them a moment.

"What's the use of your doing that? " she asked, impatiently. "It can't stay there. You'll have to tear it down when you stop playing, and then there'll be all your work for nothing."

"We don't care, do we, Norman?" answered Mary, cheerfully. "It's fun while we're doing it, isn't it, Norman?"

As Joyce walked on, Mary's lively chatter followed her, and she could hear her mother singing as she moved about the kitchen. She was glad that they were all happy, but somehow it irritated her to feel that she was the only discontented one. It made her lonely. She opened her box and spread out her material, but she was in no mood for painting. She couldn't get the right shade of green in the willows, and the reflections in the water were blotchy.

" It's no use to try," she said, finally. "Mamma was right. My hand has already lost its cunning."

Leaning back on the rustic seat, she began idly tracing profiles on the paper, scarcely conscious of what she was doing. People's faces at first, then the outline of Camelback Mountain. Abstractedly, time after time, she traced it with slow sweeps of her brush until more than a score of kneeling camels looked back at her from the sheet of paper.

Presently a cough just behind her aroused her from her fit of abstraction, and, turning hastily, she saw Mr. Ellestad, the old Norwegian, coming toward her along the little path from the house. He bad been almost a daily visitor at the Wigwam since they moved into it, not always coming in, usually stopping for only a moment's chat under the pepper-trees, as he strolled by. But several times he had spent an entire morning with them, reading aloud, while Joyce ironed and her mother sewed, and Norman built block houses on the floor beside them. Once he had taken tea with them. He rarely came without bringing a book or a new magazine, or something of interest. And even when he was empty-handed, his unfailing cheerfulness made his visits a benefaction. Mary and Norman called him "Uncle Jan," such a feeling of kinship had grown up between them.

"Mary said you were here," he began, in his quaint, hesitating fashion, "so I came to find you. I have finished my legend at last, the legend I have made about Camelback Mountain. You know I have always insisted that there should be one, and as tradition has failed to hand one down to us, the task of manufacturing one has haunted me for three winters. Always, it seems, the old mountain has something to say to me whenever I look at it, something I failed to understand. But at last I have interpreted its message to mankind."

With a hearty greeting, Joyce moved over to make room for him upon the bench, and, as he sat down, he saw the sheet of paper on her lap covered with the repeated outlines of the old mountain.

"Ah! It has been speaking to you also!" he exclaimed. "What did it say?"

"Just one word," answered Joyce, "Hopeless! Everything out here is hopeless. It's useless to try to do anything or be anything. If fate has brought you here, kneel down and give up. No use to struggle, no use to hope. You'll never get away."

He started forward eagerly. "At first, yes, that is what I thought it said to me. But now I know it was only the echo of my own bitter mood I heard. But it is a mistake; that is not its message. Listen! I want to read it to you."

He took a note-book from his pocket. "Of course, it is crude yet. This is only the first draft. I shall polish it and study every word, and fit the sentences into place until the thought is crystallized as a real legend should be, to be handed down to future generations. Then people will not suspect that it is a home-made thing, spun from the fancy of one Jan Ellestad, a simple old Norwegian, who had no other legacy to leave the world he loved. This is it:

Once upon a time, a caravan set out across the desert, laden with merchandise for a far-distant market. Some of the camels bore in their packs wine-skins that held the richest vintage of the Orient. Some bore tapestries, and some carried dyestuffs and the silken fruits of the loom. On Shapur's camel was a heavy load of salt.

The hope of each merchant was to reach the City of his Desire before the Golden Gate should close. There were other gates by which they might enter but this one, opening once a year to admit the visiting rajahs from the sister cities, afforded a rare opportunity to those fortunate enough to arrive at the same time. It was the privilege of any who might fall in with the royal retinue to follow in its train to the ruling rajah's palace, and gain access to its courtyard. And wares displayed there for sale often brought fabulous sums, a hundredfold greater sometimes than when offered in the open market.

Only to a privileged few would the Golden Gate ever swing open at any other time. It would turn on its hinges for any one sent at a king's behest, or any one bearing something so rare and precious that only princes could purchase. No common vender could hope to pass its shining portal save in the rear of the train that yearly followed the rajahs.

So they urged their beasts with all diligence. Foremost in the caravan, and most zealous of all, was Shapur. In his heart burned the desire to be first to enter the Golden Gate, and the first one at the palace with his wares. But, half-way across the desert, as they paused at an oasis to rest, a dire lameness fell upon his camel, and it sank upon the sand. In vain he urged it to continue its journey. The poor beast could not rise under its great load.

Sack by sack he lessened its burden, throwing it off grudgingly and with sighs, for he was minded to lose as little as possible of his prospective fortune. But even rid of its entire load, the camel could not rise, and Shapur was forced to let his companions go on without him.

For long days and nights he watched beside his camel, bringing it water from the fountain and feeding it with the herbage of the oasis, and at last was rewarded by seeing it struggle to its feet and take a few limping steps. In his distress of mind at being left behind by the caravan, he had not noticed where he had thrown the load. A tiny rill, trickling down from the fountain, had run through the sacks and dissolved the salt, and when he went to gather up his load, only a paltry portion was left, a single sackful.

"Now, Allāh has indeed forgotten me!" he cried, and cursing the day that he was born, he rent his mantle, and beat upon his breast. Even if his camel were able to set out across the desert, it would be useless to seek a market now that he had no merchandise. So he sat on the ground, his head bowed in his hands. Water there was for him to drink, and the fruit of the date-palm, and the cooling shade of many trees, but he counted them as naught. A fever of unrest consumed him. A baffled ambition bowed his head in the dust.

When he looked at his poor camel kneeling in the sand, be cried out: "Ah, woe is me! Of all created things, I am most miserable! Of all dooms, mine is the most unjust! Why should I, with life beating strong in my veins, and ambition like a burning simoom in my breast, be left here helpless on the sands, where I can achieve nothing, and can make no progress toward the City of my Desire?"

One day, as he sat thus under the palms, a bee buzzed about him. He brushed it away, but it returned so persistently that he looked up with languid interest. "Where there are bees, there must be honey," he said. "If there be any sweetness in this desert, better that I should go in its quest than sit here bewailing my fate."

Leaving the camel browsing by the fountain, he followed the bee. For many miles, he pursued it, till far in the distance he beheld the palm-trees of another oasis. He quickened his steps, for an odor rare as the perfumes of Paradise floated out to meet him. The bee had led him to the Rose Garden of Omar.

Now Omar was an alchemist, a sage with the miraculous power of transmuting the most common things of earth into something precious. The fame of his skill had traveled to far countries. So many pilgrims sought him to beg his wizard touch that the question, "Where is the house of Omar?" was heard daily at the gates of the city. But for a generation that question had remained unanswered. No man knew the place of the house of Omar, since he had taken upon himself the life of a hermit. Somewhere, they knew, in the solitude of the desert, he was practising the mysteries of his art, and probing deeper into its secrets, but no one could point to the path leading thither. Only the bees knew, and, following the bee, Shapur found himself in the old alchemist's presence.

Now Shapur was a youth of gracious mien, and pleasing withal. With straightforward speech, he told his story, and Omar, who could read the minds of men as readily as unrolled parchments, was touched by his tale. He bade him come in and be his guest until sundown.

So Shapur sat at his board and shared his bread, and rose refreshed by his wise words. And at parting, the old man said, with a keen glance into his eyes: "Thou thinkest that because I am Omar, with the power to transmute all common things to precious ones, how easily I could take the remnant of salt that is still left to thee in thy sack and change it into gold. Then couldst thou go joyfully on to the City of thy Desire, as soon as thy camel is able to carry thee, far richer for thy delay."

Shapur's heart gave a bound of hope, for that is truly what he had been thinking. But at the next words it sank.

"Nay, Shapur, each man must be his own alchemist. Believe me, for thee the desert holds a greater opportunity than kings' houses could offer. Give me but thy patient service in this time of waiting, and I will share such secrets with thee that, when thou dost finally win to the Golden Gate, it shall be with wares that shall gain for thee a royal entrance."

Then Shapur went back to his camel, and, in the cool of the evening, urged it to its feet, and led it slowly across the sands. And because it could bear no burden, he lifted the remaining sack of salt to his own back, and carried it on his shoulders all the way. When the moon shone white and full in the zenith over the Rose Garden of Omar, he knocked at the gate, calling: "Here am I, Omar, at thy bidding, and here is the remnant of my salt. All that I have left I bring to thee, and stand ready now to yield my patient service."

Then Omar bade him lead his camel to the fountain, and leave him to browse on the herbage around it. Pointing to a row of great stone jars, he said: "There is thy work. Every morning before sunrise, they must be filled with rose-petals, plucked from the myriad roses of the garden, and the petals covered with water from the fountain."

"A task for poets," thought Shapur, as he began. "What more delightful than to stand in the moonlit garden and pluck the velvet leaves." But after awhile the thorns tore his hands, and the rustle and hiss underfoot betrayed the presence of serpents, and sleep weighed heavily upon his eyelids. It grew monotonous, standing hour after hour, stripping the rose-leaves from the calyxes until thousands and thousands and thousands had been dropped into the great jars. The very sweetness of the task began to cloy upon him.

When the stars had faded and the east begun to brighten, old Omar came out. "Tis well," he said. "Now break thy fast, and then to slumber with thee, to prepare for another sleepless night."

So long months went by, till it seemed to Shapur that the garden must surely become exhausted. But for every rose he plucked, two bloomed in its stead, and night after night he filled the jars.

Still he was learning no secrets, and he asked himself questions sometimes. Was he not wasting his life? Would it not have been better to have waited by the other fountain until some caravan passed by that would carry him out of the solitude to the dwellings of men? What opportunity was the desert offering him greater than kings' houses could give?

And ever the thorns tore him more sorely, and the lonely silence of the nights weighed upon him. Many a time he would have left his task had not the shadowy form of his camel, kneeling outside by the fountain, seemed to whisper to him through the starlight: "Patience, Shapur, patience!"

Once, far in the distance, he saw the black outline of a distant caravan passing along the horizon where day was beginning to break. He did no more work until it had passed from sight. Gazing after it with a fierce longing to follow, he pictured the scenes it was moving toward—the gilded minarets of the mosques, the deep-toned ringing of bells, the cries of the populace, and all the life and stir of the market-place. When the shadowy procession had passed, the great silence of the desert smote him like a pain.

Again looking out, he saw his faithful camel, and again it seemed to whisper: "Patience, Shapur, patience! So thou, too, shalt fare forth to the City of thy Desire."

One day in the waning of summer, Omar called him into a room in which he had never been before. "Now at last," said he, "hast thou proven thyself worthy to be the sharer of my secrets. Come! I will show thee! Thus are the roses distilled, and thus is gathered up the precious oil floating on the tops of the vessels.

"Seest thou this tiny vial? It weighs but the weight of one rupee, but it took the sweetness of two hundred thousand roses to make the attar it contains, and so costly is it that only princes may purchase. It is worth more than thy entire load of salt that was washed away at the fountain."

Shapur worked diligently at the new task till there came a day when Omar said to him: "Well done, Shapur! Behold the gift of the desert, its reward for thy patient service in its solitude!"

He placed in Shapur's hands a crystal vase, sealed with a seal and filled with the precious attar.

"Wherever thou goest this sweetness will open for thee a way and win for thee a welcome. Thou camest into the desert a vender of salt. Thou shalt go forth an apostle of my alchemy. Wherever thou seest a heart bowed down in some Desert of Waiting, thou shalt whisper to it: "Patience! Here, if thou wilt, in these arid sands, thou mayst find thy Garden of Omar, and from these daily tasks that prick thee sorest distil some precious attar to sweeten all life! So, like the bee that led thee to my teaching, shalt thou lead others to hope."

Then Shapur went forth with the crystal vase, and his camel, healed in the long time of waiting, bore him swiftly across the sands to the City of his Desire. The Golden Gate, that would not have opened to the vender of salt, swung wide for the Apostle of Omar.

Princes brought their pearls to exchange for his attar, and everywhere he went its sweetness opened for him a way and won for him a welcome. Wherever he saw a heart bowed down in some Desert of Waiting, he whispered Omar's words and tarried to teach Omar's alchemy, that from the commonest experiences of life may be distilled its greatest blessings.

At his death, in order that men might not forget, he willed that his tomb should be made at a place where all caravans passed. There, at the crossing of the highways, he caused to be cut in stone that emblem of patience, the camel, kneeling on the sand. And it bore this inscription, which no one could fail to see, as he toiled past toward the City of his Desire:

> Patience! Here, if thou wilt, on these arid sands, thou mayst find thy Garden of Omar, and even from the daily tasks which prick thee sorest mayst distill some precious attar to bless thee and thy fellowman.

A thousand moons waxed and waned above it, then a thousand, thousand more, and there arose a generation with restless hearts, who set their faces ever westward, following the sun toward a greater City of Desire. Strange seas they crossed, new coasts they came upon. Some were satisfied with the fair valleys that tempted them to tarry, and built their homes where the fruitful hills whispered stay. But always the sons of Shapur pushed ahead, to pitch their tents a day's march nearer the City of their Desire, nearer the Golden Gate, which opened every sunset to let the royal Rajah of the Day pass through. Like a mirage that vision lured them on, showing them a dream gate of opportunity, always just ahead, yet ever out of reach.

As in the days of Shapur, so it was in the days of his sons. There were those who fell by the way, and, losing all that made life dear, cried out as the caravan passed on without them that Allāh had forgotten them;

and they cursed the day that they were born, and laid hopeless heads in the dust.

But Allāh, the merciful, who from the beginning knew what Desert of Waiting must lie between every son of Shapur and the City of his Desire, had long before stretched out His hand over one of the mountains of His continent. With earthquake shock it sank before Him. With countless hammer-strokes of hail and rain-drops, and with gleaming rills He chiselled it, till, as the centuries rolled by, it took the semblance of that symbol of patience, a camel, kneeling there at the passing of the ways. And to every heart bowed down and hopeless, it whispers daily its message of cheer:

> Patience! Thou camest into the desert a vender of salt, thou mayst go forth an Alchemist, distilling from Life's tasks and sorrows such precious attar in thy soul that its sweetness shall win for thee a welcome wherever thou goest, and a royal entrance into the City of thy Desire!"

There was a long silence when Mr. Ellestad closed his note-book. Joyce had turned her face away to watch the mountain while he read, so he could not see whether the little tale pleased her or not. But suddenly a tear splashed down on the paper in her lap, and she drew her hand hastily across her eyes.

"You see, it seems as if you'd written that just for me," she said, trying to laugh. "I think it's beautiful! If ever there was a heart bowed down in a desert of waiting, I was that one when I came out here this afternoon. But you have given a new meaning to the mountain, Mr. Ellestad. How did you ever happen to think of it all?"

"A line from Saʿadi, one of the Persian poets, started me," he answered. "'Thy alchemist, contentment be.' It grew out of that—that and my own unrest and despondency."

"Look!" she cried, excitedly. "Do you see that? A bee! A bee buzzing around my head, as it did Shapur's, and I can't drive him away!"

She flapped at it with her handkerchief. "Oh, there it goes now. I wonder where it would lead us if we could follow it?"

"Probably to some neighbor's almond orchard," answered Mr. Ellestad.

"Oh, dear!" sighed Joyce. "I wish that there was a bee that I could follow, and a real rose garden that I could find. It sounds so beautiful and easy to say, 'Out of life's tasks and sorrows distill a precious attar in thy soul,' and I'd like to, heaven knows, but, when it comes to the point, how is one actually to go about it? If it were something that I could do with my hands, I'd attempt it gladly, no matter how hard; but doing the things in an allegory is like trying to take hold of the girl in the mirror. You can see her plainly enough, but you can't touch her. I used to feel that way about 'Pilgrim's Progress,' and think that if I only had a real pack on my back, as Christian had, and could start off on a real road, that I could be sure of what I was doing and the progress I was making. I wish you'd tell me how to begin really living up to your legend."

She spoke lightly, but there was a wistful glance in the laughing eyes she turned toward him.

"You will first have to tell me what is the City of your Desire."

"Oh, to be an artist! It has always been that. To paint beautiful pictures that will live long after I am gone, and will make people better and happier. Then the work itself would be such a joy to me. Ever since I have been old enough to realize that I will have to do something to earn my own living, I've hoped that I could do it in that way. I have had lessons from the best teachers we could get in Plainsville, and Cousin Kate took me to the finest art galleries in Europe, and promised to send me to the Art League in New York if I finished my high school course creditably.

"But we had to come out here, and that ended everything. I can't help saying, like Shapur, 'Why should I, with life beating strong in my veins, and ambition like a burning simoom in my breast, be left here helpless on the sands, where I can achieve nothing and make no progress toward the City of my Desire?' It seems especially hard to have all this precious time wasted, when I had counted so much on the money I expected to earn—enough to keep mamma comfortable when she grows old, and to give the other children all sorts of advantages."

"And you do not believe that these 'arid sands' hold anything for you?" said Mr. Ellestad.

Joyce shook her head.

"It takes something more than a trained hand and a disciplined eye to make an artist," he answered, slowly. "Did you ever think that it is the soul that has to be educated? That the greater the man behind the brush, the greater the picture will be? Moses had his Midian before he was worthy to be 'Lawgiver' to his people. Israel had forty years of wilderness-wandering before it was fit for its Promised Land. David was trained for kingship, not in courts, but on the hillsides with his flocks.

"This is the secret of Omar's alchemy, to gather something from every person we meet, from every experience life brings us, as Omar gathered something from the heart of every rose, and out of the wide knowledge thus gained, of human weaknesses and human needs, to distill in our own hearts the precious oil of sympathy. That is the attar that will win for us a welcome wherever we go—sympathy. The quick insight and deep understanding that help us to interpret people. And nobody fills his crystal vase with it until he has been pricked by the world's disappointments and bowed by its tasks. No masterpiece was ever painted without it. A man may become a fine copyist, but he can never make anything live on canvas until he has first lived deeply himself.

"Do not think your days wasted, little friend. Where could you learn such lessons of patience and courage as here on this desert where so many come to die? Where could you grow stronger than in the faithful doing of your commonplace duties, here at Lionic, where they all need you and lean upon you?

"You do not realize that, if you could go on now to the City of your Desire, the little you have to offer the world would put you in the rank of a common vender of salt—you could only follow, in the train of others. Is not waiting worthwhile, if it shall give you wares with which to win a royal entrance? "

"Oh, yes," answered Joyce, in a quick half-whisper, as the musical voice paused. She was looking away toward the mountain with a rapt expression on her uplifted face, as of one who sees visions. All the discontent had vanished now. It was glowing with hope and purpose.

As Mr. Ellestad rose to go, she turned impulsively to thrust both outstretched hands into his. "I can never thank you enough!" she exclaimed. "Old Camelback will be a constant inspiration to me after this instead of an emblem of hopelessness. Please come in and read the legend to mamma! And may I copy it sometime? Always now I shall think of you as Omar. I shall call you that in my thoughts."

"Thank you, little friend," he said, softly, as they walked on toward the house. "I have failed to accomplish many things in life that I had hoped to do, but the thought that one discouraged soul has called me its Omar makes me feel that I have not lived wholly in vain."

Perseverance
(*Thabāt*)

O you who have come to faith!
Be patient, and persevere in patience,
and keep your connection,
and remain conscious of God,
so that you might attain felicity.
[*Sūrah Āl ᶜImrān* 3:200]

But those who have faith and do good deeds,
to them shall We give a home in the Garden—
lofty mansions beneath which rivers flow—
to dwell there always,
an excellent reward for those who act rightly—
those who persevere in patience
and put their trust in their Sustainer.
[*Sūrah al-ᶜAnkabūt* 29:56-59]

In the Name of God,
the Infinitely Compassionate and Most Merciful
Consider time . . .
Truly, human beings are in loss
except those who have faith and do righteous deeds
and encourage each other in the teaching of Truth
and of patient perseverance.
[*Sūrah al-ᶜAṣr* 103:1-3, complete]

And We will certainly bestow on those who patiently persevere
their reward according to the best of their actions.
Whoever works righteousness, man or woman, and has faith,
truly, to Him will We give a new life, a life that is good and pure,
and We will bestow on such their recompense
according to the best of their actions.
[*Sūrah an-Naḥl* 16:96-97]

The early years of the Muslim community were extremely difficult and challenging times, yet Muḥammad ﷺ never waivered in his mission and in his service to his community. In the later years of his life when his community had strengthened and grown and his position held a great deal of power, still his abiding stance was that of servanthood. Whether persecuted or powerful, he persevered in keeping his focus with his Sustainer and encouraged his family members and all of the faithful to do the same. Whether in the midst of contraction (*qabḍ*) or expansion (*basṭ*) his reliance was on God alone.

Fāṭimah many times had to watch her father ridiculed and reviled by the Meccans as they sought to discredit his prophecy. When she was about ten years old, she often accompanied her father to the Kaʿbah to pray. On one occasion, while she was standing in prayer at her father's side, Abū Jahl began inciting those nearby to ridicule the Prophet ﷺ. ʿUqbah left, and soon returned with the filthy entrails of a slaughtered animal which he flung on the shoulders of the prophet while he was prostrating in prayer. It was Fāṭimah who tenderly removed it; she spoke strongly to those gathered and she and her father returned home. Many incidents like this occurred in the early days and such circumstances, including increasing hunger and hardship, were endured for years before at last revelation came granting the *hijrah*. *And God will always prepare a way of emergence* [*Sūrah aṭ-Ṭalāq* 65:2].

> God Most High says, *Be sure We shall test you with something of fear and hunger* [*Sūrah al-Baqarah* 2:155]. Then, at the close of the verse, He says, *But give glad tidings to those who patiently persevere.* So He gave glad tidings to them of beautiful reward for patience in enduring hunger.[133]

You shall most certainly be tried in your possessions and in yourselves;
and indeed you shall hear much that will cause you grief
from those to whom revelation was granted before your time,
as well as from those

[133] Al-Qushayri, *Principles of Sufism*, p. 79.

who have come to attribute divinity to others beside God.
But if you persevere and remain conscious of Hu—
see how this is something on which to set one's heart.
[*Sūrah Āl ᶜImrān* 3:186]

And remember Job when he cried out to his Sustainer:
"Truly, affliction has seized me,
but You are the Most Merciful of those who are merciful."
So We listened to him: We removed his distress
and We restored his people to him, doubling their number
as a Grace from Ourselves
and as a remembrance for all who serve Us.
[*Sūrah al-Anbiyāᶜ* 21:83-84]

Ibn ᶜUyayna commented as to the meaning of the words of God Most High, *And We appointed them leaders giving guidance under Our command because they persevered in patience* [*Sūrah as-Sajdah* 32:24], [that is] "Because they grasped the essential concern, We appointed them leaders." I heard the master Abū ᶜAlī ad-Daqqāq declare, "The condition of patience is that you not object to what has been decreed, and as for letting trials become apparent, but without complaining, this does not negate patience. God Most High says in the story of Job, *Truly We found him patient. How excellent in servitude! Ever did he turn [to Us]* [*Sūrah Ṣād* 38:44], despite what God Most High has said about him, that he said, *Distress afflicts me* [*Sūrah al-Anbiyāᶜ* 21:83]. And I heard him state, "God elicited these words from Job so that they might be a way of escape for the weak ones of his community."[134]

It is very appropriate to say prayers for the sick. One should ask Allāh to bless them with recovery and help them through their sickness. Al-Bukhārī and Muslim reported that ᶜĀᵓishah

---

[134] Ibid., p. 154.

said: "If someone fell sick, the Prophet ﷺ would pass his right hand over them while saying the following prayer: 'O Allāh, Lord of mankind, take away the suffering, bring about the recovery, no cure except your cure leaves no illness.'" In another *ḥadīth* reported by Al-Bukhārī, Ibn ᶜAbbās said that the Prophet ﷺ when visiting a sick person would say: "Be patient, may Allāh cleanse you."[135]

If you become ill, remember that without illness you would not recognize the blessings of good health. Even sickness could bring blessings that only later you will become aware of. It could bring about a period of reflection and review of your lifestyle and the way you conduct your affairs. Many go through difficult and testing times to discover later that indeed, their illness was a blessing in disguise.[136]

You may mention the words of Allāh: *And give glad tidings to those who patiently endure; who say, when afflicted with a disaster: "Truly! To Allāh we belong and truly, to Him is our return." They are those on whom descend blessings and mercy of their Lord, and they are the guided ones.*[137]

The following excerpts are from the autobiography of Lance Armstrong, the world-class cyclist who at the age of twenty-five was suddenly diagnosed with testicular cancer which quickly metastacised to his lungs and his brain. He engaged in the battle against cancer and with amazing perseverance came through the terminal cancer to not only race again and become a four-time winner of the Tour de France, but to become a husband, a father, and a first-class human being.

In the early days of his racing career, patience and perseverance were not easy for the impetuous Lance to learn: "I still struggled with impatience at times. I would ride smart for a while, and then backslide. I just couldn't seem to get it through my head that in order to win I had to ride

---

[135] Abū Ghudda, *Islamic Manners*, p. 90.

[136] Ibid., p. 93.

[137] Ibid., p. 98, quoting *Sūrah Al-Baqarah* 2:155-157.

more slowly at first. It took some time to reconcile myself to the notion that being patient was different from being weak, and that racing strategically didn't mean giving less than all I had."[138] Cancer taught him much more.

It's Not About the Bike

My illness was humbling and starkly revealing, and it forced me to survey my life with an unforgiving eye. There are some shameful episodes in it: instances of meanness, unfinished tasks, weakness, and regrets. I had to ask myself, "If I live, who is it that I intend to be?" I found that I had a lot of growing to do as a man.

I won't kid you. There are two Lance Armstrongs, pre-cancer and post. Everybody's favorite question is "How did cancer change you?" The real question is "How didn't it change me?" I left my house on October 2, 1996, as one person and came home another. I was a world-class athlete with a mansion on a riverbank, keys to a Porsche, and a self-made fortune in the bank. I was one of the top riders in the world and my career was moving along a perfect arc of success. I returned a different person, literally. In a way, the old me did die, and I was given a second life. Even my body is different, because during the chemotherapy I lost all the muscle I had ever built up, and when I recovered, it didn't come back in the same way.

The truth is that cancer was the best thing that ever happened to me. I don't know why I got the illness, but it did wonders for me, and I wouldn't want to walk away from it. Why would I want to change, even for a day, the most important and shaping event in my life?

People die. That truth is so disheartening that at times I can't bear to articulate it. Why should we go on, you might ask? Why don't we all just stop and lie down where we are? But there is another truth, too. People

---

[138] This quote and the following selection "It's Not About the Bike" are from *It's Not About the Bike: My Journey Back to Life,* by Lance Armstrong, copyright © 2000 by Lance Armstrong. Used by permission of G.P. Putnam's Sons, a division of Penguin Group (USA) Inc., p. 60, and additional pages following here.

live. It's an equal and opposing truth. People live, and in the most remarkable ways. When I was sick, I saw more beauty and triumph and truth in a single day than I ever did in a bike race—but they were *human* moments, not miraculous ones. I met a guy in a fraying sweatsuit who turned out to be a brilliant surgeon. I became friends with a harassed and overscheduled nurse named LaTrice, who gave me such care that it could only be the result of the deepest sympathetic affinity. I saw children with no eyelashes or eyebrows, their hair burned away by chemo, who fought with the hearts of Indurains.[139]

I still don't completely understand it.

All I can do is tell you what happened.[140]

What are my chances? It was a question I would repeat over and over. But it was irrelevant, wasn't it? It didn't matter, because the medical odds don't take into account the unfathomable. There is no proper way to estimate somebody's chances, and we shouldn't try, because we can never be entirely right, and it deprives people of hope. Hope that is the only antidote to fear.

Those questions, Why me? What are my chances? were unknowable, and I would even come to feel that they were too self-absorbed. For most of my life I had operated under a simple schematic of winning and losing, but cancer was teaching me a tolerance for ambiguities. I was coming to understand that the disease doesn't discriminate or listen to the odds—it will decimate a strong person with a wonderful attitude, while it somehow miraculously spares the weaker person who is resigned to failure. I had always assumed that if I won bike races, it made me a stronger and more worthy person. Not so.

Why me? Why anybody? I was no more or less valuable than the man sitting next to me in the chemo center. It was not a question of worthiness.

What is stronger, fear or hope? It's an interesting question, and perhaps even an important one. Initially, I was very fearful and without

---

[139] Indurain was another legendary bike racer renowned for his stamina and dedication and endurance of heart.

[140] Ibid., pp. 4-5.

much hope, but as I sat there and absorbed the full extent of my illness, I refused to let the fear completely blot out my optimism. Something told me that fear should never fully rule the heart, and I decided not to be afraid.

I wanted to live, but whether I would or not was a mystery, and in the midst of confronting that fact, even at that moment, I was beginning to sense that to stare into the heart of such a fearful mystery wasn't a bad thing. To be afraid is a priceless education. Once you have been that scared, you know more about your frailty than most people and I think that changes a man. I was brought low, and there was nothing to take refuge in but the philosophical: this disease would force me to ask more of myself as a person than I ever had before, and to seek out a different ethic.

A couple of days earlier, I had received an e-mail from a military guy stationed in Asia. He was a fellow cancer patient, and he wanted to tell me something. "You don't know yet," he wrote, "but we're the lucky ones."[141]

One thing you realize when you're sick is that you aren't the only person who needs support—sometimes you have to be the one who supports others. My friends shouldn't always have to be the ones saying: "You're going to make it." Sometimes I had to be the one who reassured them, and said, "I'm going to make it. Don't worry."[142]

One afternoon LaTrice pointed out that I was still asking her questions, but the nature of them had changed. At first, the questions I had asked were strictly about myself, my own treatments, my doses, my particular problems. Now I asked about other people. I was startled to read that eight million Americans were living with some form of cancer; how could I possibly feel like mine was an isolated problem? "Can you believe how many people have this?" I asked LaTrice.

"You've changed," she said, approvingly. "You're going global."

Dr. Nichols told me that there was every sign now that I was going

---

[141] Ibid., pp. 95-96.

[142] Ibid., p. 110.

to be among the lucky ones who cheated the disease. He said that as my health improved, I might feel that I had a larger purpose than just myself. Cancer could be an opportunity as well as a responsibility. Dr. Nichols had seen all kinds of cancer patients become dedicated activists against the disease, and he hoped I would be one of them.

I hoped so, too. I was beginning to see cancer as something that I was given for the good of others. I wanted to launch a foundation, and I asked Dr. Nichols for some suggestions about what it might accomplish. I wasn't yet clear on what the exact purpose of the organization would be; all I knew was that I felt I had a mission to serve others that I'd never had before, and I took it more seriously than anything in the world.

I had a new sense of purpose, and it had nothing to do with my recognition and exploits on a bike. Some people won't understand this, but I no longer felt that it was my role in life to be a cyclist. Maybe my role was to be a cancer survivor. My strongest connections and feelings were with people who were fighting cancer and asking the same question I was: "Am I going to die?"

I had talked to Steve Wolff about what I was feeling, and he said, "I think you were fated to get this type of illness. One, because maybe you could overcome it, and two, because your potential as a human was so much greater than just being a cyclist."[143]

[I thought of creating a foundation for cancer research.] I wanted the foundation to manifest all of the issues I had dealt with in the past few months: coping with fear, the importance of alternate opinions, thorough knowledge of the disease, the patient's role in cure, and above all, the idea that cancer did not have to be a death sentence. It could be a route to a second life, an inner life, a better life.[144]

The foundation seemed like the perfect answer to the limbo I was in: I had completed chemo, and beaten back the cancer for the time being, but I had to figure out what to do next. To work on something outside myself was the best antidote. I was a cancer survivor first and an

---

[143] Ibid., pp. 150-151.

[144] Ibid., p. 152.

athlete second, I decided. Too many athletes live as though the problems of the world don't concern them. We are isolated by our wealth and our narrow focus, and our elitism. But one of the redeeming things about being an athlete—one of the real services we can perform—is to redefine what's humanly possible. We cause people to reconsider their limits, to see that what looks like a wall may really just be an obstacle in the mind. Illness was not unlike athletic performance in that respect: there is so much we don't know about our human capacity, and I felt it was important to spread the message.[145]

But I think we are supposed to try to face it [death] straightforwardly, armed with nothing but courage. The definition of courage is: the quality of spirit that enables one to encounter danger with firmness and without fear.[146]

It's another fact of cancer that the more informed and empowered patient has a better chance of long-term survival.

What if I had lost? What if I relapsed and the cancer came back? I still believe I would have gained something in the struggle, because in what time I had left I would have been a more complete, compassionate, and intelligent man, and therefore more alive. The one thing the illness has convinced me of beyond all doubt—more than any experience I've had as an athlete—is that we are much better than we know. We have unrealized capacities that sometimes only emerge in crisis.

So if there is a purpose to the suffering that is cancer, I think it must be this: it's meant to improve us.

I am very firm in my belief that cancer is not a form of death. I choose to redefine it: it is a part of life. One afternoon when I was in remission and sitting around waiting to find out if the cancer would come back, I made an acronym out of the word: Courage, Attitude, Never give up, Curability, Enlightenment, and Remembrance of my fellow patients.[147]

---

[145] Ibid., p. 158.

[146] Ibid., p. 266.

[147] Ibid., p. 267.

FORBEARANCE
(*Ḥilm*)

Have We not expanded your chest,[148]
and removed from you the burden
which weighed down your back,
and increased your remembrance?
So, truly, with every difficulty comes ease;
truly, with every difficulty comes ease.
So when you are free from your task continue to strive,
and to your Sustainer turn with loving attention.
[*Sūrah ash-Sharḥ* 94:1-8, complete]

But He will call you to account for what your hearts have conceived,
and Allah is Forgiving, Forbearing.
[*Sūrah al-Baqarah* 2:225]

Bear with patience what they say
and remember Our servant David,
he who was endowed with inner strength: for he always turned to Us.
It was We Who made the hills declare Our praises in unison with him
at nightfall and at break of day.
And the birds gathered: all with him did turn.
We strengthened his dominion
and gave him wisdom and sound judgment in speech and decisions.
[*Sūrah Ṣād* 38:17-20]

For the one who remains conscious of God;
He always prepares a way of emergence
and He provides for him in ways he could never imagine.
And if anyone puts his trust in God, sufficient is God for him.

---

[148] It is reported that the angel Gabriel appeared to the Prophet Muḥammad, opened his chest, and removed the impurities remaining in his heart. See the section "Purification of the Heart."

For God will surely accomplish His purpose:
truly, for all things has God appointed an appropriate measure.
[*Sūrah aṭ-Ṭalāq* 65:2-3]

A great part of Mercy is simply to restrain anger, whether or not it seems justified. This is called "forbearance." The Qur'ān says, *And know that Allāh is Forgiving, Forbearing.* [*Sūrah al-Baqarah* 2:235]; *And certainly Allāh has pardoned them; surely Allāh is Forgiving, Forbearing.* [*Sūrah Āl ʿImrān* 3:155]; *And those who restrain their anger and pardon men; and Allāh loves the virtuous* [*Sūrah Āl ʿImrān* 3:134]. The Prophet Muḥammad ﷺ said:

"The most intelligent of people are those who are strictest in matters of courtesy and friendship; and the most prudent of them are those who most restrain their anger."

"A believer will, by his forbearance and gentleness, attain the rank of a scholar who is struggling to solve problems of jurisprudence."

"There are no two things which combine better than forbearance and knowledge."[149]

Imām ʿAlī said, "Four things are most difficult to achieve: to forgive when angry, to be forbearing in the face of oppression, to be generous in times of scarcity, and to be abstinent when alone."[150]

Another *ḥadīth* . . . tells us that once a man came to the Prophet ﷺ anxious to learn and follow the teachings of Islām. But he wanted something brief and to the point which he could easily understand and put into practice. He got what he wanted. Abū Hurayrah said, "A man came to the Prophet ﷺ and said to him, 'Teach me something brief and to the point, so that I can easily understand and follow it.' The Prophet ﷺ said, 'Do not

149 Charles Upton, contributor.

150 Haeri, *Prophetic Traditions of Islām*, p. 166 (al-ʿĪnāthī, II, 63-76).

become angry and furious.' The man asked the same (question) again and again, and each time the Prophet ﷺ replied, 'Do not become angry and furious.'"'

This is how the *sunnah* promotes perfect harmony between a man's verbal supplication and his practical life. The Prophet ﷺ not only taught us to supplicate to Allāh for help in restraining our anger, but at the same time admonished us to take comparable and necessary practical steps to achieve the desired end by keeping our tempers cool and remaining patient and steadfast under difficult conditions.[151]

Suffering uncovers human frailties and literally pushes the reasonable person to his knees, so to speak, at Allāh's door, in quest of relief and the mercy of his Lord. The true believer is expected to seek refuge in Allāh in every trouble which befalls him, regardless of how insignificant it may seem. The Prophet of Allāh ﷺ said:

"Let each of you turn unto Allāh in every troublesome matter; even when you are pained by the thong of your sandal, for even that is a trial."

In other words, the Muslim must rely, in all of his affairs, upon Allāh's assistance, and not suppose that any of these affairs can be settled except by His leave. The greater the misfortune, the more ardent the Muslim's desire for refuge in Allāh, and the more protracted his entreaty.[152]

A person of fine sensibilities is inevitably distressed by personal or intellectual problems. Indeed, life for such a person would appear more constricting than even the eye of a needle. And the riches of the world, were they offered to him, would be of no consolation to him at all. This is the way that Muḥammad lived until Revelation came upon him unexpectedly.

---

151 Al-ʿAnani. *Freedom and Responsibility in Qur'anic Perspective,* p. 206.

152 Muḥammad al-Ghazālī, *Remembrance and Prayer,* p. 91.

In reference to his state at that time, the Almighty said: *Have We not opened up your heart?* [*Sūrah ash-Sharḥ* 94:1]. That is, by inspiring you with spiritual truths. *And lifted from you the burden that had weighed so heavily on your back* [*Sūrah ash-Sharḥ* 94:2-3].

The burden was such that you were forced to flee the society of others, and grieve for yourself and for them, alone and bewildered, and suffer through your incapacity and your exile from your native surroundings.

Then Allāh chose you; and who could be more exalted than one chosen by the Lord of the heavens and earth to be His instrument of guidance for all the world? *And have We not raised you high in dignity?* [*Sūrah ash-Sharḥ* 94:4]

And so is human life: *And, behold, with every hardship comes ease: and, verily, with every hardship comes ease.* [*Sūrah ash-Sharḥ* 94:5-6]

Finally, what is sought of you, after you have finished your work, is to begin it afresh: *Hence, when you are freed [from distress], remain steadfast, and unto your Lord turn with love.* [*Sūrah ash-Sharḥ* 94:7-8].

And thus we witness accommodation after estrangement, guidance after confusion and hesitation, sufficiency after want. Without a doubt the deprivations suffered by the Prophet ﷺ in his own lifetime made him all the more sensitive to the troubles of others. Thus, he shared their grief, and always did his best to eliminate, or at least to lessen, the troubling factor, regardless of whether the trouble was material or spiritual in nature. His desire was to free his life of it, and the lives of others.

And whose countenance and succour are sought in times of hardship and tribulation? Allāh, and none other! Surely, He is the secure refuge, the fortified sanctuary![153]

The neighbors of the Prophet who were opposed to him, under the leadership of Abū Lahab and his wife, intensified their

[153] Ibid., pp. 94-95.

campaign of persecution. The Prophet used to remove the unclean refuse which they repeatedly threw inside his yard and in front of his door, complaining in a markedly restrained voice:

"What kind of neighborhood is this, O Sons of Abū Manaf?" But the worst incident of persecution which the Prophet experienced after the death of Abū Ṭālib is narrated by Ibn Isḥāq as follows:

"Then Khadījah bint Khuwaylid and Abū Ṭālib died in the same year. Misfortunes continued to befall the Messenger of Allāh ﷺ as they could not hope to inflict upon him during Abū Ṭālib's life. One of their insolent mob even heaped dust and earth upon his gracious head. As he entered his home, one of his daughters wept passionately as she wiped the dust from her father's head.

"Do not cry, my daughter," he said, "for Allāh shall protect your father."[154]

The Prophet ﷺ regularly remembered his Lord, and supplicated Him earnestly and with civility. And, when he took the name of the Lord in fervent prayer, he was urging the multitude: this is the way, so follow it; this is the goal, so seek after it.[155]

Bilāl

Bilāl ibn Rabāḥ رضي الله عنه was a slave born of a foreign mother belonging to the Banu Jumaḥ. Bilāl began to hear of the faith of Muḥammad ﷺ and it inspired his heart with an intense love of the One God. When his master learned of his profession of faith in the then controversial faith of Islām, he began to torture him. As with other Muslim converts at the time, he was tied down and left in the heat of the sun.

---

[154] Zakaria Bashier, *The Makkan Crucible* (reprinted by permission of The Islamic Foundation, Leicestershire, U.K; © 1991), p. 180.

[155] Charles Upton, contributor.

[His master] Umayya b. Khalaf would place him outside at heat of noon, then order that a huge rock be placed on his chest. He would then tell him, "By God, you'll stay like this till you die, unless you disavow Muḥammad and pray to al-Lāt and al-ʿUzzā!"

Bilāl, while in this state would say only, "One! One!"[156]

... He, however, attached no importance to himself in suffering in God's cause. His people considered him valueless, so they handed him over to the children who began parading him through the streets of Mecca, while he shouted, 'One! One!'"[157]

At last, Abū Bakr ؓ who still was a wealthy man bought Bilāl ؓ to save him from this torture, and set him free. Later, when the community had settled in Medina and built the first mosque, Bilāl became the first muezzin, with his strong and beautiful voice calling all to prayer. It was he who added the phrase to the call for early morning prayer, "Prayer is better than sleep." He would make the call to prayer from the roof of the tallest house next to the mosque in Medina; early in the morning he would come to this house belonging to ʿUrwa ibn az-Zubayr ؓ of the Banī an-Najjār. She later told of how Bilāl would arrive and sit in prayer on the roof waiting for the moment to call the time of prayer for the community. During the lifetime of the Prophet, Bilāl never missed a morning and remained one of the most devoted.

He Who Seeks the Truth Chooses the Good and Holds it Fast

Kung Fu-tzu (551-497 B.C.), known in the west as Confucius, can truly be called the founder of Chinese culture (or at least of the culture

---

[156] Ibn Kathīr, *The Life of the Prophet Muḥammad*, Vol. I, pp. 356-357.

[157] Ibid., pp. 316-317.

~ "He Who Seeks the Truth Chooses the Good and Holds It Fast" contains excerpts from Karl Jaspers, *Socrates, Buddha, Confucius, Jesus;* Vol. I *The Great Philosophers: The Foundations*, Harcourt Publishers, Ltd., pp. 48-49.

that grew up in China after his death, due largely to his influence.) Confucius, though not a prophet, was the great renewer of Chinese civilization, basing his teaching on the "example of the ancients." No man who was strictly a scholar—neither the founder of a religion nor a great conqueror—has ever had anything remotely resembling the wide and deep influence of Confucius on later generations, though during his own lifetime his efforts often seemed fruitless. In a time of political disunity and feudal warfare, he tried to secure appointment as minister to the rulers of various petty states in order to institute governmental reforms for the relief of the people. He did not succeed, but the circle of scholars which slowly gathered around him during his "unsuccessful" career, and those who followed them, planted the seeds of profound cultural and ethical renewal in the years and centuries following his death.

Confucius chose to concentrate on sharing the ideal of an encompassing community, through which the human being might become a true human being. His passion was for beauty, order, truthfulness, and happiness in the world. He was cautious and reserved, yet not from fear, but from a sense of responsibility and the will to true mastery.

The German philosopher Karl Jaspers has this to say about the character and teachings of Confucius:

> All goodness, truth, beauty are combined in the ideal of the superior man (Chun-tzu). Noble both in birth and endowment, he has the manners of a gentleman and the wisdom of a sage.
>
> The superior man is no saint. The saint is born: he is what he is; the superior man becomes what he is through self-discipline. "To have the truth is the path of heaven, to seek the truth is the path of men. He who has the truth finds the right action without pains, achieves success without reflection." But he who seeks the truth chooses the good and holds it fast. He investigates, he questions critically, he ponders the truth and resolutely acts on it. "Perhaps others can do it the first time; I must do it ten times; perhaps others can do it the tenth time; I must do it a thousand times. But he who really has the perseverance to go this way—be he foolish, he will become clear-headed; be he weak, he will become strong."

The character, cast of thought, and gestures of the superior man are described. He is contrasted with the inferior man. The superior man is concerned with justice; the inferior man with profit. The superior man is quiet and serene; the inferior man always full of anxiety. The superior man is congenial though never stooping to vulgarity; the inferior man is vulgar without being congenial. The superior man is dignified without arrogance; the inferior man is arrogant without dignity. The superior man is steadfast in distress; the inferior man in distress loses all control of himself. The superior man goes searching for himself; the inferior man goes searching in others. The superior man strives upward; the inferior man strives downward. The superior man is independent. He can endure long misfortune as well as long prosperity, and he lives free from fear. He suffers from his own inability, not from others' failure to understand him. He avoids all competition, but if it must be, then only in archery. He is slow in words and quick in action. He is careful not to let his words outshine his deeds: first act, then speak accordingly.

The superior man does not waste himself on what is distant, or on what is absent. He stands in the here and now. "The superior man's path is like a long journey; you must begin from right here."

"The superior man's path begins with the concerns of the common man and woman, but it reaches into the distance, penetrating heaven and earth."

We have statements that Confucius made about himself, and others that his disciples attributed to their master:

He was conscious of his vocation. In a situation of mortal peril, he said: "Since King Wen is no more, has culture been entrusted to me? If heaven had wished to destroy this culture, a latecomer could not have received it. But if heaven does not wish to destroy this culture, what can the men of K'uang do against me?"

Despite his consciousness of his mission, he was a modest man. No doubt, he believed, he could compete with others in learning, but he recognized that he had not attained the level of the superior man who can transform his knowledge into action. "Of myself I can only say that I have striven insatiably to become so, and that I teach others untiringly."

When a disciple describes the master's dejection in rather drastic terms, Confucius replies approvingly: "Like a dog in the house of morning, you've hit it, you've hit it." To a disciple whom a prince has questioned about him, Confucius says: "Why did you not answer thus: He is a man who learns the truth without tiring, who instructs men indefatigably, who is so zealous that he forgets to eat, who is so serene that he forgets all cares, and consequently does not notice the gradual approach of old age."

Confucius sees his own failure. In a situation of dire peril, he asks his pupils: "Is my life wrong? Why does such distress come upon us?" The first says that men do not trust him because he has not yet attained true goodness, nor do what he says because he has not yet attained true wisdom. But Confucius replies: "Saints and wise men of the past have met with the most terrible ends. Clearly goodness is not necessarily rewarded with confidence, nor wisdom with obedience." The second says the master's doctrine is so great that no one on earth can endure it. The doctrine must be reduced a little in stature. In reply to this, Confucius says: "The good husbandman can sow but not bring forth the harvest. The superior man can fashion his doctrine but not cause it to be accepted. To concern oneself with its acceptance is not to look into the distance." The third says: "Your doctrine is very great, therefore the world cannot grasp it. But continue to act in accordance with it. What matter that it is not accepted? In that he is not understood, thereby the superior man is known." Confucius smiled.

Confucius did not always calmly accept his failure, but scrutinized and interpreted it. His attitude was not determined in advance and was not always the same.

He could lament: "The superior man suffers that he must leave the world and that his name is not mentioned. My way is not followed. Whereby shall I be known to posterity?" "Ah, no one knows me!" But he quickly consoles himself: "I do not grumble against heaven, I am not angry with men. I have searched here below and I am in communication with heaven. Heaven knows me."

He contents himself with his lot: "To learn and unceasingly practice, does that not give satisfaction? And if companions come to you from far away, is not that too a ground for rejoicing? And not to grow embittered if men do not know you, is not that, too, noble?" "I will not grieve that men do not know me; I should grieve only if I do not know the others."

The fool calls out to him: "Give up your vain striving. He who wishes to serve the state today only flings himself into peril." And Lao-tzu says to him: "The shrewd and clever are close to death, for they love to judge other men." But he persists in his task of helping to build a human order in the world. Success is not decisive. To be humane means to bear your part of responsibility for the state of the community. "A man of humanity does not strive for life at the cost of injuring humanity. No, there have been men who, to perfect their humanity, have given their body to death."

His basic attitude is one of readiness. "If they use you, be active; if they turn their backs on you, remain in retirement."

But here is the essential: "The one thing over which a man is master is his own heart. Good or ill fortune is no yardstick of a man's value." Not always is outward misfortune an evil; it can be "a test" (Hsun Tzu). Even in extreme affliction hope remains. "There are cases in which men rise from desperate circumstances to the highest calling."

V.

Modesty
Discretion
Humility

Modesty
(*Ḥayāᶜ*)

O children of Adam!
Indeed, We have given you garments to cover your nakedness,
and as a thing of beauty;
but the garment of God-consciousness is the best of all.
This is one of God's messages—
that human beings might take it to heart.
[*Sūrah al-Aᶜrāf* 7:26]

Tell the men of faith to lower their gaze
and to be mindful of their chastity:
this will help to increase their purity—
truly, God is aware of all that they do.
And tell the women of faith to lower their gaze
and to be mindful of their chastity,
and not to display their charms beyond what may readily be apparent.
[*Sūrah an-Nūr* 24:30-31]

"O my dear son!" continued Luqmān,
"If there were anything the weight of even a mustard-seed,
and it were within a rock or in the heavens or on earth,
God will bring it to light:
for God comprehends the subtlest mysteries and is All-Aware.
O my dear son! Be constant in prayer,
encourage what is just, and forbid what is wrong,
and bear with patient perseverance whatever comes to you;
witness, this is something upon which to set one's heart.
And do not turn away from people with pride
nor walk in insolence on the earth;
for God does not love the arrogant boaster.
And be modest in your bearing and lower your voice;
for without a doubt, the harshest of sounds is the braying of the ass."
Sūrah Luqmān 31:16-19]

Al-Bāqir said, "Allāh loves the modest and forbearing."[158]

The Messenger said: . . . "Modesty is not present in anything but that it adorns it, and evil is not present in anything but that it makes it ugly. Every religion has its character, and the character of Islām is modesty." He also said, "Modesty is from faith, and lack of modesty is disbelief."[159]

Aṣ-Ṣadiq relates that the Messenger said, "Allāh has mercy on the slave who feels true modesty in the face of his Lord, who protects his mind and what it perceives, and his stomach and its desires, who remembers the grave . . . and remembers the place of return in the next world."[160]

True obedience is that which is accompanied by taking the self to account—it is incumbent on everyone who believes in Allāh and the Last Day that he be aware of the states of his self, both when he is awake and active and when he is asleep or at rest; moreover, every morning he should empty his heart of all that is other than Him, before he takes up contact with those around him; he should also give advice to seven parts of his body; to his eyes, his ears, his tongue, his stomach, his genitals, his hands, and his legs . . . .

As for the eyes, he should guard them from looking at the private parts of [others], or from looking at [them] with contempt, and use them instead to look at the wonders of Allāh's creation and in reading books of wisdom and knowledge. . . .

As for the tongue, he should control it and prevent it from talking behind people's backs, lying, backbiting, praising the self, disdaining others or criticizing, cursing or calling evil upon them; he must not speak hypocritically of them but rather allow

---

158 Haeri, *Prophetic Traditions of Islām*, p. 166 (*Mishkāt*, 216-218).

159 Ibid., pp. 169-170 (*Mishkāt*, 233-235).

160 Ibid., p. 169 (*Mishkāt*, 233-235).

his tongue to move only in remembrance of Allāh and reminding others to do the same; he should use his tongue to teach and guide the servants of Allāh to the straight path, and to make amends between disputing parties.[161]

Remember that you are a servant of Allāh and should not regard yourself and your actions highly, nor should you expect a return for your actions. We hear from Muḥammad ibn ʿAbdullāh ar-Rāzī that someone asked Abūl-ʿAbbās ibn ʿAṭāʾ, "What thing most attracts Allāh's anger?" He replied, "When one considers himself and his actions highly, and worse still, expects a return for his good deeds."[162]

God does not love the arrogant.
[*Sūrah Luqmān* 31:18]

The most troubled of people are the kings, the most hated the proud, and the most abased are those who treat others with contempt.[163]

When the Prophet ﷺ said: "He will not enter Paradise who has a grain of arrogance in his heart," a man asked: "A man may like his dress to be nice and his shoes to be nice?" The Prophet ﷺ answered: "Allāh is beautiful and likes beauty. Arrogance is to deny rights and look down upon people.". . . Therefore, a Muslim ought to be recognized by neat dress, cleanliness, and graceful manners.[164]

It is narrated on the authority of Abū Hurayrah that the Prophet ﷺ said, "*Īmān* has over seventy branches, and modesty

---

[161] Ibid., p. 153 (*Al-Ashtarī* I, 234-248).

[162] Al-Sulami, *The Way of Sufi Chivalry*, p. 43.

[163] Haeri, *Prophetic Traditions of Islām*, p. 172 (*Mishkāt*, 224-229).

[164] Abū Ghudda, *Islamic Manners*, p. 25.

is a branch of *Īmān*." He also said, "There are two kinds of modesty: the modesty of the intellect and the modesty of foolishness. The modesty of the intellect is knowledge; the modesty of foolishness is ignorance.". . .

In the words of the Prophet ﷺ "Be as modest before Allāh as you would before one of your people who is spiritually advanced."[165]

Principles for the Musician

The most important thing in playing an instrument is tuning. Learn how to tune your instrument and always be sure that your instrument is in tune before you begin to play. This will help to increase your ability to hear the true notes and enable you to match your playing to the right pitch.

Don't waste time. Always pick up your instrument with an intention; don't play idly, randomly, as very little real progress will occur in that way.

Play the piece you are practicing as it has been indicated. Play the piece at the indicated tempo. Learn section by section, then play the piece wholly, from beginning to end. Then practice again sections that need the most work, and again play it as a whole. It is also helpful to be able to sing the piece you are trying to play as it will deepen your knowledge of it and make the playing of it more easily mastered.

Each time you play exert effort to stretch your ability. Each time you play, challenge yourself with a piece that is a bit more difficult rather than remaining with the familiar. If using a metronome, begin at slower speeds and increase bit by bit.

---

[165] Charles Upton, contributor.

~ "Principles for the Musician" is excerpted from *Oud Method #1,* translated from the Turkish by Refik Algan and Camille Helminski.

Never focus on the audience. You will lose your concentration.

Always play as though you are singing to someone who really knows music. Never forget that though there may be many people listening, the music is played for those who can really hear music and appreciate it.

Don't play or listen to "non-music" music. It will spoil your ear and your sensitivity.

Never add to someone's composition. Later you can compose your own work.

Don't play for everyone who asks. Only play for those who are really interested.

Never miss a chance to play together with other musicians and lovers of music. Join an ensemble, a chorus, an orchestra, accompany soloists, etc.

But stay away from those who degenerate music, those who continually play poor music, and who play without respect.

Learn to be able to write the notes of a melody you hear. Practice also reading the written notes so that you can sing or play written music. Keep trying and improving this ability.

Pay attention to being able to distinguish the color of different notes played on different strings.

Learn the history of the field of music in which you are involved. Develop a good knowledge of the overall history and a knowledge of the forms. This will help you to understand the spirit of the work and give you more of an opportunity to improve your own performance.

Always be modest. Never let your increasing knowledge and talent in music make you proud.

Never look down upon others. Never disdain those who can't play as well or who are less informed.

Don't hide your knowledge, but always help those who really want to learn. By helping others, your own level will be raised.

Never forget about your instrument. Remember that as you care for your instrument and improve its quality, your work will also improve. Always aim to have a fine instrument.

Become informed about scales. Learning to recognize the *makam* one hears is a necessity and will increase one's musicality.

Aim to have a healthy philosophy and culture of music. Having this as a basic aim will help you to understand others and to be understood by them.

Recognize that music and literature are two parts of an inseparable whole. In addition to spending time with music, also read appropriate literature, i.e., the classics of the tradition.

Remember that the appreciation of crowds is never a criteria. The appreciation of those who are experts in music is more important.

Discretion
(*Ḥusn at-Tadbīr*)

Those who lower their voice in the presence of God's Messenger,
their hearts God has tested for consciousness of Himself:
theirs shall be forgiveness and a great reward.
Those who shout out to you from outside the Inner Rooms,
most of them lack understanding.
If only they had patience until you could come out to them
it would be best for them.
Yet God is Often-Forgiving, Most Merciful.
[*Sūrah al-Ḥujurāt* 49:4–5]

Say: "Invoke God,
or invoke the Most Gracious:
by whichever name you invoke Him,
His are all the attributes of perfection."
And do not be too loud in your prayer
nor speak it in too low a voice, but follow a middle way.
[*Sūrah al-Isrāʾ* 17:110]

And know that among you is God's Messenger:
were he in many matters to follow your inclinations,
you would surely fall into misfortune;
but God has caused faith to be dear to you,
and has made it beautiful within your hearts,
and He has made hateful to you lack of faith, wickedness,
and rebellion against that which is good.
Such indeed are those who walk in righteousness—
through God's grace and favor;
and God is All-Knowing, Truly Wise.
[*Sūrah al-Ḥujurāt* 49:7–8]

Commenting on Allāh's words, *And say to the people words of kindness* [*Sūrah al-Baqarah* 2:83] al-Bāqir said, 'Say to the people kinder words than you yourself would like to hear, for Allāh hates those who curse much, who insult and defame the believers, the profligate and the obscene in speech, and the one who molests with his questioning; but He loves the modest, the gentle, the chaste, and the abstemious.'[166]

Always remember the *ḥadīth* of the Prophet ﷺ reported by Al-Bukhārī and Muslim: "Whoever believes in Allāh and the Last Day should say something good or remain silent."[167]

It is an inappropriate manner to whisper to someone sitting next to you if you are in a group of three. The third person will feel isolated and will harbor the worst of thoughts. The Messenger of Allāh ﷺ disapproved of this. Imām Mālik and Abū Dāwūd reported that he said: "No two shall exchange whispers in the presence of a third person." The Prophet ﷺ used "No two" . . . in an assertive negative form, indicating that such a mistake is not only inappropriate but unimaginable and instinctively despicable. Another *ḥadīth* in Al-Bukhārī says: "If you were three, two of you should not whisper to each other till you join other people, lest the third feels offended." ʿAbdullāh ibn ʿUmar was asked: "What if they were four?" "Then it does not matter," he answered; meaning it would not be then offensive.[168]

Manners are based on common sense and could be developed by socializing with prominent and tactful individuals. By observing how they act and behave, you will be able to enhance your common sense, good manners, and graceful behavior.

You might be called to a gathering where you are the youngest. In such cases, do not sit before you are invited to do so. Do not sit if you will be crowding out others, or forcing them to leave their seats for you. If you are invited to sit, do not proceed to the best place if others deserve it, and be prepared to give your seat to them. Doing this on your own, before being

[166] Haeri, *Prophetic Traditions of Islām*, p. 204 *(Mishkāt,* 189-203).

[167] Abū Ghudda, *Islamic Manners*, p. 56.

[168] Ibid., p. 46.

prompted to do so, will enhance admiration and respect for you.[169]

In *Sūrah al-Ḥajj* [22:24], Allāh described the believers: *And they have been guided to the purest of talk; and guided to the path of Him who is worthy of all praise.* When you talk during your visit, say only what befits the situation and be brief. If you are the youngest among those present, don't speak unless you are asked to, or unless you know that your talk will be well received and will please the host and the other guests. Don't prolong your speech, your talk should be clear, concise, and to the point, do not talk and talk and talk. Al-Bukhārī reported that Anas said: "The Prophet's ﷺ speech was clear and succinct, neither too long nor too short, and he disliked chattering and ranting." Similarly Al-Bukhārī and Muslim narrated a ḥadīth in which ᶜĀʾishah said: "The Prophet ﷺ spoke [so few words] that you could count his words."[170]

Al-Haitham ibn ᶜAdī[171] said: "It is an ill manner to overwhelm someone while speaking and to interrupt them before they end their talk."

If a colleague did not understand an issue and asked a scholar or an elder to explain, you should listen to what is being said. The repeated explanation may give you additional insights to what you already know. Never utter any word belittling your colleague, nor allow your face to betray such an attitude.

When an elder or a scholar speaks, listen attentively. Never busy yourself with a talk or discussion with other colleagues. Do not let your mind wander elsewhere, keep it focused on what is being said.[172]

Never interrupt a speaker. Never rush to answer if you are not very confident of your answer. Never argue about some-

---

[169] Ibid., p. 43.

[170] Ibid., p. 51.

[171] A known scholar, historian, and a member of the court of the four Khalīfahs: Abū Jaᶜfar al-Manṣūr, Al-Mahdī, Al-Hādī, and Ar-Rashīd.

[172] Abu Ghudda, Islamic Manners, p.55.

thing you do not know. Never argue for the sake of argument. Never show arrogance with your counterparts especially if they hold a different opinion. Do not switch the argument to belittle your opponent's views. If their misunderstanding becomes evident, do not rebuke or scold them. Be modest and kind. A poet once said:

> Who could get me a friend
> Who if I offend will remain calm
> Who would listen intently to what I have to say
> When he knows it better than I do?[173]

If a colleague was asked about something that you know, do not rush to answer. Instead, you should not say anything until you are asked. This is a better manner and a nobler attitude. It generates interest in what you say, while enhancing your respect.

The honorable *tābᶜī* Mujāhid ibn Jabr recalled that Luqmān the Wise said to his son: "If another person was asked a question, never hasten to give the answer, as if you are going to gain booty or to win a precious prize. By doing so, you will belittle the questioner, will offend the questioned, and will join obnoxious people with your stupidity and ill-manners."[174]

If you speak to a guest or any other person, whether in a gathering or alone, make sure that your voice is pleasant, with a low but audible tone. Raising your voice is contrary to proper manners and indicates a lack of respect for the person to whom you are talking. This manner should be maintained with friends, peers, acquaintances, strangers, the young, and the old. It is more important to adhere to this with one's parents or someone of their status, or with people for whom you have great respect. If appropriate, smile while talking to others.[175]

---

[173] Ibid., pp. 55-56.

[174] Ibid., p. 56.

[175] Ibid., pp. 52-53.

Khālid ibn Safwān at-Tamimi . . . said: "If a person tells you something you have heard before, or news that you already learned, do not interrupt him to exhibit your knowledge to those present. This is rude and ill mannered." The honorable Imām ᶜAbdullāh ibn Wahab al-Quraishi al-Masri . . . said: "Sometimes a person would tell me a story that I have heard before his parents had wed. Yet, I listened as if I have never heard it before." Ibrāhīm ibn al-Junaid said: "A wise man said to his son: 'Learn the art of listening as you learn the art of speaking'." Listening well means maintaining eye contact, allowing the speaker to finish the speech, and restraining your urge to interrupt his speech. Al-Ḥāfiẓ al-Khatib al-Baghdadi said in a poem:

> Never interrupt a talk
> Though you know it inside out.[176]

Muslim and at-Tirmidhī reported that the honorable companion of al-Miqdād ibn al-Aswad said: "We used to keep for the Prophet ﷺ his share of milk, and when he would come at night he would greet us with a voice loud enough for those awake to hear, without disturbing those who were asleep." In addition, whenever the Prophet ﷺ used to pray at night, he would recite the Qurʾān with a voice that pleased those awake, without disturbing those who were asleep.[177]

Treat poor acquaintances or guests with honor and respect. Talk pleasantly to them, using the best of language. Again, poverty is not a vice, many who are poor are more honorable than the wealthy, and many who are penniless are preferred to the rich.[178]

---

[176] Ibid., p. 54.

[177] Ibid., p. 30.

[178] Ibid., p. 73.

HUMILITY
(*Tawāḍu*ᶜ)

And always bear in mind your God is the One and Only God:
and so, surrender yourselves to Hu.
And give the glad tiding of God's acceptance to all who are humble—
all those whose hearts tremble with awe whenever God is mentioned,
and all who patiently bear whatever ill befalls them,
and all who are constant in prayer
and spend on others out of the sustenance We have provided for them.

[*Sūrah al-Ḥajj* 22:32-35]

Call to your Sustainer humbly, and in the secrecy of your hearts.
Truly, He does not love those who go beyond the bounds
of what is right.
And so, do not spread corruption on earth
after it has been so well ordered.
And call to Him with awe and longing:
truly, God's grace is very near those who do good.

[*Sūrah al-A*ᶜ*rāf* 7:55-56]

And remember your Sustainer humbly within yourself and with awe,
and without raising your voice,
in the morning and in the evening;
and don't allow yourself to be unaware.
See how those who are near to your Sustainer
are never too proud to worship Him;
and they praise His limitless glory,
and prostrate themselves before Him alone.

[*Sūrah al-A*ᶜ*rāf* 7:203-206]

And the servants of the Infinitely Compassionate One
are those who walk on the earth in humility
and when the ignorant address them they say, "Peace!"—
those who spend the night in adoration of their Sustainer
in prostration and standing straight.

[*Sūrah al-Furqān* 25:63-64]

One of the virtues most closely related to Poverty is Humility

(*Tawāḍu*ᶜ). According to the *ḥadīth*, "My Lord gave me the choice of being one of two things: either to be a slave and a messenger, or a king and a prophet, and I did not know of which of the two to choose. At my side was the angel Gabriel, and when I raised my head he said, 'Be humble to your Lord,' so I replied, 'A slave and a messenger.'"

Humility is based on a clear sense that, in the presence of God, we are as nothing—and that we are never not in the presence of God: to realize one's nothingness in the face of God is the root of Islām. We may work to develop such humility because we recognize that it is praiseworthy, or that it is one of the virtues of the Prophet ﷺ that we wish to imitate, but only the sense of God's real presence can bring this virtue to perfection. And even if we don't feel the keen sense of God's presence, we can still act as if we did. In the Prophet's words, "pray to God as if you saw Him, because even if you don't see Him, He sees you." Furthermore, if you know that you are in the presence of God right now, you will realize that, as far as you are concerned, all things, persons, and situations are signs of God which have something to say to you, while you yourself are far from perfect in your ability to pay attention to them.

Al-Ghazālī names "fawning" and "ostentatious self-abasement" as among the vices; neither has anything to do with real humility. To make submission to another person's ego is not truly humble, since it is almost always done for some kind of personal advantage, besides being a form of idolatry in itself.

In the words of the Prophet ﷺ, "The most troubled people are the kings, the most hated the proud, and the most abased those who treat others with contempt."[179]

The Messenger said, "Good fortune is theirs who are humble—but not through poverty, who spend of their wealth

---

[179] Charles Upton, contributor. Final hadith quoted: Haeri, *Prophetic Traditions of Islām*, p. 172 (*Mishkāt*, 224-229).

which they have gained lawfully, who have mercy on the abased and poor and who keep company with the scholars of law and the wise."[180]

"No one humbles himself before Allāh but that He raises him."[181]

The Messenger said to some of his companions, "Why is it that I do not see the sweetness in your worship?" When they asked him what sweetness of worship was, he replied, "Humility."[182]

"There are three things by which Allāh only increases a man in goodness: by humility Allāh will only increase a man in elevation, by submission of the self He will only increase a man in honour, and by chastity He will only increase a man in wealth."[183]

Successful indeed are the faithful,
who are humble in their prayers.
[*Sūrah al-Mu*ᶜ*minūn* 23:1-2]

. . . bowing in humility to God,
they will not sell for miserable gain the signs of God.
[*Sūrah Āl* ᶜ*Imrān* 3:199]

They used . . . to call upon Us, with yearning and awe;
and humble themselves before Us.
[*Sūrah al-Anbiyā*ᶜ 21:90]

Had We sent down this Qur'an on a mountain, truly,
you would have seen it humble itself
and split asunder out of fear of Allah.
[*Sūrah al-Ḥashr* 59:21]

---

[180] Haeri, *Prophetic Traditions of Islām*, p. 172 (*al-Ashtarī*, I, 200).

[181] Ibid., p. 172 (Al-Kāshānī, 86).

[182] Ibid., p. 172 (*al-Ashtarī*, I, 200-202).

[183] Ibid., p. 172 (*Mishkāt*, 224-229).

Thus does God set a seal over the heart
of every proud, arrogant one
[*Sūrah Ghāfir* 40:35]

Qarun was doubtless among the people of Moses;
but he acted insolently towards them:
such were the treasures We had bestowed on him
that their very keys would have been a burden
to a body of strong men.
Witness, his people said to him: "Don't gloat,
for God does not love those who take pride in riches.
But with that which God has bestowed on you
seek the Home of the Hereafter,
yet do not forget your portion in this world—
do good as God has been good to you
and do not seek to do harm in the land:
for God does not love those who act harmfully."
[*Sūrah al-Qaṣaṣ* 28:76-77]

Hasn't the time come for the faithful
that their hearts in all humility
should engage in the remembrance of God
and of the truth which has been revealed,
and that they should not become like those
to whom revelation was given but whose hearts have hardened
with the passing of time
so that many among them now rebel against that which is right?
Know that God gives life to the earth after it has been lifeless!
We have indeed made Our signs clear to you
that you might learn wisdom.
[*Sūrah al-Ḥadīd* 57:16-17]

[It is agreed] that the locus of humility is the heart. When one of the Sufis saw a man who was downcast in his outward manner, with lowered eyes and slumped shoulders, he told him,

"O so-and-so, humility is here," and he pointed to his breast, "not here," and he pointed to his shoulders. . . .

And it is said, "Humility is the melting and hiding of the heart in the presence of the Sovereign of Truth." It is also said, "Humility is the prelude to being overpowered by awe." Or, "Humility is a tremor that comes upon the heart suddenly at the unexpected disclosure of the Truth."

Fuḍayl b. ʿIyād asserted, "It is offensive that there should be seen in the outward appearance of man more humility than what is in his heart."[184]

ʿUmar

The ambassador of Rum came to the Commander of the Faithful, ʿUmar, may God be well-pleased with him, and witnessed the gifts of grace with which ʿUmar was endowed. . . .

He said, "O attendants, where is the palace of the Caliph, that I may take my horse and baggage there?"

The folk said to him, "He has no palace; ʿUmar's only palace is an illumined spirit. Though he is famous as Commander of the Faithful, his only dwelling is a hut, like the poor. O brother, how will you behold his palace, when hair has grown in the eye of your heart? Purge your heart's eye of hair and defect, and then hope to behold his palace.[185]

ʿUmar b. al-Khaṭṭāb used to walk at a quick pace, and he would explain that such walking would bring him swiftly to attend to [legitimate] needs and keep him far from vanity.

ʿUmar b. ʿAbd al-ʿAzīz was writing something one night when there was a guest with him. Seeing that the lamp was

---

[184] Al-Qushayri, *Principles of Sufism*, p. 87.
[185] Rūmī, *The Mathnawī of Jalālu'ddin Rūmī*, translated by Nicholson, p. 77 (I:1390-1395), adapted by C. Helminski.

about to go out, the guest offered, "I will go to the lamp and adjust it." But ᶜUmar replied, "No. It is not generous to use the guest as a servant." He suggested, "Then I will call the servant." ᶜUmar declined, "No, he has just gone to sleep." So he went to the container of oil and filled the lamp. The guest exclaimed, "You did it yourself, O Commander of the Believers!" So ᶜUmar told him, "I left and I was ᶜUmar, and I returned and still I am ᶜUmar."[186]

ᶜUrwa b. az-Zubayr related, "When I saw ᶜUmar b. al Khaṭṭāb ﷺ with a full waterskin on his shoulder, I told him, 'O Commander of the [Faithful], this is not fitting for you.' He responded, 'When deputations came to me, listening and obedient, a certain arrogance entered my soul, and I wished to break it.' So he proceeded with the waterskin to the chamber of a woman from the Anṣār and emptied it into her water jug.". . .

ᶜAbdallāh ar-Rāzī explained, "Humility is the abandonment of distinctions in serving.". . .

ᶜUmar b. ᶜAbd al-ᶜAzīz heard that one of his sons had purchased a valuable jewel for one thousand dirhams. So ᶜUmar wrote to him, "I have heard that you have bought a gem for one thousand dirhams. When this letter reaches you, sell the ring and fill one thousand stomachs. Then make a ring out of two dirhams, make its stone out of Chinese iron, and write upon it, 'God has mercy upon the one who knows his true value.'"[187]

Humility Opens Us to God's Grace

[The] Holy Qur'ān mentions how the prophets are chosen; it explains that the Divine does not confine "choice" to prophets alone, rather the Divine, by revealing the journey of the prophets towards truth, opens the door to all humans to expose

---

186 Al-Qushayri, *Principles of Sufism*, p. 88.

187 Ibid., pp. 91-92.

themselves to God's graces so that they might be chosen when they are in full harmony with the law of choice. To expose oneself to God's graces implies that one opens one's heart and soul to the power of light on earth; the light that all prophets and messengers of God left visible and that will always remain as a Home for all souls who long for their Lord. That is what the Holy Qur'ān clarifies when guiding believers to obey Allāh and His Messenger.

All who obey Allāh and the Messenger are in the Company of those on whom is the Grace of Allāh, of the Prophets [who teach], the sincere [lovers of Truth], the witnesses [who testify], and the righteous [who do good]: ah! what a beautiful Fellowship! [Sūrah an-Nisā' 4:69]

To follow the path of the prophets is not to make of their teachings new dogmas and literal forms and images. To obey them is not to make of one's religious affiliation an excuse for showing superiority over others. To follow their paths is essentially to give a chance to the soul to engage in a journey of spiritual transformation through which it expresses itself fully. It is because of that the Prophet Muḥammad says, "*Make yourselves accessible to God's graces.*" However, how can a soul make herself or himself accessible to God's graces?[188]

Although we have been endowed with profound resources of character, we see that, left to our egos, we are nonetheless weak, powerless, and in need.

All Muslims have a chance to deepen their understanding of the perishable nature of creation, and the eternity of God's face, during the fast of Ramaḍān; nothing humbles us, and shows us our essential nothingness, like physical weakness. If even a change in our eating schedule can confront us with our inherent poverty, how poor we must be—except as we are rich in Him.

---

[188] Aisha Rafea, "The Soul's Longing," in C. Helminski, *Women of Sufism, A Hidden Treasure*, pp. 207-208.

Perhaps the Creator wanted us to realize that we would only find strength in the help and support of a higher Source.[189]

The Humility of Muḥammad

Continually aware of the infinite awesomeness of the Divine, Muhammad ﷺ would pray, "Glory be to You, we have not been able to know You as Your knowledge requires, O You who are the object of knowledge. Glory be to You, we have not been able to worship You as You ought to be worshipped, O Worshipped One."

He was known to say, "Whoever is humble, God exalts him, and whoever is haughty, God abases him.[190]

[A true] master of the people is the one who serves them. In the words of ᶜAlī, "among people, [Muḥammad] was one of them." When he reached Quba accompanied by Abū Bakr during *Hijra*, some people of Madina who had not seen him before, tried to kiss the hands of Abū Bakr because, outwardly, there was no sign to distinguish the Prophet from Abū Bakr.

In the construction of the Mosque in Madina after the *Hijra*, he carried two sun-dried bricks while everybody else carried one. In the digging of the ditch around Madina to defend the city in the Battle of the Ditch, the Companions bound a stone around their bellies because of hunger, but God's Messenger himself bound two, because he was more hungry than anybody else. Once, a man saw him and due to his awe-inspiring appearance, began to tremble out of fear. The Messenger ﷺ calmed him, saying: 'Brother, don't be afraid! I am a man, like you, whose mother used to eat dry bread.'

Again, a woman suffering from insanity pulled him by the

---

[189] Charles Upton, contributor.

[190] Gulen, *Prophet Muḥammad, the Infinite Light*, Vol. II, p. 147.

hand and said: 'Come with me and do my housework.' God's Messenger went with the woman and did the work. As reported by ᶜĀᵓishah, mother of believers, God's Messenger patched his clothes, repaired his shoes, and helped his wives with the housework.

Although his modesty elevated him to "the highest of the high," he regarded himself as an ordinary servant of God. Once he said: "No one can enter Paradise by his deeds." When asked whether he could not either, he answered: "I cannot either, but for the Mercy of God."[191]

Muḥammad's Visit to Hilāl

Hilāl was a devoted servant to God possessed of spiritual insight and not a mere imitator. He had concealed himself in being a slave to God's creatures, not from helplessness but for good reason, as Luqmān and Joseph and others did, who were slaves in appearance. He was a groom in the service of a certain Amīr, who was a Moslem, but spiritually blind. "The blind man knows that he has a mother, but he cannot conceive what she is like." If, having this knowledge, he shows reverence towards his mother, it is possible that he may gain deliverance from blindness, for the Prophet has said that when God wills good unto a servant of His He opens the eyes of his heart, that He may let him see the Invisible World with them.

Since you have heard some of the excellent qualities of Bilāl, now hear the story of the emaciation of Hilāl. . . . Hilāl was a spiritual adept and a man of illumined Soul, though he was a groom and slave. . . . The youth served as a groom in the stable, but he was really a king of kings and a slave only in name. The Amir was ignorant of his slave's real condi-

---

[191] Ibid., Vol. II, pp. 144-145.

~ "Muḥammad's Visit to Hilāl" is from *The Mathnawī of Jalālu'ddin Rūmī*, translated by Nicholson, pp. 320-326 (VI:1109-1215), excerpted and adapted by C. Helminski.

tion, for he had no discernment. . . . He saw the clay, but not the treasure in it: he saw the five senses and the six directions, but not their source. . . .

By Divine destiny Hilāl became ill and weak: divine inspiration acquainted Mustafa with his condition, but his master was unaware of his illness, for in his eyes he was worth little. Such a well-doer[192] lay ill in the stable for nine days, and none took notice of his plight. But he who was the Emperor of all personages, he whose oceanic mind reaches every place, to him came the inspiration: "Such-and-such a one who longs for you has fallen ill." So Mustafa went to visit the noble Hilāl.

The Prophetic Moon was running behind the Sun of inspiration, while the Companions followed behind him, like the stars. The Moon is saying, "My Companions are stars—a model for those who follow them in the night-journey, and shooting stars hurled at the disobedient."

When the Amir was told of the arrival of that spiritual Sultan, he sprang up, beside himself with joy; he clapped his hands joyously, thinking that the spiritual Emperor had come on his account. When he came down from the upper chamber, he was ready to lavish his soul on the messenger as a reward for the news he had brought. Then he kissed the earth before the Prophet and greeted him; with delight he made his countenance like a rose. "In God's name," he said, "bestow honor on the house by entering it, so that this assembly-place may become a Paradise, and that my palace may surpass heaven in glory, saying, 'I have seen the Pole on which Time revolves.'"

The venerable Prophet said to him by way of rebuke, "I have not come to visit you."

He replied, "My spirit belongs to you—what, indeed, is my spirit before you? Oh, say on whose account is this solicitude, that I may become dust for the feet of the person who is planted in the orchard of your favor."

Then the Prophet said to him, "Where is that new-moon (*Hilāl*) of the highest heaven? Where is he that in his humility is spread as moonbeams like a carpet on the ground—that king who is disguised as a slave

---

[192] I.e., one who worships God as though he were seeing Him.

and has come down to this world as a witness? Do not say, 'He is my slave and stableman': know this, that he is a treasure buried in ruins. Oh, I wonder to what state he has been reduced by sickness—that new-moon by which thousands of full-moons are trodden underfoot."

The Amir said, "I have no knowledge of his illness, but he hasn't been at the palace-gate for several days. He keeps company with the horses and mules: he is a groom, and this stable is his dwelling-place."

The Prophet went eagerly into the stable to look for him and began to search. The stable was dark, foul, and dirty, but all this vanished from Hilāl's mind when friendship arrived. That fierce spiritual lion scented the Prophet just as the scent of Joseph was perceived by his father Jacob. . . . Hilāl was awakened: he said to himself, "A stable full of dung, and this kind of scent within it!"

Then through the legs of the riding-beasts he saw the holy skirt of the peerless Prophet, and that spiritual hero Hilāl came creeping out of a corner in the stable and laid his face upon his feet. Then the Prophet laid his face against Hilāl's face and kissed his head and eyes and cheeks.

"O Lord," he cried, "what a hidden pearl you are! How are you, O heavenly stranger? Are you better?"

Hilāl answered, "One whose sleep was disturbed with grief, how then is he when the Sun of Prophecy comes into his mouth? The thirsty man who eats clay to slake his thirst, how is he when the Water of Life lays him on its surface and bears him happily along?". . .

The New-moon (Hilāl) and the Full-moon (the Prophet) are in oneness. . . . The new moon's apparent imperfection is a sign of gradual increase. Night by night the new-moon gives a lesson in gradualness: with deliberation it says, "O hasty one, only step by step can one ascend to the roof."

A skillful cook lets the pot boil slowly; the stew boiled in a mad hurry is of no use. Wasn't God able to create heaven in one moment by the word "Be"? Without a doubt He was. Why, then, O you who seek to be taught, did He extend the time to six days—every day as long as a thousand years? Why is the creation of a child completed in nine months? Because gradualness is a characteristic of the action of that King.

Flow Like Water

Perfect mastery works like water:
A boon to every living creature,
In adverse relation never;
At home where most cannot abide,
Closest to the Way it lies.
For position, favor lower ground;
For thought, profundity;
For engaging, gentility;
For speaking, credibility;
For ruling, authority;
For service, capability;
For action, suitability.
Avoiding confrontation
Eliminates accusation.
There is no other way.

COMMENT: Like heaven and earth, water has no self-interest and thus flows downward to the lowest point to serve the interests of other things without confronting or contending with them. Water "goes where others will not go, does what others will not do. . . . Water is adaptable but unchanging, always itself, unitary; it does not become its opposite, though it may alter all it touches. Thus water is an apt and recurring metaphor for *Dao*.

Analects 6.21 says "the wise rejoice in water."

~ "Flow Like Water" is excerpted from Laozi, *Dao de Jing: the Book of the Way*, translated and edited by Moss Roberts, Stanza 8, pp. 45-46. (© 2001 the Regents of the University of California. Used with permission from the University of California Press.)

VI.

Purity

1. Purification of the Heart

2. Purification of the Mind

3. Purification of the Body:

Physical Cleanliness,

Moderation in Eating,

Physical Discipline, and Sports

Purification of the Heart
(*Taṭ-hīr ul-Qalb*)

This Book of blessings We have sent down to you—
so that they may meditate on its signs
and that people of insight might take them to heart.
[*Sūrah Ṣād* 38:29]

O humankind! there has come to you a direction from your Lord
and a healing for your hearts
and for those who have faith, guidance and grace.
Say: "In the abundance of God and in His grace, in that let them rejoice;
that is better than whatever they may hoard."
[*Sūrah Yūnus* 10:57-58]

Truly in this is a Message of remembrance for people of insight.
Is one whose heart God has opened to surrender
so that he is illumined by a light from his Sustainer
no better than one who is hard-hearted?
Woe to those whose hearts are hardened
against remembrance of God!
They obviously wander astray!
God has revealed the most beautiful message in the form of a Book consistent
within itself, repeating its teaching in various guises—
the skins of those who stand in awe of their Lord tremble with it;
then their skins and their hearts soften with the remembrance of God.
Such is God's guidance:
with it He guides the one who wills to be guided,
but those whom God lets stray have none to guide them.
[*Sūrah az-Zumar* 39:20-23]

Purify your inmost heart!
And turn away from all that is unclean!
And do not expect in giving any increase for yourself!
But for your Sustainer's sake be patient and steadfast!
[*Sūrah al-Muddaththir* 74:5-7]

Whoever purifies himself does so for the benefit of his own soul;
and all are journeying to God.
[*Sūrah al-Fāṭir* 35:20]

Do not attribute purity to yourselves;
He knows best who is the most pious.
[*Sūrah an-Najm* 53:32]

Consider the soul and the order and proportion given to it,
and its enlightenment as to that which is wrong and right:
truly, the one who purifies it shall reach a happy state
and the one who corrupts it shall truly be lost!
[*Sūrah ash-Shams* 91:7-9]

And be constant in prayer at both ends of the day
and at the coming of the night,
for good deeds repel those that are evil.
Let this be a reminder to those who remember God.
[*Sūrah Hūd* 11:114]

Let me not be in disgrace on the Day when we will be raised up,
the Day when neither wealth nor children will be of use,
but only the one who brings to God a sound heart.
(Prayer of Abraham)
[*Sūrah ash-Shuʿarāʾ* 26:88-89]

And anyone who honors the symbols set up by God—
truly, these derive their value
from the God-consciousness within the heart.
In that God-consciousness you shall find benefits
until a determined time is fulfilled,
and its goal and end is the Most Ancient Temple.[193]
[*Sūrah al-Ḥajj* 22:32-33]

[193] The Most Ancient Temple [*Sūrah Al-Ḥajj* 22:33], which signifies in locality the Kaʿbah, and in subtlety the heart of the human being.

The Holy Qur'ān demonstrates that all prophets guided people to a way that supports a soul who longs for a truthful life in fulfilling its longing. They tell people that they need to purify their hearts so that they might be able to receive the guidance from within and from a higher source. The Holy Qur'ān explains that when the heart is not pure, a human being cannot listen to, or see, the truth: *They have hearts wherewith they understand not, eyes wherewith they see not, and ears wherewith they hear not. They are like cattle, nay more misguided: for they are heedless (of warning).* [*Sūrah al-Aʿrāf* 7:179]. It also asserts that a "sound heart" leads a person to understanding of the truths of life, and those who have "blind hearts" cannot understand or respond to the divinity within or around: *Do they not travel through the land, so that their hearts [and minds] may thus learn wisdom and their ears may thus learn to hear? Truly it is not their eyes that are blind, but their hearts which are in their breasts* [*Sūrah al-Ḥajj* 22:46].

The Divine teachings to the Prophet Muḥammad also reveal that purification of the heart is possible when the soul is attached to a higher source of guidance. The guidance to "perform ritual prayers" on a regular basis is a means to attain attachment to a higher source. The symbol of that higher source is the Holy Home that Muslims direct their faces towards during the performance of ritual prayers. To direct one's face towards the Holy Home transcends the physical dimension; it is a symbol for the Divine Light that was manifested through all prophets, and that sustains any searching soul with Light. The need to purify one's existence of the egoistic inclinations of selfishness, greed, and covetousness is expressed in the guidance towards charity. The need for preparing oneself to listen to the divinity within is expressed in the guidance towards fasting where one stops all the desires of the physical body in one way or another for a period of time. It is because of the human need for such truths forever that the Holy Qur'ān confirms that all prophets guided their followers to "Prayers, fasting, and charity or *zakāt.*" Many verses in the Holy Qur'ān point to that fact.

Jesus, for instance says about his Lord, *And He hath made me blessed wheresoever I be, and hath enjoined on me Prayer and Charity as long as I live.* [*Sūrah Maryam* 19:31]. And about Isma'il [Ishmael] the Holy Qur'ān says, *He used to enjoin on his people Prayer and Charity, and he was most acceptable in the sight of his Lord.* [*Sūrah Maryam* 19:55].[194]

The Prophet Muḥammad ﷺ was known as Tā Hā, Ṣāfiyy, Mutahhir, Muzakka, the Most Pure. One of his frequent prayers was:

"O Allāh! Grant my soul consciousness of You and purify it. You are the Best to purify. You are the soul's Compassion and its Master."[195]

The Apostle said, "If a man's heart is sound, then his whole body is sound; if his heart is sick, then his whole body is sick."[196]

Commenting on the words of Allāh, *Thereupon their hearts became hardened until they were as stones or even harder* [*Sūrah al-Baqarah* 2:74], the Messenger said, "Beware of talking too much without remembrance of Allāh, for surely too much talking without remembrance of Allāh hardens the heart, and the people furthest away from Allāh are those with hardened hearts." [197]

The human being was born restless;
but truly in the remembrance of God hearts find rest.
[*Sūrah ar-Ra'd* 13:28]

It is useful to pause periodically during the day to witness the condition of our heart and to open to the remembrance that refreshes and

---

[194] Aisha Rafea, "The Soul's Longing," in C. Helminski, *Women of Sufism, A Hidden Treasure*, pp. 209-210.

[195] Muḥammad al-Ghazālī, *Remembrance and Prayer*, p. 97.

[196] Haeri, *Prophetic Traditions of Islām*, p. 145 (*al-Khisāl*, I, 31).

[197] Ibid., p. 101 (*Mishkāt* 53 & 57).

restores. The Prophet ﷺ continually worked to clear his heart of any cloudiness that might enter.

> [ʿĀʾishah ﵂] said, "The Prophet of Allāh ﷺ for as long as I knew him, never slept without first seeking refuge from cowardice and indolence, boredom, parsimony, undue pride, embarrassment in family or financial affairs, the chastisement of the grave, and from Satan and associating him (with the Almighty)."
>
> Thus the Prophet sleeps; but not before making the night come alive with purity and *dhikr,* so that after no more than an hour of sleep he awakes for the dawn prayer and prepares to meet another twenty-four hours with the following *du'a':*
>
> "We have awoken, and the domain belongs to Allāh. Praise to Allāh! He has no partner. There is no God but Him; and to Him is the final issuing."[198]

There are also five faults from which one should cleanse oneself: hypocrisy, argument, affectation, artificiality, and love of property and rank; and five curses from which one should free oneself: miserliness, ambition, anger, greed, and gluttony.

You can correct your state by correcting your actions. Abūl-ʿAbbās ibn al-Khashshab reports that Dhu Nun al-Misri said: "The one who settles his affairs finds peace and comfort; the one who strives to come closer, comes closer; the one who keeps pure becomes cleansed; the one who trusts in God finds security; the one who mixes himself into affairs that do not concern him may lose the things that should concern him."[199]

Behaviour becomes fixed in the self as certain actions are repeated and actions issue from the heart by means of the limbs—each limb being capable of good actions which in turn lead to laudable behaviour; if wrong actions appear which in turn pro-

[198] Muḥammad al-Ghazālī, *Remembrance and Prayer*, pp. 45-46.

[199] Al-Sulami, *The Way of Sufi Chivalry*, p. 70.

duce bad behaviour, then the movements of the heart and limbs must be checked until good is produced, and they are prevented from doing evil. Man's most fatal enemies are the desires of the stomach, sex, and tongue.[200]

[The Prophet ﷺ said:] "Longing for this world brings worry and sadness, doing without in this world brings ease to the heart and body."[201]

The Commander of the Faithful said, "Tears dry up when the heart hardens, and the heart only hardens because of the number of one's wrong actions."[202]

Surely the heart of man becomes weary as the body becomes weary and bored. Seek out rarities of wisdom for it, for surely the heart's nature is to pursue and retreat: when it is in pursuit, then urge it to extra acts of worship; and when it is retreating, then limit yourself to the obligatory acts.[203]

Just as a person's teeth are kept bright with the tooth-stick, so Allāh has created the heart pure and clear and has made remembrance, reflection, awe, and respect of Him a means of nourishing it; if the purity of one's heart is defiled by negligence and distress it is made clean by turning to Him and is purified by entrusting oneself to Him—in this way it returns to its original state. Thus Allāh says, *Surely Allāh loves those who turn much [to Him], and He loves those who purify themselves* [*Sūrah al-Baqarah* 2:222].[204]

Muḥammad ﷺ relayed God's encouraging message (*ḥadīth qudsī*), "Heaven and earth cannot contain me, but the heart of My willing servant can contain Me," and in the Qur'ān conveyed a prayer to help keep us oriented:

---

[200] Haeri, *Prophetic Traditions of Islām*, p. 158 (*Qurrat al-ᶜUyūn*, 60-64).

[201] Ibid., p. 183 (*al-Khiṣāl*, 73).

[202] Ibid., p. 145 (*Mishkāt*, 255-258).

[203] Ibid., p. 146 (*Mishkāt*, 255-258) .

[204] Ibid., p. 162 (*Qurrat al-ᶜUyūn*, 211-216).

O our Sustainer!
Do not let our hearts swerve from the truth
after You have guided us;
and bestow on us the gift of Your grace:
truly, You are the Giver of Gifts.
[*Sūrah Āl ^{c}Imrān* 3:8]

Purifying the Heart of a Prophet

Twice during the lifetime of the Prophet ﷺ, he experienced angels coming to him to assist in the cleansing and purifying of his heart:

> Abū ^{c}Amr b. Ḥamdān related . . . from ^{c}Utba b. ^{c}Abd Allāh, as follows: A man asked the Prophet ﷺ, "What was it happened to you first, O Messenger of God?" He replied, "My wet-nurse [Ḥalīma] was from the Banū Sa^{c}d b. Bakr. One time a son of hers and I went off with our flock without taking any food with us. So I said, '[O] brother, go back and get us some food from our mother's home.' So my brother hurried away while I stayed with the animals. Then two white birds like eagles came along and one said to the other, 'Is that he?' 'Yes,' the other replied. Then they both swooped down, took hold of me and laid me out on my back. They then split my abdomen, extracted my heart, cut it open, and took out from it two black clots. One bird said to his companion, 'Bring me some ice water.' And with it they cleaned my insides. The first bird then said, 'Now get some cold water.' With that they washed my heart. Then the bird said, 'Bring me *as-sakīnah* (quietude).' This they sprinkled into my heart. The one said to the other, 'Sew it up.' So he did that and then placed on my heart the seal of prophethood. After that one bird said to the other, 'Place him in one balance scale and a thousand of his people in the other.' And when I looked up, there were the thousand above me, and I was concerned that some of them might tumble down on to

me. Then the bird said, 'If his whole nation were balanced against him, he would still outweigh them.' Then both birds went away, leaving me there. I was tremendously afraid and raced off to my foster-mother and told her what had happened. She was afraid I'd lost my mind and exclaimed, 'God protect you!' Then she got an ass of hers ready for travel and put me on it. She rode behind me and we traveled till we reached my mother. She then said, 'Well, I've fulfilled my pact and agreement.' She then told my mother what had happened, but it didn't shock her. She said, 'What I saw was that a light came from inside me that lit up the castles of Syria.'"

★ ★ ★

[Abū Dharr al-Ghifārī] asked, "O Messenger of God, how were you informed that you were a prophet and when did you become convinced that you were one?" He replied, "O Abū Dharr, two angels came to me when I was in one of the valleys of Mecca. One of them dropped down to the ground, while the other remained suspended between heaven and earth. One said to the other, 'Is that he?' 'Yes, it's he.' The one said, 'Weigh him against another man.' He did so, and I outweighed him."

He then told it till the end, recounting how his chest was opened and sewn up and the seal was placed between his shoulders. He then said, "Then finally they turned away from me, as if their work was fully done.

★ ★ ★

Prayer was prescribed in Medina and . . . two angels came to the Messenger of God ﷺ, took him to *zamzam*, split open his abdomen, took out his insides and put them in a basin of gold, washed them in *zamzam* water, then filled his insides with wisdom and knowledge.

And the tradition also comes through Ibn Wahb, . . . from Anas, who said, "The Messenger of God ﷺ was visited three nights. (A voice) said: 'Take him who is the best of them and their leader.' So they took the Messenger of God ﷺ, conducted him to *zamzam*, opened his abdomen, brought a gold bowl, washed out his insides then filled them with wisdom and faith."

★ ★ ★

In the two *ṣaḥīḥ* collections it is given . . . from the Prophet ﷺ in the recounting of *al-Isrā*ᶜ (the ascension to heaven), as the story of the laying open of his chest (as occurring) on that night, and its being washed with *zamzam* water.

There is no denying the probability of that occurring twice, once when he was young and once on the night of the ascension in preparation for his going to join the heavenly assemblage of angels, and of conferring with and appearing before the Lord, the Almighty, Glorious, Blessed, and Exalted One.[205]

[205] Ibn Kathīr, *The Life of the Prophet Muḥammad*, Vol. I, pp. 164-166.

Purification of the Mind
(*Taṭ-hīr ul-ᶜAql*)

Are you not aware how God offers the parable of a good word?
It is like a good tree, firmly rooted,
reaching its branches towards the sky,
always yielding fruit, by consent of its Sustainer.
This is how God offers parables to human beings,
so that they might consider the truth.
And the parable of a corrupt word is that of a corrupt tree,
torn up from its roots onto the surface of the earth,
unable to endure.
Even so God grants firmness to those who have come to faith
through the word that is unshakably true,
in this world as well as in the life to come.
[*Sūrah Ibrāhīm* 14:23-27]

O you who have faith! Stand in awe of God
and always speak a word on behalf of that which is right and true:
that He may make your behavior whole and sound
and forgive you your mistakes.
The one who heeds God and His Messenger
has already attained a mighty success.
[*Sūrah al-Aḥzāb* 33:70-71]

Twice will they be given their reward
because they have persevered: they have turned aside evil with good,
and they give to others from what We have given to them.
And when they hear vain talk they turn away from it and say:
"To us our deeds and to you yours;
peace be with you: we do not seek the ignorant."
[*Sūrah al-Qaṣaṣ* 28:54-55]

Those will prosper who purify themselves
and remember the Name of their Sustainer and pray.
[*Sūrah al-Aᶜlā* 87:14-15]

And remember Our servants Abraham, Isaac, and Jacob,
endowed with inner strength and vision.
Truly, We purified them
by means of the remembrance of the Life to Come.
They were in Our sight, truly, among the elect and the Good.
And remember Ishmail, Elisha, and Zul-Kifl:
each of them was among the companions of the Good.
This is a reminder:
and truly, awaiting the God-conscious is a beautiful place of return.

[*Sūrah Ṣād* 38:45–49]

O you who have faith!
Do not let some men among you laugh at others;
it may be that the others are better than they.
Nor let some women laugh at others;
it may be that the others are better than they.
Nor speak ill nor with sarcasm towards each other,
nor call each other by taunting names:
a name connoting wickedness is inappropriate after one has come to faith,
and those who do not stop are doing wrong.
O you who have attained to faith!
As much as you can, avoid suspicion, for suspicion in some cases is a sin;
and do not spy on each other,
nor speak ill of one another behind each other's backs.
Would any of you like to eat the flesh of his dead brother?
No, you would detest it . . . but remain conscious of God:
for truly, God is Ever Turning One Towards Repentance,
Infinitely Merciful.
O humankind! We created you all out of a male and a female,
and made you into nations and tribes
that you might come to know each other.
Truly, the most highly regarded of you in the sight of God
is the one who does the most good.
And God is All-knowing and is Well-aware of all things.

[*Sūrah al-Ḥujurāt* 49:11–13]

Truly, Remembrance of God is the greatest.
[*Sūrah al-ᶜAnkabūt* 29:45]

It is related that the Prophet of Allāh ﷺ would blow on his hands, on getting into bed but before sleeping, recite the last two *sūrahs* of the Qurʾān, and then run his hands over his entire body. In another version of the same *ḥadīth,* it is related that when the Prophet ﷺ went to bed at night, he would clasp his hands together, and blow into them, and then recite *Sūrat al-Ikhlāṣ* and the last two *sūrahs* of the Qurʾān [*Falaq* and *Nās*], and then run his hands over as much as he could of his body beginning with his head, face, and the front of his body, repeating this three times.

The three *sūrahs* referred to mention *tawḥīd* or the Unity of God, and the purity of His person and attributes. In addition, they urge one toward divine providence, and away from the evils of body and mind.[206]

In the Name of God, the Infinitely Compassionate and Most Merciful
Say, "He is the One God; God the Eternal Originator;
He does not bear children, nor was He born;
and He is beyond compare."
[*Sūrah al-Ikhlāṣ* 112:1-4, complete]

In the Name of God, the Infinitely Compassionate and Most Merciful
Say: "I seek refuge with the Lord of the Dawn
from the mischief of created things,
and from the evil of Darkness as it overspreads,
and from the mischief of those who blow on knots,[207]
and from the evil of the envious one as he envies."
[*Sūrah al-Falaq* 113:1-5, complete]

[206] Muḥammad al-Ghazālī, *Remembrance and Prayer*, p. 112.
[207] Those who cast spells; those who spread constriction, who exacerbate difficulties.

In the Name of God, the Infinitely Compassionate and Most Merciful
Say: "I seek refuge with the Sustainer of humankind,
the Sovereign of humankind, the God of humankind,
from the evil whispering, elusive tempter
who whispers in the hearts of human beings—
from invisible forces as well as humans."
[*Sūrah an-Nās* 114:1-6, complete]

Just as the footprint of any creature that walks the earth can be placed in the elephant's footprint, which is the largest of all—even so, mindful attention is the one quality that ensures ease of mind at all times.

Mindful attention causes beneficial thoughts that have not yet arisen to arise. It also causes harmful thoughts that have already arisen to vanish. In the one who is mindful, the good that is to be will be realized.[208]

And if My servants ask you about Me—witness, I am near;
I respond to the call of the one who calls,
whenever he calls Me:
let them, then, respond to Me, and have faith in Me,
so that they may follow the right way.
[*Sūrah al-Baqarah* 2:186]

Be continuously mindful of prayers,
and of praying in the most excellent way;
and stand before God in devoted surrender.
[*Sūrah al-Baqarah* 2:238]

Al-Kāshānī said, "It can happen that the heart so totally submits to anger and desire that it is enslaved by them; in this way the heart dies and its course towards eternal bliss is interrupted. It is also possible, however, that the heart submits to

---

[208] Bancroft, *The Pocket Buddha Reader (Anguttara Nikaya)*, p. 38.

another flank of Allāh's army: knowledge, wisdom, and reflection. If the opposite happens, and the army of anger and desire conquers the self, then the man will be in great loss, which is the state of most men in this age. Their intellects have been subjected to their desires—in their very attempts to see to the needs of the desires—whereas it is the desires that should submit to the intellect whenever the latter requires this."[209]

It is hard to be born as a human being and hard to live the life of one. It is even harder to hear of the path and harder still to awake, to rise and to follow. Yet the teaching is simple: "Cease to do evil, learn to do good. And purify your mind.

"Hurt none by word or deed. Be moderate in your eating. Live in inner solitude. And seek the deepest consciousness." This is the teaching.[210]

Your perceptive mind is already luminous and shining brightly. But you color it with all your attachments. It is not easy to understand this, and many do not. They do not cultivate their perceptive mind. But that mind, luminous and brightly shining, is fundamentally free of all attachments, because they come and go. This you should understand and for you there should be cultivation of the perceptive mind.[211]

All that we are is the result of our thoughts; it is founded on our thoughts and made up of our thoughts. With our thoughts we make the world. If you speak or act with a harmful thought, trouble will follow you as the wheel follows the ox that draws the cart. If you speak or act with a harmonious thought, happiness will follow you as your own shadow, never leaving you.[212]

---

[209] Haeri, *Prophetic Traditions of Islām*, p. 148 (*Qurrat al-ᶜUyūn*, 44-47).

[210] Bancroft, *The Pocket Buddha Reader* (*Dhammapada*), pp. 70-71.

[211] Ibid., *(Anguttara Nikaya)* p. 71.

[212] Ibid., (*Dhammapada*) p. 157.

If your thought is a rose, you are a rose garden.
If your thought is thorny, you're just fuel for the bathhouse stove.[213]

Aṣ-Ṣadiq said, "If there is a group of three believers, then two of them should not converse together without involving the third, for this would cause him sorrow and pain." He also said, "Talk about your brother when he is out of your sight as you would like him to talk of you when you are out of his; leave him alone at those times when you would like to be left alone, and act like the one who knows that he is rewarded for good actions and punished for bad."[214]

Aṣ-Ṣadiq said . . . "A believer is a brother to the believer; he does not oppress him, abandon him, or cheat him, nor does he slander him, betray him, or lie to him."[215]

Aṣ-Ṣadiq said, "The Muslim is the brother of the Muslim: he is his sight, his mirror, and his guide. He does not betray him, cheat him, oppress him, lie to him, or slander him, nor does he promise him something and then go back on his promise."[216]

Abū Baṣīr said that Aṣ-Ṣadiq told him this, "O Abū Muḥammad, be scrupulous, strive hard, speak truthfully, guard whatever is entrusted to you, be good company for whoever keeps your company, and stay long in prostration, for it is the practice of those before you."[217]

The Messenger said to Abū Dharr, . . . "My Lord has ordered that my speech be remembrance, my silence reflection, and my looking an exhortation."[218]

---

[213] Rūmī, *The Mathnawī of Jalālu'ddin Rūmī*, translated by Nicholson, p. 236 (II:278), adapted by C. Helminski.

[214] Haeri, *Prophetic Traditions in Islām*, pp. 204-205 (*Mishkāt,* 189-203).

[215] Ibid., p. 214 (*Mishkāt,* 187-189).

[216] Ibid., p. 219 (al-Kulaynī, II, 166).

[217] Ibid., p. 186 (*Mishkāt,* 144-147).

[218] Ibid., pp. 100-101 (*Mishkāt,* 53 & 57).

Mujāhid relates that the Messenger, commenting on Allāh's words, "*Woe to every slanderer, defamer*" said, "The slanderer is the one who criticises people and the defamer is the one who backbites people [lit., eats their flesh]."[219]

Aṣ-Ṣadiq said, "The most beloved of Allāh's [servants] are those who are truthful in speech, who maintain the prayer and whatever Allāh has made incumbent on them—including fulfilling the trust."[220]

Imām ᶜAlı has said, . . . "All good is contained in three things: your looking, your silence, and your speech. Looking without reflection is negligence, silence without meditation is unmindfulness, and speech without remembrance is idle talk. Happiness will be theirs whose looking is a lesson, whose silence is meditation, whose speech is remembrance, who weep because of their mistakes, and by whose hand people are safe from evil."[221]

Words are under your control until you have spoken them,
but you come under their control once you have spoken them.
~ Ḥaḍrat ᶜAlī[222]

---

[219] Ibid., p. 239 (al-Ashtarī, I, 115-122).

[220] Ibid., p. 221 (*Mishkāt,* 70-84).

[221] Ibid., p. 101 (*Mishkāt*, 53-57).

[222] Thomas Cleary (translator), *Living and Dying with Grace: Counsels of Ḥaḍrat ᶜAlī* (Boston: Shambhala Publications, 1995), p. 58.

The Truthful Friend

I do not wish to treat friendships daintily but with roughest courage. When they are real, they are not glass threads or frost-work, but the solidest thing we know. For now, after so many ages of experience, what do we know of nature or of ourselves? Not one step has man taken toward the solution of the problem of his destiny. In one condemnation of folly stand the whole universe of men. But the sweet sincerity of joy and peace which I draw from this alliance with my brother's soul is the nut itself whereof all nature and all thought is but the husk and shell. Happy is the house that shelters a friend! It might well be built, like a festal bower or arch, to entertain him a single day. Happier, if he know the solemnity of that relation and honor its law! It is no idle bond, no holiday engagement. He who offers himself a candidate for that covenant comes up, like an Olympian, to the great games where the first-born of the world are the competitors. He proposes himself for contest where Time, Want, Danger, are in the lists, and he alone is victor who has truth enough in his constitution to preserve the delicacy of his beauty from the wear and tear of all these. The gifts of fortune may be present or absent, but all the hap in that contest depends on intrinsic nobleness and the contempt of trifles. There are two elements that go to the composition of friendship, each so sovereign that I can detect no superiority in either, no reason why either should be first named. One is Truth. A friend is a person with whom I may be sincere. Before him I may think aloud. I am arrived at last in the presence of a man so real and equal that I may drop even those most undermost garments of dissimulation, courtesy, and second thought, which men never put off, and may deal with him with the simplicity and wholeness with which one chemical atom meets another. Sincerity is the luxury allowed, like diadems and authority, only to the highest rank, that being permitted to speak truth, as having none above it to court or conform unto.

~ "The Truthful Friend," is excerpted from Ralph Waldo Emerson, *Essays by Ralph Waldo Emerson, First Series* (London, United Kingdom: George G. Harrap & Co., Ltd. 1926), pp. 152-154.

Every man alone is sincere. At the entrance of a second person, hypocrisy begins. We parry and fend the approach of our fellow man by compliments, by gossip, by amusements, by affairs. We cover up our thought from him under a hundred folds. I knew a man who under a certain religious frenzy cast off this drapery, and omitting all compliment and commonplace, spoke to the conscience of every person he encountered, and that with great insight and beauty. At first he was resisted, and all men agreed he was mad. But persisting, as indeed he could not help doing for some time in this course, he attained to the advantage of bringing every man of his acquaintance into true relations with him. No man would think of speaking falsely with him, or of putting him off with any chat of markets or reading-rooms. But every man was constrained by so much sincerity to face him, and what love of nature, what poetry, what symbol of truth he had, he did certainly show him. But to most of us society shows not its face and eye, but its side and its back. To stand in true relations with men in a false age is worth a fit of insanity, is it not? We can seldom go erect. Almost every man we meet requires some civility, requires to be humored; he has some fame, some talent, some whim of religion or philanthropy in his head that is not to be questioned, and which spoils all conversation with him. But a friend is a sane man who exercises not my ingenuity, but me. My friend gives me entertainment without requiring me to stoop, or to lisp, or to mask myself. A friend therefore is a sort of paradox in nature. I who alone am, I who see nothing in nature's existence I can affirm with equal evidence to my own, behold now the semblance of my being, in all its height, variety and curiosity, reiterated in a foreign form; so that a friend may well be reckoned the masterpiece of nature.

The other element of friendship is tenderness.

Be Impeccable with Your Word

Be impeccable with your word. Speak with integrity. Say only what you mean.

Avoid using the word to speak against yourself or to gossip about others.

Use the power of your word in the direction of truth and love.

The first agreement is the most important one and also the most difficult one to honor. It is so important that with just this first agreement you will be able to transcend to the level of existence I call heaven on earth.

The first agreement is to be impeccable with your word. It sounds very simple, but it is very, very powerful. Why your word? Your word is the power that you have to create. Your word is the gift that comes directly from God. The Gospel of John in the Bible, speaking of the creation of the universe, says, "In the beginning was the word, and the word was with God, and the word is God." Through the word you express your creative power. It is through the word that you manifest everything. Regardless of what language you speak, your intent manifests through the word. What you dream, what you feel, and what you really are, will all be manifested through the word.

The word is not just a sound or a written symbol. The word is a force; it is the power you have to express and communicate, to think, and thereby to create the events in your life. You can speak. What other animal on the planet can speak? The word is the most powerful tool you have as a human; it Is the tool of magic. But like a sword with two edges, your word can create the most beautiful dream, or your word can destroy everything around you.

~ This selection "Be Impeccable with Your Word" is excerpted from pp. 27-49 of the book *The Four Agreements* © 1997, Don Miguel Ruiz. Reprinted by permission of Amber Allen Publishing, Inc, P.O. Box 6657, San Rafael, California 94903. All rights reserved.

***

The word is so powerful that one word can change a life or destroy the lives of millions of people. Some years ago one man in Germany, by the use of the word, manipulated a whole country of the most intelligent people. He led them into a world war with just the power of his word. He convinced others to commit the most atrocious acts of violence. He activated people's fear with the word, and like a big explosion, there was killing and war all around the world. All over the world humans destroyed other humans because they were afraid of each other. Hitler's word, based on fear-generated beliefs and agreements, will be remembered for centuries.

The human mind is like a fertile ground where seeds are continually being planted. The seeds are opinions, ideas, and concepts. You plant a seed, a thought, and it grows. The word is like a seed, and the human mind is so fertile! The only problem is that too often it is fertile for the seeds of fear. Every human mind is fertile, but only for those kinds of seeds it is prepared for. What is important is to see which kind of seeds our mind is fertile for, and to prepare it to receive the seeds of love.

***

During our domestication, our parents and siblings gave their opinions about us without even thinking. We believed these opinions and we lived in fear over these opinions, like not being good at swimming, or sports, or writing. Someone gives an opinion and says, "Look, this girl is ugly!" The girl listens, believes she is ugly, and grows up with the idea that she is ugly. It doesn't matter how beautiful she is; as long as she has that agreement, she will believe that she is ugly. That is the spell she is under.

By hooking our attention, the word can enter our mind and change a whole belief for better or for worse.

***

Now let us see what the word *impeccability* means. *Impeccability* means "without sin." *Impeccable* comes from the Latin *pecatus,* which means "sin." The *im* in impeccable means "without," so *impeccable* means "without sin." Religions talk about sin and sinners, but let's understand what it really means to sin. A sin is anything that you do which goes against yourself. Everything you feel or believe or say that goes against yourself is a sin. You go against yourself when you judge or blame yourself for anything. Being without sin is exactly the opposite. Being impeccable is not going against yourself. When you are impeccable, you take responsibility for your actions, but you do not judge or blame yourself.

From this point of view, the whole concept of sin changes from something moral or religious to something commonsense. Sin begins with rejection of yourself. Self-rejection is the biggest sin that you commit. In religious terms self-rejection is a "mortal sin," which leads to death. Impeccability, on the other hand, leads to life.

Being impeccable with your word is not using the word against yourself. If I see you in the street and I call you stupid, it appears that I'm using the word against you. But really I'm using my word against myself, because you're going to hate me for this, and your hating me is not good for me. Therefore, if I get angry and with my word send all that emotional poison to you, I'm using the word against myself.

If I love myself I will express that love in my interactions with you, and then I am being impeccable with the word, because that action will produce a like reaction. If I love you, then you will love me. If I insult you, you will insult me. If I have gratitude for you, you will have gratitude for me. If I'm selfish with you, you will be selfish with me. If I use the word to put a spell on you, you are going to put a spell on me.

Being impeccable with your word is the correct use of your energy, it means to use your energy in the direction of truth and love for yourself. If you make an agreement with yourself to be impeccable with your word, just with that intention, the truth will manifest through you and clean all the emotional poison that exists within you. But making this agreement is difficult because we have learned to do precisely the opposite. We have learned to lie as a habit of our communication with others and more importantly with ourselves. We are not impeccable with the word.

★★★

The only thing that can break a spell is to make a new agreement based on truth. The truth is the most important part of being impeccable with your word. On one side of the sword are the lies which create black magic, and on the other side of the sword is the truth which has the power to break the spell of black magic. Only the truth will set us free.

★★★

Looking at everyday human interactions, imagine how many times we cast spells on each other with our word. Over time this interaction has become the worst form of black magic, and we call it gossip.

Gossip is black magic at its very worst because it is pure poison. We learned how to gossip by agreement. When we were children, we heard the adults around us gossiping all the time, openly giving their opinions about other people. They even had opinions about people they didn't know. Emotional poison was transferred along with the opinions, and we learned this as the normal way to communicate.

★★★

Using the analogy of the human mind as a computer, gossip can be compared to a computer virus. A computer virus is a piece of computer language written in the same language all the other codes are written in, but with a harmful intent. This code is inserted into the program of your computer when you least expect it and most of the time without your awareness. After this code has been introduced, your computer doesn't work quite right, or it doesn't function at all because the codes get so mixed up with so many conflicting messages that it stops producing good results.

Human gossip works exactly the same way. For example, you are beginning a new class with a new teacher and you have looked forward to it for a long time. On the first day of class, you run into someone who took the class before, who tells you, "Oh that instructor was such a pompous jerk! He didn't know what he was talking about, and he was a pervert too, so watch out!"

You are immediately imprinted with the word and the emotional code the person had when saying this, but what you are not aware of is his or her motivation in telling you. This person could be angry for failing the class or simply making an assumption based on fears and prejudices, but because you have learned to ingest information like a child, some part of you believes the gossip, and you go on to the class.

As the teacher speaks, you feel the poison come up inside you and you don't realize you see the teacher through the eyes of the person who gave you that gossip. Then you start talking to other people in the class about this, and they start to see the teacher in the same way: as a jerk and a pervert. You really hate the class, and soon you decide to drop out. You blame the teacher, but it is gossip that is to blame. . . . When we see the world through a computer virus, it is easy to justify the cruelest behavior. What we don't see is that misuse of our word is putting us deeper into hell.

★★★

For years we have received the gossip and spells from the words of others, but also from the way we use our word with ourselves. We talk to ourselves constantly and most of the time we say things like, "Oh, I look fat, I look ugly. I'm getting old, I'm losing my hair. I'm stupid, I never understand anything. I will never be good enough, and I'm never going to be perfect." Do you see how we use the word against ourselves? We must begin to understand what the word is and what the word *does.* If you understand the first agreement, *be impeccable with your word,* you begin to see all the changes that can happen in your life. Changes first in the way you deal with yourself, and later in the way you deal with other people, especially those you love the most.

★★★

If we adopt the first agreement, and become impeccable with our word, any emotional poison will eventually be cleaned from our mind and from our communication in our personal relationships, including with our pet dog or cat.

Impeccability of the word will also give you immunity from anyone putting a negative spell on you. You will only receive a negative idea if your mind is fertile ground for that idea. When you become impeccable with your word, your mind is no longer fertile ground for words that come from black magic. Instead, it is fertile for the words that come from love. You can measure the impeccability of your word by your level of self-love. How much you love yourself and how you feel about yourself are directly proportionate to the quality and integrity of your word. When you are impeccable with your word, you feel good; you feel happy and at peace.

PURIFICATION OF THE BODY
(*Taṭ-hīr ul-Badan*)

Eat of the good things We have provided for your sustenance
but not to excess so that My Wrath might not descend on you:
for those on whom My Wrath descends
have thrown themselves into ruin!
But without doubt I am the One Who forgives again and again
those who repent, have faith, and do right,
those who turn to receive true guidance.
[*Sūrah Ṭā Hā* 20:81-82]

O you who have attained to faith! Fasting is ordained for you
as it was ordained for those before you,
so that you might remain conscious of God.
And whoever does more good than He is bound to do
thereby does good to himself;
for to fast is to do good to yourselves—if you only knew it.
[*Sūrah al-Baqarah* 2:183-184]

The Prophet used to say in prayer: "O Allāh, I ask of You good health and gratitude for good health in this world and the next."[223]

In another *ḥadīth*, the Prophet ﷺ alluded to how nice it would be to remain clean, when he asked his companions: "If one of you had a river at his door and he washed himself five times a day would any dirt remain on him?" "No dirt will remain," they answered. The Prophet ﷺ commented: "This is the example of the five [daily] prayers as Allāh wipes with them your sins."[224]

---

[223] Haeri, *Prophetic Traditions of Islām*, p. 160 (*Mishkāt,* 255-258).
[224] Abū Ghudda, *Islamic Manners*, p. 26.

Within the Islamic tradition, prayer and the ablution preceding it are offered to the human being as a means of purification of the body as well as the heart and mind. We are encouraged to keep our bodies clean and to eat of the good things that God has provided us to keep this bodily house of Spirit in good health. Periodic fasting is also recommended for purification of body, mind, and heart.

> The thirty days of prayer and fasting is akin to the *Mandala puja* of the Hindu tradition. The name "*Ramaḍān*" comes from the Sanscrit word *Rama-dhyan. Dhyan* means to meditate and *Ram* in Sanscrit means "the one who shines in the heart." Thus Ramaḍān refers to a time to meditate on God. [225]

> One of the practical requirements before a supplication is accepted is that the supplicant must pursue an honest living and earn his livelihood through lawful means. The food that he eats or the clothes that he wears, in fact all his possessions, must be lawful and acquired through lawful means. This presumes noble qualities, like honesty, good behavior, and contentment with what one has. These qualities make one the subject of others' love and of brotherly feelings and good will. A strong will is evidently necessary to achieve all these noble qualities.
>
> Muslim has reported Abū Hurayrah as saying that the Prophet ﷺ said, "Verily, Allāh is pure and He accepts only that which is good and pure. Allāh has commanded the believers what He commanded His messengers, saying, *You apostles! Enjoy [all] things good and pure, and work righteousness! For I am well-acquainted with [all] that you do.* [*Sūrah al-Muᶜminūn* 23:51] Allāh also says, *O you who believe! Eat of the good things that We have provided for you.* [*Sūrah al-Baqarah* 2:72]"[226]

---

[225] Sri Sri Ravishankar. *Hinduism and Islām* (Bangalore, India: Vyakti Vikas Kendra, 2002), p. 7.

[226] Al-ᶜAnani. *Freedom and Responsibility in Qur'anic Perspective*, p. 201.

The voluntary poverty of the Prophet flowed naturally from the realization that *All is perishing, except His Face* [*Sūrah al-Qaṣaṣ* 28:88]. On one occasion he said: "What have I to do with this world? I and this world are as a rider and a tree beneath which he shelters. Then he goes on its way and leaves it behind him." In the words of Ḥaḍrat ᶜAlī, "Whoever attaches himself strongly to life makes himself a target for misfortune and the vicissitudes of fate." Such *ḥadīth* are an expression of the virtue of Detachment, *iḥtisāb*. Detachment has nothing to do with holding yourself apart from people or avoiding life, but rather with the ability to let come what God wants to send, and to let go of what God wants to take away. As the Prophet ﷺ said, "A man will not find sweetness of faith until he is heedless of the fruits of this world." He also said: "Doing without (*zuhd*) in this world does not mean wearing coarse clothes and eating coarse food, but rather curbing one's expectations."

According to Al-Ghazālī, egotism and vice appear not only as *excess* but also as deficiency. . . . The commanding self (*nafs al-ammāra*) may command us to worship ourselves; it may also command us to damage and destroy ourselves. In both cases, it has made sure that we are too involved in thinking and worrying about ourselves, when we should be remembering God. Both excess and deficiency in our character will interfere with our ability to sense God's presence, which is just what the commanding self wants. Al-Ghazālī therefore recommends moderation in eating, avoiding both the extremes of gluttony and self-starvation. He quotes Abū Sulayman as saying, "If something is put before you in the nature of a desire which you have renounced, then partake of it just a little, but do not give your soul all that it hopes for. In this way you will banish a desire without making it pleasurable for your soul." In the words of the Qurʾān, *Eat and drink, but do not be extravagant.* [*Sūrah al-Aᶜrāf* 7:31].[227]

---

[227] Charles Upton, contributor.

Muḥammad had no wish to live in any less Spartan fashion than did his people. His main meal was usually a boiled gruel known as *sawīq*, with dates and milk, his only other meal of the day being dates and water, but he frequently went hungry and developed the practice of binding a flat stone against his belly to assuage his discomfort.[228]

Luqmān the Wise said to his son, "If the stomach is filled, then reflection falls asleep, wisdom falls silent, and the limbs take rest from worship."

The advantages of hunger are many: clarity and vigour of the heart, delight in obedience, physical weakness which stops one committing wrong or being negligent, a stilling of sexual desire, which becomes excessive when the stomach is full, and a driving away of sleep, which by its nature makes one languid, allows one's life to slip away, and prevents one from rising in prayer at night. The Messenger said, "The stomach is the house of disease."

The aim, however, is to achieve a balance, to find the middle way—when the Messenger found out that some of the Muslims were fasting every day and staying up in prayer the whole night, he forbade them to do this.

Thus it is better that a man neither feel heavy after eating nor suffer pangs of hunger; rather, that he forget his stomach and not let it influence him. The object of eating is to keep alive and to maintain our strength for worship: excessive eating prevents one from worship and pangs of hunger engross the heart and weaken the worshipper. Allāh has said, *Eat and drink and be not extravagant,* [*Sūrah al-Aʿrāf* 7:31] which verse summarizes everything mentioned above.[229]

---

[228] Reprinted by permission from *Islam and the Destiny of Man,* p. 117, by Charles Le Gai Eaton, the State University of New York Press © 1985, State University of New York. All rights reserved.

[229] Haeri, *Prophetic Traditions of Islām*, pp. 158-159 (*Qurrat al-ʿUyūn*, 60-64).

The Holy Qur'ān also clarifies that fasting had always been a means of purification for all souls who longed for divine guidance: *O you who believe! Fasting is prescribed to you as it was prescribed to those before you, that you may [learn] self-restraint* [*Sūrah al-Baqarah* 2:183]. The Prophet Muḥammad received from the Divine a whole system for spiritual purification that he practiced, and taught to his followers. However, this is not the place to relate in detail how that system confirms and perfects the systems of prophets previous to him. Suffice it to say that all prophets, as revealed in the Holy Qur'ān, existentially lived the truth that a human cannot feel the longing of the soul to lead a truthful life unless he purifies his earthly existence. Purification takes place when the soul is attached to a higher source of guidance, when the physical body's lusts are controlled, and when the divinity within is given the chance to express itself and overwhelm the earthly existence. The means to realize that purification are unveiled by the Revelation to all prophets when they were guided by the Divine to uncover the truthful path for souls who long for submission to Allāh.[230]

Aṣ-Ṣadiq said, "If you fast, then fast with your hearing, sight, feeling, and your skin; and stop all actions undertaken for show or actions which harm people. You should treat the fast with respect. The Messenger once heard a woman insulting her slave-girl while fasting. The Prophet then called for food, bidding her to eat, but she replied, 'I am fasting.' 'How can you be fasting while you insult your slave-girl?' Fasting is not abstention from food and drink alone."[231]

The Messenger said, . . . "If one of you becomes angry he should say, 'I seek refuge from the accursed Satan,' for anger

---

[230] Aisha Rafea, "The Soul's Longing," in C. Helminski, *Women of Sufism, A Hidden Treasure*, p. 210.

[231] Haeri, *Prophetic Traditions of Islām,* p. 120 (*Qurrat al-ʿUyūn*, 268-279).

comes from Satan." "If one of you becomes angry, then he should perform the ablution with water, for anger comes from fire." "Anger is from Satan, Satan is from fire, and water extinguishes fire."[232]

Aṣ-Ṣadiq relates how the Prophet said to his companions one day, "Wealth which has not been purified [by giving away a part of it as poor-rate] is cursed, just as the body which is not purified—even if it be only once every forty days—is cursed." He was then asked, "O Messenger, we are familiar with the purification of wealth, but what is the purification of the body?'" He replied, "That it will be afflicted by disease." Then the faces of those listening changed colour. When the Messenger saw this he said, "Do you know what I meant by what I said?" They replied, "No, O Messenger!" He said, "That a man becomes anxious, is beset by misfortune, that he commits mistakes, that he is afflicted by illness, pricked by thorns, or the like, so that he suffers a throbbing pain in the eye." The Messenger said, "Everything has its means of purification, and that of the body is fasting."[233]

Aṣ-Ṣadiq said, "There is nothing more harmful to the heart of a believer than overeating. It causes two things: hardness of heart and excitement of desire. Hunger is nourishment for the believer, food for the spirit and heart, and health for the body."[234]

Truly, the rising by night
is the strongest means of governing the soul
and the most appropriate for words of prayer.
Truly, by day there is a long chain of duties for you;
but keep in remembrance the name of your Sustainer

---

[232] Ibid., p. 236 (al-Ashtarī, I, 122-126).

[233] Ibid., p. 127 (*Qurrat al-ᶜUyūn*, 267-279).

[234] Ibid., p. 157 (*Qurrat al-ᶜUyūn*, 60-64).

and devote yourself to Him wholeheartedly.
Sustainer of the East and the West, there is no god but Hu:
take Hu therefore as the guardian of your affairs.
[*Sūrah al-Muzzammil* 73:1-9]

Abū Ḥanīfah said to Imām aṣ-Ṣadiq, "O Abū ᶜAbd Allāh, what gives you patience during prayer?" He replied, "Woe to you, O Nuᶜmān! Know that prayer is the sacrifice of every God-fearing man, and that the *ḥajj* is the struggle of every weak man; for everything there is *zakāt*, and the *zakāt* of the body is the fast; the best of deeds is waiting for Allāh's help in a matter; and a man who calls to Allāh in word but not in deed is like an archer whose bow has no string. Remember these words, O Nuᶜmān."[235]

The Messenger said, "Strength is not physical combat, but rather controlling oneself when angry."[236]

There are four degrees of purification: the physical cleaning of the body from defilement; the purification of the limbs from criminal or incorrect action and sin; the purification of the heart from discourteous or odious behaviour; and the purification of the core of one's self from everything other than Allāh—and this is the purification of the prophets and the truthful believers.[237]

And your garments do purify.
[*Sūrah al-Muddaththir* 74:4]

The Prophet said, "Purity is half of faith; purity is the key to prayer; the *Dīn* [religion] has been founded on cleanliness; the

---

[235] Ibid., p. 75 (*al-Irbilī*, II, 367 & 421, 419, 414, 396, 400).
[236] Ibid., p. 236 (*al-Ashtarī*, I, 122-126).
[237] Ibid., p. 163 (*Qurrat al-ᶜUyūn*, 211-216).

worst servant [of Allāh] is he who is filthy; let whoever obtains clothing make sure it is clean."[238]

The Prophet ﷺ himself helped with daily household chores, mended his own clothes and also kept the garment of his body clean and in good shape. He was quite physically fit. He was renowned at wrestling and archery, helped with the building projects of the community, and would even sometimes run races with his young wife, ʿĀʾishah.

Archery

Know that archery is a noble skill. . . . If asked: With whom did archery originate? Say: Among our people, with Ḥamzah, who practiced it much. It is said that the Prophet shot arrows and there is no doubt that he used the bow. . . . He encouraged bowmanship and blessed the archers.

★ ★ ★

If asked: How did the bow come into existence? Say: Gabriel brought it to Adam when he had cultivated some land. Birds would come and raid his sown fields. Adam would drive them away from one side while they returned from another. Frustrated, Adam did not know what to do. He appealed to God, saying: "O my God, show me a way to keep these birds away from my fields."

God sent Gabriel with a bow and three arrows. He put the grip of the bow in Adam's hand and taught him how to shoot arrows. After a few birds had been shot by the arrows, they ceased to come, and Adam's fields remained secure.

If asked: What is the first necessity for an archer? Say: A considerate master. If a person does not have a teacher, he cannot begin to master this skill. Should he try, he will get nowhere and be of no use to anyone. . . .

Should his arrow miss the target, he should not be discouraged.

---

[238] Ibid., p. 161 (*Qurrat al-ʿUyūn*, 211-216).

~ "Archery" is excerpted from Sabzawārī, *The Royal Book of Spiritual Chivalry*, pp. 351-354.

The first arrow that Adam shot went astray. . . .

He should not envy anyone who shoots straighter and more accurately than he; instead, he should praise him.

He should not delight in his own accomplishments and become haughty, for there are many upsets in victory.

★ ★ ★

If asked: What is the mirror of the archer? Say: The target. He must keep his eye uninterruptedly on it from the moment of drawing the bow and setting the arrow until the arrow's release.

★ ★ ★

If asked what is the shape of the bow? Say: A semicircle.

If asked: What does the semicircle signify? Say: The degree of possibility which continually receives grace from the necessary. The meaning of these words is that in existence the possible needs the necessary. Therefore, whoever takes the bow in hand must remember his own need and recognize that he has come into existence through another power and should not be negligent in His service.

If asked: What does the bowstring signify? Say: The separating line that exists between possibility and necessity. In this there is a mystery of which it is not permissible to speak.

If asked: What does the bow say to the arrow? Say: It says: Fly straight so as to reach the desired goal.

★ ★ ★

If asked: What do the letters of the bow (*kamān* = *K, M, A, N*) symbolize? Say:

> *Kāf* (*K*) indicates generosity (*karam*); that is, the archer must be generous and chivalrous.
>
> *Mīm* (*M*) indicates compassion (*marḥamat*); that is, he must be merciful to those under his control.
>
> *Alif* (*A*) indicates belief (*iʿtiqād*); he must be well-intentioned and correct in his faith.
>
> *Nūn* (*N*) indicates counsel (*naṣīḥat*); he must not withhold his tutelage and advice from his colleagues and companions. Whoever does not possess these four attributes is not worthy of this handgrip.

If you speak Arabic, the letters are *Qāf, Wāw,* and *Sīn* (*qaws* = bow). The *Qāf* (Q) is for acceptance (*qabūl*), the *Wāw* (*W*) for piety (*wara*ᶜ), and the *Sīn* (*S*) for soundness (*salāmat*) of spirit; that is, the archer must make himself acceptable to hearts through service, pass his time in piety and asceticism, and have a healthy soul in order that the taking and letting go of the handgrip of the bow be lawful.

Zen in the Art of Archery

When drawn to its full extent, the bow encloses the "All" in itself, explained the Master, and that is why it is important to learn how to draw it properly. Then he grasped the best and strongest of his bows and, standing in ceremonious and dignified attitude, let the lightly drawn bowstring fly back several times. This produces a sharp crack mingled with a deep thrumming, which one never afterwards forgets when one has heard it only a few times; so strange is it, so thrillingly does it grip the heart. . . . After this significant introductory act of purification and consecration the Master commanded us to watch him closely. He placed, or "nocked," an arrow on the string, drew the bow so far that I was afraid it would not stand up to the strain of embracing the All, and loosed the arrow. All this looked not only very beautiful, but quite effortless. He then gave us his instructions: "Now you do the same, but remember that archery is not meant to strengthen the muscles. When drawing the string you should not exert the full strength of your body, but must learn to let only your two hands do the work, while your arm and shoulder muscles remain relaxed, as though they looked on impassively. Only when you can do this will you have fulfilled one of the conditions that make the drawing and the shooting 'spiritual.'" With these words he gripped my hands and slowly guided them through the phases of the movement

~ "Zen in the Art of Archery" is excerpted from *Zen in the Art of Archery* by Eugene Herrigel, pp. 17-23.

which they would have to execute in the future, as if accustoming me to the feel of it.

Even at the first attempt with a medium-strong practice-bow I noticed that I had to use considerable force to bend it. This is because the Japanese bow, unlike the European sporting bow, is not held at shoulder level, in which position you can, as it were, press yourself into it. Rather, as soon as the arrow is nocked, the bow is held up with arms at nearly full stretch, so that the archer's hands are somewhere above his head. Consequently, the only thing he can do is to pull them evenly apart to left and right, and the further apart they get the more they curve downwards, until the left hand, which holds the bow, comes to rest at eye level with the arm outstretched, while the right hand, which draws the string, is held with arm bent above the right shoulder, so that the tip of the three-foot arrow sticks out a little beyond the outer edge of the bow—so great is the span. In this attitude the archer has to remain for a while before loosing the shot. The strength needed for this unusual method of holding and drawing the bow caused my hands to start trembling after a few moments, and my breathing became more and more labored. Nor did this get better during the weeks that followed. The drawing continued to be a difficult business, and despite the most diligent practice refused to become "spiritual." To comfort myself, I hit upon the thought that there must be a trick somewhere which the Master for some reason would not divulge, and I staked my ambition on its discovery.

Grimly set on my purpose, I continued practicing. The Master followed my efforts attentively, quietly corrected my strained attitude, praised my enthusiasm, reproved me for wasting my strength, but otherwise let me be. Only, he always touched on a sore spot when, as I was drawing the bow, he called out to me to "Relax! Relax!"—a word he had learned in the meantime—though he never lost patience and politeness. But the day came when it was I who lost patience and brought myself to admit that I absolutely could not draw the bow in the manner prescribed.

"You cannot do it," explained the Master, "because you do not breathe right. Press your breath down gently after breathing in, so that the abdominal wall is tightly stretched, and hold it there for a while. Then breathe out as slowly and evenly as possible, and, after a short pause, draw a quick breath of air again—out and in continually, in a rhythm that will gradually settle itself. If it is done properly, you will feel the shooting becoming easier every day. For through this breathing you will not only discover the source of all spiritual strength but will also cause this source to flow more abundantly, and to pour more easily through your limbs the more relaxed you are." And as if to prove it, he drew his strong bow and invited me to step behind him and feel his arm muscles. They were indeed quite relaxed, as though they were doing no work at all.

The new way of breathing was practiced, without bow and arrow at first, until it came naturally. The slight feeling of discomfort noticeable in the beginning was quickly overcome. The Master attached so much importance to breathing out as slowly and steadily as possible to the very end, that, for better practice and control, he made us combine it with a humming note. Only when the note had died away with the last expiring breath were we allowed to draw air again. The breathing in, the Master once said, binds and combines; by holding your breath you make everything go right; and the breathing out loosens and completes by overcoming all limitations. But we could not understand that yet.

The Master now went on to relate the breathing, which had not of course been practiced for its own sake, to archery. The unified process of drawing and shooting was divided into sections: grasping the bow, nocking the arrow, raising the bow, drawing and remaining at the point of highest tension, loosing the shot. Each of them began with breathing in, was sustained by firm holding of the down-pressed breath, and ended with breathing out. The result was that the breathing fell into place spontaneously and not only accentuated the individual positions and hand-movements, but wove them together in a rhythmical sequence depending, for each of us, on the state of his breathing-capacity. In spite of its being divided into parts the entire process seemed like a living thing wholly contained in itself, and not even remotely comparable to a gymnastic exercise, to which bits can be added or taken away without its meaning and character being thereby destroyed.

I cannot think back to those days without recalling, over and over again, how difficult I found it, in the beginning, to get my breathing to work out right. Though I breathed in technically the right way, whenever I tried to keep my arm and shoulder muscles relaxed while drawing the bow, the muscles of my legs stiffened all the more violently, as though my life depended on a firm foothold and secure stance, and as though, like Antaeus, I had to draw strength from the ground. Often the Master had no alternative but to pounce quick as lightning on one of my leg muscles and press it in a particularly sensitive spot. When, to excuse myself, I once remarked that I was conscientiously making an effort to keep relaxed, he replied: "That's just the trouble, you make an effort to think about it. Concentrate entirely on your breathing, as if you had nothing else to do!" It took me a considerable time before I succeeded in doing what the Master wanted. But—I succeeded. I learned to lose myself so effortlessly in the breathing that I sometimes had the feeling that I myself was not breathing but—strange as this may sound—being breathed. And even when, in hours of thoughtful reflection, I struggled against this bold idea, I could no longer doubt that the breathing held out all that the Master had promised. Now and then and in the course of time more and more frequently, I managed to draw the bow and keep it drawn until the moment of release while remaining completely relaxed in body, without my being able to say how it happened. The qualitative difference between these few successful shots and the innumerable failures was so convincing that I was ready to admit that now at last I understood what was meant by drawing the bow "spiritually."

So that was it: not a technical trick I had tried in vain to pick up, but liberating breath-control with new and far-reaching possibilities. I say this not without misgiving, for I well know how great is the temptation to succumb to a powerful influence and, ensnared in self-delusion, to overrate the importance of an experience merely because it is so unusual. But despite all equivocation and sober reserve, the results obtained by the new breathing—for in time I was able to draw even the strong bow of the Master with muscles relaxed—were far too definite to be denied.

In talking it over with Mr. Komachiya, I once asked him why the Master had looked on so long at my futile efforts to draw the bow "spiritually," why he had not insisted on the correct breathing right from the start. "A great Master," he replied, "must also be a great teacher. With us the two things go hand in hand. Had he begun the lessons with breathing exercises, he would never have been able to convince you that you owe them anything decisive. You had to suffer shipwreck through your own efforts before you were ready to seize the lifebelt he threw you."

VII.

Clarity: Intention Discernment True Knowledge

INTENTION
(*Niyyah*)

And say: "O my Sustainer!
Cause me to enter upon whatever I may do in a true and sincere way,
and cause me to complete it in a true and sincere way,
and grant me, out of Your grace, sustaining strength!"
And say: "Truth has now arrived,
and falsehood has withered away:
for, witness, all falsehood is bound to wither away!"
[*Sūrah al-Isrā*ᶜ 17:80-81]

Do not say of anything "I shall be sure to do so and so tomorrow"
without adding "If God wills!"
And call your Sustainer to mind when you forget,
and say: "I hope that my Lord will guide me
ever closer even than this to the right path."
[*Sūrah al-Kahf* 18:23-24]

In the houses which God has allowed to be raised
so that His name shall be remembered in them,
there are those who praise His limitless glory
morning and evening—
those whom neither business nor striving after gain
can turn from the remembrance of God,
and from constancy in prayer, and from charity:
who are filled with awe
of the Day on which all hearts and eyes will be transformed,
who only hope that God will give them recompense
in accordance with the best of their actions,
and give them even more out of His blessing:
for God grants sustenance to whom He wills, beyond all reckoning.
[*Sūrah an-Nūr* 24:36-38]

We have bestowed messages clearly showing the truth;
but God guides to a straight way only the one who wills to be guided.
[*Sūrah an-Nūr* 24:46]

Say: "It is God I serve with my sincere devotion."
[*Sūrah az-Zumar* 39:14]

Intention is the first step in the rational method of developing our innate power of free will, because it is intimately related to our freedom of choice and action and as such forms the very basis of our accountability. . . .

Muslim scholars give prominence in their books to a discussion of intention in order to maintain a sense of priority. Intentions must be pure and sincere. For the acquisition of knowledge to be effective, rewarding, fruitful, and beneficial, it must be motivated by a desire to please only Allāh. . . .

In a sound *ḥadīth* we read that the Prophet ﷺ said, "Whoever among you sees an evil should try to change it with his hands. If he is not able to do so, then with his tongue, and if he is unable to do even that, then with his heart, and this is the weakest form of faith."

This *ḥadīth* explicitly states that if a Muslim finds himself in one of those difficult situations where he can neither use his hands nor tongue to remove the evil he should fight it by using his intention.[239]

Islām teaches that no good deed is valid without purity of intention and self-reformation, so a person's work of a life-time may be ruined if he or she is not genuinely motivated. Therefore man must be warned against pride in his good deeds in order to encourage him to do better and work still harder.[240]

In order to gain [the] benefits of intention, one should continually exercise his intention before every single act one under-

---

[239] Al-ʿAnani, *Freedom and Responsibility in Qur'anic Perspective,* p. 169.
[240] Ibid., p. 144.

takes. All through his life a Muslim makes a specific intention in submission to Allāh each time he stands in worship, makes ablution, offers prayers, gives alms, visits his relatives, parents, neighbours, or friends, visits the sick, earns a livelihood, performs a pilgrimage, looks after children, is gentle to his spouse, makes peace between members of a family, is generous to those who are defenseless and unrepresented, enjoins good and forbids evil, removes harmful things from a public path, observes fasting, helps the needy, lends to others (without interest), participates in the funeral of a Muslim, or in any way observes and abides by the general rules of good behaviour and social relationships. When repeated endlessly all these good qualities become an integral part of one's personality so that gradually and steadily one reverts to one's original nature [*fiṭrah*] and is ready to cooperate with others in a spirit of mutual understanding, appreciation, and love, and thus comes to respect his own as well as others' freedom and integrity.

One of the marvels of this aspect of Allāh's creation regarding intention is that when a Muslim consciously and carefully abides by the guidance of Allāh and follows the teachings of His Prophet Muḥammad ﷺ in due course of time this attitude slowly and gradually becomes a part of his character, which further deepens his insight and understanding. This in turn activates his intellect, because it forces him repeatedly and constantly to focus his thoughts on objectives. . . .

The ability to rise above the purely impulsive level of behaviour and to regulate one's instinctive drives is in itself a great achievement as a step towards the freedom that enables people to make their own decisions in the light of their best interests.[241]

No one will enter Paradise on account of his own good deeds alone, as stated by the Prophet ﷺ. This fact is mentioned in order to elucidate the bounty and mercy of Allāh so that we will strive even harder in His cause, and do our best to thank

[241] Ibid., pp. 172-173.

> Him for His great blessings on us. . . .
>
> Man [is warned] against pride and conceit in his accomplishments, which cannot exist independently of the great bounty bestowed by Allāh upon man.[242]

Continually we must reexamine our intentions and seek to be in clearer connection with our Sustainer in all our activities. Whether *standing, sitting, or lying down* [*Sūrah an-Nisā*ᶜ 4:103], our remembrance and our intention is with God.

> All human activities should have noble intentions. Imām Bukhārī relates that the Prophet ﷺ said, "Actions will be judged by their intentions, and a man shall be treated according to his intentions. So whoever emigrates in pursuit of worldly acquisitions or to contract marriage will have his emigration treated accordingly."[243]

> It may be that the Prophet too ﷺ had this in mind, for whenever he left his house, he never failed to recite this *du*ᶜ*ā:*
>
> "In the name of Allāh (I go out); I place my trust in Allāh! O Allāh, I seek refuge in You from being made to stumble, from straying and from being made to stray, from doing wrong to others and from being wronged by others, and from misunderstanding and from being misunderstood."
>
> The Prophet did not seek supremacy over anyone else; he wanted only to avoid falling into error or causing someone else to fall into it.[244]

> The Prophet ﷺ said: "Whoever goes into the marketplace and says, 'There is no God but Allāh, He is one and has no partner, His is the Glory and His is the Praise, Giver of life and death; He is the Living who does not die. In His hand is all

[242] Ibid., p. 144.

[243] Ibid., p. 174.

[244] Muḥammad al-Ghazālī, *Remembrance and Prayer*, p. 59.

good, and He is Powerful over everything,' that man will have a thousand thousand good deeds credited to him, and a thousand thousand bad deeds erased, and he will be elevated a thousand thousand ranks."

Such a huge reward will not be attained by the mere utterance of a few words, but by those who achieve a state of certainty regarding the presence of the Almighty and His beneficence, so that they rely on the One in whose Hand is all Goodness without ever having to resort to cunning or deception. The scholars of Islam have emphatically stated that such great rewards are never promised in return for insignificant deeds or faltering resolutions.

In the matter of earning a living for one's self and one's family, good and bad may often become confused. However, the true Muslim is one who realizes that a soul nourished on ill-gotten gains will never be admitted to Paradise, and that since Allāh is Himself Pure, He will accept only those who are themselves pure. Therefore, it is essential that the Muslim should exercise caution in all his dealings. In this regard, the Prophet ﷺ taught us to use the following *duʿā:*

"O Allāh, suffice me with Your *ḥalāl* (lawful) from seeking Your *ḥarām* (unlawful), and free me by Your Beneficence from seeking the help of others."

"O Allāh, I ask You for knowledge that is useful, sustenance that is pure and deeds that are accepted."

The nature of this world is such that, in the crush of it, a man sometimes finds himself in a situation where he could be corrupted, or where the ignorance of certain people tempt him to behave foolishly toward them, or to seek revenge on them. It is a far better thing, however, that he leave his home each morning prepared to tolerate and forbear. Anas ibn Mālik related that the Prophet ﷺ once asked his Companions:

"Are you unable to follow the example of Abū Ḍamḍam?" They said, "Who is Abū Ḍamḍam?" The Prophet replied, "Every morning he used to say, 'O Allāh, I make a gift to You

> of my life and my honour,' so that he never cursed anyone who cursed him, or wronged anyone who wronged him, or molested anyone who molested him."[245]

Muḥammad ﷺ himself continually sought to increase the Light by which and through which he lived. One of his frequent prayers was the prayer for light:

> O God! Grant me Light in my heart, Light in my grave,
> Light in front of me, Light behind me,
> Light to my right, Light to my left,
> Light above me, Light below me,
> Light in my ears, Light in my eyes,
> Light on my skin, Light in my hair,
> Light within my flesh, Light in my blood, Light in my bones.
> O God! Increase my Light everywhere.
> O God! Grant me Light in my heart,
> Light on my tongue, Light in my eyes, Light in my ears,
> Light to my right, Light to my left,
> Light above me, Light below me,
> Light in front of me, Light behind me,
> and Light within my self; increase my Light.[246]

The Blossoming Light of the Mind

Naturalness is called the Way. The Way has no name or form; it is just the essence, just the primal spirit.

---

[245] Ibid., pp. 63-64.

[246] This prayer appears in various forms in many of the *awrād* of the Islamic world. C. Helminski, *The Mevlevi Wird,* p. 67.

~ "The Blossoming Light of the Mind" contains selected excerpts taken from pages 1-2, 4, and 23-29 from *The Secret of the Golden Flower* by Thomas Cleary, copyright © 1991 by Thomas Cleary, reprinted by permission of Harper-Collins Publishers Inc.

The Secret of the Golden Flower is a lay manual of Buddhist and Taoist methods for clarifying the mind. A distillation of the inner psycho-active elements in ancient spiritual classics, it describes a natural way to mental freedom practiced in China for many centuries.

The golden flower symbolizes the quintessence of the paths of Buddhism and Taoism. Gold stands for light, the light of the mind itself; the flower represents the blossoming, or opening up, of the light of the mind. Thus the expression is emblematic of the basic awakening of the real self and its hidden potential.

In Taoist terms, the first goal of the Way is to restore the original God-given spirit and become a self-realized human being. In Buddhist terms, a realized human being is someone conscious of the original mind, or the real self, as it is in its spontaneous natural state, independent of environmental conditioning.

This original spirit is also called the celestial mind, or the natural mind. A mode of awareness subtler and more direct than thought or imagination, it is central to the blossoming of the mind. *The Secret of the Golden Flower* is devoted to the recovery and refinement of the original spirit.

This manual contains a number of helpful meditation techniques, but its central method is deeper than a form of meditation. Using neither idea nor image, it is a process of getting right to the root source of awareness itself. The aim of this exercise is to free the mind from arbitrary and unnecessary limitations imposed upon it by habitual fixation on its own contents. With this liberation, Taoists say, the conscious individual becomes a "partner of creation" rather than a prisoner of creation.

The experience of the blossoming of the golden flower is likened to light in the sky, a sky of awareness vaster than images, thoughts, and feelings, an unimpeded space containing everything without being filled. Thus it opens up an avenue to an endless source of intuition, creativity, and inspiration. Once this power of mental awakening has been developed, it can be renewed and deepened without limit.

In Wilhelm's own introduction to his translation of *The Secret of the Golden Flower,* he notes that Taoist organizations following this teaching in his time included not only Confucians and Buddhists but also Jews,

Christians, and Muslims, all without requiring them to break away from their own religious congregations. So fundamental is the golden flower awakening that it brings out inner dimensions in all religions.

From the point of view of that central experience, it makes no more difference whether one calls the golden flower awakening a relationship to God or to the Way, or whether one calls it the holy spirit or the Buddha nature or the real self. The *Tao Te Ching* says, "Names can be designated, but they are not fixed terms."

The image of the opening up of the golden flower of the light in the mind is used as but one of many ways of alluding to an effect that is really ineffable.

Turning the Light Around and Tuning the Breathing

1. The doctrine just requires single-minded practice. One does not seek experiential proof, but experiential proof comes of itself.

2. On the whole, beginners suffer from two kinds of problems: oblivion and distraction. There is a device to get rid of them, which is simply to rest the mind on the breath.

3. The breath is one's own mind; one's own mind does the breathing. Once mind stirs, then there is energy. Energy is basically an emanation of mind.

4. Our thoughts are very rapid; a single random thought takes place in a moment, whereupon an exhalation and inhalation respond to it. Therefore inward breathing and outward breathing accompany each other like sound and echo. In a single day one breathes countless times, so has countless random thoughts. When the luminosity of spirit has leaked out completely, one is like a withered tree or dead ashes.

5. So should one have no thoughts? It is impossible to have no thoughts. Should one not breathe? It is impossible not to breathe. Nothing compares to making the affliction itself into medicine, which means to have mind and breath rest on each other. Therefore tuning the breath should be included in turning the light around.

6. This method makes use of two lights. One is the light of the ears, one is the light of the eyes. The light of the eyes means the external sun and moon, combining their lights; the light of the ears means the internal sun and moon, combining their vitalities. However, vitality is congealed

and stabilized light; "they have the same source but different names." Therefore clarity of hearing and seeing are both one and the same spiritual light.

7. When you sit, lower your eyelids and then establish a point of reference. Now let go. But if you let go absolutely, you may not be able to simultaneously keep your mind on listening to your breathing.

8. You should not allow your breathing to actually be audible; just listen to its soundlessness. Once there is sound, you are buoyed by the coarse and do not enter the fine. Then be patient and lighten up a little. The more you let go, the greater the subtlety; and the greater the subtlety, the deeper the quietude.

9. Eventually, after a long time, all of a sudden even the subtle will be interrupted and the true breathing will appear, whereupon the substance of mind will become perceptible.

10. This is because when mind is subtle, breath is subtle; when mind is unified, it moves energy. When breath is subtle, mind is subtle; when energy is unified, it moves mind. Stabilization of mind must be preceded by development of energy because the mind has no place to set to work on; so focus on energy is used as a starting point. This is what is called the preservation of pure energy.

11. You don't understand the meaning of the word "movement." Movement is pulling the strings; the word "movement" is another word for "control." Since you can cause movement by vigorous action, how could you not be able to cause stillness by pure quietude?

12. The great sages saw the interrelation of mind and energy and skillfully set up an expedient for the benefit of people of later times. An alchemical text says, "The hen embraces the egg, always mentally listening." These are the finest instructions. The way a hen can give life to an egg is through warm energy; warm energy can only warm the shell and cannot penetrate the inside, so she mentally conducts the energy inward. That "listening" is single-minded concentration. When the mind enters, the energy enters; with warm energy, the birth takes place.

13. Therefore even though the mother hen goes out from time to time, she is always listening, and the concentration of her spirit is never interrupted. Since the concentration of the spirit is never interrupted,

then the warm energy is also uninterrupted day and night, so the spirit comes alive.

14. The life of the spirit comes from the prior death of the mind. If people can kill the mind, the original comes alive. Killing the mind does not mean quietism, it means undivided concentration. Buddha said, "Place the mind on one point, and everything can be done."

15. If the mind tends to run off, then unify it by means of the breath; if the breath tends to become rough, then use the mind to make it fine. If you do this, how can the mind fail to stabilize?

16. Generally speaking, the two afflictions of oblivion and distraction just require quieting practice to continue unbroken day after day until complete cessation and rest occur spontaneously. When you are not sitting quietly, you may be distracted without knowing it; but once you arc aware of it, distraction itself becomes a mechanism for getting rid of distraction.

17. As for unawares oblivion and oblivion of which you become aware, there is an inconceivable distance between them. Unawares oblivion is real oblivion; oblivion that you notice is not completely oblivious. Clear light is in this.

18. Distraction means the spirit is racing; oblivion means the spirit is unclear. Distraction is easy to cure; oblivion is hard to heal. Using the metaphor of illness, one that involves pain or itch can be treated with medicine, but oblivion is a symptom of paralysis where there is no feeling.

19. A distracted mind can be concentrated, and a confused mind can be set in order; but oblivion is unformed darkness, in contrast to distraction, which still has some direction.

20. Oblivion means the lower soul is in complete control, whereas the lower soul is a lingering presence in distraction. Oblivion is ruled by pure darkness and negativity.

21. When you are sitting quietly, if you become drowsy, this is oblivion. Repelling oblivion is simply a matter of tuning the breath. The "breath" in this case is respiration, not the "true breathing." Nevertheless the true breathing is present within it.

22. Whenever you sit, you should quiet your mind and unify your

energy. How is the mind quieted? The mechanism is in the breathing, but the mind alone knows you are breathing out and in; do not let the ears hear. When you don't hear it, the breathing is fine; and when breathing is fine, the mind is clear. If you can hear it, the breathing is rough, which means the mind is cloudy. Cloudiness means oblivion, so it is natural to feel sleepy. Even so, the mind should be kept on the breathing.

23. It is also essential to understand that this device is not mechanical or forced. Just maintain a subtle looking and listening.

24. What is "looking"? It is the light of the eyes spontaneously shining, the eyes only looking inward and not outward. Not looking outward yet being alert is inward looking; it is not that there really is such a thing as looking inward.

25. What is "listening"? It is the light of the ears spontaneously listening, the ears only listening inward and not outward. Not listening outward yet being alert is inward listening; it is not that there really is such a thing as listening inward.

26. Listening means listening to the soundless; looking means looking at the formless.

27. When the eyes do not look outside and the ears do not listen outside, they are closed in and have a tendency to race around inside. Only by inward looking and listening can you prevent this inner racing as well as oblivion in between. This is the meaning of sun and moon combining their vitalities and lights.

28. When you sink into oblivion and become drowsy, get up and take a walk. When your spirit has cleared, sit again. It's best to sit for a while in the early morning when you have free time. After noontime, when there are many things to do, it's easy to fall into oblivion. Also, there's no need to fix the length of time of meditation; it is only essential to set aside all involvements and sit quietly for a while. Eventually you will attain absorption and not become oblivious or sleepy. [247]

---

[247] See the section within this text on Purification of the Body, *Zen in the Art of Archery,* for further practice and application.

Discernment of True and False
(*Furqān*)

Blessed is the One Who sent down the Criterion to His servant
that it might be a counsel to all the world.
[*Sūrah al-Furqān* 25:1]

O you who have attained to faith!
If you remain conscious of God,
He will endow you with a standard by which to discern
the true from the false,
and will clear evil from you, and will forgive you your mistakes:
for God is limitless in the abundance of His blessing.
[*Sūrah al-Anfāl* 8:29]

Hā Mīm.
By the Book that makes things clear—
We sent it down during a blessed night:
for We wish to give counsel.
In wisdom, that night the distinction between all things is clarified,
by command from Our Presence.
For We always are sending guidance
as a mercy from your Sustainer:
for He alone is All-Hearing, All-Seeing;
the Sustainer of the heavens and the earth
and all between them, if only you have inner certainty.
There is no god but He: it is He Who gives life and gives death,
your Sustainer and the Sustainer of your earliest ancestors.
[*Sūrah ad-Dukhān* 44:1-9]

And yet, when you do not produce a sign for them,
some say, "why don't you seek to obtain it from God?"
Say: "I only follow whatever is revealed to me by my Sustainer:
this revelation is a means of insight from your Sustainer,
and a guidance and grace to those who will have faith.

And so when the Qur'an is voiced, pay attention to it,
and listen in silence, so that you might be graced with God's mercy."
[*Sūrah al-Aʿrāf* 7:203-205]

That which is on earth
We have made but as a glittering show for the earth
in order that We may test them
as to which of them are best in conduct.
[*Sūrah al-Kahf* 18:7]

In the past We granted to Moses and Aaron the Criterion
and a Light and a Message for those who are conscious of God,
those who stand in awe of their Sustainer in their most secret thoughts
and who hold in awe the Hour of Reckoning.
And this is a Message of blessing which We have sent down:
will you then reject it?
[*Sūrah al-Anbiyāʿ* 21:48-50]

And so, call out to them
and stand steadfast as you have been commanded,
and do not follow their likes and dislikes, but say:
"I have faith in the Book which God has bestowed from on high;
and I am asked to judge justly between you.
God is our Sustainer and your Sustainer.
To us belongs the responsibility for our deeds, and to you, your deeds.
Let there be no argument between us and you.
God will bring us all together, and with Him is all journeys' end."
[*Sūrah ash-Shūrā* 42:15]

Step by step He has sent down to you this book,
setting forth the truth which confirms
whatever remains of earlier revelations:
for it is He who earlier bestowed from on high
the Torah and the Gospel, as a guidance to humankind,
and it is He who has bestowed the standard for discernment.
[*Sūrah Āl ʿImrān* 3:3-4]

O you who have attained to faith!
Do not deprive yourselves of the good things of life
which God has made lawful to you,
but do not transgress the bounds of what is right:
truly, God does not love those who go beyond
the bounds of what is right.
And so partake of the lawful, good things
which God grants you as sustenance,
and be conscious of God, in whom you have faith.
[*Sūrah al-Māʾidah* 5:87-88]

And yet, they have been commanded no more than this:
to worship God, sincere in their devoted faith in Him alone;
turning away from all that is false; and to remain constant in prayer;
and to practice regular charity: and that is the true and straight Way.
[*Surah al-Bayyinah* 98:5]

Say: "Truly, my Instructor has guided me
onto a straight way through a steadfast faith—
the way of Abraham, the true one,
who was not of those who attribute divinity to anything beside God."
Say: "Truly, my prayer, and all my acts of worship,
and my living and my dying are for God alone,
the Sustainer of all worlds."
[*Sūrah al-Anʿām* 6:161-162]

Muḥammad ﷺ often used to pray, "O God, show me the true as true and give me the blessing of following it; show me the false as false and give me the blessing of avoiding it." Revelation is offered to humankind as a guidance and a grace to aid in the discernment of Truth.

The Holy Qurʾān also clarifies that it is part of the *fiṭrah* that the soul is liberated from dogmas and false deity when s/he believes in the Unseen, *al-Ghayb*. To believe in the Unseen in the

Holy Qur'ān is an inner certainty within a human that makes him sure that whatever he might come to know, there is always more that is beyond the known and the knowable. When this certainty exists, souls do not become imprisoned in dogmas, nor do they bestow divinity on anything in the transient realm. Rather, they continuously move forward towards greater knowledge and freedom ceaselessly.

But how can a human being be liberated from all dogmas and false deities? This takes us to the second point.

Since they were not satisfied with other people's practices and approach to life, the prophets began to search within and beyond. They were guided from within to open to listen to what their hearts would tell them. They naturally wanted to distance themselves from the noise of a corrupt life and the negative energy of the overwhelming darkness. They spent time in seclusion purifying the whole of their existence by controlling the physical body's desires. The vibrant *fiṭrah* guided them to allow the divinity within to come to the surface of consciousness. In the meantime, they would also direct their faces to the Supreme Transcendent, seeking guidance from a higher source. We read in the Holy Qur'ān that Abraham said, *I will go to my Lord! He will surely guide me!* [*Sūrah aṣ-Ṣaffāt* 37:99]. *And I will turn away from you all and from those whom you invoke besides Allāh: I will call on my Lord* [*Sūrah Maryam* 19:48].

The Holy Qur'ān gives us an example of the search of a soul longing for a source of guidance in the story of the experience of Abraham. The story reveals his longing for his Lord, whom he recognizes first in a star, then in the moon, and then in the sun. The moment Abraham came to be fully certain that Allāh transcends any of His manifestations was the very moment he realized that he was receiving guidance and support from his Lord. Namely, Abraham reached a moment of receiving great divine knowledge in which he could realize with no confusion that Allāh is both Unseen and also Manifest because all aspects of nature [are signs (*āyāts*) of His Presence], and also because He manifests Himself to man from within himself as well as all around him. The guidance was not letters or words; it was a superb power of enlightenment that made Truth in Abraham's heart clearer than the rays of the sun. Abraham could evidently discern his own *fiṭrah*, and God's closeness and guidance.

So also did We show Abraham the power and the laws of the heavens and the earth, that he might [with understanding] have certitude. When the night covered him over, he saw a star: he said: "This is my Lord." But when it set, he said: "I love not those that set." When he saw the moon rising in splendor, he said: "This is my Lord." But when the moon set, he said: "Unless my Lord guide me, I shall surely be among those who go astray." When he saw the sun rising in splendor, he said: "This is my Lord; this is the greatest [of all]." But when the sun set, he said: "O my people! I am indeed free from your [guilt] of giving partners to Allāh. For me, I have set my face, firmly and truly, towards Him Who created the heavens and the earth, and never shall I give partners to Allāh." [*Sūrah al-Anᶜām* 6:75-79]

The Holy Qurʾān also points to Moses' search for a higher source of guidance when it quotes Moses as saying: *I do hope that my Lord will show me the smooth and straight Path.* [*Sūrah al-Qaṣaṣ* 28:22]. It is that inner quest that pushed Moses to feel God's guidance symbolized in the burning bush.

Behold, he saw a fire: so he said to his family, "Tarry ye; I perceive a fire; perhaps I can bring you some burning brand therefrom, or find some guidance at the fire." [*Sūrah Ṭā Hā* 20:10]

Like Abraham, the very moment Moses realized existentially that God transcends any aspect of physical life, he could also feel Him strongly and devastatingly Manifest in all creation, as symbolized in *the Mount*. The guidance came in the form of a burst of knowledge and light that were delivered promptly into his heart. It was at that moment that Moses said, *I am the first to believe*. It is a statement that reflects an attitude where a soul realizes his or her source of guidance coming from within and around concomitantly and clearly.

When Moses came to the place appointed by Us, and his Lord ad-

dressed him, he said: "O my Lord! show [Thyself] to me, that I may look upon Thee." Allāh said: "By no means shalt thou see Me [direct]; but look upon the mount; if it abide in its place, then shalt thou see Me." When his Lord manifested His glory on the Mount, He made it as dust, and Moses fell down in a swoon. When he recovered his senses he said: "Glory be to Thee! to Thee I turn in repentance, and I am the first to believe." [*Sūrah al-Aʿrāf* 7:143]

The Prophet Muḥammad's search for guidance was not an exception. His life reveals that the pure *fiṭrah* was strongly awakened in him from early childhood. He never bowed to any of the 360 idols located around the Kaʿbah, nor swore by the name of any of them. He rejected all the stagnant traditions of his people and held to a very high standard of morality on all levels. Again in his search for a source of guidance towards a truthful life he was guided from within to stay for regular intervals in seclusion in a cave near Mecca named Ḥirāʾ. He lived the life of a mystic, fasting and praying to God to lead him to a way of life that would be in harmony with His will and Law.

For the Prophet Muḥammad the existence of a higher source of guidance within and beyond took several dimensions. The archangel Gabriel said to the Prophet at the very start of the Revelation,

Read! In the name of thy Lord and Cherisher, Who created, created the human being out of a connecting substance: Read! And thy Lord is Most Bountiful, He Who taught [the use of] the Pen, taught the human being that which he/she knew not. [*Sūrah al-ʿAlaq* 96:1-5]

The holy words conveyed to Muḥammad, *Read!* (or *Recite!*) *In the name of thy Lord*, clarify that the Divine is within, and when the soul is purified enough, that divinity, or *the name of thy Lord,* becomes manifest enough to discern the Truth. The verses of the very first Revelation to the Prophet Muḥammad unveil also that the soul is given the means of gaining knowledge, symbolized in *the Pen.* The Revelation also points to the existence of the Law of creation when mentioning the creation of man *out of a connecting substance.* It is implicitly disclosed that the Divine Law works through cause and effect and a human being is qualified to attain knowledge when he or she lives according to that Law. He or she then will deserve to be taught *that which he* [or she] *knew not.*

On another level, the Revelation to the Prophet Muḥammad also disclosed that the knowledge that was revealed to the prophets preceding him had not quit the earth, and so they could be a source of guidance for him. The Divine unveils to Muḥammad (in *Sūrah al-Anᶜām* 6:83-88) that *Abraham, Isaac, Jacob, Noah, David, Solomon, Job, Joseph, Moses and Aaron, Zakariya, John* [*the Baptist*], *Jesus, Elias, Ismāᶜīl, Elisha, Jonah, and Lot are all in the ranks of the Righteous.* The Divine tells him to take them as a source of guidance.

Those were the [*prophets*] *who received Allāh's guidance: follow the guidance they received.* [*Sūrah al-Anᶜām* 6:90][248]

The Buddha also reminds us: "You should inquire deeply and directly into the distress of the mind and find out what has been created and who is the self that is suffering. Without this understanding, you can't develop clarity and the ability to help others. A person may be expert at undoing knots, but if he never sees that there is a knot in front of him, how will he undo it? Without clear and direct looking, you will be locked into time and space and be unable to free yourself from the material world."[249]

To avoid mistaken judgments, we should cultivate our powers of observation. There is a vast difference between merely looking at a thing and really seeing it. Then we take many things for granted that should be tested and tried. Our own minds would rather that someone else would do the thinking and we unthinkingly follow. It is well sometimes to get away

---

[248] Aisha Rafea, "The Soul's Longing," in C. Helminski, *Women of Sufism, A Hidden Treasure*, pp. 203-206.

[249] Bancroft, *The Pocket Buddha Reader* (*Surangama Sutra*), p. 111.

from ourselves, away from our own environment, and take a bird's-eye view, as it were, of our little world from among the stars; to try to see ourselves as others see us and especially endeavor to view things as they appear from the judgment seat of God. We can hold a candle light so close to our eye as to make it appear larger than the sun: much like a prejudiced judgment. The only thing to do is to hold the candle far enough away so as to view both candle and sun in their proper proportions. In curing ourselves of prejudiced judgments, it is often necessary to change our view entirely. We may have to give up our old way of looking at things. However, even then, we should make good judgment the basis of the compromise.[250]

The truth is noble and sweet; the truth can free you from all ills. There is no savior in the world like the truth.

Have confidence in the truth, even though you may not be able to understand it, even though its sweetness has a bitter edge, even though at first you may shrink from it. Trust in the truth.

The truth is best as it is. No one can alter it, neither can anyone improve it. Have faith in the truth and live it.

The self is in a fever; the self is forever changing, like a dream. But the truth is whole, sublime and everlasting. Nothing is immortal except the truth, for truth alone exists forever.[251]

The counsel of the Prophet is regarded as the highest form of accounting for the self. ʿIbādah ibn aṣ-Ṣāmit relates that the Prophet said to a man who had asked for his counsel, "If you want to undertake something, then reflect upon its consequence; if it is correct, then go ahead with it, and if it is wrong, then abandon it."[252]

---

[250] Sister Mary Cecilia in *Women of Vision* by Dorothy Stewart, p. 196.

[251] Bancroft, *The Pocket Buddha Reader* (*Majjhima Nikaya*), p. 115.

[252] Haeri, *Prophetic Traditions of Islām*, p. 152 (Al-Ashtarī, I, 234-248).

It is related on the authority of Jābir ibn ᶜAbdullāh that the Prophet ﷺ used to teach his Companions to seek, through a special *duᶜā,* the guidance of Allāh in all matters which affected them. He said ﷺ: "When you are confused about what you should do in a certain situation, then pray two *rakᶜāt* of *nafl ṣalāt* (supererogatory prayer) and read the following *duᶜā*:

"O Allāh, I ask You, of Your knowledge, for guidance and of Your power, for strength; and I ask You of Your excessive generosity. Certainly You are powerful and I am not, and You are the Knower of the unknown. O Allāh, if you know this matter (here the supplicant should substitute for the words, 'this matter' whatever it is specifically that he has in mind, for example, this journey, or marriage, etc.) to be good for my religion, my worldly life, my life in the next world, my present state of affairs or my future state, then decree it for me and make it easy, and bless me in it. And if You know this matter to be detrimental to my religion, my worldly life, my life in the next world, my present state of affairs or my future state, then divert it from me, and turn me away from it, and decree for me that which is good, wherever it may be. And then make me to be pleased with it."[253]

Aṣ-Ṣādiq said, "The self of a man of faith should not be abased." When asked what can abase a man's self, he replied, "He does not engage in something from which he would do better to excuse himself."[254]

A servant of Allāh should always watch over his own self when he undertakes any action, supervising it closely, for if the self is neglected, then it will commit acts of oppression and corruption. He should also watch for Allāh, whether he be in motion or at rest, by always remembering that He perceives one's

---

[253] Muḥammad al-Ghazālī, *Remembrance and Prayer*, pp. 123-124.

[254] Haeri, *Prophetic Traditions of Islām*, p. 155 (*Mishkāt* 244-246).

innermost thoughts, that He is surveying his servant's action, and is a witness of what every self accomplishes.[255]

Gabriel was asked about the spiritual state called *ihsān*. He replied, "It consists in worshipping Allāh as if you can see Him; and even if you cannot see Him, He certainly sees you."[256]

Do they not reflect within themselves?
[*Sūrah ar-Rūm* 30:8]

We will show them Our signs on the farthest horizons
and within their own selves
until it becomes manifest to them that this is the Truth.
Is it not enough that your Lord is witness to all things?
Indeed! Are they in doubt concerning the Meeting with their Lord?
Ah, truly; it is He Who encompasses all things!
[*Sūrah Fuṣṣilat* 41:53-54]

The Prophet said, . . . "The crown of intellect—after faith—is a harmonious relationship with people."[257]

In the Gospel of Matthew 22:37-39, Jesus encourages:

You shall love the Lord Thy God with all thy heart, with all thy soul, and with all thy mind.

Love thy neighbor as thyself, and do unto others as you would have them do unto you.

The prophets have all brought indications as to how to best form and maintain harmonious relationships. The revelation of the Ten Commandments is the basis of Jewish law and Christian practice. How similar they are to indications of the Qur'ān! For discernment as to the best approach, the guidance of the prophets and the revelation received through them are a Light for all humankind.

---

[255] Ibid., p. 155 (*Qurrat al-ᶜUyūn*, 303-305).

[256] Ibid., p. 152 (al-Ashtarī, I, 234-248).

[257] Ibid., pp. 143-144 (*al-Khiṣāl*, I, 15).

The Ten Commandments

You shall have no other gods before Me.
You shall not make yourself a carved image, nor bow down before them, but show mercy to those who love Me and keep My commandments.
You shall not take the name of the Lord your God in vain.
Remember the Sabbath and keep it holy, allowing your servants to rest.
Honor your father and mother.
You shall not kill.
You shall not commit adultery.
You shall not steal.
You shall not lie or bear false witness against your neighbor.
You shall not covet your neighbor's house, your neighbor's spouse, . . . or anything that is his (or hers).

(The Bible, Deuteronomy 5:6-21)

Say, "Come, let me convey to you
what God has prohibited:
'Do not attribute divinity, in any way, to anything beside Him;
be good to your parents;
and do not kill your children out of fear of poverty—
for it is We who shall provide sustenance
for you as well as for them;
and do not incline towards any shameful deeds,
whether openly or in secret;
and do not take the life of a single soul—
which God has declared sacred—
except out of justice: this has He instructed you
that you might learn wisdom.
And do not touch the substance of an orphan—
except to improve it—before he comes of age.'"
And give full measure and weigh equitably:
no burden do We place on any soul, but that which it can bear;
and when you speak, speak justly,

even if a near relative is concerned.
And always observe your bond with God:
this has He asked of you, that you might remember.
And this is the way leading straight to Me:
follow it, then, and do not follow other ways,
that they might not cause you to wander from His way.
This has He asked of you,
so that you might remain conscious of Him.
[*Sūrah al-Anᶜām* 6:151-153]

Sūrah Tā Hā: "*O Humankind*"

Bismillāh ar Rahmān ar Rahīm

Prologue

Divine We [1-8]: *Tā Hā.*
We have not sent down the Qur'ān to make you unhappy, but only as a counsel to all who stand in awe of God, a revelation from the One Who created the earth and the heavens on high. The Most Gracious is firmly established on the throne of Almightiness. To the Most Gracious belongs what is in the heavens and on earth and all between them and all beneath the soil. Whether you pronounce the word aloud, it does not matter: for truly He knows what is secret and what is yet more hidden. God! there is no god but God! To Him belong the Most Beautiful Names.

Scene One: The Desert

Moses is together with his family. A light is glowing in the distance.

Narrator [9-10]: *Has the story of Moses reached you? Behold, he saw a fire, so he said to his family:*

~ A play prepared from *Sūrah Tā Hā* [20:1-82] by Camille A. Helminski.

Moses: *"Wait a while; I perceive a fire; perhaps I can bring you some burning brand from there or find some guidance at the fire."*

Narrator [11]: *But when he came to the fire a voice was heard:*

Divine We [11-17]: *"O Moses! Truly, I am your Lord!*
Take off then your shoes: you are in the sacred valley Tuwā. I have chosen you: listen then to the inspiration [sent to you]. Truly I am God: there is no god but Me: so serve Me [only] and be constant in prayer, so as to remember Me. Truly the Hour is coming; My design is to keep it hidden, so that every human being may be recompensed in accordance with what he strove for in life. And so do not let anyone who does not believe in its coming but follows his own desires divert you [from remembering it], lest you perish!"
And what is that in your right hand, O Moses?"

Moses [18]: *"It is my staff: on it I lean; with it I beat down leaves for my flocks; and in it I find other uses."*

Divine We [19]: *"Throw it, O Moses!"*

Narrator [20]: *So he threw it and behold! It was a snake moving rapidly.*

Divine We [21-24]: *"Take hold of it and have no fear: We shall return it at once to its former state. Now draw your hand beneath your armpit: it shall come forth shining white and without blemish as another Sign [of Our grace], in order that We might make you aware of some of Our greatest wonders. Go now to Pharaoh for, truly, he has transgressed all bounds."*

Moses [25-35]: *"O my Lord! Open up my heart [to Your Light]; and make my task easy for me, and remove the impediment from my speech, so they may understand what I say: and appoint for me, out of my kinsfolk, one who will help me to bear my burden: Aaron, my brother. Add to my strength through him and make him share my task, that we may celebrate Your limitless glory continually and remember You unceasingly: for You are He that sees all that is within us."*

Divine We [36]: *"Your prayer is granted, O Moses!"*

Vignette:

At the side: Moses' mother stands listening, and then, placing the infant Moses in the basket, casts it upon the river during the following verses:

Divine We [37-39]: *"And indeed We bestowed Our favor upon you another time [before]. Behold! We sent to your mother by inspiration the message: 'Place him in a chest and throw it into the river: the river will cast him up on the shore and he will be taken up by one who is an enemy to Me and an enemy to him': and so I spread [the garment of] My love over you, in order that you might be reared under My eye."*

Vignette 2:

Pharaoh's people by the riverside; the sister of Moses approaches during the following words:

Divine We [40]: *"Behold! your sister went forth and said:"*
Sister of Moses: *"Shall I guide you unto one who will nurse and rear him?"*

Vignette 2b:

Sister of Moses, Pharaoh's people, and the mother of Moses come together. Moses is restored to his mother:

Divine We: "*So We brought you back to your mother that her eye might be cooled and she should not grieve.*"

Vignette 3:

Moses as a young man, without seeking to know the truth of the situation, slaying another man who had been fighting one of his people who then enlisted his help (see *Sūrah al-Qaṣaṣ* 28:15-21); then in repentance seeking refuge in the desert:

Divine We [40-44]: "*Then you killed a man, but We saved you from grief, although We tried you with various trials. Then you did sojourn a number of years with the people of Midian. And now you have come here as ordained by Me, for I have chosen you for My own service. Go forth then, you and your brother, with My messages, and never tire of remembering Me. Go forth, both of you, to Pharaoh, for he has truly transgressed all bounds. But speak to him mildly; perhaps he may take warning or turn in awe to God."*

(Aaron comes toward Moses as he turns to go back to join his family who are waiting for him.)

Moses and Aaron [45]: *"Our Lord! we fear that he may act hastily with regard to us or that he may continue to transgress all bounds of equity."*

Divine We [46-48]: *"Fear not: for I am with you: I hear and see [everything]. So go, then, you two, unto him and say: 'Truly, we are messengers sent by your Sustainer: let then the children of Israel go with us, and do not cause them to suffer any longer. We have come unto you with a message from your Lord! And peace to all who follow guidance! Truly, it has been revealed to us that suffering will befall all who give the lie to the truth and turn away.' "*

Scene Two: The Court of Pharaoh

Moses and Aaron stand before Pharaoh. They have just delivered the message they were bidden to convey.

Pharaoh [49]: *"Who then, O Moses, is the Lord of you two?"*

Moses [50]: *"Our Lord is He Who gave to each [created] thing its form and nature and further gave [it] guidance."*

Pharaoh [51]: *"What then is the condition of previous generations?"*

Moses [52]: *"The knowledge of that is with my Sustainer, duly recorded: my Sustainer does not err nor does He forget."*

Divine We [53-56]: *"He it is Who has made for you the earth like a cradle, and has traced out for you ways [of livelihood] thereon, and sends down water from the sky; and by this means We bring forth various kinds of plants. Eat [for yourselves] and pasture your cattle: truly in this are Signs for those who are endowed with understanding. From this [earth] did We create you and into it shall We return you and from it shall We bring you out once again. And We showed Pharaoh all Our Signs but he did reject and refuse them."*

Pharaoh [57-58]: *"Have you come to drive us out of our land with your sorcery, O Moses? But we can surely produce magic to match yours! So make a tryst between us and you which we shall not fail to keep, neither we nor you, in a place where both shall have even chances."*

Moses [59]: *"Your tryst is the Day of the Festival and let the people be assembled when the sun is risen high."*

Narrator [60-61]: *So Pharaoh withdrew: he arranged his plan and then came (back). And Moses said to him:*

Moses [61]: *"Woe to you! Do not forge a lie against God lest He afflict you with most grievous suffering: for the one who contrives a lie is already undone!"*

Narrator: [62-63] *So they disputed one with another over their affair but they kept their talk secret. They said to one another:*

Sorcerers [63-65]: *"These two are certainly [expert] sorcerers: their object is to drive you out from your land with their magic and to do away with your most cherished institutions. Therefore decide upon your plan, and then assemble in one body: for, truly, the one who prevails today shall prosper indeed!"*

"O Moses! Which will you: that you throw [first] or that we be the first to throw?"

Moses [66]: *"No, you throw first!"*

Narrator [66-67]: *Then behold, their ropes and their rods due to their magic seemed to him to be moving rapidly! So in his heart Moses became apprehensive.*

Divine We [68-69]: *"Fear not! for truly you have the upper hand: throw that which is in your right hand: quickly will it swallow up that which they have faked. What they have done is but a magician's trick: and the magician thrives not wherever he goes."*

Narrator [70]: *So the magicians threw themselves down, prostrating themselves in adoration:*

Sorcerers [70]: *"We have come to believe in the Lord of Aaron and Moses."*

Pharaoh [71]: *"Do you believe in Him before I give you permission? Surely this must be your leader who has taught you magic! Be sure I will cut off your hands and feet on opposite sides and I will have you crucified on trunks of palm-trees: So shall you know for certain which of us can give the more severe and the more lasting Punishment!"*

Sorcerers [72-73]: *"Never shall we regard you as greater than the Clear Signs that have come to us or than Him Who created us! So decree whatever you desire to decree: for you can only decree in relation to the life of this world. For us, we have come to have faith in our Lord: may He forgive us our faults and the magic to which you did compel us: for God is Best and Most Abiding."*

Divine We [74-76]: *"Truly, the one who comes to his Lord lost in sin, for him is the fire: therein shall he neither die nor live. But those that come to Him as faithful ones who have worked righteous deeds—for them are high stations: gardens of perpetual bliss beneath which rivers flow. There will they dwell, for that shall be the recompense of all who attain to purity."*

Scene Three: The Red Sea

Moses alone, listening, and then leading his people through the sea, while Pharaoh and his followers pursue:

Divine We [77]: *We sent an inspiration to Moses: "Travel by night with my servants and strike a dry path for them through the sea without fear of being overtaken [by Pharaoh] and without [any other] fear."*

Narrator [78-79]: *Then Pharaoh pursued them with his forces, but the waters completely overwhelmed them and covered them up. Pharaoh led his people astray instead of leading them aright.*

Divine We [80-82]: *O children of Israel! We delivered you from your enemy and We made a covenant with you on the side of Mount [Sinai] and We sent down to you manna and quails, [saying] "Eat of the good things We have provided for your sustenance but do not transgress the bounds of equity lest My Wrath should justly descend upon you: for those upon whom My Wrath descends have indeed thrown themselves into utter ruin! But without doubt I am [also] He that forgives again and again to those who repent, have faith, and do right; those who stand ready to receive true guidance."*

TRUE KNOWLEDGE
(ᶜ*Ilm ul-Ḥaqq*)

High above all is God, the Sovereign, the Truth!
Do not be hasty with the Qur'an
before its revelation to you is complete,
but say: "O my Sustainer! Increase my knowing."
[*Sūrah Ṭā Hā* 20:114]

Many ways of life have passed away before your time.
Go, then, about the earth and see what happened
in the end to those who denied the truth:
here is a clear lesson for all human beings
and a guidance and a counsel for those who are conscious of God.
So do not lose heart, nor fall into despair:
for if you are faithful you are bound to ascend.
[*Sūrah Āl ᶜImrān* 3:137-139]

O my Sustainer! Bestow wisdom on me
and join me with the righteous;
grant me the ability to convey the truth
to those who will come after me;
make me one of the inheritors of the Garden of Bliss.
(Prayer of Abraham)
[*Sūrah ash-Shuᶜarāᶜ* 26:83-85]

To those who receive guidance, He increases their guidance
and causes them to grow in God-consciousness.
[*Sūrah Muḥammad* 47:17]

But truly, this is a message for those who stand in awe of God.
And We certainly know that there are among you
those who deny it;
but truly revelation is a source of remorse for the deniers.
And surely it is the certain truth.
So glorify the name of your Sustainer, the Most High.
[*Sūrah al-Ḥāqqah* 69:48-52]

And He it is who has created the heavens and the earth
in accordance with an inner truth—and the Day He says, "Be," it is.
His word is the Truth.
[*Sūrah al-An*ʿ*ām* 6:73]

He is the One who causes the dawn to break;
and He has made the night to be a source of stillness,
and the sun and the moon for reckoning
by the order of the Almighty, the All-knowing.
And He it is who has made the stars for you
so that you might be guided by them
through the darknesses of land and sea:
clearly have We detailed Our signs for people of inner knowing.
And He it is who has brought you all into being
out of a single soul,
and so designated for each of you a time-limit on earth
and a resting-place after death:
clearly have We detailed Our signs for people who can grasp the truth.
[*Sūrah al-An*ʿ*ām* 6:96–98]

The Holy Qurʾān reveals that the fruit of spiritual freedom that Teachers of humanity attained, by the support of the Divine, was truthful knowledge. Knowledge was delivered from the beyond to their hearts and minds because they were in full harmony with the Will of the All-Merciful to transfer truthful knowledge to humankind, and make it accessible to whoever wills to seek it. Abraham says, *O my father! to me hath come knowledge which hath not reached thee: so follow me: I will guide thee to a Way that is even and straight* [*Sūrah Maryam* 19:43]. About Joseph, the Divine says, *For he was, by Our instruction, full of knowledge [and experience]: but most men know not* [*Sūrah Yūsuf* 12:68]. *And to Lot, too, We gave Judgment and Knowledge* [*Sūrah al-Anbiyā*ʿ 21:74]. About Solomon and David the Divine says: *We inspired the [right] understanding of the matter: to each [of them] We gave Judgment and Knowledge* [*Sūrah al-Anbiyā*ʿ 21:79]. Noah said to his people: *Sincere is my advice to you, and I know from Allāh something that you know not* [*Sūrah al-Aʿrāf* 7:62]. The Prophet Muḥammad unveiled that knowledge is to be sought infinitely. He was guided to say, *"O my Lord! advance me in knowledge"* [*Sūrah Ṭā Hā* 20:114].[258]

The stories of all prophets in the Holy Qurʾān demonstrate that the fruit of their spiritual journeys is that they became accessible to the Divine Law of transferring Knowledge from Heaven to earth. That Knowledge is a Grace of Allāh to souls who seek to live in full submission to the Eternal Law of Life. The Divine revealed to the prophets the Path to a truthful life. Those revelations are expressions of God's graces on earth directed to whoever would make himself or herself available to that. Longing souls have the possibility of becoming accessible to God's graces if they follow the paths of the prophets. Following the prophets is not blind commitment to their teachings. It is making a spiritual journey so that a soul experiences and understands how to become spiritually transformed. The Holy Qurʾān clarifies that a soul is accessible to God's graces when it is purified from devotion to the transient aspects of life. That purification is attained through being attached to the divinity within and around, rendering a soul spiritually free. The sign of spiritual freedom is that a soul performs any action in this life in a state of being free from the taints of the lower self. That is the state referred to in the Holy Qurʾān as *stand straight and steadfast* and *work righteousness:*

In the case of those who say, "Our Lord is Allāh," and, further, stand straight and steadfast, the angels descend on them [from time to time]: "Fear not!" [they suggest], "Nor grieve! but receive the Glad Tidings of the Garden [of Bliss], that which you were promised! [*Sūrah Fuṣṣilat* 41:30]

---

[258] Aisha Rafea, "The Soul's Longing," in C. Helminski, *Women of Sufism, A Hidden Treasure*, p. 208.

Whoever expects to meet his or her Sustainer, let him or her work righteousness, and, in the worship of his or her Sustainer, admit no one as partner. [*Sūrah al-Kahf* 18:110]

The Holy Qurʾān asserts that the human soul is created to long to know the Divine and to seek to live according to His Law. That longing is part of its primordial nature that the Holy Qurʾān terms as *fiṭrah*. The human soul acquired that quality in the moment Allāh breathed into Adam of His Spirit. And it is that quality of nature that qualified the offspring of Adam to long for devotion to the Divine. When the human soul lives in accordance with its own primordial nature or *fiṭrah*, it fulfills its own longing, and a human life becomes a language of spirit. There is no wonder then that humankind, at all times, and in different cultures and civilizations, has witnessed the existence of human souls who have been looking for an ultimate goal of existence and have never been satisfied with the objectives of the physical realm. Their whole life has been a language of spirit.[259]

In Proverbs, the Prophet Solomon advises his son:

My son, do not forget my law; but let your heart keep my commandments.

For length of days, and long life, and peace, shall they add to you.

Do not let mercy and truth forsake you: bind them around your neck and write them on the tablet of your heart.

So shall you find favor and good understanding in the sight of God and man.

Trust in the Lord with all your heart, and do not lean for support upon your own understanding.

In all ways acknowledge Him and He shall direct your paths.

Do not see yourself as wise, but fear God and depart from evil.

---

[259] Ibid., p. 212.

It shall be health to the core of your being, and marrow to your bones.

Honor the Lord with your substance, and with the first fruits of all your increase.

So shall your barns be filled with plenty and your presses bursting with new wine.

My son, do not despise the chastisement of the Lord, nor be weary of His correction:

For whom the Lord loves, He corrects, even as a father the son in whom he delights.

Happy is the man who finds wisdom, and the man who gains understanding.

For the merchandise of it is better than the merchandise of silver, and the gain of it more precious than fine gold.

(The Bible, Proverbs 3:1-14)

When wisdom enters into your heart, and knowledge is pleasant to your soul, discretion shall preserve you, understanding shall keep you. (The Bible, Proverbs 2:10-11)

The Prophet Muhammad ﷺ is known to have said, "Acqure knowledge. It enables its possessor to distinguish right from wrong; it lights the way to heaven; it is our friend in the desert, our society in solitude, our companion when friendless; it guides us to happiness, it sustains our misery; it is an ornament among friends, and an armor against enemies."

Imām ᶜAlī said, "Knowledge of the self is the most useful form of knowledge."

"The self's introspection is a way of caring for its improvement (*ṣalāḥ*)."

"He who succeeds in knowing himself has gained a mighty victory."

"The greatest form of knowledge is that a man may know himself."

"Whoever gets to know himself has arrived at the limits of gnosis and science."[260]

"The man of knowledge is the man who knows his own capability; ignorant is the man who does not."
"The man who does not know his own capacity is doomed."[261]

Imām ᶜAlī is reported to have said, . . . "A man's knowledge of his own faults is the most useful of knowledges."[262]

Information of one sort or another may be useful to us as we go about the practicalities of our daily lives, but unless we deepen in the underlying foundational knowledge of who we are as a human being, our pure essential nature and our individual strengths and weaknesses, and understand our appropriate relationship to our Creator and all of life, the acquiring of information or learning of other kinds may only obstruct our way. It is said, "To thine own self be true." Unless we know our self, how can we be true to it? The Prophet said, "Whoever knows himself, knows his Lord."[263]

To be true to yourself is to see yourself objectively, to be honest about your own strengths and weaknesses. If you are objective with yourself, you have taken a big step toward realizing the Prophet's *ḥadīth*, "die before you are made to die."

Whoever is objective about himself can also see the things, persons, and situations around him objectively, since he will no longer be "projecting." *Projection*, a term taken from psychoanalysis, means falsely seeing something in another person, or in circumstances, that is really in you. If you know yourself, you will not project; you will see yourself and other people truly and clearly, in line with the prayer of the Prophet, "O Lord,

---

[260] Haeri, *Prophetic Traditions of Islām*, p. 147 (al-Ḥākim, I, 114).
[261] Ibid., p. 147 (*Nahj*, 304, 1159).
[262] Ibid., p. 150 (al-Ḥākim I, 114).
[263] Ibid., p. 146 (al-Ḥākim I, 211).

show me things as they really are." God in His Name *Al-Ḥaqq* is Absolute Truth, which is why the objective truth in any situation, the truth that is really there whether or not we are aware of it, is a real aspect of His Presence. This is one meaning of the *ḥadīth*, "He who knows himself knows his Lord."

If you are true to yourself, you will gain the power to speak the truth. Firstly, you will be able to speak the truth because you will *know* what's true, which includes knowing both what you *do* know and what you *do not* know. Veracity entails admitting the limits to your knowledge and not filling in the space of your ignorance with fantasies and suppositions. Secondly, you will be strong enough to speak the truth because you are used to honestly facing up to things, both in circumstances and in yourself, that are not necessarily in line with your hopes or expectations. And you will also gain the power *not* to speak the truth when silence is more appropriate; you will develop the virtue of Discretion (*ḥusn at-tadbīr*).[264]

As-Sulami reports that [Umm Aḥmad bint ᶜĀʾisha] said, "Knowledge (*ᶜilm*) is the life of humanity, spiritual practice (*ᶜamal*) is its conveyance, and intellect (*ᶜaql*) is its ornament, and gnosis (*maᶜrifa*) is its illumination and insight."[265]

On the authority of ᶜĀʾishah ﷺ, the Prophet ﷺ is reported to have stated, "The support of a house is its foundation. The support of religion is direct knowledge of God, certainty, and intelligence that safeguards against error."[266]

The Prophet Muḥammad ﷺ counseled, "Seek knowledge even unto China." The Qurʾān encourages travel throughout the world to witness

---

[264] Charles Upton, contributor.

[265] Abū ᶜAbd ar-Raḥmān as-Sulamī. *Early Sufi Women: Dhikr an-Niswa al-Mutaᶜabbidāt aṣ-Ṣūfiyyāt.* Edited and translated by Rkia E. Cornell (Louisville, KY: Fons Vitae, 1999), p. 218.

[266] Al-Qushayri, *Principles of Sufism*, p. 316.

the lives and cultures of humanity and their histories, as well as to witness the knowledge of nature, and in the process to come to know ourselves. Books may aid us in our journey, but the memorization of facts or erudition in discourse is meaningless if not based in real knowledge of the self. As we deepen in true knowledge we pass through several stages: first that of hearing about the Truth which we may not have yet directly experienced ourselves, as in hearing about a city that we may not yet have visited. Then, we may be able to actually journey there ourselves and see it with our own eyes. If we spend time there, we may come to know that place more intimately as we explore and discover its various districts, meet the inhabitants, and come to know the qualities of that place and witness the real basis of its being.

Over and over again we are told that the truest knowledge is knowledge of the self at its most essential level. Seeking that knowledge, the Buddha sat for many days under a tree; the Prophet Muḥammad ﷺ retreated to a cave, knocking on the inner door until it opened. As Jesus said, "Seek and you shall find; knock and it shall be opened unto you."

> There are three signs of the certainty of certainty: looking to God Most High for everything, returning to Him in every matter, and turning to Him for aid in every state."
>
> Al-Junayd (may God grant him mercy) declared, "Certainty is the constancy of knowledge in the heart: it does not vanish or change."[267]

The Soul is the Perceiver and Revealer of Truth

I live in society; with persons who answer to thoughts in my own mind, or outwardly express a certain obedience to the great instincts [according] to which I live. I see its presence [in] them. I am certified of a

---

[267] Ibid., p. 143.

~ "The Soul is the Perceiver and Revealer of Truth" is excerpted from Emerson, *Essays by Ralph Waldo Emerson, First Series,* pp. 208-209, 210-11.

common nature; and so these other souls, these separated selves, draw me as nothing else can. They stir in me the new emotions we call passion; of love, hatred, fear, admiration, pity; thence come conversation, competition, persuasion, cities and war. Persons are supplementary to the primary teaching of the soul. In youth we are mad for persons. Childhood and youth see all the world in them. But the larger experience of man discovers the identical nature appearing through them all. Persons themselves acquaint us with the impersonal. In all conversation between two persons tacit reference is made, as to a third party, to a common nature. That third party or common nature is not social; it is impersonal; is God. And so in groups where debate is earnest, and especially on great questions of thought, the company become aware of their unity; aware that the thought rises to an equal height in all bosoms, that all have a spiritual property in what was said, as well as the sayer. They all wax wiser than they were. It arches over them like a temple, this unity of thought in which every heart beats with nobler sense of solemnity. All are conscious of attaining to a higher self-possession. It shines for all. There is a certain wisdom of humanity which is common to the greatest men with the lowest, and which our ordinary education often labors to silence and obstruct. The mind is one, and the best minds, who love truth for its own sake, think much less of property in truth. Thankfully they accept it everywhere, and do not label or stamp it with any man's name, for it is theirs long beforehand. It is theirs from eternity.

The soul is the perceiver and revealer of truth. We know truth when we see it, let skeptic and scoffer say what they choose. Foolish people ask you, when you have spoken what they do not wish to hear, "How do you know it is truth, and not an error of your own?" We know truth when we see it, from opinion, as we know when we are awake that we are awake. It was a grand sentence of Emanuel Swedenborg, which would alone indicate the greatness of that man's perception: "It is no proof of a man's understanding to be able to affirm whatever he pleases; but to be able to discern that what is true is true, and that what is false is false; this is the mark and character of intelligence." In the book I read, the good thought returns to me as every truth will, the image of the whole soul. To the bad thought which I find in it, the same soul becomes a discerning, separating sword, and lops it away. We are wiser than we know. If we will not interfere with our thought, but will act entirely, or see how the thing stands in God, we know the particular thing, and every thing, and every man. For the Maker of all things and all persons stands behind us and casts his dread omniscience through us over things.

But beyond this recognition of its own in particular passages of the individual's experience, it also reveals truth. And here we should seek to reinforce ourselves by its very presence, and to speak with a worthier, loftier strain of that advent. For the soul's communication of truth is the highest event in nature, for it then does not give somewhat from itself, but it gives itself, or passes into and becomes that man whom it enlightens; or, in proportion to that truth he receives, it takes him to itself.

The Journey Towards Full Knowledge of the Self

Among the People, a child's first Teaching is of the Four Great Powers of the Medicine Wheel. . . . To the North on the Medicine Wheel is found Wisdom. The Color of the Wisdom of the North is White, and its Medicine Animal is the Buffalo. The South is represented by the Sign of the Mouse, and its Medicine Color is Green. The South is the place of Innocence and Trust, and for perceiving closely our nature of heart. In the West is the Sign of the Bear. The West is the Looks-Within Place, which speaks of the Introspective nature of man. The Color of this Place is Black. The East is marked by the Sign of the Eagle. It is the Place of Illumination, where we can see things clearly far and wide. Its Color is the gold of the Morning Star.

At birth, each of us is given a particular Beginning Place within these Four Great Directions on the Medicine Wheel. This Starting Place gives us our first way of perceiving things, which will then be our easiest and most natural way throughout our lives.

~ "The Journey Towards Full Knowledge of the Self" is excerpted from Hyemeyohsts Storm, *Seven Arrows* (New York, New York: Harper and Row, 1972), pp. 6-7, 8.

But any person who perceives from only one of these Four Great Directions will remain just a partial man. For example, a man who possesses only the Gift of the North will be wise. But he will be a cold man, a man without feeling. And the man who lives only in the East will have the clear, far-sighted vision of the Eagle, but he will never be close to things. This man will feel separated, high above life, and will never understand or believe that he can be touched by anything.

A man or woman who perceives only from the West will go over the same thought again and again in their mind, and will always be undecided. And if a person has only the Gift of the South, he will see everything with the eyes of a Mouse. He will be too close to the ground and too near sighted to see anything except whatever is right in front of him, touching his whiskers.

There are many people who have two or three of these Gifts, but these people still are not Whole. A man might be a Bear person from the East, or an Eagle person of the South. The first of these men would have the Gift of seeing Introspectively within Illumination, but he would lack the Gifts of Touching and Wisdom. The second would be able to see clearly and far, like the Eagle, within Trust and Innocence. But he would still not know of the things of the North, nor of the Looks-Within Place.

In this same way, a person might also be a Golden Bear of the North, or a Black Eagle of the South. But none of these people would yet be Whole. After each of us has learned of our Beginning Gift, our First Place on the Medicine Wheel, we then must Grow by Seeking Understanding in each of the Four Great Ways. Only in this way can we become Full, capable of Balance and Decision in what we do. . . .

But since it is really people that we are talking about, the Medicines must be understood within the ways of people. A Mouse Person would be one who saw everything close up, and whose vision would be limited to the immediate world around him. He would be a gatherer of things. He might gather facts, information, material objects, or even ideas. But because he could not see far enough to connect his world with that of the great prairie of the world around him, he would never be able to use or understand all that he saw and gathered.

If a Mouse Person were to be born into the North, his Beginning

Gift would be the Gift of the Mind. His Name might be White Mouse. He would be a wise Mouse Person, but he would not yet be Whole. To become Whole, he would first have to seek the South, the place of Heart, and find the Marriage of this Gift with his Beginning Gift. Then he would have to visit and have Intercourse with the things of the East, Illumination, and travel to the Looks-Within place of the West. He would be able to Grow and become a Full Person only by doing all of these things, which would give him an understanding of his own Nature.

In this way he would become able to make his decisions within the Balance of the Four Directions. A person with the Beginning Gift of the Mind must always try to include his Heart in his decisions. When he does this, he begins to turn upon the Medicine Wheel. A man can live out his entire life without ever finding more than what was already within him as his Beginning Gift, but if he wishes to Grow he must become a Seeker and Seek for himself the other Ways.

And We will show them Our signs on the farthest horizons
and within themselves
until they know that it is the Truth.
[41:53]

VIII.

Gratefulness
Generosity
Kindness

GRATEFULNESS
(*Shukr*)

It is God Who has made the night for you that you may rest in it
and the day as that which helps you to see.
Truly, God is limitless in His abundant grace to humankind,
yet most people are ungrateful.
[*Sūrah Ghāfir* 40:61]

And always does He give you something
out of what you may be asking of Him,
and if you tried to count God's blessings,
you could never compute them.
[*Sūrah Ibrāhīm* 14:34]

If you were to count the favors of God
never would you be able to compute them:
for God is Oft-Forgiving, Most Merciful.
[*Sūrah an-Naḥl* 16:18]

Have you ever considered the water which you drink?
Do you bring it down from the clouds or do We?
Were it Our Will, We could make it salty and bitter:
why, then, aren't you grateful?
Have you ever considered the fire which you kindle?
Is it you who have brought into being the tree
which feeds the fire, or is it We Who cause it to grow?
It is We Who have made it a reminder
and a comfort for those who wander in the wilderness.
Then celebrate the limitless glory
of the Name of your Sustainer, the Most Magnificent.
[*Sūrah al-Wāqiʿah* 56:68-74]

A Sign for them is the earth that is dead;
We give it life and produce grain from it

of which you eat.
And We produce there orchards with date-palms and vines
and We cause springs to gush forth from within it,
that they may enjoy the fruits there.
It was not their hands that made this;
will they not then give thanks?
[*Sūrah Yā Sīn* 36:33-35]

O my Sustainer!
so direct me that I may be grateful
for Your blessings which You have bestowed on me and on my parents
and that I may do the good work that will please You;
and admit me by Your Grace
among the ranks of Your righteous servants.
(Prayer of Solomon)
[*Sūrah an-Naml* 27:19]

We bestowed this wisdom on Luqmān:
"Be grateful to God."
Anyone who is grateful does so to the profit of his own soul;
but if anyone is ungrateful, truly God is free of all needs,
and ever to be praised.
[*Sūrah Luqmān* 31:12]

It is said that "Gratitude is a key to joy," and "Gratitude is better than the gift." Many stories are told of the gratitude expressed for the graciousness of their Creator by the Prophet Muḥammad ﷺ and the early companions. Abū Bakr ؓ was quite a wealthy man when he embraced the faith of Islām. Even more then than previously he gave of his wealth to help relieve the needs of others. Diligently he was striving to be a faithful servant of God and sincerely wanted to emulate the Prophet. In witnessing the simple poverty of the Prophet, it came to his heart to emulate him in that as well, but no matter how much of his wealth he distributed, wealth continued to come back to him. He went to the Prophet to question him about this. Abū Bakr explained that no matter how much he gave away, his wealth did not seem to lessen, and he asked Muḥammad how he might become poorer. The Prophet responded, "Stop being grateful." This of course he could not do, for through God's grace, gratitude encompassed and permeated his heart, and he recognized his gratitude for gratitude. Gratitude is indeed the greater gift.

ᶜĀʾishah ﷺ relates how the Prophet ﷺ would rise during the night to pray for long hours. One night when he had been standing and prostrating in prayer for a particularly long time she called to him asking him why he did not complete his prayer and come to bed. He responded, "Should I not be a thankful servant?" Two of the appellations given to the Prophet are *ash-Shakūr*, the thankful, and *al-Muṭīᶜ*, the obedient and responsive one.

> Thankfulness of the servant, in the true sense, includes both mention by the tongue and affirmation by the heart of the Lord's bestowal of blessings. Thankfulness is divided thus: thankfulness by the tongue, which is recognition of blessings with a degree of submission, thankfulness of the body and limbs, which means taking on the characteristics of fidelity and service, and thankfulness of the heart, which is withdrawal to the plane of witnessing by constantly observing respect. It is said that the learned are thankful with their words, the worshippers are thankful in their deeds, and the gnostics are thankful in their steadfastness toward Him in all of their states. . . .
>
> It is said: "Thankfulness for the ability to be thankful is more complete than thankfulness." This is because you see that your thankfulness comes by means of His enabling, and that enabling is among the most sublime blessings for you. Thus you give thanks for thankfulness, and then you give thanks for the thankfulness of thankfulness, and so on, ad infinitum.[268]
>
> Al-Junayd (may God have mercy on him) related, "One time when I was seven years old, I was playing in front of as-Sari, and a group was gathered before him speaking about thankfulness. He asked me, 'O lad, what is thankfulness?' I re-

[268] Al-Qushayri, *Principles of Sufism*, p. 133.

plied, 'That one not disobey God using the blessings [He has given].' He declared, 'Soon your destiny from God will be your tongue.'" Al-Junayd remarked, "I still weep over these words." Ash-Shiblī explained, "Thankfulness is awareness of the Giver of blessings, not of the blessings." It is said, "Thankfulness is a shackle for what one possesses, and a snare for what one does not yet possess." Abū ʿUthmān observed, "The common people give thanks for being fed and clothed while the elite give thanks for meanings that enter their hearts."[269]

When there was talk about poverty and wealth in the presence of Yahyā b. Mu'adh, he said, "Neither poverty nor wealth will carry any weight on the Day of Reckoning. Only patience and thankfulness will be weighed. Thus it will be said, 'He is thankful and he is patient.'"

It is told that God Most High revealed to one of the prophets (upon whom be peace), "If you wish to know whether I am pleased with you, look to whether the poor are pleased with you."[270]

Gratitude (*shukr*) is one of the greatest blessings the soul can receive, and one of the easiest and most natural forms of inner purification. It is a manifestation of God in His Name *Ash-Shakūr*, the Grateful. The grateful soul is naturally humble without either resistance or self-abasement. Gratitude is of the essence of Generosity, since it is a treasure which cannot be kept, but must be given. But we must not expect nor depend upon gratitude in the recipient of our gift. It is better for us if we so completely forget the gift we give—since to give something means to let go of it, and this means releasing it from the grasp of the mind and the emotions as well as the hand— that we take no notice of any ingratitude on the part of the recipient, and are sincerely puzzled by his gratitude.

---

[269] Ibid., p. 134.

[270] Ibid., p. 297.

According to Ibn ʿAṭaʾllāh, the descent of good fortune divides humanity into three groups: those who attribute everything to fate or their own cunning; those who recognize all as coming from God alone, with no regard for His agents; and those to whom God grants the power to extend gratitude to His agents as well—the actual human beings through whom His Generosity has appeared—without forgetting that, in reality, all gifts are from Him. Gratitude to those who are generous to us is actually gratitude to the Generous Himself. Ibn ʿAṭaʾllāh names the third of these groups as the most mature and complete.[271]

A sage once said, "Two people are truly ungrateful: a person to whom you give advice and he hates you for it, and a person who is favored with a seat in a tight place and he sits cross-legged."[272]

Grace increases in proportion as man makes use of it. Hence, it is evident that God gives man from day to day all that he needs, no more and no less, and to each according to his condition and capacity. All this he does for the love and benefit of man; because we are so cold and negligent in our endeavors, and because the instinct of the spirit is to arrive quickly at perfection, it seems as if grace were insufficient. Yet it is not so, and the fault is wholly ours in not cooperating with the grace already received, which therefore ceases to increase.[273]

Those who recite the Book of God and are constant in prayer,
and distribute out of what We have provided for them,
secretly and openly, hope for an exchange that will never fail:
for He will pay them their due,
no, He will give them even more out of His abundance;
for He is Often-Forgiving, Always Responsive to Gratitude.
[*Sūrah al-Fāṭir* 35:29-30]

[271] Charles Upton, contributor.

[272] Abū Ghudda, *Islamic Manners*, p. 45.

[273] Saint Catherine of Genoa quoted by Stewart, *Women of Vision*, p. 48.

The best behavior is to see a gift of Allāh in everything you receive. ʿAlī ibn Muḥammad al-Qazwīnī reports that Abū Yazid said: "If you have a friend whose relationship with you is at its worst, the relationship will certainly improve if you act according to the code of behavior. If something is given to you, be thankful to Allāh, because He alone turns the hearts of others in your favor. If you suffer calamity, take refuge in repentance and patience, because your being will gather strength only with patience."[274]

Ingratitude snaps shut the human heart. Grateful hearts are always open hearts. They are hearts which have received. Even God cannot squeeze a blessing through a closed heart.

We need to form the habit of gratitude. It can change everything! One little start toward being grateful to God for health, for food, for his love, begins at once to make us feel less inferior. If he cares enough to give us these things—maybe we have been exaggerating our pitiable plight! An ungrateful heart is a blind heart. It cannot see its blessings until it begins to give thanks.[275]

And which of the favors of your Lord will you deny?
[*Surah Raḥmān* 55:13]

It is said, "The thankful one has increase because he is in the presence of blessing." God Most High says, *If you give thanks, I will increase you.* [*Sūrah Ibrāhīm* 14:7][276]

[274] Al-Sulami, *The Way of Sufi Chivalry*, p. 102.

[275] Eugenia Price quoted by Dorothy Stewart, *Women of Vision,* p. 205. Reprinted by permission of the Eugenia Price/Joyce Blackburn Charitable Foundation.

[276] Al-Qushayri, *Principles of Sufism*, p. 137.

Generosity
(*Karam*)

Never shall you attain righteousness unless you spend on others
out of what you yourselves truly love;
and whatever you spend—certainly, God knows.
[*Sūrah Āl ʿImrān* 3:92]

Truly the human being was born restless—
filled with self-pity when difficulty touches him
and selfish when good fortune comes to him—
but not those who consciously turn towards God in prayer—
those who continually persist in their prayer,
and in whose wealth is a recognized right
for those who ask and for the one who cannot ask,
and who grasp the truth of the Day of Reckoning.
[*Sūrah al-Maʿārij* 70:19-26]

In the Name of God the Infinitely Compassionate and Most Merciful
Consider the night as it conceals, and the brilliance of the day!
Consider the creation of male and female! Truly, your aims are diverse!
So, the one who gives to others and stands in awe of God,
and sincerely affirms that which is Best—
We will indeed ease for him the path to bliss.
But as for the one who is stingy,
and thinks that he or she is self-sufficient,
and betrays the good—
for that one We shall make easy the path towards hardship;
nor will his wealth be of use to him when he falls.
In truth, it is up to Us to guide;
and, truly, to Us belong the End and the Beginning:
and so I warn you of the raging fire—
which none shall have to endure but the most unfortunate wretch
who denies the truth and turns away.
But distant from it shall remain the one who is truly conscious of God:

the one who spends his possessions upon others so that he might grow in purity—
not as payment for favors received,
but only out of a longing for the countenance of his Sustainer,
the All-Highest: and such, indeed, shall in time be well-pleased.
[*Sūrah al-Layl* 92:1-21, complete]

And give their due to your close relations,
as well as to the needy and the traveler,
but do not squander senselessly.
Witness, those who squander are truly like satans—
for Satan has indeed proved most ungrateful to his Sustainer.
And if you must turn aside from those seeking
to obtain your Sustainer's grace and hoping for it,
at least speak to them gently,
and neither allow your hand to be chained to your neck,
nor stretch it forth to your utmost limit,
that you might not find yourself blamed, or even destitute.
Witness, your Sustainer grants abundant sustenance,
or gives it in scant measure, to whomever He wills:
truly, He is completely aware of His creatures, and sees them all.
[*Sūrah al-Isrā*ᶜ 17:26-30]

Say: "Truly my Sustainer grants abundant sustenance
or bestows it in meager measure
to such of His servants as He wills;
and whatever you spend on others, He replaces it:
for He is the Best of Providers."
[*Sūrah Sabā*ᶜ 34:39]

[Muḥammad ﷺ] never refused a request, for it was he who said: "The generous are near to God, near to Paradise, near to people, but distant from the Fire. The miserly are distant from God, distant from Paradise, distant from people, but near to the Fire."

Again he said: "O people! Surely God has chosen for you

Islam as religion, so better your practice of Islam through generosity and good manners."

The mercifulness of God's Messenger rose up as moisture into the sky, and then "rained" as generosity to make hardened hearts propitious for the growing of *good trees whose roots are firm and whose branches are in the heavens, and which yield their fruits every season by the leave of their Lord* [*Sūrah Ibrāhīm* 14:24-25].[277]

The Prophet ﷺ was an ocean of generosity; he was generous not only with his goods, but also with his labor, his teaching, and his presence:

It was only too well known that "he could refuse nothing." One day a woman gave him a cloak—something he badly needed—but the same evening someone asked him for it, to make a shroud, and he promptly gave it up. He was brought food by those who had a small surplus, but he never seemed to keep it long enough to taste it. There was always someone in greater need.[278]

After his conquest of Mecca, the Prophet ﷺ was not only merciful to the defeated Quraysh, but generous. To complete the reconciliation Quraysh were treated with the utmost generosity over the following months; Abū Sufyān, instead of losing his head, received a gift of two hundred camels.

The Prophet said of Generosity: "The Garden is the abode of the Generous." "Generosity is one of the trees of the Garden which reaches down to the earth; whoever takes a branch from it will be led to the Garden by that branch."

"Gabriel has related that Allāh has said, 'As for Myself, I am content with this religion: only generosity and good character

---

[277] Gulen, *Prophet Muḥammad, the Infinite Light*, Vol. II, p. 143.

[278] Reprinted by permission from *Islam and the Destiny of Man*, p. 117, by Charles Le Gai Eaton, the State University of New York Press © 1985, State University of New York. All rights reserved.

are fitting for it, so ennoble it with these two as far as you are able.'"[279]

Some of the *du*ᶜ*ā*ᶜ the Prophet ﷺ used to supplicate his Lord, and urged his followers to do the same:

"O Allāh! Inspire me with guidance, and spare me the evil of my selfishness."

"O Allāh! I seek refuge in you from hunger; for it is a terrible bedfellow. And I seek refuge in You from treachery; for it is indeed a foul inner-lining."

... "O Allāh! I seek refuge in You from incapacity, sloth, cowardice, miserliness and decrepitude. And I seek refuge in You from the torment of the grave."[280]

The Prophet was also great in hospitality (*nuzūl*). [Just as in] the English proverbs, "A man's home is his castle," and "home is where the heart is," in an important sense the traditional Arabian Muslim house, built of strong, usually windowless outer walls surrounding an inner courtyard and garden open to the sky, is a true symbol of the Heart. And the deepest and most sacred hospitality is that through which the truths of the Heart are shared. Hospitality involves giving, not just of one's goods, but of oneself.

A central aspect of generosity and hospitality is to give with an "open hand," which entails not looking down upon those in need. To give "with strings attached," creating a sense of shame or obligation in the recipient, is not generosity but commerce; this is why secret charity is always preferable. As Ḥaḍrat ᶜAlī said, "Hide the good you do, and make known the good done to you."[281]

Be satisfied with little for yourself, and wish much for others. Through Abū Bakr al-Diwanji we hear that the Prophet

---

[279] Charles Upton, contributor.

[280] Muḥammad al-Ghazālī, *Remembrance and Prayer*, pp. 96-97.

[281] Charles Upton, contributor.

said, "The best of my people will enter Paradise not because of their achievements, but because of the Mercy of Allāh and their quality of being satisfied with little for themselves and their extreme generosity toward others."[282]

[In the time of the Prophet ﷺ] enterprise was encouraged, but there were also those of a more contemplative temperament who had neither the skills nor the inclination to earn their own living, and they—as though to prove that the Muslim does not have to be an 'activist'—were given an honoured place in the community. A space was found for them to sleep in the covered section of the new mosque and they came to be known as "the People of the Bench [*Ahl aṣ-Ṣuffah*]." They were fed with food from the Prophet's own table, when there was any to spare, and with roasted barley from the community chest; and of all these the most famous was Abū Hurayrah, which means "Father of the little cat," who followed Muḥammad everywhere—just as his little cat followed him—and to whose prodigious powers of memory we owe a great number of recorded *ḥadīths*. Perhaps he might be regarded as the first of those of whom Muḥammad was to say: "The ink of the scholars is more valuable than the blood of the martyrs."[283]

If the giver is truly generous, he will not violate the self-respect of the one in need. And for the needy one to receive a gift with true gratitude, neither fawningly nor arrogantly, is also an act of generosity, since it prevents the giver from feeling unappreciated or degraded. And the same *ādāb* applies when it comes to accepting gifts from God. He is *Al-Karīm,* The Most Generous.[284]

---

[282] Al-Sulami, *The Way of Sufi Chivalry*, p. 41.

[283] Reprinted by permission from *Islam and the Destiny of Man,* pp. 116-117, by Charles Le Gai Eaton, the State University of New York Press © 1985, State University of New York. All rights reserved.

[284] Charles Upton, contributor.

Why do you not rely on the generosity of Allāh in this world? If an enemy intends to do you harm, why do you seek to trick him rather than entrusting him to the kindness and mercy of Allāh? If you are overcome by one of the desires of the world, why do you abandon your soul in seeking after this desire? Do you think that Allāh is generous in the next world but not in this? Has He not said: *And there is not [an] animal in the earth but on Allāh is [the responsibility for] its sustenance [Sūrah Hūd* 11:6]? And talking about the next world, He says: *And that man shall have nothing but what he strives for [Sūrah an-Najm* 53:39].

He has entrusted you with the affairs of this world; but you do wrong by your actions and rush after it like an animal. He has entrusted the affair of the hereafter to your efforts, but you neglect it in your pride.[285]

Imām aṣ-Ṣādiq said, "The roots of disbelief are three in number: greed, pride, and envy."[286]

The Prophet said, "There are two qualities in creation that Allāh loves, and two He hates: the two He loves are good character and generosity, and the two He hates are ill-manners and miserliness."[287]

You must give without being asked. Anything given after being asked for is merely reparation for the embarrassment suffered by the asker. The generous should not cause embarrassment to others. Abū ʿAbdullāh ibn Battah tells of the advice that ʿUbaydullāh ibn ʿAbbās gave to his brother's son: "The best of gifts is the one given without being asked, because if you are asked, what you give is only payment for the supplicant's embarrassment."[288]

---

[285] Haeri, *Prophetic Traditions of Islām*, pp. 153-154 (al-Ashtarī, I, 234-248).

[286] Ibid., p. 173 (*Mishkāt*, 224-229).

[287] Ibid., p. 174 (al-Ashtarī, I, 170-171).

[288] Al-Sulami, *The Way of Sufi Chivalry*, p. 101.

*Wara*ᶜ, scrupulousness, in its lowest phase is avoidance of the *ḥarām* and the doubtful. In its middle phase it is moving from the doubtful to what is certain to bring benefit. It is avoidance of anything that will cast a shadow on the heart. In its highest phase it is avoiding any desire except desire for Allāh.

Al-Ḥasan al-Baṣrī was asked, "What is the pivot of the *dīn* (life-transaction)?" He replied: "*Wara*ᶜ."

If you are scrupulous with yourself and generous in judgment of others it is better for you than that you should be scrupulous in judgment of others and lax in your own behavior.

The *faqīr* must guard against contemplating his own scrupulousness, or basking in it, or resting in it, lest it, too, become a snare for him. Remember that there are people who make all the right actions and are careful in everything, yet their hearts become hardened.[289]

"My Lord! I ask forgiveness of You to whom all praise is due. There is no God but You who are Tender and Giving, the Creator of the heavens and the earth, the Originator, O You who are the Possessor of Majesty and Infinite Generosity." The Prophet ﷺ heard a man call out this prayer and said, "Truly, he has called Allāh by the Great Name, the one by which prayers are answered and needs are fulfilled."[290]

Abundance is seeking beggars, just as beauty seeks a mirror.[291]

Imām ᶜAlī said, "Miserliness is a disgrace and cowardliness is a defect. Be liberal but not wasteful, prudent but not miserly, and do not be ashamed of giving a small amount; for to withhold is to give even less. I am amazed at the miser, who so quickly brings upon himself the very poverty from which he is

---

[289] Shaykh ᶜAbdalqadir al-Murabit, *The Hundred Steps* (London: Madinah Press, 1998), p. 11.

[290] C. Helminski, *The Mevlevi Wird*, pp. 53, 70.

[291] Jalālu'ddin Rūmī, *The Pocket Rumi Reader*, edited by Kabir Helminski (Boston, Massachusetts: Shambhala Publications, 2001), p. 229 (*Mathnawī* I:2750).

fleeing, and who fails to gain the riches he desires. He lives as a poor man in this world, and he will be taken to account as a rich man in the next. Miserliness represents the sum of man's shortcomings and leads one to all kinds of evil."[292]

[Imām Jaᶜfar aṣ-Ṣādiq] was asked why Allāh had forbidden usury, to which he replied, "So that people do not stop performing acts of kindness amongst themselves." Then he added, "Man has been created with different qualities, yet whatever he has been created with does not include treachery and lying."[293]

Those saved from the covetousness of their own souls,
they are the ones who achieve prosperity.
[*Sūrah al-Ḥashr* 59:9]

Understand that what you really own is not what you keep of your property, but that which you spend for your brethren. . . . ᶜĀʾishah recounted that someone presented a lamb as a gift to the Messenger of Allāh. He distributed the meat. ᶜĀʾishah said, "Only the neck is left for us." The Prophet said, "No, all of it is left for us except the neck."[294]

Aṣ-Ṣādiq said, "Make gifts to each other and love each other, for surely gifts remove malice and spite."[295]

If a friend, a relative, or an acquaintance gives you a gift, thank them as soon as possible regardless of the value of the gift. It is a good manner to show warm appreciation for such a kind gesture and if you can, reciprocate with an appropriate gift. The Prophet ﷺ said: "Whoever does you a favor then reward him,

---

[292] Haeri, *Prophetic Traditions of Islām*, p. 175 (*Mishkāt*, 229-230).

[293] Ibid., pp. 75-76 (al-Irbillī, II, 396).

[294] Al-Sulami, *The Way of Sufi Chivalry*, p. 42.

[295] Haeri, *Prophetic Traditions of Islām*, p. 212 (*al-Khiṣāl*, I, 27).

if you can not reward him, pray for him." The *ḥadīth* calls upon the receivers to reciprocate, within their means. The reward means a gift equivalent to that received, if that is not possible, a simple gift will do, and if that is not possible, then a sincere prayer would suffice.

It is recommended that the reward be better than the original gift. It is the essence of Islamic manners to return a nice gesture with a better one. A man brought Imām Abū Ḥanīfa a gift worth ten *dirhams* and the Imām presented him with a gift worth five hundred *dirhams*. The man was surprised and said: "But Imām, my gift was little, about a tenth of your gift." "Your gift is more valuable," the Imām answered: "You remembered me while I forgot you, I remembered you only after you had given me your gift. So your gift is better."[296]

A person who gives freely is loved by all. It's hard to understand, but it is by giving that we gain strength. But there is a proper time and proper way to give, and the person who understands this is strong and wise. By giving with a feeling of reverence for life, envy and anger are banished. A path to happiness is found. Like one who plants a sapling and in due course receives shade, flowers, and fruit, so the results of giving bring joy. The way there is through continuous acts of kindness so that the heart is strengthened by compassion and giving.[297]

---

[296] Abū Ghudda, *Islamic Manners*, pp. 73-74.

[297] Bancroft, *The Pocket Buddha Reader (Majjhima Nikayase)*, p. 21.

Red Brocade

The Arabs used to say,
When a stranger appears at your door,
feed him for three days
before asking who he is,
where he's come from,
where he's headed.
That way, he'll have strength
enough to answer.
Or, by then you'll be
such good friends
you don't care.

Let's go back to that.
Rice? Pine nuts?
Here, take the red brocade pillow.
My child will serve water
to your horse.

No, I was not busy when you came!
I was not preparing to be busy.
That's the armor everyone puts on
to pretend they had a purpose
in the world.

I refuse to be claimed.
Your plate is waiting.
We will snip fresh mint
into your tea.[298]

---

[298] "Red Brocade" is excerpted from pp 40-41 of *19 Varities of Gazelle, Poems of the Middle East* by Naomi Shihab Nye. Greenwillow/ HarperCollins Publishers, NY, NY. © Naomi Shihab Nye, 2002.

Giving of What We Love

Nana Asmaʾu (1793-1864)[299] helped to guide an entire community in what is now Nigeria. She was raised under the careful eye of her father, who was the spiritual and tribal leader of the Shehu people, as well as that of her mother and a number of other scholarly women. At an early age Nana had memorized the entire Qurʾān, and she soon spoke and wrote in Fulfulde, Hausa, Tamachek, and Arabic.

When she was quite young, her family and their expanding community of Qādiri Muslims began their journey of emigration to settle in a place where their community might be free to practice with appropriate care the *sunnah* of the Prophet Muḥammad ﷺ. As they moved from one place to another during a time of intense civil war when strong efforts were being made to reform and purify the practice of Islām in the region (1804-1830), one of the few things they carried with them was the family library consisting of hundreds of carefully copied loose-leaf manuscripts. These books were continually passing through a process of renewal as in that climate even though the hand-copied tomes were enveloped by sturdy goatskin bags, it was not long before the parchment pages would begin to disintegrate. Books were of such importance that wherever the family journeyed, a room was always set aside for the copying of texts so that the library of important Islamic and Sufi texts might be preserved.

Nana Asmaʾu became an enthusiastic teacher of both men and women and one who was well-loved by her students and her whole community. At the same time that she was both a wife and a mother, devoted daughter and sister, she was also an educator, an author, and "a respected scholar of international repute who was in communication with scholars throughout the sub-Saharan African Muslim world."[300] "[Her]

---

[299] Nana Asmaʾu was born in the small village of Degel in the dry sandy plains of Hausaland at a time when the French Revolution was at its height. The Islamic revolution in which she played an important part affected an area the size of Western Europe.

[300] Beverly B. Mack and Jean Boyd, *One Woman's Jihād* (Bloomington, Indiana: Indiana University, 2000), p. 1.

efforts to promote reconciliation, education, and justice helped change forever the Muslim culture in which she lived. This was her personal *jihād* [301] and it took three aspects: First was the preservation and propagation of all that the Shehu stood for [the rightful following of the *sunnah* of the Prophet and justice for all]. . . . Second was the education of women, who were the primary mentors of future generations. . . . Third, she devoted her life to reconciliation and peaceful coexistence, using her wit, her imagination, and her immense prestige to find pragmatic solutions to the problems that faced her."[302] "Asma'u was as comfortable in intellectual debate as she was in domestic endeavors, understanding both to be of equal importance to life in this world."[303] For her, daily life was imbued with Islamic devotion.

"Asma'u never patronized her students, but she provided in her works access to multiple layers of meaning at every level. Her works were replete with a wide variety of meanings hidden among features from the simplest to the most erudite, including clever vernacular wordplay, chapter and line citations from the Qur'ān, and paraphrases from the classics. Through these techniques, Asma'u's students enjoyed a rich experience in reciting her poetry. For those unprepared for such techniques, her works provided the most basic of satisfactions by establishing for them mantras in the simple repetition of the rhymes. Asma'u recognized that in truly pious endeavors there is no room for intellectual elitism: she met each individual at his or her own level, in keeping with the Sufi tenets of humility and patient piety.[304]

"Asma'u's . . . piety and good deeds made her an admirable person, but her literary skills and her ability to compose effectively in several languages spread her fame among the educated and illiterate alike. She

---

[301] *Jihād* means struggle, effort. Though occasionally it may be used to refer to an external struggle, it is understood that the "greater *jihād*" is the struggle within one's own self, grappling with the forces of the ego to unify one's self with the Divine, in alignment with the Divine Will, in *tawḥīd* (complete Oneness).

[302] Ibid., p. 6.

[303] Ibid., p. 10.

[304] Ibid., p. 58.

was not only famous among the Muslim scholars in her community and beyond, but she was also loved by ordinary unschooled villagers because she offered them, in languages they could understand, a place in Paradise with the Shehu through the works she composed. . . . In addition to religious instruction and enlightenment, Asmaʾu's poetic works offered views on recent history, with which they were familiar, and practical tools for their participation in a community newly unified under Islam. . . .

"Her poetry demonstrates that she was a strong-willed woman, engaged in her cause, the unification of a Muslim state, in addition to being a poet sensitive to matters of grief and loss. She never wrote in isolation, but always was an activist, whose writings were merely instruments in bringing her fellow citizens to a higher good."[305]

As mother, wife, sister, statesperson, poet, scholar, healer, and friend, she experienced the whole range of human emotions and human duties. When her brother, Muḥammad Bello, who had succeeded their father as caliph of the infant Islamic state died, she was grief-stricken. An outpouring of this grief found its expression in her book, *Tabshir al-Ikhwan* relating "Qur'anic remedies for specific emotional, mental, and physical maladies. 'When light enters the heart,' she wrote, 'darkness departs from it and it is guided aright.'. . . 'God has enjoined us all to praise Him . . . that we might obtain light and radiance of heart, that we may be cleansed.'"[306]

Asmaʾu was an "organizer and innovator; it was her reputation (she was described by her kinsman Sheikh Sa'ad as 'the tireless lady who excels in everything she has to do') which persuaded men to allow their womenfolk to trek on foot across country, without male escorts, for educational purposes. . . . Asmaʾu had pupils [*ᶜyan-taru* or "women disciples"] from many towns and they included women from several ethnic groups, namely Fulani, Hausa, and Sulubawa."[307] In recent years,

---

[305] Excerpted from pp. 61-62 of *One Woman's Jihad*, by Beverly B. Mack and Jean Boyd (Bloomington Indiana University Press 2000). Reprinted by permission of Indiana University Press.

[306] Jean Boyd, *The Caliph's Sister, Nana Asmaᶜu 1793-1865, Teacher, Poet, and Islamic Leader* (London, United Kingdom: Frank Cass & Co., 1989, reprinted 1995), p. 72.

namely Fulani, Hausa, and Sulubawa."[307] In recent years, her great-great-granddaughter, the Modibo of Kware (Hajara), has been among those who have continued the tradition of spiritual education of rural women.[308]

Asma'u's teaching songs in Hausa are still well-known today as they continue to be learned by both young girls and boys. Her people "speak of her as if she were alive and recite the injunctions she taught their great-grandmothers. . . . She herself [spoke and] wrote about the women of her father's generation who had been 'teachers of women, teachers of the exegesis of the Qur'ān, and women of great presence.' They, in turn, had been taught by earlier generations of women who included her [grandmother and great-grandmother]. In her own generation there were six other women writers whose poetry has survived: they were her sisters Hadiza, Fāṭimah, Habsatu, Safiya, and Maryam—the sixth was her cousin Aisha."[309]

Following here is one of Asma'u's song poems—a commentary on Surah 94, *Sūrah Inshirah* (or *Ash-Sharḥ*) noting God's generosity to us even in the midst of difficulty:

Truly, with Every Difficulty Comes Ease

1. Lord God Almighty, all Powerful, he who asserts there is more than one god will perish.
2. One God, Almighty, nothing is perfect except it comes from Him.
3. Come to God, receive His generosity: all good things are derived from Him.

---

[307] Ibid., p. 76.

[308] Ibid., pp. 99-100.

[309] Ibid., pp. 98-99

~ "Truly, with Every Difficulty Comes Ease" is excerpted from *One Woman's Jihad*, by Beverly B. Mack and Jean Boyd (Bloomington Indiana University Press 2000), p. 132. Reprinted by permission of Indiana University Press. This poem was written by Nana Asma'u in 1822 A.D./1238-39 A.H. in the Fulfulde language; the source of the text wasWaziri Junaidu.

4. Anyone who says he requires nothing of God is either ignorant or an unbeliever.
5. Everyone who seeks God's help will receive it, for God allows people to make requests.
6. I pray God will show me the Way of religion and that I will keep to it until I die.
7. God is Pure, and forgets nothing: those whom He forgives find peace.
8. May He bless us and show us the Path, and may He help us to remain one people.
9. We pray for victory and that the rebellion of Ibra may be overcome.
10. We pray, too, for forgiveness in this world and the next.
11. Call upon God always, so that things which are too difficult may be made easy.
12. Pray to God, do your meditations, praying for forgiveness and giving thanks.
13. Look at His generosity! It is unbounded, His munificence is infinite.
14. We give thanks to God and pray for our Lord of the Universe.

Kindness
(*Ṭībah*)

It is God Who sends to His servants clear signs
that He may lead you out of the depths of darkness
into the Light.
And truly, God is to you Most Kind and Merciful.
[*Sūrah al-Ḥadīd* 57:9]

Truly those who say, "Our Sustainer is God"
and remain steadfast—
no fear shall they have, neither shall they grieve.
These shall be companions of the Garden, dwelling there
as a completion for their deeds.
We have enjoined on the human being kindness to his parents:
in pain did his mother bear him and in pain did she give him birth.
The carrying of the child to his weaning is thirty months.
At length when he reaches the age of maturity
and attains forty years he prays, "O my Sustainer!
Inspire me to be grateful for Your blessings
which You have bestowed on me and on both my parents
and that I may act rightly in a way which You may approve;
and be gracious to me in my offspring.
Truly, I have turned to you, and truly, I bow in surrender."
Such are they from whom We shall accept the best of their deeds
and disregard their mistakes:
they shall be among the companions of the Garden:
this is a true promise made to them.
[*Sūrah al-Aḥqāf* 46:13-16]

Do not join any other deity side by side with God,
that you might not find yourself disgraced and in want:
for your Sustainer has commanded
that you shall worship none but Him.
And do good to your parents.

Should one of them, or both, reach old age in your care,
never speak with contempt to them or scold them,
but speak to them with reverence,
and tenderly lower to them the wings of humility,
and say: "O my Sustainer! Bestow Your grace upon them,
even as they cherished and nurtured me when I was but a child!"
[*Sūrah al-Isrā*ᶜ 17:22-24]

And We have enjoined upon the human being
goodness towards his parents;
in travail upon travail did his mother bear him
and in two years was his weaning.
Be grateful to Me and to your parents:
with Me is all journey's end.
[*Sūrah Luqmān* 31:14]

The Prophet ﷺ said, "Kindness is prosperity and offensiveness is misfortune."

"Never was kindness placed on something but that it beautified it, and never was it removed but that it marred it."

"In kindness there is increase and blessing; whoever withholds kindness withholds goodness."

"No two persons keep company with each other but that the one with the greatest reward and the most beloved of Allāh is the one who is most kind to his companion."

"If kindness were a visible creation, nothing which Allāh has created would be more beautiful than it."[310]

He is also known to have said, "Kindness is a mark of faith and whoever has not kindness has not faith."

"All God's creatures are His family, and he is the most beloved of God who tries to do most good to God's creatures."

---

[310] Haeri, *Prophetic Traditions of Islām*, p. 223 (al-Kulaynī, II, 120).

> A man said, "O Prophet of God! Which is the best part [of Islam]?" He said, "That you give food [to the hungry], and extend greetings to all whom you know and whom you do not know."
>
> The Prophet also said, "Gabriel kept on recommending [that I treat] the neighbors in a kind and polite manner, so much so that I thought that he would order me to make them my heirs."[311]

Kindness is especially due to those closest to us. No one who does not love his family will be able to love his neighbor—or God, for that matter. The Prophet ﷺ, in his Farewell Address, directed Muslims to, "Take special care to be kind to your mothers and fathers, sisters and brothers, then those nearest of kin."[312]

Aṣ-Ṣādiq tells of the time when a man came to the Prophet ﷺ asking for permission to fight in the *jihād*, which was granted. "The man said, 'O Messenger, I have two elderly parents who claim that they are so fond of me that they do not want me to leave.' The Messenger replied, 'Then stay with your parents, for by the One who has my soul in His hand, their fondness for you—be it only a day and a night—is better than fighting for a whole year.'"[313]

> A man came to the Apostle, saying, "O Messenger of Allāh, whom should I treat kindly?" "Your mother," he replied. "And then whom?" "Your mother." "And then whom?" "Your mother." "And then whom?" "Your father."[314]

A student of Imām Mālik named Imām Abdul-Raḥmān ibn

[311] Charles Upton, contributor (*Mishkāt*, 212-215).

[312] Zakaria Bashier, *Sunshine at Madinah* (Leicestershire, United Kingdom: The Islamic Foundation, 1990), p. 130.

[313] Haeri, *Prophetic Traditions of Islām*, p. 192 (al-Kulaynī, II, 157-160).

[314] Ibid.

al-Qāsim al-Utaqi al-Masri said: "Once while Imām Mālik was reading *al-Muwatta* to me, he suddenly stood up and left me for a long while. Then he came back and sat down. He was asked why he acted as such, and he answered: 'My mother came down asking me something. Since she was standing I stood up respectfully, when she went, I sat back down.'"[315]

Kindness is being of a gentle disposition, compassionate, avoiding harshness and rudeness in one's actions and words with people at all times.

The Messenger said, "Kindness is prosperity and offensiveness is misfortune."[316]

Aṣ-Ṣādiq said, "The smile of one believer to another believer is a fine action rewarded by Allāh."[317]

And lower your wing [*be kind*]
to whoever follows you of the faithful.
[*Sūrah ash-Shu*ᶜ*arā*ᶜ 26:215]

The Messenger also said, "Treat the elderly with deference, for deference to the elderly is honouring Allāh, and whoever does not treat them with deference is not one of us."[318]

"He is not one of us who shows no respect for our elders, or who has no compassion for our young, or who has no appreciation for the rights of our learned." The noble Prophet ﷺ met everyone in the same spirit.[319]

This should not be taken to belittle the youth or put them down. Imām Al-Bukhārī reported that Ibn ᶜAbbās narrated that ᶜUmar allowed him to attend his council with seniors who at-

---

[315] Abū Ghudda, *Islamic Manners*, pp. 70-71.

[316] Haeri, *Prophetic Traditions of Islām*, p. 223 (al-Kulaynī, II, 119-120).

[317] Ibid., p. 224 (*Mishkāt*, 179-180).

[318] Ibid., p. 215 (*Mishkāt*, 168-170).

[319] Muḥammad al-Ghazālī, *Remembrance and Prayer*, p. 102.

> tended the battle of Badr. Some of them felt uneasy and asked: "Why are you permitting him to attend when he is as young as our children?" ᶜUmar replied: "He is knowledgeable, as you well know." Another version elaborates that ᶜUmar asked the seniors to explain *Sūrah al-Fātiḥah* and only ᶜAbdullāh ibn ᶜAbbās explained it correctly. Ibn ᶜAbbās said: "I thought he asked the question just to demonstrate my knowledge to them."[320]

There is a beautiful story of how Muḥammad ﷺ would sometimes take his grand-daughter Umāma ﵂, the daughter of his eldest daughter Zaynab ﵂, into the mosque with him and would put her on his shoulders while he prayed. When the moments for prostration would arrive, he would set her down beside him and then put her back on his shoulders when he rose again to standing witness in the ritual prayer.[321]

> The Prophet ﷺ said: "Gentleness adorns every act. Its absence will tarnish it." In addition, Muslim reported that the Prophet ﷺ also said: "Whoever lacks kindness, lacks all good things."[322]

Gentleness and consideration and kindness to others may be manifested in many ways. For instance: "When entering or leaving a house, do not push the door violently or slam it shut, nor leave it to close by itself. . . . Close the door quietly with your hand."[323]

> At the end of his book of Māliki *Fiqh, al-Kafi,* Imām Ibn ᶜAbdul al-Barr said: "Kindness to the parents is an obligatory duty and by the grace of Allāh, it is not so difficult. Kindness means to be humble with them, to speak to them nicely, to look at them with love and respect, to speak in a mild tone that

---

[320] Abū Ghudda, *Islamic Manners*, p. 60.

[321] See Muḥammad Saeed Ṣiddiqi, *The Blessed Women of Islam* (Lahore, Pakistan: Kazi Publications, 1982), p. 108.

[322] Abū Ghudda, *Islamic Manners*, p. 34.

[323] Ibid., p. 29.

does not surpass theirs unless they are hard of hearing, to give them complete access to your own wealth, and to offer them the best of your food and drink."[324]

Making your parents' life enjoyable is one of the most virtuous acts.[325] In return, it is the parents' duty to make it easier for their children by being kind and supportive to their children, for only with Allāh's help, people are able to obey Him and heed His commands.[326]

As a Muslim, one should demonstrate to all people the goodness of Islam with gentle manners and kind behavior. Al-Bukhārī and Muslim reported the *ḥadīth* of Anas: "None of you [truly] believes until he loves for his brother what he loves for himself." The version reported by Muslim says: "Unless he loves for his brother, or neighbor, as he loves for himself.'" The scholars commented that the word 'brother' is used in the most common context, and thus means brother in humanity, including both Muslims and non-Muslims.[327]

Keeping Appointments

Keeping appointments is vital to our lives. Time is the most precious commodity; once wasted, it can never be recovered. If you made an appointment, whether with a friend, colleague, or for business, you should do your utmost to keep this appointment. This is the right of the other persons who, despite other commitments, favored you with a part of their valuable time. If you do not come on time, not only have you disrupted their schedule but you have also marred your image and reputation.

---

[324] Ibid., p. 71.

[325] Ibid.

[326] Ibid., pp. 71-72.

[327] Ibid., p. 75.

If your punctuality becomes poor you will lose people's respect. You should keep all your appointments whether they are with an important person, a close friend, or a business colleague. You will then be responding to the call of Allāh in *Sūrah al-Isrā*ᶜ: *And keep the promise; the promise is a responsibility.* [17:34][328]

Our kind Prophet ﷺ gave an appointment to one of his companions. The companion came three days later. The Prophet ﷺ gently reprimanded him saying: "You have caused me some trouble. I have been waiting for you for three days." The companion probably had an excuse for this delay; however, he had no means by which to inform the Prophet ﷺ about his inability to keep the appointment.

Today, fast and reliable communication means are available everywhere. Therefore, as soon as you realize you will be unable to keep an appointment, you should inform the other parties to enable them to utilize their time elsewhere. Do not be careless or irresponsible, assuming that since the appointment is relatively unimportant, it does not merit a notice or an apology. This is totally irrelevant. Regardless of its importance, an appointment is a commitment that should be kept or properly cancelled in advance.[329]

Visiting Manners

Imām An-Nawawi said: "It is strongly recommended for Muslims to visit the pious people, their brethren, neighbors, friends and relatives, and to be generous, kind, and obliging to them. However, the extent of the visit varies according to the host's circumstances. The visit ought to be conducted in a pleasant manner and at convenient times."[330]

---

[328] Ibid., p. 37.

[329] Ibid., pp. 37-38.

[330] Ibid., p. 44.

Choose an appropriate time for your visit. Do not visit at inconvenient times such as meal-time, or when people are sleeping, resting, or relaxing. The length of the visit should correspond with how well you know the hosts, as well as their circumstances and conditions. Do not overstay your welcome by making your visit too long or burdensome.[331]

Imām Al-Bukhārī in *al-Ādāb al-Mufrad* reported that our forefathers used to look their best when visiting each other. Be kind and considerate with your guests. As a rule do not ask them to help you with house chores. Imām Shāfiʿī said: "Gentlemen do not employ their visiting guests."

If you visit a relative or a friend, you should be mindful of your host's circumstances and work commitments. Make your visit as brief as possible, as everybody has various jobs and duties to attend to. Be considerate of your hosts and volunteer to help them with their business, house chores, and obligations.[332]

The Messenger of Allāh ﷺ taught the youth the manners of companionship and the custom of giving precedence to elders. Al-Bukhārī and Muslim reported that the honored companion Mālik ibn al-Huwairith said: "I was with a group of youth who visited the Messenger of Allāh ﷺ in Madīnah for twenty nights. The Messenger of Allāh ﷺ was very kind and compassionate. He sensed that we might have missed our families and were home-sick, and asked us about whom we had left behind. When we informed him, he said: 'Go back to your families, live with them, teach them Islām, and te1l them of the good deeds. At the times of prayer, let one of you call the *azan,* and have your eldest lead the prayer.'"

In this particular case, the Prophet ﷺ specified that the eldest should lead the prayers, since they were equal in their

[331] Ibid.

[332] Ibid., p. 47.

knowledge and learning. Being older in such a case merits leading the prayers. However, if a person is more knowledgeable, then he should lead the prayer, for knowledge is an honor above old age as supported by many *aḥādīth* on this subject.

If the prayers are offered at a house, the host is entitled to lead it. Out of respect, he may invite a person who is more knowledgeable, older or more prominent. If the guest declines, the host should not hesitate to lead the prayers. Imām Aḥmad reported in his *Musnad* that ᶜAbdullāh ibn Masūd visited Abū Mūsā al-Ash'ari. When it was time to pray, Abū Mūsā asked Ibn Masūd: "Please lead the prayers as you are older and have more knowledge." Ibn Masūd said: "No, you lead the prayer. This is your house and praying area. You should lead the prayer." Abū Mūsā then led the prayer.'[333]

Treat poor acquaintances or guests with honor and respect. Talk pleasantly to them, using the best of language. Again, poverty is not a vice; many who are poor are more honorable than the wealthy, and many who are penniless are preferred to the rich.[334]

It is the duty of every Muslim to visit their Muslim brethren if they fall ill; this will enhance and nourish the bond of Islām and the brotherhood among them. As a committed Muslim, one should not undervalue the great reward from Allāh. Imām Muslim reported that the Messenger of Allāh ﷺ said: "A Muslim visiting his ill brethren will continue to be in the *khurfa* of Paradise until he comes back home. He was asked: "What is the *khurfa* of Paradise?" He answered: "This means the harvest of Paradise."[335]

---

[333] Ibid., pp. 61-62.

[334] Ibid., p. 73.

[335] Ibid., p. 89.

If you can not visit your relatives, friends, or acquaintances, you should still keep in touch by calling them or sending them a letter. This will leave them with a deep amicable impression, and will keep the relationship alive. . . . Inquiring about friends is like meeting them. [336]

---

[336] Ibid., p. 48.

IX.

Responsiveness—Faithful and Right Action

(*Al-Ijāba—Al-Īmān wa ᶜAmal uṣ-Ṣāliḥāt*):

Creativity and Beauty

Strength, Courage, and Vigilant Awareness

Justice and Conflict Resolution

FAITHFUL AND RIGHT ACTION
(*Al-Īmān wa ᶜAmal uṣ-Ṣāliḥāt*)

For those who have faith and do righteous deeds
are Gardens as welcoming homes for that which they have done.
[*Sūrah as-Sajdah* 32:19]

Truly: all who surrender their whole being to God,
and do good, shall have their reward with their Sustainer;
these need have no fear, neither shall they grieve.
[*Sūrah al-Baqarah* 2:112]

And the one who brings the Truth and the one who stands with it,
it is they, they who do right.
They shall have all that they yearn for in the presence of their Sustainer,
such is the reward of those who do good,
so that God will divert from them the worst in their deeds
and give them their recompense
according to the best of that which they have done.
[*Sūrah az-Zumar* 39:33–35]

Tell those who have faith to forgive
those who do not consider the coming of the Days of God:
it is for Him to recompense each People
according to what they have earned.
If anyone does a righteous deed, it is to his/her own benefit;
if he/she does harm, it works against his/her own soul.
In the end you will all be brought back to your Sustainer.
[*Sūrah al-Jāthiyah* 45:14-15]

Remember God—standing, and sitting, and lying down;
[*Sūrah an-Nisāᶜ* 4:103]

Recite what is sent of the Book by inspiration to you
and establish regular prayer:

for prayer restrains from shameful and unjust deeds,
and remembrance of God is surely the greatest of all things in life.
And God knows that which you do.
[*Sūrah al-ᶜAnkabūt* 29:45]

That you have faith in God and His Messenger,
and that you strive in God's cause
with your possessions and your lives:
that is best for you, if only you knew!
[*Sūrah aṣ-Ṣaff* 61:11]

And those who have faith in God and do righteous deeds,
He will admit to gardens beneath which rivers flow, to dwell there forever:
God has indeed granted for them a most excellent provision.
[*Sūrah at-Talāq* 65:11]

And God endows with an ever-deeper consciousness of the right way
those who seek guidance;
and good deeds, the fruits of which endure forever,
are best in the sight of your Sustainer
and yield the best return.
[*Sūrah Maryam* 19:76]

Throughout the Qurʾān, in many verses, faith and good deeds are linked. Rightful action is a natural outflowing of true faith. These "rightful deeds" may manifest with a preponderance of beauty (*jamal*) or of strength (*jalāl*), but in all cases, with justice.

Creativity and Beauty
(*Badāʿah* and *Jamāl*)

God! there is no god but Hu!
To Him belong the Most Beautiful Names.
[*Sūrah Ṭā Hā* 20:8]

God is He other than Whom there is no god,
Who knows what is hidden and what is manifest;
Hu, the Infinitely Compassionate, the Infinitely Merciful.
God is He other than Whom there is no god,
the Sovereign, the Holy One, the Source of Peace,
the Inspirer of Faith, the Preserver of Security,
the Exalted in Might, the Compelling, the Supreme:
Glory to God!
Who is above the partners they attribute to Him—
He is God, the Creator, the Evolver, the Bestower of Forms.
To Hu belong the Most Beautiful Names:
whatever is in the heavens and on earth
declares His Praises and Glory,
and He is the exalted in Might, the All-Wise.
[*Sūrah al-Ḥashr* 59:22-24]

Invite to the way of your Lord with wisdom and beautiful urging;
and discuss with them in the best and most gracious manner.
[*Sūrah an-Naḥl* 16:125]

He has created the heavens and the earth in accordance with Truth
and has shaped you and made your shapes beautiful;
and with Him is your journey's end.
He knows what is in the heavens and on earth;
He knows what you conceal and what you reveal:
yes, God knows well the secrets of hearts.
[*Sūrah at-Taghābun* 64:3-4]

Whoever does good, whether male or female, and is of the faithful, truly, We will give a new life that is good and pure, and We will bestow on such their reward according to the most beautiful of their actions.
[*Sūrah an-Naḥl* 16:97]

Many stories are related as to how in the early days of the *Ummah* of Islām, the recitation of the Qur'ān overwhelmed hearts by its beauty. It was a new expression of God's Presence that had the power to change people's hearts, drawing them to faith in the Unity of God and all of creation. Recognition was given in this new revelation of the beauty and wisdom of creation and especially the beauty and ordered proportion of the human being. Muḥammad ﷺ was honored with recognition as being of the most beautiful character. It was through him that the creative word of the Qur'ān burst forth into manifestation that might be shared with other human beings, calling them to refresh and deepen their connection with their Creator.

The Prophet Muḥammad ﷺ is a beautiful example of a purely creative person whose actions unfolded with beauty and strength in response to his intimate connection with his Lord. Each human being has the capacity to be a mirror of God's qualities and to bring into greater manifestation the beauty of the Divine. It is said that God is Beautiful and loves Beauty (*ḥadīth qudsī*).

> The master Abū ʿAlī ad-Daqqāq (may God grant him mercy) declared, "God will beautify the inner faculties with contemplation for one who adorns his outer being with striving, for God Most High says, *And those who strive in Us, We will certainly guide them to Our paths* [*Sūrah al-ʿAnkabūt* 29:69].[337]

Muḥammad ﷺ offers us many examples of creative and beautiful personal prayer like the prayer he would offer upon awakening:

"We have awakened and all of creation has awakened for God, Sustainer of all the worlds. God, I ask You for the best the day has to offer,

[337] Al-Qushayri, *Principles of Sufism*, p. 12.

opening, support, light, blessings, guidance, and I seek refuge in You from any harm in it and any harm that might come after it."

Manners of Prayer

Once upon a time Moses encountered a shepherd, whose idea of worshipping God was to comb His hair, wash His feet and give Him milk to drink. The prophet thundered against the shepherd for dragging God down to the human level: "Far be it from Him to need His hair combed! God is Lord of the Worlds; He is infinitely beyond your paltry conception of His Majesty. Rectify your practice, then. Worship Him in Spirit, not in form." But as Moses traveled on, God came to him in a vision and chastised him: "My servant the shepherd worshipped me according to his conception—as do you. You have misjudged him; his sincerity is perfect in My sight." Distraught and repentant, Moses ran back to the shepherd to ask his forgiveness. "I beg your pardon, shepherd, for God has revealed to me that I had seriously misjudged you. Please continue to worship Him as seems right to you." "But I was about to thank you for your instruction!" the shepherd answered. "The shock you administered opened my eyes to a vastly greater conception of God than the one I had previously held. After what I have seen, I can never return to my former practice."

In that timeless time before we were brought into existence, when God asked us *Am I not your Lord?* and we answered *Yea!* [*Sūrah al-Aᶜrāf* 7:172], in that very instant each of us consented to be precisely who He made us to be—as if each of us, in a sense, were the reflection of a unique Name of God. We study the lives of great exemplars of virtue so that they can throw light on our own lives, not so that our unique talents and weakness and needs and capacities can be blotted out in the blinding light of the Hero. It is said that no one reaches God on his own feet; that to come to His threshold we must walk with God's feet.

But it is equally true to say that no one can reach that threshold on the feet of someone else; if we aspire to step into God's shoes, it must be with our own feet.

Those who worship their own uniqueness and originality instead of God are idolaters; but those who suppress this uniqueness so they can pour themselves blindly into an external mold have cheated God, who demands from us who we really are. . . . [The greater *jihād* is the struggle to polish the heart so that it may be receptive to Spirit and be freed of the compulsive desires of the self.] Between the Spirit (*ar-rūh*) and the commanding self (*an-nafs al-ammara*) is the domain of the Heart (*al-qalb*), the Center of consciousness and intent, the organ or power within the human being which is capable of direct knowledge of God.

The development of the virtues with the help of God's grace is the Way of the greater *jihād*. The virtues develop through three stages:

1) *Knowing* what is right;
2) *Doing* what is right (this is *islām,* submission);
3) *Loving to do* what is right (this is *īmān,* faith).

The perfection of these is *iḥsān,* (being and doing the beautiful).

We come to "know" what is right through the guidance of the Qur'ān, the *ḥadīth*, the example of the prophets and people of wisdom, and through praying to God for guidance. The faculties by which we know what is right, except in the case of prayer, are the rational intellect (*ᶜaql*) and the memory . . . . On the field of virtue, we *know* what is right through the rational intellect and memory, *do* what is right through the will (*irāda*), and *love to do* what is right through the emotions.

But when the Heart is fully realized, when the Eye of the Heart is open, we no longer have to pass through these stages, because, in the city of the Heart, emotions, will, and mind are one. It's not that we know what is right and then do it—it's that we have become rectitude. This is *ihsān*, [beautiful] excellence. The Heart is a balanced qualitative consciousness that has become inseparable from spontaneous right action. We no longer have to study what is right, plan our actions on the basis of this study, and then finally act, because knowledge, action, and love now form an indivisible whole. Our character has become unified. We have realized the self-at-peace. The Prophet Muḥammad ﷺ did not have to consult the Qurʾān in every case before acting. As his wife ʿĀʾishah ؓ said, when asked what the Prophet's character was like: "His character was exactly like the Qurʾān." And as God says,

> *Truly, in the Messenger of God*
> *you have a beautiful standard*
> *for anyone whose hope is in God and the Last Day*
> *and who remembers God unceasingly.*
> [Sūrah al-Aḥzāb 33:21]

When the Heart acts at the command of God in such a way that the rational intellect, the will, and the feelings no longer appear as separate stages of a process, then Unity of Character has been established. It's a little like what happens in the process of learning an art—calligraphy, for example. At the beginning we must consciously practice, study various styles, learn from our mistakes—but at the end, we no longer have to painstakingly direct our hand to do what our memory tells us to do, because we have *become* calligraphy.[338]

> *Let the Beauty we love be what we do.*
> *There are hundreds of ways to kneel and kiss the ground.*
> ~ Mevlana Jalālu'ddin Rūmī[339]

---

[338] Charles Upton, contributor.
[339] Jalālu'ddin Rūmī, *Open Secret: Versions of Rumi*, translated by John Moyne and Coleman Barks (Putney, Vermont: Threshold Books, 1984), p. 7.

Truth is Beauty and Beauty is Truth

"What is evident in this world is the endless procession of moving things; but what is to be realized is the supreme human Truth by which the human world is permeated.

"We must never forget today that a mere movement is not valuable in itself, that it may be a sign of a dangerous form of inertia. We must be reminded that a great upheaval of spirit, a universal realization of true dignity of man once caused by Buddha's teachings in India, started a movement for centuries which produced illumination of literature, art, science and numerous efforts of public beneficence. This was a movement whose motive force was not some additional accession of knowledge or power or urging of some overwhelming passion. It was an inspiration for freedom, the freedom which enables us to realize *dharma,* the truth of Eternal Man.

"Lao-tze in one of his utterances has said: 'Those who have virtue (*dharma*) attend to their obligations; those who have no virtue attend to their claims.' Progress which is not related to an inner *dharma,* but to an attraction which is external, seeks to satisfy our endless claims. But civilization, which is an ideal, gives us the abundant power to renounce, which is the power that realizes the infinite and inspires creation."[340]

"In India, poetry and philosophy have walked hand in hand, only because the latter has claimed its right to guide men to the practical path of their life's fulfillment. What is that fulfillment? It is our freedom in truth, which has for its prayer: Lead us from the unreal to reality.

For *satyam* is *anandam,* the Real is Joy."[341]

Well-known musicians, painters, and writers live on in the lives of millions of future generations who enjoy the gifts they have created. The valuable legacy they leave to the world is not

---

[340] Rabindranath Tagore, *The Religion of Man,* p. 154.

[341] Ibid., p. 183.

of riches but in how they used their great artistic gifts. Yet all of us have been endowed with some gift which we can use to benefit humanity. I have always been surprised by the number of well-meaning people with a genuine desire to help who have looked at the enormity facing humanity and said, "The problem is too big—there is nothing I, as an individual, can do to help." The truth is that there are few problems confronting humanity that are incapable of solution if only a sufficient number of human beings apply their hearts and energies.[342]

Eternal Beauty

The Supreme Critic on all the errors of the past and the present, and the only prophet of that which must be, is that great nature in which we rest as the earth lies in the soft arms of the atmosphere; that Unity, that Over-soul, within which every man's particular being is contained and made one with all other; that common heart of which all sincere conversation is the worship, to which all right action is submission; that overpowering reality which confutes our tricks and talents, and constrains every one to pass for what he is, and to speak from his character and not from his tongue, and which evermore tends to pass into our thought and hand and become wisdom and virtue and power and beauty. We live in succession, in division, in parts, in particles. Meantime within man is the soul of the whole; the wise silence; the universal beauty, the eternal ONE. And this deep power in which we exist and whose beatitude is all accessible to us, is not only self-sufficing and perfect in every hour, but the act of seeing and the thing seen, the seer and the spectacle, the subject and the object, are one. We see the world, piece by piece, as the sun, the moon, the animal, the tree; but the whole, of which these are the shining parts, is the soul. Only by the vision of that Wisdom can the horoscope of

[342] Sue Ryder in *Women of Vision* by Dorothy Stewart, p. 147.

~ "Eternal Beauty" is excerpted from Emerson, *Essays by Ralph Waldo Emerson, First Series*, pp. 202-205.

the ages be read, and by falling back on our better thoughts, by yielding to the spirit of prophecy which is innate in every man that we can know what it saith. Every man's words who speaks from that life must sound vain to those who do not dwell in the sane thought on their own part. I dare not speak for it. My words do not carry its august sense; they fall short and cold. Only itself can inspire whom it will, and behold! Their speech shall be lyrical, and sweet, and universal as the rising of the wind. Yet I desire, even by profane words, if sacred I may not use, to indicate the haven of this deity and to report what hints I have collected of the transcendent simplicity and energy of the Highest Law.

If we consider what happens in conversation, in reveries, in remorse, in times of passion, in surprises, in the instructions of dreams, wherein often we see ourselves in masquerade—the droll disguises only magnifying and enhancing a real element and forcing it on our distinct notice—we shall catch many hints that will broaden and lighten into knowledge of the secret of nature. All goes to show that the soul in man is not an organ, but animates and exercises all the organs; is not a function, like the power of memory, of calculation, of comparison—but uses these as hands and feet; is not a faculty, but a light; is not the intellect or the will, but the master of the intellect and the will—is the vast background of our being, in which they lie—an immensity not possessed and that cannot be possessed. From within or from behind, a light shines through us upon things and makes us aware that we are nothing, but the light is all. A man is the façade of a temple wherein all wisdom and all good abide. What we commonly call man, the eating, drinking, planting, counting man, does not, as we know him, represent himself, but misrepresents himself. Him we do not respect, but the soul, whose organ he is, would he let it appear through his action, would make our knees bend. When it breathes through his intellect, it is genius; when it breathes through his will, it is virtue; when it flows through his affection, it is love. And the blindness of the intellect begins when it would be something of itself. The weakness of the will begins when the individual would be something of himself. All reform aims in some one particular to let the great soul have its way through us; in other words, to engage us to obey.

Of this pure nature every man is at some time sensible. Language cannot paint it with his colors. It is too subtle. It is undefinable, unmeasurable; but we know that it pervades and contains us. We know that all spiritual being is in man. A wise old proverb says, "God comes to see us without a bell:" that is, as there is no screen or ceiling between our heads and the infinite heavens, so is there no bar or wall in the soul, where man, the effect, ceases, and God, the cause, begins. The walls are taken away. We lie open on one side to the deeps of spiritual nature, to all the attributes of God. Justice we see and know, Love, Freedom, Power. These natures no man ever got above, but always they tower over us, and most in the moment when our interests tempt us to wound them.

The sovereignty of this nature whereof we speak is made known by its independency of those limitations which circumscribe us on every hand. The soul circumscribeth all things. As I have said, it contradicts all experience. In like manner it abolishes time and space. The influence of the senses has in most men overpowered the mind to that degree that the walls of time and space have come to look solid, real, and insurmountable; and to speak with levity of these limits is, in the world, the sign of insanity. Yet time and space are but inverse measures of the force of the soul. A man is capable of abolishing them both. The spirit sports with time—

Can crowd eternity into an hour,
Or stretch an hour to eternity.

We are often made to feel that there is another youth and age than that which is measured from the year of our natural birth. Some thoughts always find us young, and keep us so. Such a thought is the love of the universal and eternal beauty. Every man parts from that contemplation with the feeling that it rather belongs to ages than to mortal life. The least activity of the intellectual powers redeems us in a degree from the influences of time. In sickness, in languor, give us a strain of poetry or a profound sentence, and we are refreshed; or produce a volume of Plato or Shakespeare, or remind us of their names, and instantly we come into a feeling of longevity. See how the deep divine thought demolishes centuries and millenniums, and makes itself present through all ages.

Centering Clay

The artist in man knows that we can't suddenly be a certain way—we can't suddenly be free, be independent, be mature, be peaceful. We have to become what we are growing to be. Inner growth takes time. And trust. It takes a sense of the seed forces in ourselves, and some knowledge of the stages of development, seasons, deaths and rebirths, something about a feel for life processes at work, patience. It takes patience and steadiness and humor and commitment, like a farmer has.

Therefore art teachers understand the need both for unsupervised time and for instruction. They understand that the occupations of one's leisure are the deepest labors of one's being; are, indeed, one's work

We are not meant to work for wages but for wholeness. What is wholeness? Ah, a good question . . . it isn't half persons; it isn't half truths. It is a good question. The question is the quest.

In an Irish fairy story the hero goes a long journey on a shaggy nag who carries him safely through thick and thin and then asks to be slain in order that the threshold to the city be safely crossed and the trusted horse-sense be allowed to change into its next shape: a radiant being. It is especially difficult in our day to give up the picture one has of oneself and of truth and to keep ourselves open to transformation.

How does transformation come about? Not only of consciousness but of character? This is one of the questions in the new science of man. In my book *Centering* I wrestle with it in various ways, through the experiences which have taught me something: through the potter's craft, the poet's craft, the teacher's craft, and the evolution of person through the ordeals of life. Someone else would come to the question from other directions.

The central images in the book are taken from the potter's craft: centering. and the ordeal by fire. But both are archetypal and occur in other contexts as well. Centering is a term used by the Quakers for a feeling of flowing toward a common center in their meetings for worship.

~ "Centering Clay" is excerpted from pp. 53-57 of *The Crossing Point* © 1973 by M.C. Richards and reprinted by permission of Wesleyan University Press.

It is also an ancient Sanskrit term used in spiritual disciplines of the East. What it means, I think, is to feel the whole in every part. When you center clay on the potter's wheel, you take a lump of clay, and by moving it upwards into a cone and outwards into a plane, you create a condition of balance between the outside and the inside, so that when you touch the clay at a single point. the whole mass is affected. Centering has nothing to do with a center as a place. It has to do with bringing the totality of the clay into an unwobbling pivot, the equilibrium distributed throughout in an even grain. The substance of the clay has to be brought to a condition of stillness at the same time that it is spinning, it has to be worked so that there is no difference in quality between the surface and the interior, a balance between the inner consistency and influences from without. So that when we stick our fingers into it to open it up into a vessel, the inside will be as firm and malleable as the outside. And will be able to create a space which will be a container. It is poetic and mysterious and yet very actual and concrete and messy and common clay. COMMON CLAY! WHAT'S THAT?

Centering is a spiritual discipline working through the body, on earth as it is in heaven, as the bard said. It is a dialogue between the clay and the hand, or rather between the clay and the person.

The art of the fire is likewise archetypal: practiced by the alchemists of old, as well as by present-day studio potters, and there is a way of looking at inner development also as an art of the fire.

The goal of alchemy was the transformation of crude substance into refined substance. The alchemists were trying to create a philosopher's stone which would turn lead into gold. The philosopher's stone, they said, contained all the opposites: it was both impermeable and waxlike. It was both indestructible and able to be melted down. It was a stone, but it was a healing unguent as well. Its value was judged by the number of times it could melt down and recoagulate.

That which contains opposite extremes within a whole has healing and transforming properties.

In the potter's art, mud turns to stone. Goosh turns into a vessel. By means of fire.

In life itself, it is the capacity of being open, a feminine receptivity of soul, into which new awareness may play. It is interesting to me that the Greek word for cell is kytos, which means hollow vessel. And it was interesting to the psychologist Jung that the feminine aspect of the soul is least developed among us; part of our task today is to develop it consciously. And it was also interesting to him in this connection that the Catholic Church officially declared the assumption of the Virgin Mary (the feminine) into the heavenly family, indicating a development in the inner world of beings whom he calls Archetypes. He found also an increasing experience of the Christ archetype in the individual psyche.

Centering is a discipline of surrendering in this sense of receptivity, and of integrating. Moving in from the outside toward a center which is not a space but a function, a balance, a feature; distributing the center itself from within outwards. By undergoing a change on the inside, the clay comes as we say into center: which is a quality, not a place.

It is a discipline because one is often tempted to say "nay" rather than "yea" to life, and centering is a process of bringing in rather than of leaving out. As Emerson said, "Do the thing, and you have the power. He who does not do the thing, has not the power." There is no substitute for experience.

To see the whole in every part leads to a new kind of teaching. Last year, when asked to teach a design class, I presented design in relation not only to graphic art but to economics, government, poetry, sculpture, architecture, philosophy, natural science. Since it is an ingredient of the whole, many features may be examined in its light.

Or take clay. In a three weeks course at a loosely structured school where my students ranged in age from five to fifteen and parents and teachers dropped in as well, I mentioned the relation of clay to geology, chemistry, ancient civilizations, the development of writing, industrial ceramics, building materials, artistic forming, agriculture, and asked them to contribute their "wild connections"—as Robert Frost says, it is the poet's freedom to make wild connections. Of course they are not wild at all in the sense of being implausible. They are wild in the sense of being natural, like wilderness is. The connections we make, wild, are in the nature of things. Poetry is a branch of the same vine from which science grows. The children made up songs and poems about the clay: what it is and does. In musical speech. That is to say, speech where we are conscious of the music, which we aren't mostly, though it is playing all the time. Our ears are so sleeping we only begin to listen when someone says HARK! . . .

Writers are entering the classroom, rather than sending their texts. Children are being encouraged to make their own books as well as to respect those made by others: to have an eye for the beauty of a book to the eye and the hand, as well as its content. Handicraft is being offered as an ingredient of other subjects. Movement and drama are part of history. Visual perception is part of geography. Technical knowledge is part of art. Number is part of music. And rhythm is part of physiology. Man and his knowledge and feeling and deeds are a continuous organism. The time is ripe for leadership by people who have a point of view about education which awakens the spirit and enriches relationships.

An acknowledgement of man as intuitive, imaginative, inspired, whatever form his life takes, whatever his work, may add to the curriculum of our schools.

What we know may be only what we are able to ask. The asking may be a doorway into our next development.

Courage, Strength, and Vigilant Awareness
(*Shajā'ah*, *Quwwah*, and *Taqwā*)

O you who have attained to faith!
Stand firmly in your devotion to God,
bearing witness to the truth in complete fairness;
and never let hatred of anyone
lead you to make the mistake of deviating from justice.
Be just: this is the closest to being God-conscious.
And remain conscious of God:
truly, God is well-aware of all that you do.
[*Sūrah al-Mā'idah* 5:8]

Whoever supports a good cause shall have a share in its blessings;
and whoever supports an evil cause shall be answerable for his part in it:
for, indeed, God watches over everything.
[*Sūrah an-Nisā'* 4:85]

If anyone slays a single soul—
unless it be in punishment for murder
or for spreading corruption on earth—
it shall be as though he had slain all humankind;
whereas, if anyone saves a life,
it shall be as though he had saved the lives of all humanity.
[*Sūrah al-Mā'idah* 5:32]

And God sets forth as an example to those who have faith
the wife of Pharaoh:
witness, she said: "O my Sustainer!
Build for me in nearness to You a mansion in the Garden
and save me from Pharaoh and his actions
and save me from those who do wrong";
also Mary, the daughter of 'Imran, who guarded her chastity,
and We breathed into her of Our spirit,

and she witnessed to the truth of the words of her Sustainer
and of His revelations and was one of those devoted.
[*Sūrah at-Taḥrīm* 66:11-12]

See how God has purchased of the faithful
their lives and their possessions;
in return, theirs is the Garden,
and so they struggle in God's way.
[*Sūrah at-Tawbah* 9:111]

Courage and truth are always found together—like falsehood and cowardice. ~ Ḥaḍrat ᶜAlī

Imām ᶜAlī [also] said, "Fear of Allāh restrains the self and prevents it from acts of disobedience." "The best of actions is to achieve a balance between fear and hope."[343]

Fear of Allāh is the lamp of the heart; by it the believer observes the good and the bad in it, and the reins of knowledge restrain the self from oppression and injustice. The sign of this fear is its constant vigil in secret and in the open, and it issues only from an exceeding gentleness and a complete gnosis. In this respect Allāh says, *Only those of His servants who are possessed of knowledge fear Allāh; surely Allāh is Mighty, Forgiving.* [*Sūrah al-Fāṭir* 35:28].[344]

The virtue of courage *(shujaᶜah)* grows, in part, out of the virtue of *khawf;* when the Fear of God occupies the heart, it leaves no room for any other fear. There is the courage to see, the courage to feel, the courage to question, the courage to take an unpopular stand, the courage to ask for help, the courage to bear one's burdens in silence, the courage to act, and the courage to refrain from acting. Courage is the virtue—along with

[343] Haeri, *Prophetic Traditions of Islām*, p. 178 (al-Ḥākim, I, 406).
[344] Ibid., p. 108 (al-ᶜĪnāthī, II, 1).

vigilance (*taqwā*)—which gives us the ability to practice every other virtue. What is generosity, or trustworthiness, or patience, or dignity, without courage? The central nature of the virtue of courage is denoted by the English word for it, which means "the quality of having heart." In the words of the Qur'ān, *Establish worship and enjoin kindness and forbid iniquity, and persevere whatever may befall thee. Lo! That is of the steadfast heart of things.* [*Sūrah Luqmān* 31:17]. The Prophet Muḥammad ﷺ possessed both the courage to act and the courage to endure (*iḥtimāl*). During his ten years in Madīnah he organized seventy-four military campaigns, leading twenty-four of them in person—though Abbās Hussein has estimated that during his entire life he spent no more than 89 days in battle. But his endurance, and his suppression of rage (*khaẓm al-ghayẓ*) were also great. This was evident during the period of oppression the Muslims endured in Makkah before the *hijrah*, especially in the year when both his beloved wife Khadījah and his protector Abū Ṭālib died.

In order to develop courage, we need to be honest with ourselves about what we are really afraid of. There is physical courage, moral courage and spiritual courage. Physical courage is the courage to risk our physical well-being. Moral courage is the courage to risk psychological discomfort in order to do what is right, which may require courage to face the uncomfortable fact that we are not who we thought we were, or that people we believed we knew are radically different from our mental image of them. And spiritual courage is the willingness to acknowledge, in the face of Absolute Reality, that we ourselves are nothing—the willingness to be annihilated in the presence of God.[345]

"During the war, I was simply terrified by air raids, and it was my lot to be in every one that happened in London. I tried

---

[345] Charles Upton, contributor.

to build up my courage by reason and prayer, etc., etc. Then one day I realized quite suddenly: As long as I try not to be afraid I shall be worse, and I shall show it one day and break. What God is asking of me, to do for suffering humanity, is to be afraid, to accept it, and put up with it. Instead of kidding myself and trying to minimize the danger or to find some distraction from it, I said to myself: 'For as long as this raid lasts—an hour, or eight hours—you are going to be terrified, so you must carry on and be terrified, that's all.'

"At once the strain ceased. Oh yes, I was terrified. But all that time I felt that God had put his hand right down through all the well upon well of darkness and horror between Him and me and was holding the central point of my soul; and I knew that however afraid I was then, it would not, even could not, break me. It's only when we try not to experience our special suffering that it can really break us."[346]

Wait on the Lord: be of good courage, and he shall strengthen your heart; wait, I say, on the Lord. (The Bible, Psalm 27:14)

Spiritual courage—whether virtual or fully actualized—is the root of moral and physical courage. It is possible to have a degree of moral courage in service to principles and ideals, and to take personal satisfaction in it, but such courage is imperfect because in this case our real "lord" is our own self-image, not the principles we claim to serve. True courage in service to principles will make us willing to sacrifice in their name not only our physical well-being but also our moral self-satisfaction.

As for physical courage, there is a kind of raw bravery which delights in danger. Such bravery is one element of true courage, and can sometimes ripen until it reaches the level of that virtue. But physical bravery can also be a form of sensationalism and

[346] Caryll Houselander in *Women of Vision* by Dorothy Stewart, p. 82.

self-indulgence; a way of avoiding the call to develop moral and spiritual courage; even an unconscious impulse to suicide, which Islām expressly forbids.

According to Al-Ghazālī, one of the virtues directly related to courage is *khazm al-ghayz*, "suppression of rage." In the words of Ḥaḍrat ʿAlī, "Anger is a raging fire. Whoever can subdue his anger puts out the fire; whoever cannot gets burnt himself." Anger so often deludes us; it convinces that it is power. But my own anger, the anger of the *nafs al-ammara*, is only weakness. God's anger alone can truly be called power.

Sometimes a person with a great deal of physical bravery will dream of dying a hero. . . . An attraction to physical danger requires, and helps us develop, a strong physical vigilance and awareness, but we may also indulge in it as an excuse for not developing subtler kinds of vigilance and awareness on the moral and spiritual levels. . . . The true martyr is not the one who throws his life away, but the one who places that life in service of a moral ideal which is itself subordinate to the one spiritual Reality, even if this means certain death. . . . In the words of the Prophet Muḥammad, "Die before you are made to die." [Be courageous enough to fully surrender the self to God.] This is the true aim and ultimate purpose of courage.[347]

> *Those who are patient in adversity, and true to their word,*
> *and truly devout, and who spend in God's way,*
> *and pray for forgiveness from their innermost hearts before dawn.*
> *God offers signs—and so do the angels*
> *and all who are endowed with knowledge—*
> *that there is no god except God, the Upholder of Justice:*
> *there is no deity but Hu, the Almighty, the Truly Wise.*
> *Witness—*
> *the only true religion in the sight of God is self-surrender to Him.*
> [Sūrah Āl ʿImrān 3:17-19]

---

[347] Charles Upton, contributor.

Surely Allah loves those who are conscious of Him
[*Sūrah at-Tawbah* 9:4]

Commenting on Allāh's words, *Surely Allāh enjoins the doing of justice and the doing of good* [*Sūrah an-Naḥl* 16:90], the Messenger of Allāh has said, "Allāh has gathered the meaning of *taqwā* ([vigilant] awareness of Allāh in one's every action) in this verse." He has also said, "Have *taqwā* of Allāh, for in it lies all goodness." Elsewhere he said, "Whoever desires to be the most noble of men let him have *taqwā* of Allāh."[348]

God's Messenger established a system of rules governing international relations among sovereign states. In other words, he was the first to legislate an international law. Although the concept was not unknown before Islam, international law was very limited—for example, there were no recognized rules for the treatment of prisoners of war. Again, God's Messenger ﷺ established a set of rules to bring a "discipline" to fighting. For example, the following is the order given by him and his true successors to come until the present day to armies dispatched for fighting, an order which had been strictly obeyed by Muslims in their wars as Muslims:

"Always keep fear of God in your mind. Remember that you cannot afford to do anything without His grace. Do not forget that Islam is a mission of peace and love. Do not destroy fruit-trees nor fertile fields in your paths. Be just, and spare the feelings of the vanquished. Respect all religious persons who live in hermitages or convents and spare their edifices. Do not kill civilians. Do not outrage the chastity of women and the honour of the conquered. Do not harm old people and children. Do not accept any gifts from the civil population of any place. Do not billet your soldiers or officers in the houses of civilians."[349]

---

[348] Haeri, *Prophetic Traditions of Islām*, p. 11 (*Mishkāt*, 45-46).

[349] Gulen, *Prophet Mohammed, The Infinite Light*, Vol. II, pp. 84-85.

Luqmān told his son, "There are three kinds of people who can be recognized only at three times: a forbearing man at the time of anger, a courageous man at the time of war, and a brother at the time he is needed."[350]

Imām ᶜAlī has said, 'There is no honour more worthy than Islām, nothing more noble than *taqwā,* and no fortress stronger than carefulness in one's behavior.'[351]

Commenting on the meaning of *taqwā*, Imām ᶜAlī has said, "Truly *taqwā* of Allāh is a medicine for your hearts' illness, and sight for the blindness of your hearts, a cure for your bodies' sickness and a correction of whatever is wrong in your breasts. It is a purification of your character, a making clear of the dimness of your sight; it is a safety from your agitation and fear, and a light for the blackness of your gloom.[352]

Taqwā is the gatherer of all goodnesses, and the inner truth of *taqwā* is protecting one's self from God's punishment by means of obedience to Him, just as it is said, "So-and-so protected himself with his shield."[353]

God Most High says, *God is watchful over all things* [*Sūrah al-Aḥzāb* 33:52].

On the authority of Jarir ibn ᶜAbdallāh al-Bajalli, it is told that Gabriel came to the Prophet ﷺ in the form of a man. He asked, "O Muḥammad, what is *īmān*?" He replied, "It is that you believe in God, His angels, His books, His messengers, and destiny—its good and evil, its sweetness and bitterness." He said, "You have spoken the truth." Jarir remarked, "We were

[350] Al-Qushayri, *Principles of Sufism*, p. 245.

[351] Haeri, *Prophetic Traditions of Islām*, p. 12 (al-Ashtarī, II, 39).

[352] Ibid., p. 12 (*Nahj*, I, 275).

[353] Al-Qushayri, *Principles of Sufism*, p. 25.

astonished at his confirming the truth of what the Prophet said, when he had asked him a question and then confirmed the answer." He then commanded, "Tell me, what is *islām*?" He replied, "*Islām* is that you establish regular prayer, give the *zakāt*, fast the month of Ramadān, and perform the pilgrimage to the House." He confirmed, "You have spoken the truth." He then asked, "Tell me, what is *iḥsān*?" The Prophet replied, "*Iḥsān* is that you worship God as if you see Him, for if you do not see Him, yet He sees you." He averred, "You have spoken the truth." The saying of the Prophet, "For if you do not see Him, yet He sees you," is an indication of the state of vigilant awareness, because vigilant awareness is the servant's knowledge of the Lord's constant awareness of him. So his constancy in this knowledge is vigilant awareness of his Lord, and this is the source of all good for him. He will come to this vigilant awareness only after he has fully called himself to account, for when he has called himself to account for what has happened in the past, makes right his state in the present, keeps firmly to the path of Truth, makes good his relationship with God by compliance of his heart, and guards his breaths against forgetfulness of God Most High, observing God Most High in all his states, then he knows that God (may He be exalted!) is watchful over him and that He is near to his heart. He knows his states, He sees his deeds, and He hears his words. The one who is heedless of all this is distant from the beginning of attainment and [how much more so] from the inner truths of nearness.[354]

It is said that Ibn ʿUmar was on a journey when he saw a boy tending some sheep. He asked him, "Will you sell one of these sheep?" The boy replied, "They are not mine." So Ibn ʿUmar suggested, "[You could] tell the owner of the flock that a wolf made off with one of them." The boy said, "And where is God?" After that for some time Ibn ʿUmar would repeat,

---

[354] Ibid., pp.157-158.

"That slave said, 'And where is God?'"[355]

> When Ibn ᶜAtaʾ was asked, "What is the best act of worship?" he answered, "Vigilant awareness of God at all times." Ibrāhīm al-Khawāṣṣ said, "Observance bequeaths vigilant awareness; this awareness bequeaths inner and outer devotion to God Most High." Abū ᶜUthmān al-Maghrībī noted, "The best things man imposes on his soul in this path are calling the self to account, vigilant awareness, and regulating his actions by knowledge."[356]

Continually we are called to courage . . . the courage to wrestle with the demands and desires of our egos, the courage under the light of knowledge to be true to our most essential self and to develop our capacities and potential as human beings, the courage to bear whatever burdens we are given and to engage in the struggle for that which is most rightful within ourselves and within our communities and our world . . . the courage to become true servants. Real strength lies in self-control, whether it be discipline of the body, mind, or heart. Real courage is to continually take responsibility for the life we are living and at any moment to be ready to face our Creator, realizing that no matter where we turn, the Face of our Creator is before us.

> I heard the master Abū ᶜAlī ad-Daqqāq explain, "There are three degrees of steadfastness: setting things upright (*taqwīm*), making things sound and straight (*iqāma*), and being upright (*istiqāma*). *Taqwīm* concerns discipline of the soul; *iqāma*, refinement of the heart; and *istiqāma*, bringing the inmost being near to God."[357]

---

[355] Ibid., pp. 159-160.
[356] Ibid., p. 161.
[357] Ibid., p. 183.

Wrestling

Know that wrestling is a popular skill, approved by kings and rulers. Those who practice it do so for the most part in purity and honesty.

If asked: With whom did this art originate? Say: With the children of Jacob. He knew it and taught it to his sons, saying: Know that proficiency in this will be useful in repelling enemies.

It is also said that wrestling was one of the four hundred and forty skills that Adam knew. It is further related that the Prophet wrestled Abū Jahl, . . . In summary, this skill is attributed to the prophets and saints. . . .

If asked: What is the significance of wrestling? Say: It alters a man's character. The truth of this is demonstrated by the fact that there is always a wrestling match between praiseworthy qualities and blameworthy behavior. That is, each of those inclinations strives to overcome its opposite. Indeed, when one looks at the truth of it, . . . generosity and niggardliness, piety and debauchery, certainty and doubt, righteousness and corruption, beauty and ugliness, humility and arrogance, love and hate, modesty and shamelessness, attendance and neglect, mercy and cruelty, prudence and censure, etc., are always wrestling each other. The art of wrestling helps the approved qualities, using the strength of asceticism, to pin the evil characteristics.

If asked: What is the foundation of wrestling? Say: Wisdom and skill.

If asked: What about strength? Say: Strength has no credit for the reason that there are animals possessing great strength; but, since they lack knowledge, they are not held in awe.

If asked: What about wisdom with strength? Say: That is extremely good, for as the learned have said, strength without wisdom is like an unjust king. Wisdom without strength is like a just king without an army. When wisdom and strength work together, they achieve results.

If asked: Is wrestling a science or an art? Say: It is science united with art. If someone learns something, it is possible that he may not use it. In

---

~ "Wrestling" is excerpted from Sabzawārī, *The Royal Book of Spiritual Chivalry*, pp. 299-303.

this art, if there is no science, one cannot practice it. As a result, science and art complement each other.

If asked: How many are the rules of conduct for the masters of wrestling? Say: Twelve.

1. A wrestler must keep himself clean and healthy.
2. He must lead his trainees in cleanliness.
3. He must not be stingy and withhold things from them.
4. He must be kind to them.
5. He must not covet their property.
6. He must teach them according to their potential.
7. He must not be rude or deceptive with them.
8. He must not wish ill for his trainees.
9. If someone does not wrestle well, the master should not say: You have wrestled badly. Instead, he should speak to him gently.
10. If he gives instructions on the field of trial, he should speak discreetly so that the opponent not hear.
11. He must be proficient in the techniques of wrestling.
12. He must not forget to commemorate his own spiritual mentor and master at each competition.

If asked: How many are the rules of conduct for the trainees? Say: They are also twelve.

1. A trainee must be honest.
2. He must be devout and have an honest livelihood.
3. He must be well-behaved and of good character.
4. He must be well-intentioned.
5. He must not be deficient in obeying God.
6. He must serve his master sincerely.
7. He must not envy anyone.
8. He must not be stingy, but devote all he possesses to his guide.
9. He must be united with the other trainees in heart and soul.
10. He must not solicit alms.
11. He must not become conceited about his strength.
12. He must not delight in his opponent's defeat. . . .

If asked: Who may be called a champion? Say: He who has twelve qualities:

1. Fear of God
2. Obedience to religious law
3. A strong body
4. A good manner of speaking
5. Courage
6. Impeccable wisdom
7. Complete patience
8. Absolute knowledge
9. Unceasing effort
10. A pleasing character
11. Abstention from what is unlawful
12. Enduring blessing

Justice and Conflict Resolution
(ᶜ*Adl* and *Iṣlāḥ*)

And to you We have sent this Book
of the Truth, confirming the truth
of whatever remains of earlier revelations
and guarding what is true within.
Judge in accordance with what God has bestowed from on high,
and do not follow erring views,
forsaking the truth that has come to you.
For every one of you have We designated a law and a way of life.
And if God had so willed,
He could surely have made you all one single community:
but He willed it otherwise in order to test you
by means of what He has bestowed on you.
Strive, then, with one another in doing good!
Your goal is God;
and then He will make you understand
the truth of everything in which you have differed.
[*Sūrah al-Māᶜidah* 5:48]

God commands justice, the doing of good,
and generosity to your relatives
and He forbids all shameful deeds and injustice and rebellion;
He instructs you so that you may receive counsel.
Fulfill the bond with God when you have entered into it
and do not break your oaths after you have confirmed them;
indeed you have made God your assurance;
for God knows all that you do.
And don't be like a woman who breaks into untwisted strands
the yarn that she has spun after it has been strengthened.
Nor take oaths to deceive between yourselves
lest one group should be more numerous than another;
for God will test you by this,

and on the Day of Reckoning He will certainly make clear to you
the truth of all that about which you disagree.
[*Sūrah an-Naḥl* 16:90-92]

O you who have attained to faith!
Always be steadfast in upholding justice,
bearing witness to the truth for God's sake,
even though it may be against your own selves
or your parents and kinsfolk.
Whether the person concerned be rich or poor,
God's claim takes precedence over the claims of either.
Do not, then, follow your own desires,
that you might not turn aside from that which is just.
For if you distort the truth, witness,
God is indeed well-aware of all that you do!
[*Sūrah an-Nisā*ᶜ 4:135]

If one honors God's sacred commandments,
it will multiply to your own good in your Sustainer's sight.
[*Sūrah al-Ḥajj* 22:30]

Witness, God instructs you
to deliver all that you have been entrusted with
to those who are entitled to it,
and whenever you judge between people, to judge with justice.
Truly, how excellent is that which God urges you to do;
truly, God is All-hearing, All-seeing.
[*Sūrah an-Nisā*ᶜ 4:58]

Invite to the way of your Lord with wisdom and beautiful urging;
and discuss with them in the best and most gracious manner
for your Lord knows best who strays from His Path
and who receives guidance.
And if you do engage them,
respond to them no worse than they respond to you;

but if you show patience that is indeed best for those who are patient.
Then be patient, always remembering that your patience is from God;
and do not grieve over them;
and do not worry yourself because of their plots.
For God is with those who are carefully conscious of Him
and those who do good.
[*Sūrah an-Naḥl* 16:125-128]

And so, do not kill your children for fear of poverty:
it is We Who shall provide sustenance for them as well as for you.
Truly, killing them is a great sin.
And do not approach adultery—
for, behold, it is an abomination and an evil way.
And do not take any human being's life—
which God has willed to be sacred—
except in the pursuit of justice.
[*Sūrah al-Isrā*ᶜ 17:31-33]

We have sent our messengers with clear signs,
and through them We bestowed revelation and a balance
so that people might behave with justice;
and We sent down iron in which is awesome power
as well as many benefits for humankind,
that God might test who it is that will help unseen
Him and His messengers;
for truly, God is the Lord of All Power, Almighty.
[*Sūrah al-Ḥadīd* 57:25]

Woe to those who commerce in fraud,
those who when they are to receive from other people
exact full measure,
but when they must measure out give less than is due.
Do they think they won't be called to account—
on an awesome day,
a day when all humankind will stand
before the Sustainer of all Worlds?
[*Sūrah al-Muṭaffifīn* 83:1-6]

The faithful are but a single brotherhood.
So make peace between your two contending siblings,
and remain conscious of God
so that you may be graced with God's Mercy.

[*Sūrah al-Ḥujurāt* 49:10]

And do not call on another god besides God.
There is no god but He.
Everything is perishing except His Face.
With him rests all Judgment,
and to Him will you all return.

[*Sūrah al-Qaṣaṣ* 28:88]

Justice is essentially balance; to do justice is to correct imbalances, in outer situations as well as within one's own soul. The central criterion of justice in Islām is the Holy Qur'ān, which at times contradicted the personal opinions and criticized the behavior even of the Prophet himself. Once when he was giving audience, a blind man tried to get his attention in a way that annoyed him; he frowned and turned away. In response to this, he received the *sūrah* "He Frowned" [*Sūrah ʿAbasa* 80], which corrected his behavior.

In the words of Ḥaḍrat ʿAlī, "the best form of justice is succoring the oppressed"—not only the politically oppressed, but also those who are made outcasts, ignored, or ridiculed by society. Injustice is basically imbalance—and one of the great imbalances in worldly society is *imbalance of attention.* Those who are powerful or charismatic command all the attention, while those who are not, no matter how sincere or virtuous they may be, are deprived of it. Attention is like food: to crave it is like gluttony, but to be severely deprived of it is a kind of starvation. And while it is the better part of virtue not to *demand* attention, the virtue of justice requires that we *give* everyone the attention he or she needs—no more, but certainly no less. In the *ḥadīth* literature we see how the *sunnah* of the Prophet was to make no distinction between the great and the humble in granting audiences (though in the course of things he naturally spent more time with his close companions than with anyone else). This openness to approach became the model and the ideal for all future Muslim rulers.[358]

According to the Qur'ān every human being is honored solely by virtue of being human, without any further consideration of race, origin, or creed. The Qur'ān says, *We have honored the children of Adam, provided them with transport on land and sea, and conferred on them special favors above a great part of Our creation* [*Sūrah al-Isrā*ᶜ 17:70].

Islām emphasizes the oneness of humanity as a family: *O mankind, fear your Guardian Lord, who created you from a single self and created—out of it—its mate, and made from them twain scattered* [*like seeds*] *countless men and women* [*Sūrah an-Nisā*ᶜ 4:1]. All people equally possess basic human rights, including the right to freely choose one's religion without coercion, for within Islām the space of the "other" is well-preserved and protected. Islām is not an exclusive religion, and no human being, clergy or otherwise, is permitted to set limits on God's mercy and forgiveness, or to speak on His behalf in assigning reward or punishment. The ultimate judge is God Himself: *Your return in the end is toward Allāh. . . . He will tell you the truth of the things wherein you disputed* [*Sūrah al-An*ᶜ*ām* 6:164].[359]

People are equal like the teeth of a comb. You are all from Adam: and Adam is from dust. There is no superiority of white over black, nor of Arab over non-Arab, except by piety. (A *ḥadīth* of the Prophet Muḥammad)[360]

From amongst humanity, Jews and Christians are the nearest to Muslims and are given the honorary title of *People of the*

---

[358] Charles Upton, contributor.

[359] Hathout, *Reading the Muslim Mind*, p. 13.

[360] Ibid., p. 82.

Book. They are fellow believers in the One God and the recipients of scriptures from Him. They share the belief in the line of prophethood, and many of our Jewish and Christian friends are taken by surprise when they learn that the biblical prophets are also Islamic prophets. The three religions share a common moral code. The Qur᾽ān says,

Say: "We believe in God, and the revelation given to us, and the revelation given to Abraham, Ishmael, Isaac, Jacob and the Tribes, and that given to Moses and Jesus, and that given to [*all*] *the prophets from their Lord: We make no distinction between one and another of them, and to Him we are submitters."*"[*Sūrah al-Baqarah* 2:136].

The word *Islām* literally means "submission to the will of God."[361]

The Prophet said, "Support your brother whether right or wrong." Thereupon he was asked: "We (understand) supporting him if he is right, but how could we support him if he was wrong?" The Prophet answered: "By preventing him from doing wrong: for this is his real (help) support."[362]

And if two parties of the faithful fall to fighting, then make peace between them. And if one party of them does wrong to the other, fight that which does wrong till it returns to the ordinance of Allāh; then, if it returns, make peace between them justly, and act equitably. Witness! Allāh loves the equitable. [*Sūrah al-Ḥujurāt* 49:9].

Justice is a comprehensive term. It includes justice to the self, justice to [one's] fellow man, and justice to the created world.

Justice to the self is the core of justice. The Qur᾽ān declares: *O you who have faith! Stand firmly for justice, as witnesses before God, even if it is against your own selves.* [*Sūrah an-Nisā*ᶜ 4:135]

In another passage it declares: *O you who have faith! Be stead-*

[361] Ibid., p. 14.

[362] Ibid., p. 86.

fast before God, as witnesses for justice. [*Sūrah al-Mā*ᶜ*idah* 5:8]

The Prophet Muḥammad said, "Neither be an oppressor, nor be an oppressed one."

Justice to the self implies that man has a proper balance and perspective of his own self, knows who he is, understands his position in the cosmos and his relationship to the Creator. If man assumes that he is totally self-sufficient and autonomous, as did the Pharaohs, he forgets that there are ethical bounds to his actions and he becomes an oppressor. On the other hand, if he forgets his pristine relationship to the Divine, he leaves himself open to injustice. There is in man an innate, universal craving to belong, to build his life around an anchor. If this anchor is not the presence of God then some other anchor moves in to take His place. Man is neither an unfettered "superman" without bounds, nor is he a helpless creature who cannot defend his rights.

History has shown time and again that when man loses sight of his proper position in the scheme of creation he brings ruin on himself and others.[363]

Woman is the co-equal of man, partner in the moral regency bestowed upon humankind. The rights of both men and women derive from the Creator, and each is responsible before Him for his/her deeds.

The Qur'ān declares: *O humankind! Be conscious of your Guardian-Lord, Who created you from a single Soul, created of like nature your spouses, and from them twain scattered [like seeds] countless men and women. Be conscious of your Creator, through Whom you demand your mutual rights, and revere the wombs [that bore you], for God ever watches over you.* [*Sūrah an-Nisā*ᶜ 4:1].

Certain aspects of the relationships between men and women deserve closer examination.

---

[363] Dr. Nazeer Ahmed, *What Makes Us Human? A Spiritual Perspective* (Concord, California: American Institute of Islamic History and Culture, 2000), pp. 124-125.

Men and women have like nature and are created by God.

It is astonishing that this most obvious fact has to be reiterated in this day and age. . . .

Men and women alike are heirs to the moral regency bestowed upon humankind.

The spiritual view offered by the Qur'ān has no concept of "original sin" in it. Both Adam and Eve erred but when they repented together, Divine Love turned to them in forgiveness and promised them guidance. This spiritual view emancipates woman from the dogma that she was the instigator in committing the "original sin." Man and woman have like nature, an equal tendency to err and to seek forgiveness. Each is judged according to what each one earns, *To men is due what they earn, to women what they earn.* [*Sūrah an-Nisā'* 4:32][364]

The question of *social justice* is central to Islamic tradition. In Islām, man's essential "right" is to choose God or reject Him; according to the Qur'ān, *There is no compulsion in religion* [*Sūrah al-Baqarah* 2:256]. It is true that human actions are divided into five categories: Praiseworthy, permitted, indifferent, discouraged, and prohibited. And certainly acts which are praiseworthy, permitted, or indifferent could be defined as those we have a "right" to perform. But human conduct in Islām is defined more in terms of duties than of rights. Clearly we have a *right* not to be oppressed—but since Islām is a religion, our moral duty before God and our neighbor must always come first, which is why our right not to be oppressed is most accurately defined in terms of our *duty not to oppress*.

Justice, in Islām, is fundamentally related not to self-assertion, but to mercy. This is certainly not to say that the oppressed are not enjoined to seek and establish mercy and justice, if necessary by militant means. But this *jihād* to establish a just and merciful society is not to be carried out according to the paradigm of *rebellion*, where the *desires* of the dispossessed are as-

[364] Ibid., pp.133-134.

serted over against the *desires* of the privileged. The paradigm of *jihād* is not the rebellious assertion of desire, but faithfulness to one's human duty to God, by which personal desire in the realm of the soul is dethroned, and God is established as the sovereign ruler of that realm; and so the greater *jihād*, the struggle against the self, is the source and archetype of the lesser. Desire is the "pretender", but God is the true King. Since God is Just, His rule also allows room for the moderate and dignified fulfillment of desire—but this is first an expression of His Mercy, and only secondarily of our rights. Insofar as humanity stands, as *ᶜabd*, before the Absolute Truth, Power, and Mercy of God, the concept of "rights" disappears—except for the one truly inalienable right, the "right to be what we are," the right—which is equally a duty—to embody the *fiṭrah*, to be who God made us to be, and commands us to be. Whatever social forces stand in the way of our fulfillment of this command do indeed violate our human rights.

But humanity is not only *ᶜabd*; we are also *khalīfah*. And as such, we certainly do possess "inalienable rights." The root of human rights, from the Islamic perspective, lies in the "theomorphic" nature of man: we have the right, as well as the duty, to stand as representatives of God's Mercy and Justice in this world. And inseparable from this right is the right not to have our dignity as *khalīfah* violated. We do have the right—which is also a duty—not to submit to degradation at the hands of others, because whoever degrades a human being degrades God's image on earth. It is possible to suffer oppression with dignity, as the Prophet did in the early years of his mission in Mecca; but the time may come when submission to oppression becomes complicity in the degradation of that dignity, at which point it is one's *duty* to assert one's rights. . . .

God may subject us to material and psychological hardship, but He never violates our essential human dignity, since He Himself is the principle of that dignity. And if we really believe this, then we possess the secret which will give us the power to deal with any hardship, any degradation that life throws our way. If we see hardship as coming to us by way of other people's arrogant and selfish actions alone, we will feel degraded; if we see it as coming by way of impersonal circumstances alone, we will feel oppressed. But if we know it ultimately as coming from no one but God, then we will recognize it as a test, or as purification, and our human dignity will in no way be compromised by hardship and suffering.

The society founded by the Prophet in Madīnah was based on a social contract which included both duties and rights; no society which does not define the rights of its citizens can ever be just. Nonetheless, any truly Islamic social system must be based first and foremost on man's duty to God; human rights can only be defined, and pursued, in light of this duty. As *khalīfah* we can and should assert our rights; as *ᶜabd* we must recognize every right as a gift of God, and be careful not to "bite the hand that feeds us.". . .

The highest level of justice requires that we do justice without demanding it, recognizing that our own demands—on our friends, our family, our neighbors, our employer, or our government —may themselves be the major imbalance in our immediate situation, and the only one we really have the power to put right. A story is told of Dhu'l Nūn, the great Egyptian saint. There was a drought in Egypt, and the people implored him to pray to God for rain. He did so, and during his prayer God informed him that he himself was the source of the drought. So he left Egypt, and the rain came.

One of the Names of God is *Al-ᶜAdl*, "The Just." Some people have a hard time understanding how God can be just, since the world is filled with injustice, and nothing happens that is not God's will. Jalālu'ddin Rūmī in the *Fīhi mā fīhi* explains it like this: God is like a baker. A baker needs people to be hungry, otherwise he could not sell his bread; but he also wants people to be well fed, otherwise he would not feed them. Or God is like a doctor: he needs for there to be sick people, otherwise he could not pursue his profession; but he also wants people to be healthy, otherwise he would not heal them.

There is a Mullah Naṣruddīn story which deals with the apparent ambiguities of justice. God's perfect justice is not always visible to us, since our perception is limited to time; but God's Knowledge is eternal:

Once Hodja Naṣruddīn went to the Turkish bath. He was dressed in cheap, shabby clothes, so the attendants were not very excited about serving him; they handed him old towels and the last of the soap. But when he left, they were amazed when he presented each of them with a gold coin.

A few days later he returned, this time dressed in magnificent robes. "If this wealthy man tipped us so handsomely last time" the attendants thought, "if we now attend him as he deserves, he will probably be even more generous." So they treated him like a king. But when Naṣruddīn left the bath, he handed each of them a copper penny. Seeing their puzzled looks, he explained: "The pennies are for *last* time. The gold coins were for *this* time."[365]

Beware of oppressing someone with no defense against you except God. ~ Ḥaḍrat ᶜAlī

An essential aspect of Islamic Justice is balance and strict limitation in warmaking. Women and children are not to be deliberately attacked; noncombatants are not to be harmed.[366] And no one is to be attacked because of his or her religion.

To every community We have appointed ways of worship,
which they ought to observe.
And so, do not let others draw you into arguing about it,
but invite them to your Sustainer:

---

[365] Charles Upton, contributor.

[366] Bukhārī relates, on the authority of ᶜAbdullāh bin ᶜUmar: "Allāh's Messenger disapproved the killing of women and children."

for you are indeed on the right way.
And if they argue with you, say: "God knows best what you are doing."
Indeed God will judge between you on the Day of Resurrection
concerning everything about which you differ.
[*Sūrah al-Ḥajj* 22: 67-69]

[*When*] *the earth shines with the light of her Lord,*
and the Book is set up,
and the Prophets and witnesses are brought,
and it is judged between them with truth,
and they are not wronged.
[*Sūrah az-Zumar* 39:69]

The Prophet said, "If Allāh and his Apostle did not act justly, who would act justly?"

Imām ᶜAlī said, "It is preferable to me that I help to reconcile two people than to give away two dinars in charity."[367]

The Prophet ﷺ was invited to Medina to assist in bringing resolution between the conflicting tribes of Aws and Khazraj:

Through Muṣṭafā their ancient feuds vanished in the light of Islām and purity.

First those enemies became brothers like grapes within a cluster in the garden;

And upon the admonition given in the words, *The truly faithful are like brothers* [*Sūrah al-Ḥujurāt* 49:10], they merged and became as one.

Clustered grapes appear to be brethren; when you squeeze them they become one juice.

Immature and fully mature grapes may be opposed to each other, but when they ripen, they become good friends.[368]

---

[367] Haeri, *Prophetic Traditions of Islām*, p. 203 (al-ᶜĪnāthī, I, 67).

[368] Rūmī, *The Mathnawī of Jalālu'ddin Rūmī,* translated by Nicholson, pp. 414-415, (II:3714-3718), adapted by C. Helminski.

It was here in Medina that the Prophet ﷺ and his small community of early Muslims who had been so persecuted in Mecca at last found sanctuary. To avoid difficulties in merging the immigrant Muslim community with the tribes of Medina, Muḥammad also connected them one to one as brothers.

Continually the Prophet Muḥammad ﷺ worked for the highest justice and the greater unity of human being with human being as brothers/sisters together in service to God. This was evident even in his youth when he helped to resolve the conflict that arose during the rebuilding of the Kaʿbah.

The Rebuilding of the Kaʿbah

Ibn Isḥāq continued, "Then the tribes of Quraysh gathered stones to rebuild [the Kaʿbah], each one collecting them separately. They built it up until it reached the place for the (black) stone but then fell into dispute about it. Each tribe wanted to raise it into its position, regardless of the rest. Eventually they broke up, established alliances, and readied to do battle. . . . Quraysh remained in this confrontation for four or five nights, then they met together in the mosque, debated one another but divided into equal sides. Some scholars of the traditions claim that Abū Umayya b. al-Mughīra b. ʿAbd Allāh b. ʿUmar b. Makhzūm, who was at that time the oldest man in all Quraysh said, 'O Tribe of Quraysh, resolve your dispute by agreeing that the first man who enters by the door of this mosque will decide the issue.' They agreed.

"The first man to enter was the Messenger of God ﷺ and when they saw him they said, 'This is *al-Amīn*, "the trustworthy"; we are satisfied. This is Muḥammad.' When he reached them and they told him of the problem, the Messenger of God ﷺ said: 'Bring me a robe.' One was brought to him and he took the cornerpiece (the 'black stone') and placed it on the robe. Then he said, 'Let each tribe grasp one side of the cloth. Then all raise it up.' This they did until it was at the right spot, whereupon the Messenger of God ﷺ himself positioned it. Then they built above it."[369]

The competing claims of the different clans are like the endless conflicts that arise between different opinions, conflicts which tempt those involved to care more about *being right* than about discovering *what is true*. They are also like the many different and competing voices we often hear inside us when we face a hard decision. When the Quraysh submitted their dispute to the unexpected, they submitted it to God's will. When they accepted Muḥammad ﷺ as arbiter (according to the Name of God *Al-Ḥakam,* The Arbitrator), they submitted to God's decision. And when Muḥammad came up with a plan which allowed every clan to have a part in replacing the Black Stone, he was manifesting a sign of God's Objectivity, which transcends the many and various desires and opinions of you and me. He was also demonstrating how God's Objectivity is also His Unity: only what is beyond us (God in His Name *Al-Jāmi*ᶜ, The Uniter) can truly unite us.[370]

Seeking a Language of Spirit

So the different dogmas of our own age have turned into new idols. We also need the language of Spirit to find liberation. The language of Spirit can increase the well-being of humanity. It would encourage all efforts that aim at adding to the knowledge acquired through science because seeking knowledge infinitely is in itself a part of submission to the Divine Law. However, spirituality would help everyone be more cooperative and just in sharing the fruits of knowledge. And it would lead people to use that knowledge for constructive purposes, not destruction. The language of Spirit could also assist in settling many conflicts and wars on Earth because many of them are the outcome of spiritual ignorance.

---

[369] Ibn Kathīr, *The Life of the Prophet Muḥammad,* Vol. 1, p. 202.

[370] Charles Upton, contributor.

~ "Seeking a Language of Spirit" is excerpted from Aisha Rafea, "The Soul's Longing" in C. Helminski, *Women of Sufism, A Hidden Treasure*, p. 214.

Lack of spiritual knowledge tends to make humans, individuals, and states think that they cannot be safe and strong unless they destroy others or use them for their own egoistic objectives. With spiritual awareness people would come to realize that when they hurt others for no reason, they hurt their own spirits, and diminish themselves spiritually. With spiritual freedom humans might come to know that the natural resources of the earth can suffice all. Starvation happens not because of lack of resources but because of the selfishness and arrogance of some souls who are heedless of spiritual truths. Spiritual awareness could lead to increased human creativity in solving many problems of the modern age, because a spiritual person considers what is useful to all, not just to her/himself. Dissemination of spiritual knowledge is the hope that might save humanity from many present difficulties and unexpected disasters. We need such a powerful spirituality that it might be capable of transforming our whole planet into a more enlightened one. This is not impossible for those who have faith that it is always from the depths of darkness that light is born.

Using Truth-Force

Mohandas K. Gandhi, known as the Mahatma ("great soul"), was the leader of the Indian independence movement from Britain during the first half of the 20th Century. Based on his understanding of the Hindu mystical classic the *Bhagavad-Gita,* and also influenced by his Christian reading and contacts, he developed a form of non-violent (but certainly not passive) resistance named *satyagraha* ("truth-force"), which was ultimately successful in displacing the British *raj*. The *Bhagavad-Gita* forms part of the great Indian epic the *Mahabharata*, which is the story of a war on the battlefield of *kurukshetra* between two clans representing good and evil. Gandhi took this war as a symbol of the "greater *jihād*." "*Kurukshetra*," he said, "is in the heart of man."[371]

> On January 13th [1948], the Mahatma began to fast "for Hindu-Muslim unity." This was his last fast, and from all the

[371] Charles Upton, contributor.

context of his utterances it could be seen to be a form of penance or atonement, although what was its precise purpose, or what might be done to induce him to stop it, the newspapers did not say. (At that time I really did not understand the Mahatma's fasting: I thought some of it had been a simple method of bringing pressure on others, or obtaining a desirable social result. I did not know then what I know now, that in this own mind it was always a form of prayer to God and not a form of coercion, even though often great actions were taken to persuade him to desist.)[372]

Gandhi's fast was shaking all India. The Stock Exchanges in Bombay and Calcutta closed on the day the fast began; the government of India—which had been withholding almost $2,000,000,000 of the gold reserve allotted to Pakistan on the ground that this would be used to support the campaign in Kashmir—now presented Pakistan with this huge sum of money, hoping to ease Mr. Gandhi's mind thereby. Gestures of repentance, of peaceful intention, of desire to return to nonviolence, were made throughout the country. There were parades in the streets with great frequency, calling on the people to "save our Bapu" by making peace. Various persons (both Indian and foreign) in Delhi told me that talk of war with Pakistan had been quite common only a few days before; it now vanished utterly. On January 15th, the third day of the fast, the Prime Minister, Mr. Nehru, made a great peace speech in which he announced that India was turning over to Pakistan the famous "55 crores" (the sum of gold reserve mentioned before); the fifth day of the fast (Saturday, January 17th) was a day of prayer throughout India—prayer for Hindu-Muslim peace and for the ending of the Mahatma's fast.[373]

A delegation representing all the main bodies in orthodox Hinduism had waited upon the Mahatma that very evening and had told him they were ready to pledge anything for peace if he

---

[372] Vincent Sheean, *Lead, Kindly Light: Gandhi and the Way to Peace* (New York, New York: Random House, 1949), p. 170.
[373] Ibid., p. 171.

would resume eating. Mr. Gandhi had listed for them seven main points, all looking toward the peace, protection, and well being of the Muslims in Delhi, their freedom of worship, and the restoration of their mosques. These were not conditions, but they were his idea of what the suppliants could do to restore peace. He did not say he would stop fasting even if these seven points were all pledged.

On the following day the heads of the Hindu organizations all took the peace pledge, following the seven conditions laid down by the Mahatma. At 12.30 on that day—Sunday, January 18th—he broke his fast, accepting a glass of lime juice from the great Muslim divine, the Maulana Sahib, his friend of many years. The breaking of the fast, like its initiation, was accompanied by hymns and prayers, in which "Lead Kindly Light" figured as always.[374]

India rejoiced. All talk of war had ceased, not only in Delhi but everywhere. The Deputy Prime Minister, Mr. Patel, was in Bombay, making a speech a day, but the belligerent tone he had used ten days before was completely gone. The Mahatma was, according to the newspapers, regaining strength.[375]

As I came in he was walking up and down on a rectangular blue carpet which covered less than half the floor. This, and his white pallet in the corner, made the only furniture of the room. In the corner at the right were three or four of "the girls": granddaughters, grandnieces, seated on the floor and talking in whispers.

I began by saying that I wanted to make a rather extensive study of his system of thought and action. (I think I actually said "Good evening, sir," at the outset.) He said: "Yes, Pandit Nehru told me." He paused and looked up at me with a curious birdlike motion (I was much taller). "Pandit Nehru did not tell me," he said, "whether you wished to see me *absolutely* alone."

---

[374] Ibid., p. 173.

[375] Ibid., p. 175.

The delicate emphasis on *absolutely* was full of meaning; I knew quite well that Mr. Gandhi never saw anybody "absolutely" alone.

"No, sir," I said. "I make no conditions."

"Very well," he said. "Would you like to walk or to sit?"

"Whatever you wish," I said. "Perhaps you are tired after the meeting . . . ?"

"On the contrary," he said with a sort of gentle decision (oddly, I can still hear this phrase when some more important ones are preserved only by written notes). "At this hour I prefer to walk a little."

We walked up and down the blue carpet. I was absurdly conscious of the hole in my sock, which I hardly suppose Gandhi saw. I was also aware that his swift steps up and down the carpet were much more numerous than mine. For me walking up and down that carpet was hardly walking at all; in three steps I had reached the end of it and turned back with him.

"Then you would not object," he went on, "if some notes were taken . . . ?" He motioned with his hand toward Mr. Pyardal, who was keeping pace with him on the other side.

"No, sir," I said. "On the contrary. . . ."

"They might even be useful?" He finished the sentence for me on a rising note, with a curious half-smile.

"I have been reading your edition of the Gita," I said, "and my questions are based on that."

He smiled and exclaimed something ("*Acha, Acha!* " I believe, conveying assent). I went on: "I propose to begin with action and the fruits of action."

He stopped still in his walk and looked up at me with his head slightly on one side. This is the characteristic motion I have called birdlike. He then straightened his head and pointed a long finger at the carpet.

"Let me get one thing clear," he said. "I have typhoid fever. Doctors are sent for and by means of injections of sulpha drugs or something of the kind they save my life. This, however, proves nothing. It might be that it would be more valuable to humanity for me to die."

He stopped again for a few seconds; we were both standing still now. The moment was of tremendous importance.

"Is that quite clear?" he asked, looking at me with his head up. "If it is not, I will repeat it."

This was the nearest thing to asperity—a very gentle kind of asperity—in the whole conversation.

"No, sir," I said. "I think I understand it."

We resumed the walk.

"What I wish to ask is this: how can a righteous battle produce a catastrophic result?" I said. "The battle is righteous in the terms of the Gita. The result is a disaster. How can this be?"

"Because of the means used." He said. "Means are not to be distinguished from ends. If violent means are used there will be a bad result."

"Is this true at all times and places?" I asked.

"*I* say so," he said with his curious lisp, and rather shyly, too, as if he had never gone quite so far before (as indeed he had not). Then he produced a statement which was much bolder.

"As I read the Gita, even the first chapter, the battlefield of Kurukshetra is in the heart of man. I must tell you that orthodox scholars have criticized my interpretation of the Gita as being unduly influenced by the Sermon on the Mount."

He took a few more steps and then made a really defiant profession of faith.

"There is one learned book in existence," he said, "which supports my interpretation of the Gita. But even if there were no such book, and even if it could be *proved* that my interpretation was wrong, I would still believe it."[376]

---

[376] Ibid., pp. 182-184.

X.

Contentment
Love
Inner Peacefulness

CONTENTMENT
(*Riḍā, Qanā*ᶜ*ah*)

And keep your soul content with those
who call on their Sustainer morning and evening, seeking His Face;
and do not let your eyes pass beyond them
seeking the fame and glitter of this life;
nor obey any whose heart
We have permitted to neglect the remembrance of Us—
one who follows his own desires and has gone beyond all bounds.
Say: "The Truth is from your Lord". . . .
As to those who have faith and work righteousness,
truly, We shall not allow to perish
the recompense of anyone who does a good deed.
[*Sūrah al-Kahf* 18:28-29;30]

Don't despair over things that pass you by
nor exult over blessings that come to you.
For God does not love those who are conceited and boastful,
those who are grasping and encourage others to be greedy.
And as for the one who turns his back—
truly, God alone is Self-Sufficient, the One to Whom All Praise Is Due.
[*Sūrah al-Ḥadīd* 57:23-24]

Say: "That which is from the Presence of God is better
than any bargain or passing delight!
For God is the best of providers."
[*Sūrah al-Jumu*ᶜ*ah* 62:11]

Whenever Zachariah visited her in the sanctuary,
he found her provided with food. He would ask,
"O Mary, from where did this come to you?"
She would answer: "It is from God;
see how God grants sustenance to whom He wills,
beyond all reckoning."
[*Sūrah Āl* ᶜ*Imrān* 3:37]

It is He Who gives wealth and contentment;
and that it is He alone Who sustains the brightest star.[377]
[*Sūrah an-Najm* 53:48-49]

Aṣ-Ṣādiq relates that the Messenger said, "The world is a series of changes in fortune: such benefit you may draw from it comes to you despite your frailty, and what is to your disadvantage will afflict you without your being able to ward it off. Anyone who ceases to long for what has passed him by finds peace of mind, and whoever is content with what Allāh has provided him will find coolness for his eyes."

The Messenger said, "Contentment is a wealth which never dries up," and "Contentment is an inexhaustible treasure."[378]

Al-Bāqir said, "Take care that your eyes do not covet what is beyond you—Allāh says to His Apostle: *Let not then their property and their children excite your admiration* [*Sūrah at-Tawbah* 9:55], and *Do not strain your eyes after what We have given certain classes of them to enjoy* [*Sūrah al-Ḥijr* 15:88]. If any of these things does enter your heart then remember the life of the Prophet: his bread was made from barley, his sweets were dates, and his fuel was palm fronds, if he could find them."[379]

The Messenger said to Ḥusayn ibn ᶜAlī, "Perform the obligatory duties of Allāh and you will be among the most pious of people. Be content with what Allāh has apportioned you and you will be among the richest of people, and abstain from what Allāh has forbidden and you will be among the most scrupulous of people. If you maintain good relations with your

---

[377] Sirius, of the constellation Canis Major, the brightest star in the heavens. This phrase might also be understood as, "it is God alone who sustains the brightest of the saints, those who shine with His Light."

[378] Haeri, Prophetic Traditions of Islam, p. 187 (Mishkāt, 130-132).

[379] Ibid., p. 188 (al-Kulyanī, II, 138-140).

neighbours, you are [of the faithful], and if you are good company for your companions, then you are a Muslim. Keeping company with the people of religion is an honour in this world and the next."[380]

It has been related that the Prophet said to someone, "O ʿUwaymir, if you increase your use of the intellect you will increase your proximity to your Lord, and in this there is contentment [*qanāʿah*]." "How am I to employ the intellect?" asked ʿUwaymir. He replied, "Avoid what Allāh has forbidden and carry out what He has made obligatory, that is how you will be making use of the intellect. Undertake supererogatory good actions—this will increase your intellect in this world and increase your proximity to and respect with your Lord."[381]

It is easy to believe we have trust in God when we feel the power of His presence. But just as God created the night to follow the day and the day the night, so he also created the day and night of the Spirit. Sometimes we feel His presence, sometimes His absence. He makes Himself present to us in order to manifest His Mercy, and absent from us so that we will not mistake *our experience* of His presence for His ultimate Reality. His presence gives us hope (*rajāʾ*) and trust; His absence breaks our attachment to His gifts, and reminds us that our love and submission must be for Him alone. Every virtue is perfected in just this way, through our experience of the relentless alternation between God's strength and our weakness; to endure this alternation requires, and teaches, the virtue of patience (*ṣabr*). Our weakness is the place where His strength is perfected; our nothingness is the throne where His Reality is established. And when we come to the station where we experience both His absence and His presence equally as signs of His Reality, then patience has ripened into trust, and trust into contentment. (In

[380] Ibid., p. 227 (*Mishkāt*, 219-220).

[381] Ibid., pp. 143-144 (*al-Khiṣāl*, I, 15).

reality, God's presence never departs or diminishes; it is our own receptivity to Him which is fickle, which comes and goes; but God is constant.)[382]

It is reported on the authority of Ibn Masᶜūd that the Prophet ﷺ commented, "There are three things at the root of all sin. Guard yourselves against them and beware of them. Beware of pride, for pride caused Iblīs to refuse to prostrate before Adam. Beware of greed, for greed caused Adam to eat of the tree. And beware of envy, for it was from envy that one of the two sons of Adam killed his brother."[383]

God Most High says, *Whoever works righteousness, whether male or female, and is a believer, We shall quicken with a life that is good* [*Sūrah an-Naḥl* 16:97]. Many of the commentators say that "a life that is good" in this world is one of contentment.[384]

It is said that Moses (upon whom be peace) prayed, "O my God, direct me to a deed whose performance would please You." He was told, "You would not be able to do that." Moses fell down prostrate to Him, imploring. So God Most High revealed to him, "O Son of ᶜImran, My pleasure is in your pleasure with My decree."[385]

It is said as to the meaning of the saying of God Most High, *God will bestow on them a goodly sustenance* [*Sūrah al-Ḥajj* 22:58], that this refers to contentment. . . . It is also said, "The one who returns to God in every state is provided by God with contentment."[386]

---

[382] Charles Upton, contributor.

[383] Al-Qushayri, *Principles of Sufism*, p. 101.

[384] Ibid., p. 109.

[385] Ibid., p. 165.

[386] Ibid., p. 110.

As we move through life, we encounter many challenges. Many have found support in the following phrases as they journey on the road to abiding contentment with their Lord.

I have readied the following words: facing all fears, "There is no God but God" (*lā ᶜilāha ᶜillallāh*).

Facing all sorrows and sadness, "May it be as God wills" (*mā shāᶜ allāh*).

Facing all benefits, "Praise be to God" (*alḥamdulillāh*), and facing all abundance, "Thanks be to God" (*shukrulillāh*).

And facing all astonishment, "God is subtle beyond all knowing" (*subḥānallāh*).

Facing all sins, "I ask God's forgiveness" (*ᶜastaghfirullāh*); facing all scarcities, "Allāh is enough for me" (*ḥasbiyallāh*).

Facing all calamities, "We belong to God and to Him we shall return" (*'innā lillāhi wa ᶜinnā ᶜilayhi rājiᶜūn*).

Facing every event of destiny, "I trust in God" (*tawakkaltu ᶜalallāh*).

Facing all obedience and disobedience, "There is no means or power in anyone except through God who is the Most High, the Most Great" (*lā ḥawla wa lā quwwata ᶜillā billāhil ᶜalyyil ᶜaẓeem*).[387]

The Guest House

Darling, the body is a guest house;
every morning someone new arrives.
Don't say, "O, another weight around my neck!"
or your guest will fly back to nothingness.

---

[387] Traditional prayers included in many Islamic litanies. C. Helminski, *The Mevlevi Wird*, pp. 44-45.

~ "The Guest House" is from Mevlāna Jalāluddin Rūmī, translated by Kabir Helminski, in *The Rumi Collection,* selected and edited by Kabir Helminski (Boston, Massachusetts: Shambhala Publications, 1998), pp. 188-189 (*Mathnawī* V:3644-3646; 3676-3688; 3693-3696; 3700-3701).

Whatever enters your heart is a guest
from the invisible world: entertain it well.

Every day, and every moment, a thought comes
like an honored guest into your heart.
My soul, regard each thought as a person,
for every person's value is in the thought they hold.

If a sorrowful thought stands in the way,
it is also preparing the way for joy.
It furiously sweeps your house clean,
in order that some new joy may appear from the Source.
It scatters the withered leaves from the bough of the heart,
in order that fresh green leaves might grow.
It uproots the old joy so that
a new joy may enter from Beyond.

Sorrow pulls up the rotten root
that was veiled from sight.
Whatever sorrow takes away or causes the heart to shed,
it puts something better in its place—
especially for one who is certain
that sorrow is the servant of the intuitive.

Without the frown of clouds and lightning,
the vines would be burned by the smiling sun.
Both good and bad luck become guests in your heart:
like planets traveling from sign to sign.
When something transits your sign, adapt yourself,
and be as harmonious as its ruling sign,
so that when it rejoins the Moon,
it will speak kindly to the Lord of the heart.

Whenever sorrow comes again,
meet it with smiles and laughter,

saying, "O my Creator, save me from its harm,
and do not deprive me of its good.
Lord, remind me to be thankful,
let me feel no regret if its benefit passes away.

And if the pearl is not in sorrow's hand,
let it go and still be pleased.
Increase your sweet practice.
Your practice will benefit you at another time;
someday your need will be suddenly fulfilled.

Happiness

Every human being, every sentient creature, including even the lowest of animals, begins to search for happiness from the moment it feels the impulse of life. This law is so constant that, even if every other natural law were to change, this tendency would probably remain the same. Most creatures, because their wants, pleasures, and thoughts are within limits, find some degree of happiness. Yet it is the ordinary human being, who, though his capacity for happiness is great, does not really understand the true nature of the happiness he seeks and so seldom finds it. He or she never envisions a limit for the attainment of happiness. Unfortunately, due to this never-ending aspiration, there are even some happy people who develop the opinion that they aren't happy and so end up making a hell out of their fleeting lives. What an enigma the human being is! Is it a necessity of creation that human beings should be so strange? People obtain many things; yet the more they possess, the more ambitious they become.

What is happiness? Few really know. Perhaps only the crazy ones, those oblivious to the turmoil of life, might be considered happy.

~ "Happiness" is excerpted from Ahmet Hilmi, *Awakened Dreams*, translated by Refik Algan and Camille Helminski (Putney, Vermont: Threshold Books, 1993), pp. 122-127.

Please pay attention for a moment. One may compare a city to a theater and its inhabitants to actors. Not long ago I was in a city where due to the necessities of living I was in contact with most of the population. I observed many people. Because almost all of them were afflicted by real or imagined deficiencies, they were unhappy. In that crowded place, three personalities caught my attention. Two of them were quite odd.

One of these was the *imām* of the district in which I was living. He was well-educated and had even gone to Al-Azhar University[388] in Cairo. Nevertheless, he was loquacious, flagrantly wealthy, and given to imitating celebrities. Though he was boastful and extremely conservative, he was highly esteemed and influential. He would continually preach that the end of time had arrived, that faith and conviction had weakened, and that doomsday was at hand. He saw fault in everyone but himself and would never accept the purity of anyone else's prayers or ablutions. He could not see that anyone else was truly following the rules of the religion with the proper fear of God. This *imām* could have been quite content with what he already had, but instead, while publicly abstemious, his private search for happiness and pleasure led him to involvement in various immoral activities. He began to practice usury, lending money to peasants secretly, awaiting the interest. Though the eating of pork was forbidden, he could swallow a whole pig, tail and all, when necessary. He gave sermons about surrendering oneself to unfortunate destiny and yet would quickly cover his ears at the sound of thunder. He spent more and more of his time pursuing secret, illicit entertainments which had brought him face to face with unnecessary and unpleasant situations.

Another odd personality was the *shaikh*[389] of a local *tekke*.[390] He lived luxuriously with the regular income of this *tekke* which he had inherited from his father. He knew many stories about the saints and prophets and

---

[388] Al-Azhar University: the oldest Islamic university, founded in the 9th century in Cairo.

[389] *Shaikh*: a venerated leader, especially of a mystical order. Originally used as a title of respect for the chief of an Arab tribe; derived from *shakha*, to grow old.

[390] *Tekke:* center for spiritual education and service.

could defend himself from many false beliefs and ways of thinking. He knew the rules of many rituals, had important dreams all the time, and could gather and bind *jinns* and elemental forces. However, his fear of the *jinns* was so great he wouldn't even go to the bathroom at night without his wife accompanying him. He sometimes attended to his family's needs, and sometimes not. He was a simple, foolish, and lazy man. With just a few changes he could have become quite balanced and more helpful to those around him; yet he persisted in his useless behavior and so continued to suffer.

It's the third person whom I really want to tell you about. According to my observations, he is the one who was actually content and who to a certain extent had succeeded in creating a happy family. It was during some of my excursions through the city that a carpenter named Hamdun, who lived quite near me, caught my attention. He was about forty years old, and from his countenance and the way he moved, it was easy to see that he was strong and healthy. Whenever I passed by, we would greet each other, and he always seemed full of joy.

One day with the freedom due a holy fool, I took a seat in the corner of his shop. He welcomed me with respect and happiness and sent his youngest apprentice to order some coffee. Brother Hamdun returned to planing a piece of wood. "Dede,[391] a carpenter must not spend his time idly talking. These three apprentices are my sons, and I don't wish to be a bad example for them. So, if you will excuse me, I will work while we talk."

Two young men with arms like wrestlers, one about twenty, the other perhaps sixteen, were busy at their work nearby. Further inside the shop, a plump boy of about nine, who had just returned with the coffee, was attempting to separate the woodchips from the sawdust and put them into a sack. As I watched, I drank my coffee. "Brother Hamdun," I remarked, "so these, may God bless them, are your sons?"

"Yes, all three of them. The oldest, my first child, is almost twenty. He has already become one of the most skillful and hard-working master carpenters in the region. He even learned new skills on his own, like the

[391] "Dede" means "grandfather," and is used as a title of respect for a wise elder.

carving of olive wood which I myself don't know. Soon he will be better at it than the most experienced carvers in the city. At present he earns one silver coin a day."

"Oh! From whom does he get his wages?"

"From whom would he get them? From me. Suppose I didn't have a son and hired a master craftsman to work with me. Wouldn't a master craftsman receive a silver coin a day? Instead of hiring someone from the outside, I chose to employ my own sons."

Astonished, I asked, "Does a father give daily pay to his sons?"

"Of course! If a boy doesn't receive daily wages from his father who employs him, how is he going to learn about the value of working? He will probably become lazy. With no real value given to his efforts, he will tend to neglect things. He'll feel that his father is supplying him with shelter in exchange for his work, and not simply because he is a part of the family. As a result he loses his virtue. Instead, working together could be a useful opportunity for a child to learn how to earn money and understand its value. This is why I pay my sons daily wages. My second son receives ten kurush now, but in three days, when the new week begins, he graduates to master workman status, and I will be raising his pay to fifteen kurush. My youngest son still receives twenty para, the same amount that I first earned from my late master. He is hard-working and very enterprising, and may well surpass his brothers one day. Though he really deserves a kurush now, I have not increased his wages because from hurry and carelessness he has cut his hand twice. I don't appreciate careless people, but if he doesn't cut his hand again, he will soon deserve a kurush a day."

"This must mean that they also share the household expenses?"

"How could that be?" Hamdun replied, "Let's suppose that I didn't have any sons. Would my master craftsman and apprentices share my household expenses? Or let's suppose that like many others, my sons are incapable of earning money for themselves. How could they share my expenses? Instead, my sons save what they earn. Besides his wages, my oldest son has a considerable amount of capital which I put aside for him long ago. Because he adds his wages to it, it will soon be almost equal to my capital. Before long, I'll help him open a proper workshop of his own or make him a partner in mine, and then perhaps marriage will follow so that our home may be filled with the joys of grandchildren. And similarly with my second son, and the third, according to their wishes."

"Brother, this means that you are rather rich, aren't you?"

Hamdun called to his sons, "Raise your arms, please." The boys raised their arms. "Look, Mirror Dede, don't you agree that these eight arms are riches? As I said, I finished setting aside my oldest son's initial capital a long time ago. Soon I will complete my second son's also. Dede, do you know that I was married at the age of twenty? At that time my daily wages were seven kurush. My oldest son was born the following year. My late master, Haji Murteza, raised my daily wages to fifteen kurush. He showed me a way. From that day I began to save: sixty para [one and a half kurush] for my son's money, as well as three kurush for the time when I won't be able to work due to sickness, ten para for the clothing expenses of poor children on holidays, ten para as alms, three kurush to gather into capital, two kurush for our house rent, *et cetera*. The five kurush remaining was enough for us to live on.

I replied, "I'm astonished by this orderly life. This means your master Haji Murteza was a very good man."

The carpenter's eyes filled with tears, "May the grace of God be upon him. Whatever I have is under his auspices."

"May God increase your happiness. May God grant health and a long life for your wife and your sons," I responded.

This prayer of mine made the carpenter very happy. First his youngest and then the other sons came over and kissed my hand. I became so happy at their situation that my eyes, which for a long time hadn't had sufficient reason to weep, either out of sadness or sweetness, now filled with tears.

"Tell me more about the life you live," I said.

"We get up very early in the morning. Whether it is summer or winter, we wash our faces with cold water, and then young or old, we each drink a cup of coffee. After chatting together for a while, we take the pot that was simmered earlier by my wife to the table and drink some soup. Then my sons and I leave and walk to the workshop. On the way one of us goes off to do the necessary household shopping for the day, takes it home, and meets the others at the workshop. When we are all together again, I discuss the work of the day with my sons, and we all set about our tasks. Around noon, when we get hungry, the youngest goes home and brings our meal, and we have a nice lunch. After lunch I order coffee from the nearby cafe and get a newspaper. My oldest son looks it over and tells me the important news in it."

"So! Your sons know how to read!"

"They can all read and write."

"So you must have sent them to school at some time?"

"No. When a boy goes to the district school for years, he not only loses his virtue but learns very little. Instead, I found a teacher who, before going to the school to teach, is willing to come by our shop early each morning. For the fee of a coffee and two *para*, he teaches the children for half an hour. In a year, my sons could read the Holy Qur'ān and the newspaper; they also learned how to write as much as is necessary for us. In addition every year I have bought books which this teacher has recommended. During noon breaks and sometimes at night, they read these books.

How do we live? At noon we have a break of an hour and a half. Sometimes we read the newspaper aloud, but one can do whatever one wants for that time after lunch. We shut the workshop half an hour after the call to prayer in the afternoon. In the late afternoon we take a short walk through the pleasant neighborhoods of the city. On winter nights other artisans and neighbors and their wives visit our home. The other women love my wife very much because she never gossips. Every Friday my wife, my children, and I have a picnic in our garden. So, our days pass in this way. Praise be to God that no sickness enters our home. All through our lives, only twice have I fallen ill, and my wife only three times, because we eat and sleep and get up regularly and we don't eat indiscriminately. In short, a thousand praises and thanks be to God."

LOVE
(*Hubb*)

It is He who has created you all out of one soul,
and out of it brought into being a mate,
so that man might incline with love towards her.
[*Sūrah al-Aʿrāf* 7:189]

Truly, your Sustainer's grasp is strong.
It is He Who creates from the very beginning
and it is He Who can restore.
And He is Ever Ready to Forgive, the Loving One,
Lord of the Throne of Glory,
the Unceasing Doer of all that He intends.
[*Sūrah al-Burūj* 85:12-16]

Among the signs of God is this: that He created you from dust,
and then, see how you become human beings ranging far and wide!
And among His Signs is this: that He created for you mates
from among yourselves
that you may dwell in tranquility with them,
and He engenders love and compassion between you;
truly in that are signs for those who reflect.
[*Sūrah ar-Rūm* 30:20-21]

Truly, those who have faith and do righteous deeds
will the Most Gracious endow with Love.
[*Sūrah Maryam* 19:96]

He loves them and they love Him.
[*Sūrah al-Māʾidah* 5:54]

Consult with others in the conduct of affairs; and when you make a decision to do something, then put your trust in Allah.
Allah loves those who put their trust in Him.
[*Sūrah Āl ʿImrān* 3:159]

It is claimed, "'Love' comes from *ḥabb* [seeds, singular *ḥabba*], and *ḥabbat al-qalb* [the seed of the heart] is that which sustains it. Thus 'love' [*ḥubb*] is so named because it is lodged in the *ḥabbat al-qalb.*" It is said, "The words for seeds and love [*ḥabb* and *ḥubb*] are [only spelling variations of the same meaning,] like the words for 'lifespan' *(ᶜamr* and *ᶜumr).*" It is also said, "'Love' is taken from *ḥibba,* meaning the seeds of wilderness. Love is called *ḥubb* because it is the seed of life, just as *ḥabb* means the seeds of the plants." It is said, *"Ḥubb'* are the four planks on which the water jug is set. Love is called *ḥubb* because it bears the burdens of glory and disgrace that come in the path of seeking the beloved." It is also said, "'Love' comes from *ḥibb* (water jar) because it holds water, and when it is full, there is no space for anything else. Just so, when the heart is full of love, there is no space in it for anything other than the beloved."[392]

The Prophet ﷺ has said, "A person is with the one he loves, and they are with God Most High." Yahyā b. Muᶜadh declared, "The inner reality of love means that it will not decrease when one experiences hardships, nor will it increase when one is shown kindness."[393]

An-Nashrabadhi . . . said, "Love is the avoidance of forgetfulness in all circumstances."[394]

The Messenger said, "You will not enter the Garden until you [have faith], you will not [have faith] until you love each other, and you will not love each other until you greet each other with the greeting of peace."[395]

---

[392] Al-Qushayri, *Principles of Sufism*, p. 329.

[393] Ibid., p. 331.

[394] Ibid., p. 332.

[395] Haeri, *Prophetic Traditions of Islam*, p. 220 (*Mishkāt*, 70-84).

> Imām ᶜAlī said, . . . "To display a friendly mien is the foundation of a loving friendship; and tolerance is the graveyard of faults."[396]

> According to the *ḥadīth qudsī*, "My love belongs by right to those who love one another in Me, to those who sit together (in fellowship) in Me, to those who visit one another in Me, and to those who give generously to one another in Me."[397]

In reflecting on the quality of Love, we might consider three aspects of love: 1) instinctual attraction (*eros*); 2) brotherly/sisterly sharing of interests (*philos*); 3) unconditional, all-encompassing love without particular object (*agape*).

> Allāh did not create our instincts so as to oppress or deceive us, nor so that some people should worship Him by attempting to suppress or ignore them. On the contrary, He created natural outlets for all of our instincts. In the case of our sexual instincts, He made available to us the institution of marriage and caused love and mercy to flow from it in order to establish in the home an atmosphere of tenderness and grace. And He charged His pious servants to appreciate the value of this felicity, to delight in its comforts, and not to allow even their eyes to stray beyond its limits. He charged them to direct their energies within marriage to the bringing up of children, to caring for their future, and to raising a generation of rightly-minded and rightly-behaved youth. . . . Consider the *duᶜāᶜ* of the Prophet Ibrāhīm (God's peace on him):[398]

---

[396] Ibid., p. 203 (*Mishkāt*, 190-192).

[397] William A. Graham, *Divine Word and Prophetic Word in Early Islam: A Reconsideration of the Sources, with Special Reference to the Divine Saying or Ḥadīth Qudsī* (The Hague: Mouton, 1977), p. 142.

[398] Muḥammad al-Ghazālī, *Remembrance and Prayer*, pp. 49-50.

My Lord, cause me and my offspring to remain constant in prayer,
and accept this my prayer.
[*Sūrah Ibrāhīm* 14:40]

O humankind, heed your Lord,
who created you from a single soul, and created from it its mate,
then caused to issue forth from them many men and women.
Heed Allah in whose name you seek your rights
from one another, and be conscious of your Creator,
through Whom you demand your mutual rights,
and revere the wombs [that bore you];
surely God ever watches over you.
[*Sūrah an-Nisāᶜ* 4:1]

O Adam, dwell thou and thy wife, in the Garden.
[2:235]

Marriage is a complete and total synthesis of two souls, alike and complementary in their nature. There is total mutuality in marriage. The Qurʾān declares, *They are your garments, and you are their garments.* [*Sūrah al-Baqarah* 2:187]

Like two bundles of light intertwined with each other, a husband and wife are enjoined to mutual love, affection, honor and respect, struggle and sustenance, each complementing and augmenting the other.

Marriage is a social and spiritual covenant which bestows mutual rights and responsibilities upon men and women. . . . *O humankind! Be conscious of your Creator through Whom you demand your mutual rights.* [*Sūrah an-Nisāᶜ* 4:1]. Thus men and women are joint heirs to the grace of life, created for mutual comfort and companionship. Both men and women are children of Adam and have the same soul. Neither one is inferior to the other. The womb as a symbol of life is used to bestow a special place of honor and respect for all women. [*Bismillāhir-Raḥmānir-Raḥīm.*] A special injunction is made to honor mothers [and fathers]: *And we have enjoined upon you to be good to your parents* [*Sūrah al-Aḥqāf* 46:15]. [And the Prophet said, "Paradise is at the feet of mothers."]

Thus, the spiritual view of marriage is that it is the fulfillment of the complementary nature of man and woman. God created man and woman in justice and in truth and in their union lies the consummation of this justice and truth.[399]

In many medieval romances, both Muslim and Christian, the beloved can only be won after overcoming dangerous trials, like digging through a mountain with your bare hands, trials which often include slaying a monster or a dragon or an evil knight. One way we can look at stories like this is as a picture of what is going on in our own inner world . . . the struggle with ego, the polishing of the heart, and surrender to love of the most virtuous beloved.

In addition to our potential or actual virtues, a human beloved will inevitably confront us with all our shortcomings, attachments, and vanities. If we are dedicated to Truth, *Al-Ḥaqq*, then emotion itself can be a step on the way to Truth; if our will is constant in obedience to God, our feelings will eventually follow, to strengthen and refine our efforts and help them ripen into wisdom.[400]

Ananda, an attendant of the Buddha, passed by a well near a village. A young low-caste woman, Pakati, was fetching water. He asked her for a drink.

Pakati said: "I am low caste and therefore may not give you water. Please ask nothing from me in case I contaminate your holy state with my low-caste status."

Ananda said: "I am not interested in caste. It is water I am after."

---

[399] Ahmed, *What Makes Us Human? A Spiritual Perspective*, pp. 135-136.
[400] Charles Upton, contributor.

Pakati's heart leaped joyfully. She gave him water to drink and when he left she followed him at a discreet distance. Finding out that he was a disciple of the Buddha, she went to the Buddha and said, "Please accept me and let me live in this place where your disciple Ananda dwells, so that I may see him and supply him with what he needs. For I find that I love Ananda."

The Buddha understood what was going on in her feelings and he said gently, "Pakati, your heart is full of love but you don't understand your own emotions. It is not Ananda that you love, but his kindness. Accept the kindness that he has shown to you and in your turn practice it toward others. You have been born low caste, but in this way you will be a model for high-born nobles. Keep to this path and in time you will outshine the glory of kings and queens."[401]

We could talk in the chapel without the guilt of hypocrisy only as we lived in the house:

Some of us were good at taking prayers, others at talking in study groups, others at practical work, but it was in none of these things as such, it was in the actual attitude and deed over a saucepan, or in your quality of thinking of someone else, whether you took sides or healed the separation between sides that was the actual test. You can sit in your principal's room, or before your class, and talk with real earnestness, but the great things are not won like that. Humility, generosity, peacemaking only rise from the actually-controlled deed, the love-restrained reaction, the detached-from-self sight of truth in a situation in which the truth is not pleasant for you. In the actual working together you have to change your natural self-guarding laziness and carelessness if you are to live at peace. The adventures are endless and it is a continual actual choosing whether you go the way of self or the way of love. You cannot cover over what you are by any amount of brilliant talk, even spiritual talk. We

---

[401] Bancroft, *Buddha Reader (Agamas)* p. 30.

could talk in the chapel without the guilt of hypocrisy only as we lived in the house.[402]

It is in this way that we must train ourselves: by liberation of the self through love. We will develop love, we will practice it, we will make it both a way and a basis, take our stand upon it, store it up, and thoroughly set it going.[403]

A mother, even at the risk of her own life, protects her child, her only child. In the same way should you cultivate love without measure toward all beings. You should cultivate toward the whole world—above, below, around—a heart of love unstinted, unmixed with any sense of differing or opposing interests. You should maintain this mindfulness all the time you are awake. Such a state of heart is the best in the world.[404]

Arouse your will, supreme and great,
Practice love, give joy and protection,
Let your giving be like space,
Without discrimination or limitation
Do good things, not for your own sake
But for all the beings in the universe
Save and make free everyone you encounter,
Help them attain the wisdom of the way.[405]

Instead of death and sorrow, we have to bring joy and peace to the world. We have to beg God for His gift of peace and we have to learn to love each other and to accept each other as brothers and sisters, children of God. We know that the best place for children to learn to love and pray is the family, because they see the love and prayers of their father and mother.

[402] Florence Allshorn in *Women of Vision* by Dorothy Stewart, p. 172.

[403] Bancroft, *The Pocket Buddha Reader* (*Samyutta Nikaya*), p. 25.

[404] Ibid., (*Majjhima Nikaya*) p. 24.

[405] Ibid., *(Prajnaparamita)* pp. 30-31.

When families get broken or divorced, many children grow up without learning how to love and how to pray. A country where many families are destroyed like this . . . will have many problems. I have seen many times in rich countries how children want drugs or other things to escape the feeling of being unloved and unwanted. But when our families are strong and united, children can see Gods' special love in their father and mother and they can grow so as to make their country a place full of love and prayer. A child is Gods' most beautiful gift to a family and it needs both mother and father because they show God's love each in their own special way. A family that prays, stays together. And when they stay together they will love each other like God loves each one of them. And works of love are works of peace. Let us keep in our hearts the joy of love and share these joys with everyone whom we meet. ~ Mother Teresa[406]

Abū Yazīd al-Bisṭāmī said that a man asked him, "Show me the shortest way to reach Allāh Most High." Abū Yazīd said, "Love those beloved of Allāh and make yourself lovable to them so that they love you, because Allāh looks into the hearts of those whom He loves seventy times a day. Perchance He will find your name in the heart of the one He loves; then He will love you, too, and he will forgive you your wrongdoings."[407]

As Rābiᶜa al-ᶜAdawiyyah says:

In love, nothing exists between breast and Breast.
Speech is born out of longing,
true description from the real taste.
The one who tastes, knows;

---

[406] Mother Teresa excerpt from a talk given to the UN Women's Conference, 1995. http://www.john654.org/MotherTtoUN.html (accessed 10/7/03).
[407] Al-Sulami, *The Way of Sufi Chivalry*, p. 42.

the one who explains, lies.
How can you describe the true form of Something
in whose Presence you are blotted out?
And in whose Being you still exist?
And Who lives as a sign for your journey?[408]

O God, Whenever I listen to the voice of anything
    You have made
The rustling of the trees
The trickling of water
The cries of birds
The flickering of shadow
The roar of the wind
The song of the thunder, I hear it saying:
"God is One!
Nothing can be compared with God!"[409]

My Joy
My Hunger
My Shelter
My Friend
My Food for the journey
My Journey's End
You are my breath,
My hope,
My companion,
My craving,
My abundant wealth.
Without You my Life, my Love
I would never have wandered across these endless countries.
You have poured out so much grace for me,

---

[408] Charles Upton, *Doorkeeper of the Heart: Versions of Rābiʿa* (originally published by Threshold Books, Putney, Vermont, 1998), p. 36.
[409] Ibid., p. 48.

Done me so many favors, given me so many gifts
I look everywhere for Your love
Then suddenly I am filled with it.
O Captain of my Heart,
Radiant Eye of Yearning in my breast,
I will never be free from You as long as I live.
Be satisfied with me, Love,
And I am satisfied.[410]

Sing to the Lord all creatures!
Worship Him with your joy;
Praise Him with the sound of your laughter.
Know that we all belong to Him,
That He is our Source and our Home.
Enter His light with thanksgiving;
Fill your hearts with His praise.
For His goodness is beyond comprehension,
And His deep love endures forever.

~ The Prophet David, The Bible, Psalm 100 [411]

[410] Ibid., p. 47.

[411] Stephen Mitchell, *A Book of Psalms: Selected and Adapted from the Hebrew* (New York, New York: Harper Collins Publishers, 1993), Psalm 100, p. 45.

Brotherly Love

Just as brotherhood calls for silence about unpleasant things, so it requires the utterance of favorable things. Indeed, this is more particularly a feature of brotherhood, because anyone satisfied with silence alone might as well seek the fellowship of the People of the Tombs. You wish for brothers so as to benefit by them, not just to escape being hurt by them, and the point of silence is to avoid hurt.

You should use the tongue to express affection to your brother, and to enquire agreeably about his circumstances. For instance, in asking about some accident that has befallen him, you should show the heart's concern on his behalf and over his slow recovery. Thus you should indicate by word and deed that you disapprove of all circumstances that are disagreeable to him, and use your tongue to let him know that you share his joy in all conditions that give him pleasure. For brotherhood means participating together in joy and sadness.

The Prophet ﷺ said: "If one of you loves his brother, let him know it!" He gave this command because the communication brings about an increase in love. If the brother knows that you love him he will naturally love you, without a doubt. If you know that he loves you too, then without a doubt your love will increase. Thus love will grow progressively from either side and will multiply.

Mutual love among believers is required by the Sacred Law, and is desired in religion. Therefore the Messenger pointed out the way of it saying: "Guide one another, love one another." Part of the matter is calling your brother by his favorite names, be he absent or present. ʿUmar رضي الله عنه said: "There are three ways of showing sincere brotherly love: give him the greeting 'Peace!' when first you meet him, make him comfortable, and call him by his favorite names."

Another part is praising him for the good qualities you know him to possess, in the presence of one before whom he would choose to be

---

~ "Brotherly Love" is excerpted from Abū Hamid al-Ghazālī, *Al-Ghazālī: On the Duties of Brotherhood,* translated from the Arabic by Muhtar Holland. (Woodstock, New York: The Overlook Press, 1979), pp. 49-53. Reprinted by permission of the Overlook Press.

praised. This is one of the most efficacious ways of attracting affection. Likewise praising his children, his family, his skill and his actions; then on to his intelligence, his character, his appearance, his handwriting, his poetry, his composition, and everything he enjoys. All this without lying or exaggeration, though it is necessary to embellish whatever admits of embellishment.

Still more fundamental is that you communicate to him the praise of anyone who praises him, showing your pleasure, for to hide such praise would be pure envy.

Furthermore, you should thank him for what he does on your behalf, indeed for his very intention even if he does not succeed completely. ʿAlī said: "He who does not praise his brother for his good intention will not praise him for his good deed."

What is even more potent in attracting affection is defending him in his absence whenever he is abused or his honour impugned, explicitly or by innuendo. Brotherhood calls for briskness in protection and aid, for rebuking the fault-finder and addressing him harshly. Not to speak out here disturbs the breast and alienates the heart. It is a shortcoming in fulfilling the duty of brotherhood. When the Messenger of God compared two brothers to a pair of hands, one of which washes the other, he meant that one should aid the other and stand in for him.

God's Messenger said: "The Muslim is brother to the Muslim. He does not wrong him, does not forsake him, does not betray him." What treachery and desertion to abandon him to the rending of his honour! It is like abandoning him to the rending of his flesh. How vile in a brother to see you savaged by a dog, tearing your flesh, yet remain silent and unmoved by compassion and zeal to defend you! The rending of honour is harder on souls than the rending of flesh, which is why God (Exalted is He!) compared it with the eating of carrion meat. For He said: "*Would any of you like to eat the flesh of his brother's corpse?*" [*Sūrah al-Ḥujurāt* 49:12]

The angel, who in dreams provides sensory representation of what the spirit has learned from the Preserved Tablet, symbolises slander by the eating of carrion. Thus if someone dreams he is eating carrion-flesh this means he is slandering people. For in his symbolism, that angel has regard for the correspondence and correlation between the thing and its symbol, the meaning of the symbol being understood spirtually and not in the outer forms.

Therefore, the protection of brotherhood by repelling the blame of enemies and the criticism of fault-finders is a duty in the contract of brotherhood.

Mujāhid said: "Refer to your brother in his absence only as you would have him refer to you in your absence."

There are two measures you can apply. In the first case, when something is said about your brother, you consider what you would want him to reply on your behalf, if the same were said of you in his presence; then you must deal accordingly with the impugner of his honour. In the second case, you suppose that he is present behind a wall, listening to your words, but thinking that you are unaware of his presence. Ask yourself how your heart would be moved to help him when you were in his hearing and sight, for so it should be in his absence.

Someone said: "Whenever a brother of mine is mentioned in his absence I imagine him sitting there, and I say of him what he would wish to hear if he were present."

Another: "Whenever a brother of mine is mentioned to me I imagine myself in his form, then I say about him what I would wish said about me."

This is part of genuine Islam; that you do not see fit for your brother what you do not see fit for yourself.

Inner Peacefulness
(*Sakīnah*)

But God invites to the Abode of Peace;
He guides those that will to a way that is straight.
To those who do good is a good recompense, even more!
No darkness nor shame will veil their faces!
They are companions of the Garden; there will they dwell!
[*Sūrah Yūnus* 10:25-26]

O you who have faith!
celebrate God's praises, and do this often;
and glorify Him morning and evening.
He it is Who sends blessings on you as do His angels
that He may bring you out of the depths of Darkness into the Light:
and He is Full of Mercy to the faithful.
Their greeting on the Day they meet Him will be "Peace!"
And He has readied for them a most generous recompense.
[*Sūrah al-Aḥzāb* 33:41-44]

And whoever repents and does good
has truly turned to God by repentance.
Those who never bear witness to that which is false
and if they encounter frivolity pass by it with honor;
those who when they are counseled with the signs of their Sustainer
don't act as if they were deaf or blind;
and those who pray, "O our Sustainer!
grant us spouses and offspring who will be the comfort of our eyes
and give us the grace to lead the righteous"—
those are the ones who will be rewarded
with the highest place in heaven because of their patient perseverance;
there they shall be met with greetings and peace,
dwelling there—what a beautiful abode and place of rest!
[*Sūrah al-Furqān* 25:71-76]

It is He Who sent down tranquillity
into the hearts of the faithful
so that they may add faith to their faith;
for to God belong the forces of the heavens and the earth;
and God is All-Knowing, All-Wise.
[*Sūrah al-Fatḥ* 48:4]

Remember how it was when He caused inner calm to enfold you,
as an assurance from Him,
and sent down over you water from the skies
so that by it He might purify you
and free you from the unclean whisperings of Satan
and strengthen your hearts and so make your steps firm.
Witness! Your Sustainer inspired the angels
to convey His message to the faithful:
"I am with you!"
[*Sūrah al-Anfāl* 8:11-12]

And paradise will be brought near to the God-conscious,
no longer will it be distant:
"This is what was promised for you—
to everyone who would turn to God
and keep Him always in remembrance—
who stood in awe of the Most Compassionate though unseen
and brought a heart turned in devotion to Him;
Enter here in peace and security; this is the Day of eternal Life!"
There will be for them there all that they may wish
and yet more in Our Presence. . . .
Bear then with patience all that they say
and celebrate the praises of your Sustainer
before the rising of the sun and before its setting
and in the night also celebrate His praises,
and at the end of prostration.
And listen for the Day
when the Caller will call out from a place quite near.
[*Sūrah Qāf* 50:31-35, 39-41]

Truly, those who have attained to faith and do righteous deeds—
it is they who are the best of creatures.
Their recompense is with God: gardens of perpetual felicity,
beneath which rivers flow, they will dwell there forever;
God well-pleased with them, and they with Him:
all this for those who stand in awe of their Sustainer!
[*Sūrah al-Bayyinah* 98:7-8]

Truly, those who have faith and do righteous deeds
their Sustainer will guide by means of their faith:
beneath them will flow rivers in Gardens of Bliss.
There they will call out:
"Glory to You, O God!"
and they will be answered with the greeting, "Peace!"
And the completion of their cry will be:
"Praise be to God, the Cherisher and Sustainer of all the Worlds!"
[*Sūrah Yūnus* 10:9-10]

But to the righteous soul will be said:
"O soul in complete rest and satisfaction!
Return to your Sustainer well-pleased and well-pleasing!
Enter then among my devoted ones!
Yes, enter my Garden!"
[*Sūrah al-Fajr* 89:27-30]

Whoever would live well,
Long lasting, bringing bliss—
Let him be generous, be calm,
And cultivate the doing of good.
By practicing these three,
These three bliss-bringing things,
The wise one lives without regret
His world infused with happiness.[412]

---

[412] Bancroft, *The Pocket Buddha Reaader* (*Itivuttaka Sutta*), p. 175.

The master Abū ʿAlī ad-Daqqāq (may God grant him mercy) said, "One of the signs of gnosis is the attainment of awe. For one whose gnosis increases, awe of God increases." He also stated, "Gnosis brings about utter tranquility to the heart, just as knowledge brings about peacefulness. So for one whose gnosis increases, tranquility increases."[413]

The Lord is my shepherd. I shall not want.
He makes me lie down in green pastures:
He leads me beside the still waters.
He restores my soul:
He leads me in the paths of righteousness for His name's sake.
Though I walk through the valley of the shadow of death,
I will fear no evil, for You are with me;
Your rod and Your staff they comfort me.
You prepare a table for me in the presence of my enemies:
You anoint my head with oil; my cup runs over.
Surely, goodness and mercy shall follow me
all the days of my life;
and I will dwell in the house of the Lord forever.
(The Bible: Psalm 23)

The Messenger said to Abū Dharr . . . "If you find the meadows of paradise, then linger there." When asked what the meadows of paradise were, he replied, "Gatherings of remembrance of Allāh."[414]

"Whenever a group sits down to remember Allāh, then a voice calls from heaven, 'Stand up! For I have exchanged your wrong actions for good [ones], and I have forgiven you everything.' Whenever a number of the inhabitants of the earth sit down to remember Allāh, a number of angels sit down with them."

---

[413] Al-Qushayri, *Principles of Sufism,* p. 317.

[414] Haeri, *Prophetic Traditions of Islam*, p. 100 (*Mishkāt*, 53 & 57).

"Whenever a group of people remember Allāh, angels circle around them, covering them with mercy; tranquility descends on them, and they make mention of those making remembrance of Allāh amongst themselves."[415]

"Remember Allāh much, for truly it is a remembrance for you in heaven and a light for you on earth."[416]

[However,] real peace does not mean we suddenly are transported to a problem-free realm where nothing bad ever happens. Real peace means we can survive the chaos and confusion around us without becoming chaotic or confused.

There is no such thing as "easy peace." If you recite the Twenty-third Psalm every night before you go to sleep and really think about it, you will be soothed temporarily. But you will only be really strengthened inwardly, you will only be given real, tough, durable, inner peace, if you come to realize and recognize the firm grip of the hand of the one who is already your Shepherd![417]

Overcome your uncertainties and free yourself from dwelling on sorrow. If you delight in existence, you will become a guide to those who need you, revealing the path to many.[418]

A monk can be very gentle, very peaceful, while there are no hard words to assail him. But when hard words are directed at him, it is then that he must be really gentle and peaceful.[419]

Two things will lead you to supreme understanding. What are those two? Tranquility and insight.

---

[415] Ibid.

[416] Ibid.

[417] Eugenia Price in *Women of Vision* by Dorothy Stewart, p. 83. Reprinted by permission of the Eugenia Price/Joyce Blackburn Charitable Foundation.

[418] Bancroft, *The Pocket Buddha Reader* (*Sutta Nipata*), p. 5.

[419] Ibid., (*Majjhima Nikaya*), pp. 158-159.

If you develop tranquility, what benefit can you expect? Your mind will develop. The benefit of a developed mind is that you are no longer a slave to your impulses.

If you develop insight, what benefit will it bring? You will find wisdom. And the point of developing wisdom is that it brings you freedom from the blindness of ignorance.

A mind held bound by unconsidered impulse and ignorance can never develop true understanding. By way of tranquility and insight, the mind will find freedom.[420]

Peace as a Triumph of Principles

Society is a wave. The wave moves onward, the water of which it is composed does not. The same particle does not rise from the valley to ridge. Its unity is only phenomenal. The persons who make up a nation today, die, and their experience with them.

And so the reliance on Property, including the reliance on governments which protect it, is the want of self-reliance. Men have looked away from themselves and at things so long that they have come to esteem what they call the soul's progress, namely, the religious, learned, and civil institutions as guards of property, and they deprecate assaults on these because they feel them to be assaults on property. They measure their esteem of each other by what each has, and not by what each is. But a cultivated man becomes ashamed of his property, of what he has, out of new respect for his being. Especially he hates what he has if he sees that it is accidental—came to him by inheritance, or gift, or crime; then he feels that it is not having; it does not belong to him, has no root in him, and merely lies there because no revolution or no robber takes it away. But that which a man is, does always by necessity acquire, and what the man

---

[420] Ibid., (*Anguttara Nikaya*), p. 159.

~ "Peace as a Triumph of Principles" is excerpted from Emerson, *Essays by Ralph Waldo Emerson, First Series*, pp. 64-66.

acquires, is permanent and living property, which does not wait the beck of rulers, or mobs, or revolutions, or fire or storm, or bankruptcies, but perpetually renews itself wherever the man is put. "Thy lot or portion of life," said the Caliph ʿAlī, "is seeking after thee; therefore be at rest from seeking after it." Our dependence on these foreign goods leads us to our slavish respect for numbers. The political parties meet in numerous conventions; the greater the concourse and with each new uproar of announcement, "The delegation from Essex! The Democrats from New Hampshire! The Whigs of Maine!" the young patriot feels himself stronger than before by a new thousand of eyes and arms. In like manner the former summon conventions and vote and resolve in multitude. But not so, O friends! will the God deign to enter and inhabit you, but by a method precisely the reverse? It is only as a man puts off from himself all external support and stands alone that I see him to be strong and to prevail. He is weaker by every recruit to his banner. Is not a man better than a town? Ask nothing of men, and, in the endless mutation, thou only firm column must presently appear the upholder of all that surrounds thee. He who knows that power is in the soul, that he is weak only because he has looked for good out of him and elsewhere, and, so perceiving, throws himself unhesitatingly on his thought, instantly rights himself, stands in the erect position, commands his limbs, works miracles; just as a man who stands on his feet is stronger than a man who stands on his head.

So use all that is called Fortune. Most men gamble with her, and gain all, and lose all, as her wheel rolls. But do thou leave as unlawful these winnings, and deal with Cause and Effect, the chancellors of God. In the Will work and acquire, and thou hast chained the Wheel of Chance, and shalt always drag her after thee. A political victory, a rise of rents, the recovery of your sick or the return of your absent friend, or some other quite external event raises your spirits, and you think good days are preparing for you. Do not believe it. It can never be so. Nothing can bring you peace but yourself. Nothing can bring you peace but the triumph of principles.

XI.

Courtesy
Chivalry
Noble Character

Courtesy
(*Ādāb*)

Say: "I counsel you one thing only:
be ever conscious of standing before God—
whether you are in the company of others or alone.
[*Sūrah Sabā*ʿ 34:46]

O you who have attained to faith!
Remain conscious of God,
and let every soul look to what it has prepared for the day to come.
And remain conscious of God:
for God is well-aware of all that you do.
And do not be like those who forget God,
whom He then causes to forget their own souls!
[*Sūrah al-Ḥashr* 59:18-19]

And God is with you wherever you may be
and sees well all that you do.
To God belongs the dominion of the heavens and the earth.
And all things return to God
He makes the night grow longer by shortening the day,
and He makes the day grow longer by shortening the night
and He knows completely the secrets of hearts.
[*Sūrah al-Ḥadīd* 57:4-6]

One of the central Muslim virtues, so apparent in the character of the Prophet Muḥammad ﷺ, is courtesy (*ādāb*). This quality of courtesy or "appropriate behavior" is sometimes said to emerge from the blending of love with humility.

> Aṣ-Ṣādiq once said to a man, . . . Make your heart a companion and devote yourself to him, make your activity a father

and care for him, make your self your enemy and fight it, and make what you own as a thing borrowed, and so return it."[421]

Jābir ibn ʿAbd Allāh al-Anṣārī relates that the Messenger said, "It is part of the good behaviour of the prophets and the truthful that when they see each other they are filled with joy, and when they meet they shake hands. The man who visits for the sake of Allāh has a right over the person he visits—namely, that he be treated generously."[422]

Respect your friends and show your respect for them. . . . A man entered the mosque when the Prophet ﷺ was alone. The Prophet got up to show him respect. When the man protested, the Prophet responded that to be paid respect is the right of the believer.[423]

Courtesy is based on a recognition that the dignity of the human state is not limited to oneself, nor to those who are great or fascinating or powerful in worldly terms. Every human being is an expression of the human essence, the *fiṭrah*; therefore every human being is, potentially, *khalīfah*, God's fully-empowered representative in this world, whether or not he or she is faithful to this Trust.

We can never know for sure whether a particular person is living up to their responsibility as *khalīfah*, or betraying it. When, after the Prophet took Mecca, his former sworn enemies, like Abū Sufyān and Hind, embraced Islam, no one could be blamed for wondering about their sincerity. Yet to openly question that sincerity would have been the height of discourtesy. We can never know the secret of the relation between another human soul and its Creator; this is the origin of

---

[421] Haeri, *Prophetic Traditions of Islam*, p. 151 (*Mishkāt*, 244-246).

[422] Ibid., p. 202 (al-Ashtarī, I, 29).

[423] Al-Sulami, *The Way of Sufi Chivalry*, p. 40.

the Muslim blessing "may God keep his secret." In the words of the Prophet ﷺ:[424]

"Do not look for the faults of the believers. Whoever seeks after the faults of his brother, then Allāh will seek after his faults; and whoever Allāh looks for in search of his faults then He will discover, even if he is hidden in his house."[425]

The Messenger said, . . . "The person with the best faith is he who is the best-mannered; the most righteous of them is the one who is most beneficial to the people, and the best of people is he who is the most useful to them."[426]

Everything must be in accord with reason, and reason itself must be courteous. ~ Ḥaḍrat ᶜAlī

Imām ᶜAlī said, "The best character is perfection in manners." He also said, "Cheerfulness is the basis of love, tolerance the burial of faults, conciliation the concealing of shortcomings; and there is no better relative than good character."[427]

Courtesy in Islam has many aspects, and perhaps the largest part of it is to maintain good relations with one's own family, and fulfill one's duties to them. *And we have enjoined in man respect of his parents* [*Sūrah Luqmān* 31:14]; *And that you be kind to your parents. . . . Do not say to them* [*so much as*] *'Fie' nor chide them, but speak to them a generous word* [*Sūrah al-Isrāᶜ* 17:23]. Among the duties one owes to one's children is to give them a good education, starting in infancy. The Prophet said, "Whoever has a new-born child should say the call to prayer in his

[424] Charles Upton, contributor.

[425] Haeri, *Prophetic Traditions in Islam*, p. 203 (*Mishkāt*, 190-192).

[426] Ibid., p. 227 (*Mishkāt*, 219-220).

[427] Ibid., p. 164 (*Mishkāt*, 223-224).

right ear and the call to start the prayer in his left . . . this is a protection." Equally important is courtesy and affection between husbands and wives. *And treat them [the wives] kindly* [*Sūrah an-Nisā*ʾ 4:19]. The Prophet said, "The faithful one with the most perfect faith is he who is most courteous and kind with his family."[428]

The Prophet [also] said, "The most intelligent of people are those who are strictest in matters of courtesy and friendship; and the most prudent of them are those who most restrain their anger."[429]

Courtesy when meeting people is part of Islam, and is more important than presenting a gift; moreover, a joyful mien is preferable to a good deed. It has been related in a Prophetic tradition, "If two Muslims meet, then be the most beloved of them in the eyes of Allāh, and the best of them by your more joyful encounter with your companion; when two Muslims shake hands, then Allāh makes a hundred mercies descend on them, ninety of them being for the one who began the handshake."

In expounding on this, one of the scholars has said, "The believer possesses an aura of faith, [with] its respect, brilliance, and beauty; the most joyful of them [i.e., of the two Muslims] is the most understanding and perceptive of the two, in that his intellect comprehends what Allāh has blessed him with, and he demonstrates this knowledge of Allāh, and the fact that He is bestowing this on his [servant], by his joy."

Another scholar has said that the foundation of companionship is based on four things: agreement, sympathy, preferring the other to oneself, and service. Moreover, among the courtesies of intimate relationships are speaking kindly and listening

---

[428] Charles Upton, contributor.

[429] Haeri, *Prophetic Traditions of Islam*, p. 165 (*Mishkāt*, 216-218).

when spoken to. The best and most noble kind of companionship is to maintain relations with a bad-mannered person until he reforms.[430]

During gatherings begin your own meal only after everyone else has started eating. Muḥammad ibn Yaᶜqub al-Asamm reports that the father of Jaᶜfar ibn Muḥammad said, "Whenever the Prophet ﷺ ate with others, he was the last one to begin eating."[431]

The Messenger said, . . . "You will never be able to meet the demands of the people with your wealth, so meet them with your courtesy and manners."[432]

God Most High says, *His [the Prophet's] sight did not swerve nor did it stray* [*Sūrah an-Najm* 53:17]. It is said that this means, "He upheld the correct behavior of being in the presence of God." God Most High says, "*Protect yourselves and your families from a fire. . . .*" [*Sūrah at-Taḥrīm* 66:6]. Ibn ᶜAbbās said in commenting on this verse that it means, "Instruct them and teach them correct behavior."[433]

The inner truth of correct behavior is that all good traits are combined. Thus the one with correct behavior *(ādib)* is the one in whom all good traits are combined. From this comes the word *ma'duba* (a banquet), i.e., a gathering for food.[434]

It is related that Sahl b. ᶜAbdallāh stated, "He who subdues his soul with correct behavior worships God sincerely." It is

---

[430] Ibid., p. 205 (*Mishkāt*, 189-203).

[431] Al-Sulami, *The Way of Sufi Chivalry*, p. 42.

[432] Haeri, *Prophetic Traditions of Islam*, pp. 226-227 (*Mishkāt*, 219-220).

[433] Al-Qushayri, *Principles of Sufism*, p. 308.

[434] Ibid., p. 309.

said, "Perfection in correct behavior is reached only by the prophets and the veracious." ᶜAbdallāh b. al-Mubarak asserted, "People hold many views on what constitutes correct behavior. We say, 'It is knowledge of the soul.'"[435]

The true proficiency of the soul consists not so much in deep thinking, or eloquent speaking, or beautiful writing, as in much and warm loving. Now, if you ask me in what way this much and warm love may be acquired, I answer:

By resolving to do the will of God, and by watching to do His will as often as occasion offers. Those who truly love God love all good wherever they find it. They seek all good to all people. They commend all good, they always acknowledge and defend all good. They have no quarrels. They bear no envy. O Lord, give me more and more of this blessed love! It will be a magnificent comfort in the hour of death to know that we are on our way to be judged by Him whom we have loved above all things. We are not going to a strange country, since it is His country whom we love and who loves us. ~ Saint Teresa of Avila[436]

Abbās Hussain gives this description of the Prophet's character and *ādāb*:

He was shy and would not stare into people's faces. He answered the invitation of the slave and the free-born and he accepted presents even if they consisted of merely a drop of milk or a rabbit's leg. He . . . visited the sick and attended the funerals of his enemies without a guard. He was the humblest of men. Silent, without being insolent. Most eloquent, without being lengthy. He was always joyful and never awed by the affairs of this world. He rode a horse, a male camel, an ass. He walked bare-footed and bare-headed at different times. He

---

[435] Ibid., p. 312.

[436] Stewart, *Women of Vision*, p. 173.

loved perfumes and disliked foul smells. He sat and ate with the poor. He tyrannized nobody and accepted the plea of those who begged his pardon. He joked, but only spoke the truth. He laughed but did not burst out laughing. . . . He was always the first one in greeting. In a handshake, he was never the first to release his hand. He preferred his guest to himself and would offer the cushion on which he reclined until it was accepted. He called his companions by their *kuniyah* [names of paternity or maternity] so as to show honour to them; children, so as to soften their hearts. One did not argue in his presence. He only spoke the truth. He was the most smiling and laughing of men, in terms of his companions, admiring what they said. He never found fault with his food . . . if he disliked it, he did not make it hateful to someone else. . . . Ḥaḍrat ᶜAlī, his closest companion said: "Of all men, he was the most generous, most open-hearted, most truthful, the most fulfilling of promise, the gentlest of temper and the noblest to his family. Whoever saw him unexpectedly, and whoever was his intimate, loved him." He himself said: "I am the complete, perfect man.". . . The ultimate miracle of the Prophet lies in the perfect courtesy on a day-to-day basis . . . *consistency* is it.[437]

The Prophet said: "Pray to God as if you saw Him, because even if you don't see Him, He sees you."

While those who are undergoing intensive spiritual training may be directed by their teacher to go into retreat for a time, the more central ideal is "solitude in company," where fellowship is balanced by circumspection and discretion. The ultimate effect of this balance is to unify the character so that our behavior, except for necessarily private activities, is the same whether we are in company or alone. Dhu'l Nūn al-Miṣrī said: "A person who does in secret what he would be ashamed to do in public has no self-respect; in fact, he does not even consider

[437] Charles Upton, contributor.

himself a living being." Dignity, in Islam, is inseparable from courtesy and justice in our dealings with others. It is a social virtue. But this does not mean that it is mere worldly "respectability." To practice dignity is to protect, in the midst of social relations and activities, one's secret relationship with God.[438]

Sahl ibn ᶜAbdullāh said, "Five things express the beauty of a being: when the poor appear rich; when the hungry appear satisfied; when those with heavy hearts appear joyful; when love is shown to an enemy; when feebleness does not appear despite fasting the whole day and praying the whole night."[439]

"Visit graves and thereby remember the next world; wash the dead, for doing this is rewarded and it is a profound lesson; pray over the dead that it may make you grieve, for the one who grieves is under the protection of Allāh."

"Visit your sick and comfort them with prayer, for surely this is equal to the prayer of the angels."

"Whoever assists the poor and is just with people of his own accord is truly of the faithful."

"If one of you meets a brother, then he should greet and shake hands with him, for Allāh has bestowed this on the angels—so do as the angels do."

"When a man is content to sit without distinction and honors in company, Allāh and his angels bless him until he rises."

"Treat the elderly with deference, for deference to the elderly is honoring Allāh, and whoever does not treat them with deference is not one of us."

"Whoever causes harm to his neighbor, God will deprive of the breeze of the Garden. . . . Whoever does not fulfill the rights of his neighbor is not one of us."[440]

---

[438] Ibid.

[439] Al-Sulami, *The Way of Sufi Chivalry*, p. 77.

[440] Hadith of the Prophet Muhammad collected by Charles Upton, contributor.

Once again, the Prophet said: "Pray to God as if you saw Him, because even if you don't see Him, He sees you." This is the root of courtesy. If we are not just intellectually but also *emotionally* certain that we are always in the presence of God, if we understand that He has first claim on our intimacy, then we will not demand *absolute* intimacy from others, which is something that no person can really give. We will no longer try to command other people's attention. . . .

If we have forgotten our total dependency upon God, then we are drawn to try to depend upon other people's attention to us. Instead of paying attention to God, we become beggars for the attention of others, constantly trying to make them either pity us, [appreciate us], or look up to us. But this is not true human relatedness; it is only mutual idolatry.

It goes without saying that we must depend on each other in many ways. We need emotional support and human love, and society cannot function well to maintain human life unless every member contributes. But the true Sustainer, the true Beloved, is always God. Everything else, the institutions of society, the ways in which human beings support and bless and exhort and protect each other, is really nothing but the play of His Names in the field of this world.[441]

It is related that when the Prophet ﷺ, mounted his camel with the intention of setting out on a trip he would say, after beginning with *Allāhu Akbar:*

"O Allāh, we ask You of this, our journey, righteousness and *taqwā;* and of deeds, those which are pleasing to You. O Allāh, make this, our journey, easy for us, and fold its distances (so as to make it shorter for us). You are our Companion in travel and the Protector of those we leave behind. O Allāh, I seek refuge in You from the hardship of the journey ahead, and from wandering into evil, and from harm befalling my family or wealth."

---

[441] Charles Upton, contributor.

On return from the journey, he would repeat the same *duʿāʿ* and then ﷺ add the following:

"Returning, repenting, worshipping, praising Our Lord."

It is also recorded that the Prophet ﷺ and his Companions would say *Allāhu Akbar* whenever they journeyed over the crest of a hill, and that they said *Subḥān Allāh* whenever they reached the valley floor. It was as if the entire caravan was performing *ṣalāt*, saying *Subḥān Allāh* in *sajdah* on the valley floors and *Allāhu Akbar* on every hill.

What a noble life it is that makes its chief occupation the glorification of Allāh. And makes *dhikr* and praise of Him the sort of wealth which soothes the aching body and causes time to pass unnoticed!

In another *ḥadīth* it is recorded that, whenever he approached a village he intended to enter, he would say ﷺ:

"O Allāh, I ask You for the good of this (place) and the good You have gathered within it. I seek refuge in You from the evil of it, and the evil You have gathered in it."

"O Allāh! Sustain us through those who live here, and protect us from disease in this place, and make the inhabitants to love us as you make us to love the righteous ones among them."[442]

The *ādāb* or code of exemplary conduct of the Prophet ﷺ with regard to travel encourages the traveler to actively seek the protection of Allāh, and to expect to see the workings of His infinite mercy.

Whenever one of his people set out on a journey, ʿAbdullāh ibn ʿUmar would say to him:

"Come close to me so that I may say goodbye to you the way that the Prophet used to say goodbye to us. He used to say: 'I commit your *dīn* (religious conviction) to the keeping of Allāh, and (so also) your responsibilities, and the outcome of your doings.'"

---

[442] Muḥammad al-Ghazālī, *Remembrance and Prayer*, pp. 80-81.

ᶜAbdullāh said: "Whenever the Prophet said goodbye to anyone, he would grasp his hand. Finally, it would be the one departing who would disengage his hand from the grasp of the Prophet ﷺ."

Here we encounter emotions both stirring and animated. The Prophet retains the traveler's hand in his own and the traveler himself decides that the time has come to go about his business. It is then that the Prophet asks of Allāh three things for the traveler; to protect his *dīn*, to aid him in living up to his responsibilities, and to ensure that his efforts result in a fruitful outcome. The traveler may make a mistake or even stumble headlong, but he will pull himself up again, straighten himself out, and then go on to complete, in the best possible manner, whatever it was he set out to do.

Indeed, what more could a traveler need? Except perhaps, the continually renewed perception that Allāh is blessing him with gift after gift.[443]

Watch for the Unity

In the occurrence of unpleasant things among neighbors, fear comes readily to heart and magnifies the consequence of the other party, but it is a bad counselor. Every man is actually weak and apparently strong. To himself he seems weak; to others formidable. You are afraid of Grim; but Grim also is afraid of you. You are solicitous of the good will of the meanest person, uneasy at his ill will. But the sturdiest offender of your peace and of the neighborhood, if you rip up his claims, is as thin and timid as any; and the peace of society is often kept, because, as children say, one is afraid and the other dares not. Far off, men swell, bully and threaten: bring them hand to hand, and they are a feeble folk.

---

[443] Ibid., pp. 77-78.

~ "Watch for the Unity" is excerpted from Emerson, *Essays by Ralph Waldo Emerson, First Series*, pp. 179-181.

It is a proverb that "courtesy costs nothing"; but calculation might come to value love for its profit. Love is fabled to be blind, but kindness is necessary to perception; love is not a hood, but an eye-water. If you meet a sectary or a hostile partisan, never recognize the dividing lines, but meet on what common ground remains—if only that the sun shines and the rain rains for both—the area will widen very fast, and ere you know it, the boundary mountains on which the eye had fastened have melted into air. If he set out to contend, almost St. Paul will lie, almost St. John will hate. What low, poor, paltry, hypocritical people an argument on religion will make of the pure and chosen souls. Shuffle they will and crow, crook and hide, feign to confess here, only that they may brag and conquer there, and not a thought has enriched either party, and not an emotion of bravery, modesty or hope. So neither should you put yourself in a false position to your contemporaries by indulging a vein of hostility and bitterness. Though your views are in straight antagonism to theirs, assume an identity of sentiment, assume that you are saying precisely that which all think, and in the flow of wit and love roll out your paradoxes in solid column, with not the infirmity of a doubt. So at least shall you get an adequate deliverance. The natural motions of the soul are so much better than the voluntary ones that you will never do yourself justice in dispute. The thought is not then taken hold of by the right handle, does not show itself proportioned and in its true bearings, but bears extorted, hoarse and half witness. But assume a consent and it shall presently be granted, since really and underneath their all external diversities, all men are of one heart and mind.

Wisdom will never let us stand with any man or men on an unfriendly footing. We refuse sympathy and intimacy with people, as if we waited for some better sympathy and intimacy to come. But whence and when? Tomorrow will be like today. Life wastes itself whilst we are preparing to live. Our friends and fellow-workers die off from us. Scarcely can we say we see new men, new women, approaching us. We are too old to regard fashion, too old to expect patronage of any greater or more powerful. Let us suck the sweetness of those affections and consuetudes that grow near us. These old shoes are easy to the feet. Undoubtedly we can easily pick faults in our company, can easily whisper names prouder, and that tickle the fancy more. Every man's imagination hath its friends; and pleasant would life be with such companions. But if you cannot have them on good mutual terms, you cannot have them. If not the Deity but our ambition hews and shapes the new relations, their virtue escapes, as strawberries lose their flavor in garden beds.

Thus truth, frankness, courage, love, humility and all the virtues range themselves on the side of prudence, or the art of securing a present well-being. I do not know if all matter will be found to be made of one element, as oxygen or hydrogen, at last, but the world of manners and actions is wrought of one stuff, and begin where we will we are pretty sure in a short space to be mumbling our Ten Commandments. (see p.227.

Laws of the Khwajagan

The following code of awareness and behavior as formulated by ᶜAbd al-Khalīq Ghudjuvani in the 11th Century has also continued to be a good basis of remembrance for many.

Remember every breath. As we breathe we should place our attention on each successive breath and be aware of our own presence. Inattention is what separates us from God. The more that one is able to be conscious of one's breath, the stronger is one's inner life.

Watch each step. Remember where you came from and where you are going. You wish for freedom and you must never forget it. Keep your attention on the step you are taking at this moment.

Journey toward your homeland. You are traveling from the world of appearances to the world of reality. Man cannot know his destiny as long as he is in the subjective dream state.

Solitude in the crowd. Enter into the life of the outer world without losing one's inner freedom. Remember God and do not allow yourself to be identified with anything.

Remember your Friend. You may discover the Friend, i.e., God, through the *being* of your guide. Let the prayer of your tongue be the prayer of your heart.

Return to God. No aim but to attain Reality. We must be single-minded about our goal. The possibility of transformation is a gift to be valued above all other possessions.

Remain watchful. Struggle with alien thoughts. Keep your attention on what you are doing, whether outwardly or inwardly. Observe what captures your attention and why.

Be constantly aware of the Divine Presence. Accustom yourself to recognize the quality of the divine presence in your heart. The "loss of self" allows us to participate in a greater Being.

CHIVALRY
(*Futuwwah*)

O you who have faith!
Be conscious of God with all the consciousness that is due Him,
and do not allow death to overtake you
before you have surrendered yourselves to Him.
And hold fast, all together, to the rope of God,
and do not draw apart from one another.
And remember with gratitude the blessings
which God has bestowed on you:
how, when you were adversaries, He brought your hearts together,
so that through His blessings you became as though of one family;
and how when you were on the brink of a fiery abyss,
He saved you from it.
In this way, God makes clear His signs to you,
so that you might be guided,
and that there might grow out of you a community
who invite to all that is good, and encourage the doing of what is right
and forbid the doing of what is wrong:
and it is they who shall attain happiness!
[*Sūrah Āl ʿImrān* 3:102-104]

[Abul-Ḥusayn al-Bushanji] said, "One of the principles of *Futuwwah* is to beautify one's essence with God: to love and want for one's friends the things that one loves and wants for oneself; in fact, to prefer one's friends to oneself, because Allāh Most High says: *But those who, before them, had homes [in Medina] and had adopted the faith, show their affection to those who came to them for refuge, and do not entertain in their hearts desire for things given to them, but give them preference over themselves, even though poverty was their own lot.* [*Sūrah al-Ḥashr* 59:9]. And the Prophet ﷺ said, 'Your faith is not complete until you love for your brother that which you love for yourself.'"

One must understand the element of time and give impor-

> tance only to time in time: that is, give immediate attention to time in the present, before it becomes the past. Sahl ibn ^{c}Abdullāh at-Tustarī was asked, "When is the dervish saved from his ego?" He answered, "When he will not allow his ego to concern itself with any other time but the moment within which he is. That is when the Sufi will find peace."
>
> Grace in behavior is a sign of *Futuwwah*. When Abū Sa^{c}īd al-Kharrāz was asked what *Futuwwah* is, he answered, "To forget what one already knows, to show patience against the wishes of one's ego, to give up expectations from ordinary people, not to want, not to expect thanks and rewards, to be generous, to hide one's state, and to be modest."
>
> Leave things in the hands of God. . . . Shāh ibn Shuja^{c} said, "In order to put someone else in charge of something, one must abandon one's own will."
>
> In generosity and benevolence, follow the example of Allāh's Messenger ﷺ, who said: "Visit those who do not visit you, give to those who do not give to you, respond with kindness and good deeds to the harm that is done to you."[444]

> Humility is one of the requirements of *Futuwwah*. To be humble is to accept the Truth and to be noble. . . . Fudayl was asked about humbleness. He said that humbleness was to submit to Truth, to be led to it, and to accept it from whomever one hears it from.[445]

The virtue of chivalry might be defined as "heroic generosity." It was a characteristic virtue of the pre-Islamic Arabs and Persians that was later incorporated into Islam. "The tradition of chivalry involved consideration for others (*morowwat* [*muruwwat*]), self-sacrifice (*ithār*), devotion (*fada-kari*), the helping of the unfortunate and unprotected, kindness

---

[444] Al-Sulami, *The Way of Sufi Chivalry*, pp. 67-68.

[445] Ibid., pp. 70-71.

toward all beings and self-effacement."[446]

Futuwwah (companionship) was institutionalized as a military order to deal with civil strife and counter the Mongol threat by Nasir ad-Dīn Allāh, who became Caliph in 1180 A.D. Later on, after this "courtly" chivalry dissolved, *futuwwah* became associated with the craft guilds, just as certain influences from the Knights Templars, a similar order in western chivalry who may in fact have been influenced by the courtly chivalry of Islam, later turned up in Freemasonry. *Futuwwah* is derived from the word *fatā*, "young man" with the connotation of "eternal or mystical youth." "The ideal *fatā*, who is exemplified by ᶜAlī, cousin and son-in-law of the Prophet, is characterized by selflessness, courage, generosity, and honor."[447]

The following are some of the virtues of the *fatā*: To bring joy to one's friends; to respond to cruelty with kindness; to visit friends and never find fault with them; to maintain old friendships; to allow friends to treat one's possessions as if they were their own; to be truthful; to love and care for the lonely and the poor; to be cheerful and playful, within the bounds of modesty and honor, which was the *sunnah* of the Prophet; to shun idleness; to be repentent; to forgive, even if you have the power to retaliate; to accept trouble with equanimity; never to pry into the affairs of others; to receive the one who approaches you and not to run after the one who withdraws from you; to avoid hypocrisy, argument, affectation, artificiality, and love of property and rank; to shun miserliness, anger, ambition, greed, and gluttony; to maintain *ādāb* even when alone; not to lower yourself either by fawning or condescension; to be kindly to the ignorant; to seek no praise for doing good, nor stop doing good out of fear of criticism; not to make fun of one's friends; not to listen to slander; to be a good neighbor; not to criticize or hold grudges; to be properly terrified of one's ego; to do one's best to match one's outer self with one's inmost self.[448]

---

[446] Javad Nurbakhsh, *Discourses on the Sufi Path* (London: Khaniqahi Nimatullahi Publications, 1996), p. 13.

[447] Al-Sulami, *The Way of Sufi Chivalry*, p. 20.

[448] Summarized by Charles Upton, contributor.

Qushayri provides a number of sayings concerning chivalry . . . in his famous *Risāla*:

> The root of chivalry is that the servant strive constantly for the sake of others.
>
> Chivalry is that you do not see yourself superior to others.
>
> The one who has chivalry is the one who has no enemies.
>
> Chivalry is that you be an enemy of your own soul for the sake of your Lord.
>
> Chivalry is that you act justly without demanding justice for yourself.
>
> Chivalry is a beautiful character.

Anṣārī provides us with two descriptions of chivalry in the context of the spiritual path. The first is from his Persian *Ṣad maydān*:

> God says, *They were chivalrous youths who had faith in their Lord.* [*Sūrah al-Kahf* 18:13].
>
> What is chivalry? To live in young-manliness and freedom. Chivalry is of three kinds: a kind with God, a kind with the creatures, and a kind with oneself.
>
> To be chivalrous with God is to strive in servanthood with all one's strength. To be chivalrous with creatures is not to blame them for a defect that you know comes from yourself. To be chivalrous with oneself is not to accept the temptations, embellishments, and adornments of your own soul.
>
> Chivalry with God has three marks: You never tire of seeking knowledge, you never cease remembering Him, and you stick to companionship with good people.[449]

One of our friends (may God grant him mercy) declared, "There is no place in chivalry for taking profit from one's friend." He was a young chivalrous man named Aḥmad b. Sahl, the merchant, and I bought a linen cloak from him. He charged

---

[449] Sachiko Murata, *The Tao of Islam: A Sourcebook on Gender Relationships in Islamic Thought* (Albany, New York: State University of New York Press, 1992), p. 267.

> me only what he had paid for it, so I asked him, "Will you not take some profit?" He responded, "As for the price of the cloak, I will take it from you, and not impose an obligation on you. But I will not take a profit because there is no place in chivalry for taking profit from one's friend."[450]

Umm ᶜAbdallāh, the wife of Abū ᶜAbdallāh as-Sijzī, who lived in the late 800's was known to have said, "Being in the company of one's spiritual brethren in this world is the consolation for being in the abode of materiality." [Her husband] was one of the great shaykhs of Khurasan and a master of chivalry (*futuwwah*). . . . When asked the meaning of *futuwwah,* he said: "It means accepting the excuses of humankind and your own shortcomings; seeing their perfection and your imperfections; and having compassion for all creatures, in their goodness and evil. The perfection of *futuwwah* is that you not busy yourself with humankind at the expense of God, the Glorious and Mighty."[451]

ᶜĀʾisha of Merv, the wife of Aḥmad ibn as-Sarī was heard to have said, "Whenever one of the practitioners of . . . chivalry (*fityān*) from anywhere seeks me out, I sense the light of his intention in my inner soul until he arrives. If I am successful in serving him and fulfilling his needs, that light becomes fully mine, but if I cut short my service to him, the light goes out."[452]

> Relations between brethren must be such that when they see each other, their hearts should fill with joy. Ismāᶜīl ibn Abū ᶜUmayyah said: "It should be easy to go and see a friend among the brethren, and one should not hesitate to do so. Be wise, see how important it is, and consider it a blessing and a gift." Ibn Mubarak said, "To see one's brethren strengthens one's faith, and is a cure for illness." Sufyan at-Thawri declared that he had no other pleasure left in this world except to be with friends.[453]

---

450 Al-Qushayri, *Principles of Sufism*, p. 218.

451 Abū ᶜAbd ar-Raḥmān as-Sulamī, *Early Sufi Women: Dhikr an-Niswa al-Mutaᶜabbidāt aṣ-Ṣūfiyyāt*, p. 200.

452 Ibid., p. 196.

453 Al-Sulami, *The Way of Sufi Chivalry*, p. 81.

Uphold these five virtues for the preservation of your being: Keep safe what has been lent to you; protect and preserve the good in yourself; be truthful and honest; be patient, pure, and selfless toward your brothers; and seek the salvation of your soul. Whoever loses one of these virtues loses his aim. Some wise men have said, "The one who possesses these six qualities knows that he indeed possesses *Futuwwah*: He is thankful for the little that he has, patient amid the greatest trouble, kindly to the ignorant, and generous so as to educate the miser; he seeks no praise for doing good, and does not stop doing what he believes to be good out of fear of criticism." Yahyā ibn Muᶜadh said that *Futuwwah* is peace, generosity, loyalty, and modesty.[454]

May Chivalry Endure

One day, during the caliphate of Hazrat ᶜUmar, while he was sitting with his companions, three noble and beautiful young men entered his presence. Two of them said, "We two are brothers. While our father was working in his field, he was killed by this young man, whom we have brought to you for justice. Punish him according to God's Book." The caliph turned to the third young man and asked him to speak.

"Although there were no witnesses, Allāh, the Ever-Present, knows they are telling the truth," said the accused. "I regret very much that their father found death at my hands. I am a villager. I arrived in Medina this morning to visit the tomb of our Prophet, may Allāh commend and salute him. At the outskirts of the city I got off my horse to take ablution. My horse started eating from the branch of a date tree that was hanging over a wall. As soon as I noticed this, I pulled my horse away from the branch. At that moment an angry old man approached with a big stone in his hand. He threw the stone at my horse's head, killing it instantly. Since I

---

[454] Ibid., pp. 83-84.

~ "May Chivalry Endure" is excerpted from Al-Sulami, *The Way of Sufi Chivalry*, pp. 9-12.

loved my horse very much, I lost control of myself. I picked up the stone and threw it back at the man. He fell dead. If I had wanted to escape, I could have done so, but to where? If I do not meet my punishment here, I shall meet an eternal punishment in the hereafter. I had not intended to kill this man, but he died by my hand. Now the judgment is yours."

The caliph said, "You have committed murder. According to Islamic law, you must receive treatment equal to that which you have dispensed."

Although this was a pronouncement of death, the young man kept his composure and calmly said, "So be it. However, a fortune has been left in my care to be given to an orphan when he comes of age. I buried this fortune for safekeeping. Nobody knows where it is but me. I must dig it up and leave it in somebody else's care; otherwise the orphan will be denied his right. Give me three days to go to my village and attend to this duty."

ᶜUmar replied, "Your request cannot be accorded unless somebody takes your place and vouches for your life."

"O Ruler of the Faithful," said the young man, "I could have escaped before if I had wished. My heart is filled with the fear of God; be certain I will be back."

The caliph refused on the basis of the Law. The young man looked at the noble companions of the Prophet ﷺ who were gathered around the caliph. Choosing at random, he pointed to Abū Dharr al-Ghifari and said, "This man will be the one to vouch for me." Abū Dharr was one of the most beloved and respected companions of the Prophet ﷺ. Without hesitation he agreed to replace the young man.

The accused was released. On the third day, the two young accusers came back to the caliph's court. Abū Dharr was there, but not the accused. The accusers said, "O Abū Dharr, you vouched for someone you did not know. Even if he does not return, we will not leave without receiving the price of our father's blood."

The caliph said, "Indeed, if the young man does not return, we will have to apply his punishment to Abū Dharr." Hearing this, everyone present began to weep, for Abū Dharr, a man of perfect virtue and splendid character, was the light and inspiration for all of Medina.

When the third day had come to an end, the excitement, sorrow, and amazement of the people reached their peak. Suddenly the young man appeared. He had been running and was tired, dusty, and hot. "I am sorry to have worried you," he said breathlessly. "Pardon me for arriving at the last minute. There was much work to be done, the desert is hot, and the trip was long. I am now ready; execute my punishment."

Then he turned to the crowd and said, "The man of faith is loyal to his word. The one who fails to keep his word is a hypocrite. Who can escape death, which comes sooner or later anyway? Did you think I was going to disappear and make people say, 'The Muslims do not keep their word anymore'?"

The crowd then turned to Abū Dharr and asked whether he had known of the young man's fine character. He answered, "Not at all, but I did not feel that I could refuse him when he singled me out, as it would not have been in keeping with the laws of generosity. Should I be the one to make people say that there is no more kindness left in Islam?"

The hearts of the accusers trembled and they dropped their claim, saying, "Should *we* be the ones to make people say that there is no more compassion left in Islam?"

The True Hero or Heroine

Ibn ʿArabī [the 13th century mystic and philosopher] was deeply marked by the humility, the simplicity, and the renunciation of Andalusia's spiritual adepts. Undoubtedly, these characteristics were to his mind the cardinal virtues of the hero (*fatā*), in the sense that Qushayrī gives to the word; "The hero is he who smashes idols and the idol of every man is his ego"—a definition inspired by the Qur'anic story where Abraham, after destroying the idols worshipped by his people, is referred to by this word. In the chapter of the *Futūḥāt* dedicated to heroes (*fityān*, plural of *fatā*) and to "heroic generosity" (*futuwwa*), the Shaykh al-Akbar abruptly

~ "The True Hero or Heroine" is excerpted by permission of The Islamic Texts Society from their publication *Ibn Arabi: The Voyage of No Return* by Claude Addas. English language translation © The Islamic Texts Society 2000, pp. 36-38.

affirms that, "The 'hero' is he who does not perform a single useless gesture."[455] Those who have reached this degree of spiritual development are "princes in the guise of slaves"; just as God provides sustenance for the impious, so do "heroes" treat all creatures with kindness, regardless of how wrongly they may have been treated themselves. And citing the famous *ḥadīth,* "The master is at the service of those over whom he is master," Ibn ᶜArabī comments that, "He whose authority consists in serving others is a 'pure servant' of God (*ᶜabd maḥḍ*)."

Taken to its most extreme degree, "heroic generosity" is but another name for *'ubūdiyya,* "servitude," to the extent that it is fully integrated and actualised by [the human being]. In fact, there is no question of acquiring "servitude," as it is the indefeasible status of all creatures. The fundamental difference between the "hero" and a normal believer is that the hero is forever conscious of his ontological indigence; there is nothing left in him that can hide it. "Nothing is more removed from the master than his slave; the condition of servitude, in itself, is not a state of proximity, but the consciousness that the slave has of his servitude brings him closer to his master."[456] In this regard, Ibn ᶜArabī loves to cite the story in which the famous ninth century Sufi, Abū Yazīd al-Bisṭāmī, asked God how he could draw nearer to Him. The answer he received was, "Approach me through that which is not Mine: humility and indigence."

In his vow of servitude, in the eradication of any pretence of autonomy, man reaches *walāya,* a word usually translated by "sainthood," but which literally means *proximity* to God. Having smashed the idol of the ego, he discovers that he only acts through God, as a *ḥadīth qudsī* of which Ibn ᶜArabī was so fond, states, "My servant draws near to Me by nothing I like more than by the works that I have prescribed for him. And he does not cease approaching Me by supererogatory works until I love him. And when I love him, I am his ear with which he hears, his sight with which he sees, his hand with which he grasps, his foot with which he walks. . . ." The real metamorphosis that comes about, says Ibn ᶜArabī, is in the perception of the servant who, by virtue of engaging in supere-

---

[455] Ibn al-ᶜArabī, *Futūḥāt* I, p. 242.

[456] Ibn al-ᶜArabī, *Futūḥāt* II, p. 561.

rogatory acts, becomes conscious that God is—and has never ceased being—his hearing, his sight. . . .

As sublime as this degree of spiritual realization may be, it is nevertheless marked by imperfection, by the trace of individual will which helps the servant to perform acts of supererogation: acts *chosen by the servant himself.* In other words, he reserves for himself some measure of autonomy, as infinitesimal as this may be. For the "pure servant," the possibility of a personal choice has disappeared. Consequently, he adheres to those works that God has imposed upon him and at the times that He imposes them on him. The "abandonment of self-reliance" (to use the wonderful title of a mystical treatise by the fourteenth-century Egyptian saint, Ibn ᶜAṭā Allāh) is his permanent state. Paradoxically, it is through this abdication of the powers that he attributes to himself that man qualifies to reign over the world as promised by God when He set him up as "vicegerent." In effect, when he arrives at this station, as Ibn ᶜArabī explains, it is no longer God who is "his ear, his sight . . ."; it is he who, from that moment on, is the hearing and the sight of God. "God wills, through his will, *without him knowing that what he wants is exactly what God wants;* if he becomes conscious of it, he has not fully realized this station" (Ibn al-ᶜArabī, *Futūḥāt* IV, p. 559). Completely extinguished to himself in the radiant Divine Presence, lost in the contemplation of the Divine Names, he no longer knows that he is. "When the servant has been stripped of all his names, those that confer his ontological servitude upon him as well as those that his original theomorphism grant him, nothing remains but his essence *devoid of either name or quality.* Then he is among 'those who are near'[. . .] Nothing is manifest either in him or by him that is not God" (Ibn al-ᶜArabī, *Futūḥāt* IV, p. 13). Just like Abū Yazīd, this saint when he is asked, "How are you this morning?" will answer, "I have no qualities, I have neither morning nor evening."

NOBLE CHARACTER
(*Akhlāq*)

Be constant in prayer and spend in charity
and loan to God a beautiful loan.
And whatever good you send forth for your soul,
you shall find it in God's Presence richer and better in reward.
And always seek God's grace:
for God is Ever Ready to Forgive, Most Merciful.
[*Sūrah al-Maʿārij* 70: 20]

Remember Me and I will remember you.
[*Sūrah al-Baqarah* 2:152]

See how God has purchased of the faithful
Their lives and their possessions;
In return, theirs is the garden,
And so they struggle in God's way.
[*Sūrah at-Tawbah* 9:111]

Look, the wine is in the green grape, existence in nothingness!
Joseph, I beg you, see in your pit the crown and the kingdom!
A thorn that has not blossomed cannot illumine the field;
how can a being made of water and clay find life
If Divine Breath does not Itself kindle it?
Clap your hands, clap your hands again, and know each sound
has its origin in the Wine's own self-surrender!
Be silent! Spring is here! The rose is dancing with its thorn.
Beauties have come from the Invisible to call you home.[457]

Noble character sheds light. The Prophet Muḥammad ﷺ is often referred to as the Full Moon, the one whose being and character is perfectly complete and conveys a brilliant light through God's grace. The Prophet

[457] Rūmī, *The Rumi Collection*, p. 23.

said, "I was sent in order to perfect noble character."[458] The truly noble human being is one who is carefully scrupulous, always intimately aware of the Presence of his or her Sustainer, and who then is able to be a conduit for the blessings of that Presence.

> The closest description of the man of *taqwā* is scrupulousness: he combines kindness with knowledge, words with deeds and rarely commits a wrong action, his heart is humble, he is content in himself, he eats little food; he takes the easiest path in his affairs and is zealous in matters of his religion, his desires have been extinguished and his anger stilled. Good is expected of him and he himself is protected from evil. If he is negligent, he is recorded as not being among those who remember Allāh; if he is amongst those who remember Allāh, he is not counted amongst those who are negligent. He forgives those who cause him harm and gives to him who withholds; he re-establishes relations with those who have broken with him. He is far from their corruption but gentle in his speech to them. He is absent from their bad actions and present for their kind actions. He accepts goodness from them and turns away from evil; he is dignified in the face of calamity and patient when faced with their plotting. He is thankful when things go easily.[459]
>
> Shaykh Ibn ᶜAṭaʾllāh said of [the one of noble character]:
>
> "He acts justly towards everyone and gives everyone his proper due."
>
> This is the possibility of the human creature. This is the capacity of the one possessed of a core. Recognize your perfection from the place of recognition. Praise belongs to Allāh at the beginning and at the end. There is no power and no strength but from Allāh, the Exalted, the Vast.[460]

---

[458] *Ḥadīth* quoted by Abū Nasr as-Sarraj in "The Book of the Example and Imitation of the Messenger of God," translated by Carl Ernst in *Teachings of Sufism* (Boston, Massachusetts: Shambhala Publications, 1999), p. 31.

[459] Haeri, *Prophetic Traditions of Islam*, p. 13 (*Nahj*, I, 273).

[460] Al-Murabit, *The Hundred Steps*, p. 100.

Rightful Dignity

In Islam it is still possible, so to speak, to stand as Adam before God; in the words of the prophetic *ḥadīth*, "Verily God created Adam in His own image." Islam is the religion of the *fiṭrah*, our original human nature; it recognizes that somewhere in each man and woman, the state of Adam and Eve before the fall still exists . . . the mirror of our original nature is tarnished and encrusted by *ghaflah*, heedlessness. It is polished, and returned to its original purity, by *dhikr*, the remembrance of God. *Remember Me and I will remember you* [*Sūrah al-Baqarah* 2:152]. To stand as Adam or Eve before God is to stand in one's primordial human dignity.

According to the Qur᾿ān, *They have forgotten God, and so God has caused them to forget themselves* [*Sūrah al-Ḥashr* 59:19]. In English, the phrase "to forget yourself" means to engage in some kind of compulsive behavior that compromises your dignity. In any society which has forgotten God, human dignity becomes impossible without a conscious rejection of the norms of that society. If we see security, pleasure, and power as the final ends of human life, then we have no dignity. If we identify with our desires for these things, if we blend with them, if we define ourselves solely in terms of them, then we have forgotten ourselves in their presence. We have become two-dimensional, a caricature or cartoon of a human being; in the words of the Qur᾿ān, *Shall I show you one who makes desire his god?* [*Sūrah al-Furqān* 25:43]. The person who worships security we call a "coward," the one who worships pleasure a "libertine," and the one who makes power his god a "tyrant." None of these three "religions" support, or understand, human dignity; the tyrant, the libertine, and the coward are not complete human beings, except in essence. In terms of realization, they are merely fragments of the human form, even though they wear clothes and walk upright. The tyrant, the libertine, and the coward are called to be *khalīfah*, the viceregent of God on earth, but they have not heeded that call; they have betrayed the human trust.

Democracy in the west began as an assertion of universal human dignity against the rule of tyrants. Dignity is not the sole possession of the king, the aristocrat, the rich man; every human being, simply by being human, possesses a share of that dignity. In the words of the Scottish poet Robert Burns, "A man's a man for 'a [all] that." The "revolution" of Muḥammad ﷺ was also democratic, in the sense that it overturned the hereditary power of the aristocracy and made provision for the poor one of the five pillars of Islam. But unlike the secular democratic revolutions of the west, it was based on a deep understanding of human dignity in terms of humanity's *khalifate*, our position as God's fully-empowered representative on earth. In Islam, our human dignity is inherent, and inseparable from our essential humility, since we are also *ʿabd*, God's servant. And because we are servants of God alone in our human essence, where our true dignity is rooted—though not necessarily in our outer social relations, where we are necessarily beholden to others—it follows that, in our soul, in our human essence, we can be the slave of no man.

It is not society, however, that gives us our dignity—not even religious society. Dignity, like every virtue, is part of our *fiṭrah*. If we live up to it, it blesses us; if we betray it, we earn its curse. Many today have a hard time understanding the concept of dignity; they mistake it for pompousness or vanity. But humility, too, can be dignified. As American poet Lew Welch said, describing a Japanese Zen master: "Suzuki bows with so much confidence we all feel bold." Dignity makes no difference between myself and another; if a difference is made, it is the other who makes it. In the words of an obscure Catholic priest, speaking in the 1960's: "True pride and true humility are the same thing." So dignity is the same as self-respect. Those who respect themselves will respect others; those who have no self-respect will despise others because they despise themselves. Dignity, unlike pompousness and vanity, is not based on other people's opinion of you—or on your opinion of yourself, for that matter. It has to do with being who God made you to be, irrespective of appearances.

Dignity is inseparable from courage, courtesy, humility, and justice; it does not try to make others feel undignified, but invites them to participate in the common dignity of the human form. Powerfully and silently, it calls those who encounter it to awaken to their *fiṭrah*, their primordial human nature. Once upon a time, a traveler in the American southwest visited the country of the Hopi Indians, where he was introduced to a man of the tribe. His first condescending impression of this man was that he was nothing, really, but a poor Indian—ignorant, underprivileged, living in difficult and primitive conditions, without the blessings of modern civilization; the visitor "looked down on him." As he gazed at the man, however, he realized that the Hopi had not responded to his impression of him in any way, either by abasing himself or by standing up for himself. Usually when we look down on someone, he or she will sense it and react. This man did not. He was simply there. This impassiveness on the part of the Hopi began to impress the visitor, who now began to see him as exalted somehow, a sage, a "noble savage," perhaps even a saint. He started to "look up" to the Indian instead of down on him. Where at first he had felt superior to him, he now felt inferior and inadequate. But once again, the Hopi did not react. He neither expanded in response to the visitor's positive opinion of him, "lording it over" him, nor did he modestly try to counteract that opinion. He was simply there. Finally the visitor's intensely positive impression began to moderate, till finally he, too, was simply there. He was no longer a "privileged, educated American" nor an "effete, over-protected American." He was nothing but a man, standing with another man on the common earth. It was only his ego that had suffered inflation and deflation; his *fiṭrah* did not. Unlike the American—at least as he was at the beginning of the story—the Hopi remembered his Creator, and so knew his place in the universe. The "moral" of this tale is that if we forget God, our psyche will wander aimlessly; while if we remember Him, we will rest in our true place: this is what it means to have dignity.

So the root of dignity is the remembrance of God. If we have forgotten ourselves because we have forgotten Him, only the remembrance of Him can restore that dignity and self-remembrance. Some have claimed that the practice of remembering God is none other than the practice of remembering ourselves; to be careful of our thoughts, our actions, our words, and our physical motions and postures is seen as a way of standing consciously, and with dignity, in the sight of God. And certainly this idea has some truth to it. But it is even truer to say that we will ultimately be unable to remember ourselves unless we remember God first. "Self-remembering" is another name for self-respect, a self-respect which is inseparable from an ability to view ourselves "disinterestedly," objectively. And only a consciousness of the Absolute Object can give us this ability. If we try to remember ourselves without Him, we will never find the way out of the circle of our subjective egotism; to set one part of our subjective psyche the task of observing and remembering the other part is like "setting the fox to guard the henhouse." It can only end in obsessive self-involvement, or in the mental illness known as "narcissism." But if we awaken to the fact that there is no god but God, and that He is the Omniscient, the All-Seeing, the Universal Witness, the Knower of each separate thing, the Totally Aware, then, knowing ourselves to be seen, we will see ourselves within the circle of His seeing; as God has said, *Remember Me and I will remember you.* [*Sūrah al-Baqarah* 2:152]. And if we know that we are in the presence of the King, who has appointed us viceroy over this earthly reality, then we will carry ourselves with grace and dignity, humility and self-respect; we will live up to our *khalifate*; we will be faithful to the Trust.[461]

---

[461] Charles Upton, contributor.

Muḥammad's Farewell Pilgrimage

After the principal rites had been completed the Prophet climbed to the summit of Mt. ᶜArafāt and preached from his camel to the multitude. After praising God, he said: "Hear me, O people, for I do not know if I shall ever meet with you in this place again."

He exhorted them to treat one another well and reminded them of what was permitted and what was forbidden. Finally he said: "I have left amongst you that which, if you hold fast to it, shall preserve you from all error, a clear indication, the Book of Allāh and the word of his Prophet. O people, hear my words and understand!" Then he imparted the revelation which had just come to him, the final revelation of the Qurʾān: *This day I have perfected for you your religion and fulfilled My favour unto you and chosen for you as your religion al-Islām* [*surrender*]. [*Sūrah al-Māᶜidah* 5:3]. He ended by asking twice: "O people, have I fulfilled my mission?" A great cry of assent arose from the many thousands assembled on the lower slopes and at the foot of the hill. As he came down the hillside the last rays of the setting sun caught his head and shoulders; then darkness fell. Islam had been established and would grow into a great tree sheltering far greater multitudes.

The Ideal Human Being

Ideal man passes through the very midst of nature and comes to understand God; he seeks out mankind and thus attains God. He does not

---

~ "Muḥammad's Farewell Pilgrimage" is reprinted by permission from *Islam and the Destiny of Man,* p. 128, by Charles Le Gai Eaton, the State University of New York Press © 1985, State University of New York. All rights reserved.

~ "The Ideal Human Being" is excerpted from ᶜAlī Sharīᶜati, *On the Sociology of Islam: Lectures* (Oneonta, New York: Mizan Press, 2000), pp. 122-124. Reprinted by permission.

bypass nature and turn his back on mankind. He holds the sword of Caesar in his hand and he has the heart of Jesus in his breast. He thinks with the brain of Socrates and loves God with the heart of Hallaj. As Alexis Carrel desired, he is a man who understands the beauty of science and the beauty of God; he listens to the words of Pascal and the words of Descartes.

Like the Buddha, he is delivered from the dungeon of pleasure-seeking and egoism; like Lao Tse, he reflects on the profundity of his primordial nature; and like Confucius, he meditates on the fate of society.

Like Spartacus, he is a rebel against slaveowners, and like Abū Dharr, he scatters the seed for the revolution of the hungry.

Like Jesus, he bears a message of love and reconciliation, and like Moses, he is the messenger of *jihād* and deliverance.

He is a man whom philosophical thought does not make inattentive to the fate of mankind, and whose involvement in politics does not lead to demagoguery and fame-seeking. Science has not deprived him of the taste of faith, and faith has not paralyzed his power of thought and logical deduction. Piety has not made of him a harmless ascetic, and activism and commitment have not stained his hands with immorality. He is a man of *jihād* and *ijtihād*, of solitude and commitment, of emotion and genius, of strength and love, of faith and knowledge. He is a man uniting all the dimensions of true humanity. He is a man whom life has not made a one-dimensional, fractured, and defeated creature, alienated from his own self. Through servitude to God, he has delivered himself from servitude to things and to people, and his submission to the absolute will of God has summoned him to rebellion against all forms of compulsion. He is a man who has dissolved his transient individuality in the eternal identity of the human race, who through the negation of self becomes everlasting.

He has accepted the heavy Trust of God, and for this very reason, he is a responsible and committed being, with the free exercise of his will. He does not perceive his perfection as lying in the creation of a private relationship with God, to the exclusion of men; it is, rather, in struggle for the perfection of the human race, in enduring hardship, hunger, deprivation, and torment for the sake of the liberty, livelihood, and well-being of men, in the furnace of intellectual and social struggle, that he attains piety, perfection, and closeness to God.

He is not a man who has been formed by his environment; on the contrary, it is he who has formed his environment. He has delivered himself from all the forms of compulsion that constantly press down upon man and impose their stereotypes on him by means of science, technology, sociology, and self-awareness, through faith and awareness. He is free of the compulsion of nature and heredity, the compulsion of history, the compulsion of society and environment; guided by science and technology, he has freed himself from these three prisons. As for the fourth prison, that of the self, he has liberated himself from it by means of love. He has rebelled against the ego, subdued it, and refashioned it.

Liberating his character from the inherited norms of his race and the conventions of his society—all of which are relative and the product of environment—and discovering eternal and divine values, he takes on the characteristics of God and attains the nature of the absolute. He no longer acts virtuously as a duty imposed upon him, and his ethics are no longer a collection of restraints forced upon him by the social conscience. To be good has become identical with his nature, and exalted values are the fundamental components of his essence; they are inherent to his being, his living, his thinking, his loving.

Art is not a plaything in his hands; it is not a means for gaining pleasure, for diversion, for stupefaction, for the expenditure of accumulated energy. It is not a servant to sexuality, politics, or capital. Art is the special trust given to man by God. It is the creative pen of the Maker, given by Him to his viceregent so that he might make a second earth and a second paradise, new forms of life, beauty, thought, spirit, message, a new heaven, a new time. God possesses absolute freedom, absolute awareness, and absolute creative power. Ideal man, the bearer of God's trust, he whom God has fashioned in His own form, is an eternal will overflowing with beauty, virtue, and wisdom. In all of nature, only man has attained to a relative freedom, a relative awareness, and a relative creative power. For God created him in His own image and made of him His relative, telling him, "If you seek Me, take your own self as an indication."

Ideal man has three aspects: truth, goodness, and beauty—in other words, knowledge, ethics, and art. In nature, he is the viceregent of God; he is a committed will with the three dimensions of awareness, freedom, and creativity.

A Prophet's Qualities

Whoever has rose gardens to feast and dwell within,
why should he or she linger drinking wine in a fiery furnace?
The pure spirit's home is the seventh heaven;
it's the worm that finds its home in dung.
The purifying cup is for the God-intoxicated;
briny water is the drink for birds that are blind. . . .
Those who lack real faith are satisfied with painted pictures
of the prophets;
but having known the brilliance of those moons,
we aren't interested in shadows.
The person of the prophet sits here,
while his other body is in heaven, like the moon.
This mouth of his discourses with those beside him,
while that mouth intimately whispers with the Beloved.
His outward ear apprehends these words,
while his spiritual ear draws close the mysteries of Being.
His outward eye apprehends human forms and features,
while his inward eye is dazzled by the Face of that Friend.
Here his feet stand evenly in the row of worshippers within the mosque,
there he circumambulates the heavens.
Every part of him is reckoned in this way:
here within Time, there Eternity's companion.
One of his names is "owner of the two realms;"
another is "Imām of the two places of prostration."

~ "A Prophet's Qualities" is excerpted from Rūmī, *The Mathnawī of Jalālu'ddin Rūmī,* translated by Nicholson, pp. 215-216, (V:3593-3616), adapted by C. Helminski.

Religious seclusion and fasting no longer are his obligation.
His infidelity has become faith and disbelief has disappeared.
Like the letter *alif*, he stands foremost by his rectitude;
nothing of his qualities remains.
Putting aside the garment of his own weaving,
his spirit has gone, naked, to the One who gives it increase.
Since naked he arrived in the presence of that incomparable King,
He has woven him a holy raiment.
Putting on that robe of noble qualities,
spirit flew from the pit to the palace of majesty.
That's the way it is: when dregs become pure, lightening, they rise.

Appendix: Supplemental Biographies

ʿĀʾishah

ʿĀʾishah (c. 612-678 C.E.) was the daughter of the Prophet Muḥammad's closest friend, Abū Bakr, known for her striking beauty and her formidable memory. She was betrothed to the Prophet ﷺ at an early age[462] after the death of his dear wife Khadījah. Gabriel appeared to Muḥammad in a dream, carrying to him a bundle wrapped in red silk, saying, "This is your wife." Muḥammad later told ʿĀʾishah, "When I uncovered the face, I discovered it was you, so I said, 'If this is from Allāh, it will be done.'[463] ʿĀʾishah had previously been betrothed to another, but that family had not accepted Islam. They decided they would rather not have one who was a member of the beleaguered Muslim community marry into their family. So, she was instead betrothed to Muḥammad. This lightened his heart after the long "year of sorrow" in which he had lost both his beloved wife, Khadījah, and his devoted uncle, Abū Ṭālib.

Meanwhile, at the encouragement of friends, Muhammad ﷺ married the widowed Sawdah who was a kind and supportive companion and helped him to raise his daughters. It was not until several years later, after the *hijrah,* that the marriage between ʿĀʾishah and Muḥammad took place and she went to live with Muḥammad in a little hut in what had become his family compound adjacent to the first mosque in Medina. Their hut was just adjacent to the hut of Fāṭimah and ʿAlī and opened into the common courtyard shared with the community mosque.

Before and after her wedding ʿĀʾishah maintained a natural jollity and innocence and did not seem at all overawed by the thought of being wedded to him who was the Messenger of God ﷺ whom all his companions, including her own mother and father, treated with such love and

---

[462] In Arabia in that era, it was customary for girls to be betrothed at an early age and to marry shortly after the onset of menses.

[463] Al-Bukhārī (*ḥadīth*).

reverence.[464] During the years that followed the *hijrah*, Muḥammad married nine women in the process of consolidating tribal loyalties and providing for the widows of muslim men who had died defending their faith. ʿĀʾishah was the only wife of Muḥammad who had not been previously married. At the time of Muḥammad, polygamy had been commonly practiced indiscriminately without regard for women's rights, however the revelation of the Qurʾān enjoined new respect for women and their rights, and Muḥammad was careful to provide each of his wives with a hut of her own, and to treat each with equal respect.

A verse of the Qurʾān was revealed then limiting to four the general number of wives possible for a man, but stating that even this condition was allowable only if such a man were able to treat them all equally [*Sūrah an-Nisā* 4:3]. "Modern Muslims often interpret this verse as essentially an exhortation in favor of monogamy, since at another point the Qurʾān states that a man who is married to several wives at once cannot be equally just to all of them—Qurʾān, *Sūrah an-Nisā* 4: 128-129."[465] Truthful, committed partnership with equality, fidelity, and tenderness between marriage partners was encouraged, based on love.

Several verses of the Qurʾān speak of the creation of "man and his mate" from a single soul: *It is He who created you from a single soul and likewise his mate of like nature, in order that he might dwell with her (in love)* [*Sūrah al-Aʾraf* 7:189] The first couple of Prophecy, Adam and Eve, are pointed to as exemplary of the original harmonious "one to one" relationship intended for us as human beings: *O Adam, dwell thou and thy wife in the Garden . . .* [*Sūrah al-Baqarah* 2:35]. The Qur'an indicates that it is intended that husband and wife be a "garment" of comfort for each other [*Sūrah Baqarah* 2:187].

A moment did arise when Muḥammad's dear friend and son-in-law, ʿAlī, considered taking a second wife, but Muḥammad, knowing that

---

[464] Charles Upton, contributor.

[465] Wiebke Walther, *Women in Islam*, p.57. Today, polygamy is outlawed in a number of Muslim countries. A woman does have the right to specify monogamy in her marriage contract as did the great-granddaughter of the Prophet Muḥammad, Amīnah.

it would cause distress to Fāṭimah 🌺, asked him to refrain from doing so or divorce her. ʿAlī relinquished the idea. He did not remarry until quite some time after Fāṭimah's death. It is clear from historical records that Muḥammad's own situation of polygamy was not an easy one.

In Islam it is said, "Marriage is half the faith." In close relationship, the sharp edges of our *nafs* (ego-soul) can be little by little smoothed; there is in marriage much to be learned. Growing up as the wife of the Prophet, ʿĀʾishah 🌺 learned a great deal from Muḥammad's example and shared intimately with him the journey of soul.

ʿĀʾishah is said to have laid down the fundamental rules of Arab-Islamic ethics. She is said to have affirmed that noble qualities of character were "honesty of speech, reliability, truthfulness and steadfastness in misfortune, the provision of protection for friend and neighbor, and readiness to give aid in the ups and downs of life, to feed the needy, to treat slaves with kindness, and to revere one's parents."[466]

ʿĀʾishah reported that the Messenger of God said: "Certainly the most perfect of the faithful in faith is one who is the best of them in conduct, and is the most affable of them to his/her family."[467]

It was often when Muḥammad ﷺ was with ʿĀʾishah 🌺 that revelation would come to him. She never hesitated to ask him questions or discuss with him the meaning of the revelation or of his own actions. From an early age she had been present during innumerable conversations between Muḥammad and her parents regarding the revelation and the needs of the emerging community. Her mental acumen enabled her to

---

[466] Wiebke Walther, *Women in Islam: from Medieval to Modern Times*. Translated from the German by C.S.V. Salt, with an introduction by Guity Nashat (Princeton, NJ: Markus Wiener Pub., rev. ed. 1993), p. 106.

[467] *Mishkāt ul-Maṣābīḥ*, translated from the Arabic by Al-Haj Maulana Fazlul Karim (Lahore, Pakistan: Pakistan Educational Press), Vol. 1, p. 213.

easily learn the evolving Qurʾān by heart and to memorize additional revelations as they came.

After Khadījah رضي الله عنها, ʿĀʾishah رضي الله عنها was Muḥammad's favorite wife. When he became ill he was grateful that he was allowed by his other wives to stay in her hut, and he remained for many hours at a time resting with his head in her lap. It was thus that he died.

Two years after the passing of the Prophet ﷺ, ʿĀʾishah's father, Abū Bakr رضي الله عنه, who had become the caliph, or leader, of the developing Islamic state after the Prophet's passing, also died in her arms. It is related that she was the one who delivered his eulogy "in moving words of resounding rhymed prose."[468] He was buried beside Muḥammad under the floor of her room. The companion ʿUmar رضي الله عنه became the next caliph. When he was dying he asked that he, too, might be buried with Muḥammad and Abū Bakr under the floor of her room. Though she felt somewhat shy of this, she agreed. However, after that she curtained off that portion of the room and would not enter there without first enwrapping herself with her veil. Before Muḥammad's death, she had had a dream of three moons setting in her room; now they had indeed all come to rest.

ʿUthmān رضي الله عنه followed ʿUmar رضي الله عنه as caliph but a few years later was murdered during the still-stormy years that followed Muḥammad's passing. After some debate, ʿAlī رضي الله عنه then assumed the position of caliph. ʿĀʾishah رضي الله عنها was concerned that ʿAlī was not actively bringing the murderer of ʿUthmān to justice. Two of the early companions of the Prophet ﷺ, Ṭalḥah and az-Zubayr, the husbands of her sisters, gathered forces against ʿAlī and persuaded ʿĀʾishah to join them. She journeyed on camel-back to participate in the battle. When the army was passing a certain town, the barking of a dog reminded her of something the Prophet had said to her in caution, years earlier. She began to doubt the rightfulness of their endeavor and wanted to turn back, but her companions persuaded her to continue. A terrible battle ensued in which thousands of lives were lost, including those of her brothers-in-law. When her side was completely defeated, her own brother, Muḥammad, who had been on the side of ʿAlī, was the one to help her off the back of her

---

[468] Walther, *Women in Islam: from Medieval to Modern Times,* p. 106.

camel. She was given safe passage back to Medina.

In Medina, she resumed residence in the hut where she had lived with her husband. One half of the hut was now taken up with the three graves—those of the Prophet Muḥammad ﷺ; her father, the beloved companion and second caliph, Abū Bakr ؓ; and the companion and third caliph, ʿUmar ؓ. She lived in the other half of the hut. In her little room she would receive visitors from many regions who came to her to learn and understand the Qurʾān and the sayings and ways of the Prophet. She is reported to have conveyed over two thousand sayings (*ḥadīth*) of his. She was also well versed in medicine, history, and poetry. This small room became her classroom where she taught young boys and girls, and women and men of the community. One was considered very blessed to have been able to study with ʿĀʾishah ؓ. Though she had no children of her own, she adopted a number of young people, whom she carefully instructed and through whom many of the traditions of the faith were conveyed. She made the annual pilgrimage (*hajj*) to Mecca every year and would pitch a tent there in order to be able to receive those who came to study with her during that time of annual gathering of the extended Muslim community.

> The life of ʿĀʾishah is proof that a woman can be far more learned than men and that she can be the teacher of scholars and experts. Her life is also proof that a woman can exert influence over men and women and provide them with inspiration and leadership [and] . . . that the same woman can be totally feminine and be a source of pleasure, joy, and comfort to her husband.
>
> She did not graduate from any university—there were no universities as such in her day. But still her utterances are studied in faculties of literature, her legal pronouncements are studied in colleges of law, and her life and works are studied and researched by students and teachers of Muslim history as they have been for over a thousand years.[469]

---

[469] ʿAbdul Wāhid Hamīd, *Companions of the Prophet*, Vol. I, p. 242.

Her nephew ʿUrwah asserts that she was proficient not only in *fiqh* but also in medicine (*ṭibb*) and poetry. Many of the senior companions of the Prophet came to her to ask for advice concerning questions of inheritance which required a highly skilled mathematical mind. Scholars regard her as one of the earliest *fuqahāʿ* of Islam along with persons like ʿUmar ibn al-Khaṭṭāb, ʿAlī, and ʿAbd Allāh ibn ʿAbbās. The Prophet, referring to her extensive knowledge of Islam, is reported to have said: "Learn a portion of your religion (*dīn*) from this red-[haired] lady." "*Ḥumayriyyah*" meaning "red-[haired]" was an epithet given to ʿĀʾishah by the Prophet.

ʿĀʾishah not only possessed great knowledge but took an active part in education and social reform. As a teacher she had a clear and persuasive manner of speech and her power of oratory has been described in superlative terms by Al-Aḥnaf who said:

"I have heard speeches of Abū Bakr and ʿUmar, ʿUthmān, and ʿAlī, and the *Khulafāʿ* up to this day, but I have not heard speech more persuasive and more beautiful from the mouth of any person than from the mouth of ʿĀʾishah."[470]

Throughout her lifetime, ʿĀʾishah continued to live in the style of utter simplicity that she had experienced together with Muḥammad ﷺ as his wife. As they had often had little to eat and drink—no more than a few dates and water—she never learned to cook. In later life, she continued to fast often, and when the stipend allotted to her by the government treasury was brought to her, she would often distribute it to those in need the same day, keeping back nothing for herself. She also continued throughout her life to immerse herself in prayer, adding to the five daily ritual prayers the extra early morning prayer (*ḍuḥā*, after sunrise) and the extra night prayer (*tahajjud*), which she had so often observed together with Muḥammad. Often in the night they had stood for hours in prayer, tears cascading down their cheeks as they worshiped their Sustainer. Sometimes when ʿĀʾishah tired, she would sleep, and Muḥammad would

[470] Ibid., pp. 249-50.

continue to pray. Their hut was quite small, so when she would lie down, it would often happen that she would be lying down right in front of him as he prayed, and when he would bow in prostration, she would tuck up her feet to make space for his forehead and hands.

Though ʿĀʾishah ﵂ lived many years after the rebellion against ʿAlī ﵁, she continued until her death to regret her part in it. When at age sixty-five she was dying, one of those who had been a close friend for many years came to visit her. She was hesitant to hear his praise of her, saying she wished she were but a stone or a clod and had never behaved as she had. When he suggested that there yet remained space beside Muḥammad ﷺ and her father and ʿUmar ﵁ for one more grave where she might be buried, she reproached him, saying, "Would you have me undo all my repentance?" She insisted on being buried at night in the communal cemetery, al-Baqīʿ, on the outskirts of Medina. Even though the funeral was held at night, thousands came out to honor her passing, out of love and respect for this "Mother of the Faithful."

ᶜUMAR

One of the most determined opponents of the new faith of Islam was a certain ᶜUmar ibn al-Khaṭṭāb, a young giant of fearful aspect—they said of him that his scowl could kill, and his walking staff was more terrible than most men's swords. ᶜUmar was highborn, related to the most powerful families in Mecca, and like many young aristocrats he was disposed to seek easy solutions to his problems. He came to the conclusion that the best way to put an end to the new faith was by killing Muḥammad. One day he decided to put his resolve into effect, and marched, sword in hand, to the house of al-Arqam, where he knew Muḥammad was hiding. On the way he met a friend who asked what he was doing. "I am going to kill Muḥammad!" ᶜUmar declared, and he was a little puzzled when the friend, a secret convert, suggested that there might be better things to do, and less dangerous ones. "Are you not afraid they will take vengeance on you?" the friend said. "Why kill a man who is so much beloved by your favorite sister?" For the first time ᶜUmar learned that his sister had become a convert. He went straight to her house. He paused outside to listen to the chanting of one of the verses of the sacred book containing the messages received by Muḥammad—it was the verse describing the miracles of Moses and the glory reserved for those who accepted the revelation of the One God—and when he could bear the sound of chanting no more, ᶜUmar burst into the house and attacked his sister and her husband with his sword. His sister's face was covered with blood, and he was about to kill her when she said: "We are followers of Muḥammad, believing in the One God and in His messenger, and you may do with us as you please!" ᶜUmar was impressed by her passionate sincerity and let the sword fall from his hand. She showed him the palm leaf on which the verses were written. He studied it with care, and asked if he could take it home with him. "No," said his sister. "You are unclean from long worshiping of idols, and you may not touch it until you have been cleansed!" ᶜUmar went out and washed himself, and took the leaf home. The next day he went swordless to the house of al-Arqam and paid homage to Muḥammad as the messenger of God.[471]

ʿUmar later became the second Caliph to lead the Muslim community after the death of Abū Bakr. Not long after the beginning of his caliphate, he realized that many people were afraid of him. He had begun to be aware of this already during the Prophet's lifetime and had tried to address it, as ʿĀʾishah recounted:

> Once there was a woman in my house who was singing when ʿUmar asked permission to enter. The woman, upon recognizing ʿUmar's voice, hid herself. When ʿUmar entered the house, the Prophet, who had been listening to this singing, was smiling. ʿUmar said, "O Prophet of God, why are you smiling?" He replied, "There was a woman here who was singing, but when she heard your voice she hid herself." Then ʿUmar said, "I will not leave this house unless I hear what the Prophet heard." So the Prophet called the woman and she resumed her singing while the Prophet and ʿUmar listened.[472]

When Caliph, he told the community that during the time of the Prophet and Abū Bakr who were both so kind and gentle, he had wielded his sword fiercely for Truth and Justice, but now that the Prophet and Abū Bakr were gone, he realized that he needed to manifest both stringency and compassion. He hoped that the people would find in him a friend—generous in mercy and kindness to those in need, and swift and strong in justice for any who were oppressed.

---

[471] From *The History of Islam* by Robert Payne (original title: *The Holy Sword*), pp. 20-21. Copyright © 1959 by Robert Payne. Copyright renewed © 1987 by Sheila Lalwani Payne. Reproduced by permission. (New York, New York: Dorset Press, 1959, 1987.)

[472] Nurbakhsh, Dr. Javad. *The Path*. p76.

[In continuing to convey the Way of the Prophet Muhamamd,] ʿUmar stated that he heard the Holy Prophet say "Give the road its due." He was asked what was the road's due. The Holy Prophet replied: "Lowering the eyes; removing anything offensive; returning salutations; recommending what is reputable; forbidding what is disreputable; helping the sorrowful; guiding people on their way."[473]

In one of his early sermons he called out to his community:

O servants of God, continue to fear God. Suppress your selfish motives and work for the solidarity of the Muslims as a whole. In running the State, you are my partners. Help me with your sound advice. If I follow the right path laid down by God and His Prophet follow me. If I deviate, correct me. Strengthen me with your advice and suggestions.[474]

[ʿUmar ﷺ] showed a particular genius for co-ordination and for correcting errors due to the rashness of commanders, together with remarkable diplomatic talents, taking the edge off disputes and controlling the ambitions of the less tractable among the companions. Although he is known as "the Conqueror," he has some claim also to be known as "the Peacemaker." If we think of the wild young man who had sworn to murder the Prophet, and whose conversion had been so sudden and so dramatic, it becomes possible to observe how Muḥammad had moulded this rough substance into greatness, a flowering of what was already latent within it; ʿUmar's essential characteristics had not been annihilated—God and His messenger do not 'annihilate'—but had been purified, channeled, and then integrated into an excellence both spiritual and human.[475]

---

473 *Alīm 6.0:* . See "Khalīfa ʿUmar bin al-Khaṭṭāb."

474 Ibid.

475 Reprinted by permission from *Islam and the Destiny of Man,* pp. 132-133, by Charles Le Gai Eaton, the State University of New York Press © 1985, State

ᶜUmar was known for being hard on his generals, especially when success threatened to turn their heads. When ᶜAmr, the conqueror of Alexandria, reported to the Caliph that "I have captured a city from the description of which I shall refrain. Suffice it to say that I have taken therein 4,000 villas, 4,000 baths, . . . and 400 pleasure palaces fit for kings". . . [he] received an angry letter accusing him of [attachment to wealth], and soon afterward a special envoy arrived to confiscate half his property. . . .

This same envoy visited Saᶜd, the conqueror of Iraq, at his base in Kūfa and handed him a letter from ᶜUmar: "I hear that you have built yourself a mansion and erected a door between yourself and the people. . . . Come out of it! And never erect a door to keep people out and banish them from their rights, so that they have to wait until you are ready to receive them." Such was the influence of the early caliphs upon the subsequent history of Islam that, to this day, a senior official in the Arab world may face grave criticism if he tries to keep people out of his office and expects them to wait until he is "ready to receive them." Khālid, of whom the nineteenth-century orientalist Sir William Muir wrote that "his conduct on the battlefields . . . must rank him as one of the greatest generals of the world," was even more harshly treated. He was honourably—but compulsorily—retired from his command and died in poverty.

What one senses in ᶜUmar's conduct of affairs throughout his caliphate is a desperate struggle to prevent the forces of this world—pride, power, and wealth—from infiltrating the sacred community; yet still they seeped in. He may well have known that this was one battle he could not hope to win, but it had to be fought none the less; and if the great men of the time—such military geniuses as Khālid, ᶜAmr, and Saᶜd—had to be brought low, this was of little consequence and was, in any case, for their souls' good. In his own life ᶜUmar observed the most rigid discipline and self-denial. "Nothing of the Lord's goods is allowed me," he said, "except a garment for winter and one for summer, and enough for the Pilgrimage and the rites, and food for me and my household at the middle rate allowed one of my people; beyond that I have no more right than any other Muslim."

In fact he did not even observe the middle way, but was so frugal in his habits that his daughter Ḥafṣah begged him to take better care of himself, if only for the Muslims' sake. "I take your meaning," he replied, "but it was in a certain path that I said farewell to two companions of mine"—he meant the Prophet and Abū Bakr—"and if I turned away from the path in which I walked with them I should never find them again at journey's end." So tall that he towered above the people "as though on horseback," grey and prematurely aged, he went about the town barefoot, drawing his patched cloak about him, never satisfied that he was doing his duty as he should. He planned to spend a year traveling among the Muslims, for he knew not—he said—what demands might have been cut short before they came to his attention. "By God," he said once, "I do not know whether I am a caliph or a king; and if I am a king, that is a fearful thing"; this was said in connection with the necessity for taxation, which suggests that he was aware—as are few earthly rulers—of the profound moral problems involved in the seizure of the people's goods or earnings for the purposes of the state. . . .

Riches were now pouring into the treasury, but ʿUmar had an intense distaste for keeping wealth locked up and insisted upon immediate distribution. A register of "pensioners" was instituted, headed by ʿĀʾishah ※, followed by the other surviving "Mothers of the Faithful," then by relatives of the Prophet, men who deserved well of Islam (such as the survivors of Badr), men who had learned the Qurʾān by heart, and soldiers who had fought bravely in the wars. An administration was being built up, but since the Arabs had little experience of such matters, it was a question of devising appropriate institutions as they went along. Yet, for all his labours in Medina, the Caliph found time to travel, and in doing so lost no opportunity to set an example for future generations of Muslims. On one of his journeys, in a year of famine, he came upon a poor woman seated at the roadside with her children beside a fire upon which was an empty pot; he hastened to the nearest village, procured bread and meat, and returned to cook her a meal.

He made a tour of Syria, and before he left the province, an event occurred which stirred the hearts of the faithful. Bilāl, the first *mu*ᶜ*ezzin* of Islam, had retired there, having refused after the Prophet's death ever again to make the public Call to Prayer. The leaders now came to him and begged him to make the Call on this very special occasion. The old African consented, and as the familiar voice rose over the multitude, still loud and clear, the people remembered so vividly the radiant time when the Prophet used to lead the prayers after Bilal's Call that the whole assembly was moved to tears and ᶜUmar sobbed aloud.[476]

It was the usual practice of ᶜUmar that he would patrol the streets and suburbs of Madīna to watch the interests of the people, and attend to their needs. One day ᶜUmar noticed a tent pitched in an open space outside Madīna. A person was sitting outside the tent, and some one inside the tent was groaning. ᶜUmar went to the man, greeted him, and wanted to know who he was. The man said that he was a man of the desert, and had come to Madīna to wait on the Commander of the Faithful and seek his assistance. ᶜUmar next asked who was groaning inside the tent. The man said that inside the tent his wife was groaning with labour pains. He said that he was a stranger in Madīna and did not know what to do. ᶜUmar enquired

[476] Reprinted by permission from *Islam and the Destiny of Man*, pp. 135-137, by Charles Le Gai Eaton, the State University of New York Press © 1985, State University of New York. All rights reserved.

whether he had any woman to look after the confinement of his wife. He said that there was none.

ᶜUmar said, "Do not worry. I will make the necessary arrangements."

ᶜUmar came home, and asked his wife Umm Kulsum to accompany him on a mission of service. Umm Kulsum got ready and took with her such things as might be needed for the purposes of confinement. ᶜUmar took with him some provisions for the purposes of cooking a meal. ᶜUmar returned to the camp with his wife. Umm Kulsum went inside the tent to attend to the woman in pain, while ᶜUmar sat outside the tent with the Bedouin and began cooking some meals for him. After an hour or so when the meals had been cooked, Umm Kulsum from inside the tent addressed ᶜUmar: "*Amīr ul-muᶜminīn!* Congratulate your guest on the birth of a son."

Hearing this the Bedouin felt much embarrassed. Turning to ᶜUmar he said, "*Amīr ul-muᶜminīn,* why did you not reveal your identity? You have overwhelmed me with your benevolence."

ᶜUmar put all his fears to rest saying: "That's all right. There is nothing to worry about. Thank God I have been of some service to you at the time of your need. You may come to me tomorrow and I will see what can be done further to help you."

It was late at night when ᶜUmar and Umm Kulsum left. The Bedouin thanked God and said: "God be praised. I came to seek the Commander of the Faithful, and God sent the Commander of the Faithful to seek me."[477]

ᶜUmar had been caliph for ten years when, in November 644, a young man, who thought himself badly treated in the matter of his salary [and ᶜUmar's judgment of his case], stabbed him three times as he came out of the mosque in Medina and then killed himself. Knowing that he was mortally wounded, ᶜUmar appointed a committee of six Qurayshites to choose one of their number to succeed him. "To him who shall follow

---

[477] *Alīm 6.0:* , see "Khalīfa ᶜUmar bin al-Khaṭṭāb."

me," he said, "I give it as my wish that he be kind to this city which gave a home to us and to the Faith, that he make much of their virtues and pass lightly over their faults. And bid him treat well the Arab tribes, for they are the strength of Islam. . . . O my Lord, I have finished my course." They carried the body to ʿĀʾishah's chamber, where the Prophet and Abū Bakr were buried. The dead man's son saluted her and said: "ʿUmar requests permission to enter." "Bring him in," she said.[478]

[478] Reprinted by permission from *Islam and the Destiny of Man,* p. 137, by Charles Le Gai Eaton, the State University of New York Press © 1985, State University of New York. All rights reserved.

RĀBIᶜA

Rābiᶜa al-ᶜAdawiyyah, a major saint of Islam, was born, according to one reckoning, in 717 A.D., and died in 801. She lived and died in Baṣra. Stories about her and poems attributed to her have come down to us through many writers, including ᶜAṭṭār, her major biographer, and Al-Ghazālī, the central pole where Sufism and orthodox Islam meet. Little is known of her actual life, and that little is a mixture of factual information and hagiography (saint-stories)—another kind of "fact."

The "real" facts are brief: She was born into a poor family. During a famine both her parents died, and she and her sisters were separated. Homeless and vulnerable, she was captured and sold as a slave. Later she was freed by her master, and may have made her living as a flute player at one time. She may have made the pilgrimage to Makkah. In later life she became famous as a saint. She was offered money, houses, and proposals of marriage, but she preferred to remain single and live in humble surroundings—some texts say a "ruin"—where she spent her time praying, keeping house, performing spiritual exercises, and receiving visitors. The stories of her interactions with those who came to challenge her or learn from her make up the bulk of the Rābiᶜa material as we know it.

The following three stories are representative:

When being pursued by the slave-trader who finally captured her, she tried to run, but slipped and sprained her wrist. When she knew her freedom was lost, she cried: "O God! I am an orphan, and am about to be a slave—on top of that, my wrist is broken. But that's not what I care about. The thing I have to know is, are you satisfied with me?" Immediately a Voice answered her: "Don't worry, Rābiᶜa—on the Day of Resurrection your rank will be so high that even the closest companions of God will envy you."

Then Rābiᶜa submitted to God's will, and became a slave.

~ These stories and poems of Rābiᶜa are excerpted from *Doorkeeper of the Heart* by Charles Upton (Threshold Books, Putney, Vermont 1988), pp. 8-12, 21, 44, 52.

In her life as a slave, Rābiʿa found time for her worship of God by doing without sleep. She fasted and prayed. One night her master awoke, looked down from the window of his house into the courtyard, and saw Rābiʿa in prayer. As he was watching her he was amazed to see a lamp appear above her head in mid-air; the light from this miraculous lamp lit up the whole house. Terrified and astonished, he went back to bed, and sat wondering until dawn. Then he called Rābiʿa to him, confessed what he had seen, and gave her her freedom, with the option of staying on with him if she wanted to. She asked permission to leave and it was granted; so she went out of the house, out of the city, and into the desert to pray.

On one occasion several different men wanted to marry Rābiʿa, including ʿAbd al-Walīd ibn Zayd, Ḥasan of Baṣra, the provincial governor, and the Amīr of Baṣra himself. . . . By the time Rābiʿa's fame as a saint had spread, bringing with it offers of property and proposals of marriage, her earlier life of hardship had already formed her character: to accept gifts from this world would have been to turn her back on the God who sustained her when this world had nothing to offer but a whip. Generally speaking, marriage and full involvement with the affairs of the community of believers is the norm in Islam, but [for some servants,] God may have other plans. . . . This was her answer to the Amīr:

"I'm not interested, really, in 'possessing all you own,'
Nor in 'making you my slave,'
Nor in having my attention distracted from God
Even for a split second."

And she told the governor:

"Control *yourself:* Don't let others control you.
Share your inheritance with them, not with me,
And suffer along with them the common suffering of the time.
As for you, remember the day of your death.
As for me, whatever bride-price you offer,
Understand that the Lord *I* worship can double it."
"So goodbye."

Chief among her companions were Sufyān al-Thawrī, her closest male companion; Rabah al-Qays, a well-known ascetic of the same school of Sufyān; and Maryam of Baṣra, her most devoted female disciple, who became her servant. Another name frequently associated with hers is that of the famous saint Ḥasan of Baṣra—but since scholarship seems to show that he was around eleven years old when Rābiᶜa died, the many stories of their encounters may actually represent a controversy between their schools.

Al-Ghazālī calls Rābiᶜa a prime exemplar of the Station of Love. But she speaks to us just as clearly out of other stations as well . . . and she seems to be among those who introduced into Islam the idea that the highest form of the worship of God entails sacrificing the desire both for this world and the next. As she says in one of her poems:

> O God! If I adore you out of fear of Hell, burn me in Hell. If I adore you out of desire for Paradise, lock me out of Paradise. But if I adore You for Yourself alone, do not deny me the vision of Your eternal Beauty.

The following poems were either composed by her or are based on her sayings:

I am fully qualified to work as a doorkeeper, for this reason:
What is inside me, I don't let out,
What is outside me, I don't let in.
If someone comes in, he goes right out again;
He has nothing to do with me at all.
I am a doorkeeper of the Heart, not a lump of wet clay.

Where a part of you goes, the rest will follow—given time.
You call yourself a teacher: therefore learn.
My soul, how long will you keep on falling asleep and
waking up again?
The time is near when you will fall into so deep a sleep
That only the Trumpet of Resurrection will have the
power to wake you.

O God, the stars are shining;
All eyes have closed in sleep;
The kings have locked their doors.
Each lover is alone, in secret, with the one he loves.
And here I am, too, hidden from all of them,
Alone with You.

LADY NAFĪSA

Lady Nafīsa (9th century), who was known as "the jewel of knowledge" and "the mother of the helpless," was the great-granddaughter of Ḥasan, son of Lady Fāṭimah and Imām ʿAlī. She was born in Mecca in the year A.H. 145 (760 A.D.) and brought up in Medina. Her life was the expression of good works and immersion in the worship of God.

> Nafīsa married Isḥāq, son of the Imām Jaʿfar aṣ-Ṣādiq, and bore him two children, al-Qāsim and Umm Kulthūm. After her marriage, [they] went to Egypt with her cousin Sakīna al-Madfuna, and settled down to live not far from the Khalīfah's palace in Cairo. Like the other ascetics of Islam, she used to fast all day and spend the night in prayer.
>
> She was reputed to know the Qurʾān and the commentaries by heart and was so versed in religious knowledge that even her great contemporary, the Imām Ash-Shāfiʿī,[479] used to come and listen to her discourses and enter into discussions with her; the degree of his respect for the scholarship of this saintly woman and for her sanctity also may be judged from the fact that he used to pray with her the special prayers for Ramaḍān.[480]

~ This biography of Lady Nafisa is excerpted from *Women of Sufism* by C. Helminski, portions of pp 56-59.

[479] Ash-Shāfiʿī was one of the four great Sunnī Muslim jurists. Lady Nafīsa had studied in her youth with one of the other great jurists, Mālik ibn Anās. The four major schools of legal thought in Islam are the Shāfiʿī, Maliki, Hanbali, and Hanafi. The Jaʿfari school of law, upon which the Shiʿite Muslims base their practice, follows the interpretation of Imām Jaʿfar Aṣ-Ṣādiq (the sixth Imām descended from ʿAlī), Lady Nafīsa's father-in-law. Lady Nafīsa was one of the many early Sufi women who were well-versed in the principles of law (based on the Qurʾān and the *ḥadīth*). Her opinion on rightful ways of action and being was sought by many notables of her time, as was her illuminative presence. (C.A.H.)

[480] Smith, Margaret, *Rabiʿa the Mystic and Her Fellow Saints in Islam*, Cambridge University Press, 1928, p. 148.

Whenever Ash-Shāfiʿī would fall ill, he would send word with a messenger to Nafīsa asking for her prayers and as soon as the messenger would return to Ash-Shāfiʿī he would find him recovered from his ailment. When he came down with his fatal illness, he again sent the messenger to Nafīsa, but this time she told the messenger to go back and tell Ash-Shāfiʿī that, "God has blessed him with the pleasure of seeing His Noble Face." When the messenger returned to the Imām he asked the messenger what happened, and when he relayed the words of Lady Nafīsa, Ash-Shāfiʿī knew his time had come to make his final preparations. He made his last will and testament asking that Lady Nafīsa perform the funeral prayers for him when he died. When the Imām died, his body had to be brought to her house because she was so weak due to her constant fasting and worship that she could not leave her house to go to him to perform the prayer. . . . She prayed extensively for him and offered the eulogy: "May God have mercy on Ash-Shāfiʿī because he performed his ablutions in the most beautiful way." She said this because she understood that ablution[481] is the key to prayer and

Ramaḍān is the annual lunar month of fasting for Muslims. Observation of this month of fasting is one of the pillars of Islam and is understood to bring great blessing in many ways. From first light of day until sunset, Muslims refrain from eating, drinking, and sexual intercourse. During this month they also especially refrain from gossip and carefully watch their speech so that no ill words might be spoken. During Ramaḍān special prayers are recited and families and friends gather frequently in intensified remembrance and worship of God. (C.A.H.)

[481] Ablution is the ritual washing that precedes all prayer. Certain conditions nullify the ablution and one must renew it. As one cleans the body one is simultaneously with intention clearing the inner capacities as well and renewing one's connection with one's Sustainer. The faithful strive to as much as possible always be in a state of ablution so that they might also rightfully be continuously in prayer and ever ready for the meeting with their Lord. As one never knows when the moment of death may arrive, one wishes always to be as clear as possible, outwardly and inwardly prepared for that meeting. (C.A.H.)

that whoever excels in ablution excels in the other works of the Way.[482]

Lady Nafisa's neice, Zaynab, was asked about her aunt's sustenance. She said, " She used to eat once every three nights. She would hang a small basket in front of her place of prayer; whatever she needed she would find in that basket. I used to find in it things I would never imagine finding there, and I never knew where they came from. This amazed me and I asked my aunt about it. She told me, "O Zaynab, whoever sets things right with God, the whole universe is theirs."[483]

During the time of Lady Nafisa, there was an old, poor widow with four daughters who made their living by weaving cloth and then selling it. One day, the old woman was on her way to the market with their weaving when a bird swooped down and snatched the sack in which she was carrying it. The woman was so distressed that she fainted. When she regained consciousness, she reflected, "What shall I do? How will I provide for my family?" and she began to weep. People gathered around her and when they heard what had happened, they took her to Lady Nafisa. Nafisa listened to her story and then began to pray for her, saying, "O my God, You are exalted in ability, and You are the Compelling Sovereign. Relieve your servants from their sorrows. They are Your creation and Your dependents and You have ability over all things." Then she said to the widow, "Stay here a while, and know that God has power over all things." The old woman sat down, full of concern for her children's plight.

After a while a group of people came to the house asking for

[482] Sheikh Tāhā ʿAbdur-Raʾūf Saʾad and Saʾad Ḥasan Muḥammad ʿAlī, *As-Sayyidah Nafisa, Nafisat ul-ʿIlm Karīmat ad-Dārayn*, translated by Mahmoud Mostafa (Cairo, Egypt: Al Safaa Library, 2000), p. 33.

[483] Ibid., pp. 31-32.

Lady Nafisa. When they entered her presence they told her, "An amazing thing happened to us. We were traveling by ship and when we approached your coast, our vessel was damaged and water began filling our ship. We tried to plug the hole but could not, and we thought we would drown. Then suddenly a bird swooped down from the sky and dropped a sack on us. We found in it woven cloth which we used to plug the hole enough to be able to reach safety by God's will. And we are here to give 500 dinars as a gift of our gratitude for our safety." When Nafisa heard this, she burst into tears and said, "My God, my Master, my Friend! How merciful You are! How gentle you are with Your servants!"

She then called the old widow near to her and asked her how much she would have expected to receive in exchange for her goods at the market. The woman told her she had hoped to earn 25 dirhems; Nafisa handed her the 500 dinars (a much greater amount). The woman took the money home to her daughters and related to them what had taken place. They all returned to Lady Nafisa and devoted their lives in her service.[484]

Lady Nafisa was famed throughout Egypt and wherever she went her reputation followed her, and she gained the full approbation of all, both individuals and the people generally, who revered her for her good works,[485] her frequent pilgrimages,[486] her lengthy fasts, and her nights spent in prayer. She died in Cairo in the month of Ramaḍān, in the year A.H. 208 (824 A.D.).

One of her biographers relates that when she was at the

---

[484] Ibid., pp. 32-33.

[485] When people complained to her about the injustice of the Egyptian governor of that time, she is said to have stood in his path and handed him a note in which she accused him of tyranny and called on him to be more just. (Walther, *Women in Islam: from Medieval to Modern Times*, p. 110)

[486] She is reported to have made thirty pilgrimages. (Ibid.)

point of death, and, as usual, fasting, those with her tried to compel her to break her fast, but she refused, saying, "This would seem a strange thing to me. For thirty years I have been asking God that I should meet with Him when I was fasting, and shall I break my fast now? This shall not be." Then she repeated the *Sūrah al-Anᶜām* and when she reached the part where God said, "For them is an abode of peace with their Lord,"[487] she passed away.

The same writer tells us that during her life-time she had dug her grave with her own hands and had descended into it and prayed and there repeated the whole Qurʾān six thousand times. When Nafisa died, the people assembled from all the villages and towns in the neighbourhood and lighted candles that night and the sound of the wailing for the dead was heard from every house in Cairo, and they prayed over her body, while many bore witness that they had seen none like her. Then she was buried in the grave that she had dug in her own house. Up to the time of the writer, and even to the present time, her shrine has been a place of pilgrimage for travelers from afar. Her husband, indeed, wished to convey her body to Medina, for burial in the sacred city, but the people of Cairo begged that she should be buried among them.

Many miracles, showing her charity towards others, were attributed to Nafisa. The story is told of how one year the Nile failed to rise in flood at the usual time and the people were in great distress. They were afraid that for lack of water for their crops they would perish from famine, and in this extremity they came to the saint, appealing for her help. She gave them her veil and bade them cast it into the river, and when they had done so, immediately the river rose in an unusually high flood and the people were saved.[488]

---

[487] *Sūrah Al-Anᶜām* 6:127.

[488] Smith, Margaret, *Rabi'a the Mystic and Her Fellow Saints in Islam*, Cambridge University Press, 1928, p. 148-150.

Her tomb, like that of many of the *Ahl al-Bayt* (family of the house of Muḥammad ﷺ), continues to be a place of pilgrimage and prayer where many receive blessings. The shrine of her great-aunt, Sayyida Zaynab ؓ, is another shrine of one of the women of the early *Ahl al-Bayt* where many find great blessing (both Muslim and Christian). Lady Nafisa was particularly known for the ability to heal eye ailments.[489] The Egyptian government, not blind to her healing influence, established a hospital specifically for the healing of eye diseases in the neighborhood of her tomb in Cairo.

---

[489] True vision, *basīrah*, clear-sightedness both outwardly and inwardly, is one of the gifts of God to the faithful.

SALADIN

Ṣalāh ad-Dīn (1138-1193), known in the west as Saladin, was the great Muslim leader who defeated the Christians in the Second Crusade and destroyed the Latin kingdoms they had established in Syria and Palestine. In his conquest of Jerusalem in 1187 he showed a clemency to the Christian inhabitants which was in stark contrast to the usual practice of the Crusaders following their own victories. He was known for his justice, for his defense of the weak against the strong, and for his ready accessibility to people of all classes and stations in life.

He was indulgent to those who failed and slow to wrath. I was on duty at his side at Marj ᶜUyun before the Franks attacked Acre—may God make its reconquest easy! It was his custom to ride on for as long as possible and then to dismount and have food served, which he would eat in company with his men before retiring to sleep in his private tent. When he awoke he would pray, and then withdraw, with me in attendance on him, to read a section of *ḥadīth* or Law: among other works that he read with me was an anthology of Sulaym ar-Rāzī including the four sections of the Law. One day he dismounted as usual and food was served. He was about to rise when he was told that it was almost the hour of prayer, so he sat down again and said: "Let us pray, and then let us go to bed." He sat and talked wearily. Everyone except his personal servants had withdrawn, when suddenly there appeared an ancient mamluk whom he held in high esteem, who presented him with a plea from someone fighting in the Holy War. "I am tired now," said the Sultan, "present it again a little later', but the man would not comply with this request. He held the plea up to the Sultan's august face, opening it so that he could read it. Saladin read the name written at the top, recognized it and said: "A worthy man." "Well then," said the other, "Your Majesty will in-

---

~ "Saladin" is excerpted from Francesco Gabrieli, *Arab Historians of the Crusades—Selected and Translated from the Arabic Sources.* Edited and translated by E.J. Costello. (Copyright © 1969 Routledge and Kegan Paul, Ltd., Andover, United Kingdom; used with their permission and that of the University of California Press), pp. 105-107, 111.

scribe your placet." "But there is no inkwell here," said the Sultan, for he was sitting at the opening of the tent, blocking the entrance, while the inkstand was at the back of the tent, which was a big one. But his interlocutor observed: "There is the inkstand, at the back of the tent!" which was nothing if not an invitation to Saladin to bring that very inkwell out. The Sultan turned, saw the inkstand and said: "By Allāh, you are right!" He leaned on his left elbow, stretched out his right hand, took the inkstand, signed the plea. . . . Then I said: "God said to His prophet: "*You are truly a magnanimous man,*" and it seems to me that Your Majesty shares this quality with him," to which Saladin replied: "It did not cost anything: we heard what he wanted, and we wanted to recompense him." If a similar thing had happened to a private individual he would have lost his temper; and who would have been capable of replying to one of his subordinates in this way? This is the perfection of kindness and generosity, *and God will not let such goodness go unrewarded.*

One day when I was on duty I was riding with him ahead of the Franks when a sentry brought up a woman who was in a distracted state, weeping and beating her breast. "This woman," said the sentry, "has come from the Frankish camp and asked to be brought before the Sultan, so we brought her here." The Sultan told the interpreter to ask her what was the matter, and she said that Muslim raiders had come into her tent the day before and had carried off her little daughter. "All night long I have been seeking help, until this morning our leaders told me: 'The Muslim King is merciful; we will let you leave the camp to go to him, and you can ask him for your daughter.' So they let me come, and you are my only hope of getting my baby back again."

Saladin was moved to pity by her plight, and tears came into his eyes. His generous spirit prompted him to order someone to take her to the market-place in the camp to ask who had bought the child, repay him and bring her back. All this occurred in the morning; not an hour passed before the knight returned with the child on his shoulders. As soon as her mother caught sight of her she fell to the ground, rubbing her face in the dust, while everyone there wept with her. She raised her face to heaven, but we could not understand what she said. Her daughter was handed over to her and she was conducted back to her own camp.

AL-GHAZĀLĪ

There are geniuses in this world who preach things but do not practice them. But Imām al-Ghazālī was one of those who preached, wrote, and spread only those things which he practiced. This immortal genius and thinker was born in 1058 in Ṭūs in the province of Khurasan. His real name was Abū Ḥāmid ibn Muḥammad an-Nīshāpūrī. "Ghazālī" was a title taken probably from his birthplace, Ghazala, or from his father's trade, Ghazzal, meaning wool merchant. His father was a very religious Sufi who used to find special pleasure in associating with Sufis and dervishes.

He started his career with a great Sufi who gave him lessons in the Qur'ān, *ḥadīth*, and Sufism. He then studied the *Sharī'ah* for some time with Shaykh Aḥmad aṭ-Ṭūsi and then he went to Jurjan to become a disciple of Imām Abū Nasr of Jurjan. While he was returning from Jurjan to Ṭūs, he was attacked by bandits and robbed of all his belongings, including his books and manuscripts. Then he went to the leader of the bandits and requested him to return his books and manuscripts in return for keeping everything else. At this the bandit leader remarked with laughter that if they had looted his knowledge, then there was no need for such knowledge. If his knowledge was confined to books, could he really be called a man of knowledge? This taunting remark went deep into his heart and thereafter he started memorizing everything that he had learnt.

Then for some time he devoted himself to studying Sufism and in 1078 he was admitted into the famous Niẓāmiyya Madrasah of Nishapur and became a disciple of the principal of the Madrasah, Shaykh Abū'l-Ma'ālī, the Imām of the Ḥaramayn. Under his leadership, he leamed religion, philosophy, jurisprudence, and natural law. Everyone in the Niẓāmiyya Madrasah was struck by his profound learning and unusual

---

~ "Al-Ghazālī" is excerpted from M. Atiqul Haque, *Muslim Heroes of the World* (London, United Kingdom: Ta-Ha Publishers, 1990, 1998), pp. 66-69, 69-70, 71. Reprinted by permission of Ta-Ha Publishers, Ltd., 1 Wynne Road, London SW9 0BB United Kingdom.

genius. The Imām al-Ḥaramayn himself had said to him out of jealousy, "You have outdone me while I am alive! You could have at least waited until I died!"

At this time he became more prone to criticizing faith than having faith. He used to declare that those who did not judge and discern could not find the truth—they would remain in the dark. He used to believe, at this time, that the scholars should only reach a conclusion through research and discerning the truth. They should not accept anything blindly and easily. They must find the truth by exerting themselves through trial and error [or] through critical judgment and penetrating study. In short, he became a great arguer and an excessive debater. He said Allāh had given him excessively the faculty of reasoning and argumentation.

Soon he became a famous scholar and great philosopher. At this time Niẓām al-Mulk was the Prime Minister of Malik Shah, the Seljuq Sultan, who used to summon assemblies and debates between scholars and philosophers and others of the intellectual elite. The enlightened assembly used to be entertained by al-Ghazālī's power of reasoning and his far-reaching knowledge. After the death of Imām al-Ḥaramayn in 1091, the Prime Minister appointed al-Ghazālī, at the age of 34, as the Principal of Niẓāmiyya Madrasah. The people of Baghdad were enthralled by al-Ghazālī's lectures, his penetrating analysis of religion, and by his clear and straightforward presentation of solutions to several difficult matters of religion. He soon became their hero. He gained wealth as well as fame. He became the Imām of the whole of Iraq and Khurasan.

He was the principal of the Niẓāmiyya Madrasah for only four years. But during this time his fame and name spread far and wide; and the people of the Muslim world were full of praise for his brilliant scholarship. But suddenly, at the age of forty, when he was the undisputed leader of Baghdad, he gave up and left all his fame, name, and wealth, and went away in search of the Truth in different places and locations.

The gloss of this world did not hold him back. He cut himself off implacably from its clutches and went away into the desert, in hiding, to find his Lord. He remained in hiding for ten years, far away from the distracting crowds, meditating on his Lord and the Hereafter. Like a dervish he roamed from place to place, to Syria, to Palestine, Jerusalem,

Cairo, Alexandria, etc., and also to the tombs of many distinguished *awliyā*ᶜ, and to many mosques in many countries. At that time nobody would ever have thought from his wretched clothes, from his worn-out appearance, and from his thin voice that this man was once the greatest scholar of Baghdad and had been rising on the highest ladder of riches and luxury. While he was in this wretched condition he found his Lord. His inner eyes opened and he found the Truth.

In 1106 he came back to Baghdad and at the request of the then Prime Minister of Baghdad he agreed to start teaching again in the Niẓāmiyya Madrasah. During this period he wrote his famous book *Iḥyā*ᶜ ᶜ*Ulūm ad-Dīn*. From this book he used to deliver lectures (*khuṭbahs*) which were so full of spiritual enlightenment and all-embracing knowledge that people used to call him the Ḥujjatu'l-Islām or the Proof of Islām. But after only two years he again left the Niẓāmiyya Madrasah for his home town of Ṭūs where he spent the rest of his life.

Al-Ghazālī is one of the greatest thinkers and geniuses the world has known. The focus of his thoughts and the principal aim of his teachings and of his learned discourses were to attract people to morality. He well realized that the society of his time was steeped in the glitter and worship of this world and hence the necessity of tremendous moral teaching and religious injunctions. He devoted most of his time and most of his writings to distracting people from the enjoyment of this world and to diverting them to the upliftment of their soul and spirit. His unique scholarship, wide experience, sharp insight, deep thinking and wonderful sense of judgment went a long way to give a direction to the then-disillusioned Muslim society. And his Muslim readers and followers of his thought have gained immensely, and his writings have become universally celebrated.

But al-Ghazālī's greatest contribution was in his turning the whole spiritual world of Islam into a fine presentation of *taṣawwuf*. That is to say, it is the spirit that is the most important thing in Islam. And this is what Al-Ghazālī in his beautiful writings has presented to the world.

He was proclaimed a reviver of Islam and the gratified Muslims greeted him as the Ḥujjatu'l-Islām, i.e. the Witness of Islam. It was owing to his influence and writings that the Muslim world got its rightful place back in the intellectual circles of the world and in the world of science and philosophy. And he did all this by drawing only from the Qur'ān. Henceforth the *ᶜUlamāᶜ* and the Sufis did not clash; they were riding on the same boat. The coordination between the two was made complete through him.

JALĀLU'DDIN RŪMĪ

Jalālu'ddin Rūmī (1207-1273), was born in Balkh in what is now Afghanistan. When he was a young boy, his family emigrated from Balkh just before the invasion of the Mongols. After many years of journeying his family finally settled in what is now Konya, Turkey, but was then known as *Rūm*, hence, "Rūmī."

His father was one of the highly respected scholars of the *ᶜUlamāᶜ* and Rūmī was raised with a deep knowledge of Qur'ān, Islamic law, *ḥadīth,* and commentary and an ever-deepening awareness of and connection with his Sustainer. After his father's death, he continued his education with a close friend and disciple of his father's and completed further study in Aleppo and Damascus. Rūmī then took on his father's teaching role at the Konya *madrasah*, and became renowned just as his father had been as the "Sultan of the learned." He and his wife and family continued to be pillars of the community and the region.

Then one day, a wandering dervish, Shams ad-Dīn Ṭabrīzī, arrived in Konya. In the streets of Konya, they met and an intense spiritual friendship commenced. Shams was burning with the love of God, and Jalālu'ddin Rūmī caught fire. From then on they were inseparable, spending long hours in spiritual conversation and prayer. However this caused a tension in the community of the *madrasahs* because Rūmī's students missed his presence and attentions. The difficult atmosphere drove Shams to disappear for a time. Rūmī sent his son in search of him and at last he brought Shams back from Damascus. It wasn't long though before again jealousies arose and eventually Shams was one day killed.

Rūmī's heart cracked wide open and the grief he felt at separation from this dearest of spiritual friends exploded in him into a fountain of love. Poetry began to flow from his tongue and those around him wrote down what came to be called the Dīvān-i Shams-i Ṭabrīz. As this love continued to deepen and to find its steady source in the Infinite Love of God, Rūmī composed what has come to be known as "the Qur'ān in the Persian tongue," the *Mathnawī*, his masterwork of 26,000 couplets. Inspiration would come to him and he would recite while his dear friend Ḥusāmuddīn would write down the lines. The couplets of the *Mathnawī* encopass all aspects of life and direct our attention continually to the Divine Source. The spiritual and poetic traditions that produced Rūmī, Sanā'ī, ʿAṭṭār, Saʿdī, and Jāmī understands all of creation as providing metaphors of Divine Qualities. Rūmī did not write poetry for the sake of writing poetry but only as a means to communicate the encompassing and continual Presence of the Divine. Within Rūmī's *Mathnawī*, God's abundant Generosity and Compassion and Mercy breathe from every page as the underlying message is continually conveyed of the Oneness of Reality.

The love that overflowed from Rūmī drew many to him to drink from that Source. Whether Muslim, Christian, Jew, or other, all were nourished by his presence and his words. Even little children were drawn to be near him. One of his biographers relates his words and the following story:

> "Every tree that yields no fruit, as the pine, the cypress, the box, etc., grows tall and straight, lifting its head up high, and sending all its branches upward, whereas all the fruit-bearing trees droop their heads, and trail their branches.". . . In like manner, Jalāl also had the commendable habit to show himself humble and considerate to all, even the lowest; especially so to children and old women. He used to bless them and always bowed to them, even if they were not Muslims. Once he chanced upon a number of children who were playing and who left their game, ran to him, and bowed. Jalāl bowed to them also; sc much so that one little fellow called out from afar, "Wait for me until I come." Jalāl did not move away until the child had come, bowed, and been bowed to.

On the 17th of December 1273, Rūmī died and countless people of the Konya region turned out to mourn him, whether Muslim, Christian, or Jew. Everyone felt the loss of his presence.

One Christian was heard chanting the words, "He was our

Moses and David and he was our Jesus and we were his followers."[490]

In short, Rūmī was a great personality, greater than any description we can give of him. He was a lover of all that is good, pure and beautiful. But, above all, he was a lover of the love of Allāh. This love of Allāh is the pinnacle of man's possibilities. And to reach that pinnacle of love, man's intelligence and reasoning are not sufficient. Intelligence and reasoning are very limited. It is the love of Allāh that will lead him to his goal. But this should not make him forget his obligations to his country, to his society, and to the service of man. He should try to find Allāh through following what is true, what is good, what is beautiful, and what is good for his country and his people. In other words, through human love he can find the love of Eternity, and that is the *Sirāj al-Munīra*, the greatest light.[491]

God, in spite of the sceptics,
Caused spiritual gardens with sweet flowers to grow
In the hearts of His friends.
Every rose that is sweet-scented within,
That rose is telling of the secrets of the Universal.
Their scent, to the confusion of the sceptics,
Spreads around the world, rending the veil.
[*Mathnawī* I:2021-2023][492]

---

[490] Haque, *Muslim Heroes of the World*, pp. 98-100.

[491] Ibid., p. 101.

[492] *Rumi: Daylight, A Daybook of Spiritual Guidance, Three Hundred Sixty-Five Selections from Jalaluddin Rumi's* Mathnawi, Translated by Camille and Kabir Helminski, Threshold Books, 1990. p. 15.

FLORENCE NIGHTINGALE

> Nursing is an art; and if it is to be made an art, requires as exclusive a devotion, as hard a preparation, as any painter's or sculptor's work—for what is the having to do with dead canvas or cold marble, compared with having to do with the living body, the temple of God's spirit? It is one of the fine arts; I had almost said, the finest of the Fine Arts.
>
> ~ Florence Nightingale, "Una and the Lion," 1868[493]

Florence Nightingale was born in 1820 in Florence, Italy to a noble English family. Though her family belonged to the ruling elite of England, Florence from an early age was drawn not to social grandeur, but to service. "God has always led me of Himself . . . the first idea I can recollect when I was a child was a desire to nurse the sick. My daydreams were all of hospitals and I visited them whenever I could. I never communicated it to anyone as it would have been laughed at; but I thought God had called me to serve Him in that way."[494] Though she was born during an era when education for women was considered unsuitable, with the help of close relatives, Florence managed to persuade her parents to let her study mathematics.

Little by little her path in nursing unfolded until in 1854 she found herself head of the nursing forces of the main hospital in Constantinople during the Crimean War. Living quarters were infested with vermin; the roof leaked; there were hardly any cleaning supplies or facilities for washing patients or their bedding; lice infestation was rampant and proper food was quite scarce, so fasting became common practice. During these challenging days, a journalist described her as having tremendous tact and diplomacy:

---

[493] Barbara Montgomery Dossey, *Florence Nightingale, Mystic, Visionary, Healer* (Philadelphia, Pennsylvania: Springhouse Pub. Co., http://lwww.com Lippincott Williams & Wilkins, 2000), p. vi.

[494] Ibid., p. 3 (Florence Nightingale, Curriculum Vitae, 1851).

> Her manner and countenance are prepossessing, and this without great self-possession of positive beauty; it is a face not easily forgotten, pleasing in its smile, with an eye betokening great self-possession, and giving, when she wishes, a quiet look of firm determination to every feature. Her general demeanor is quiet and rather reserved; still I am much mistaken if she is not gifted with a very lively sense of the ridiculous. In conversation, she speaks on matters of business with a grave earnestness one would not expect from her appearance. She has evidently a mind disciplined to restrain under the principles of the action of the moment every feeling which would interfere with it. She has trained herself to command, and learned the value of conciliation towards others and constraint over herself. I can conceive her to be a strict disciplinarian; she throws herself into a work as its head. As such she knows well how much success depend upon literal obedience to her every order. . . .
>
> Every day [at Scutari] brought some new complication of misery to be somehow unraveled. Each day had its peculiar trial to one who had taken such a load of responsibility, in an untried field with a staff of her own sex, all new to it . . . and in my opinion, [she] is the one individual who in this whole unhappy war had shown more than any other what real energy guided by_good sense can do to meet the calls of sudden emergency.[495]

Continually Florence encouraged her nurses to improve not only their skills, but their manner of being as well:

> How can we be "stewards of grace" to one another? By giving the "grace" of our good example to all around us. . . . Do we look enough into the importance of . . . keeping careful

---

[495] Excerpted from Barbara Montgomery Dossey, *Florence Nightingale, Mystic, Visionary, Healer* (Philadelphia, Pennsylvania: Springhouse Pub. Co., http://lwww.com Lippincott Williams & Wilkins, 2000), p. 127.

Notes of Lectures, of keeping notes of all type cases . . . so as to improve our powers of observation: all essential if we are in future to have charge? Do we keep in view the importance of helping ourselves to understand these cases by reading at the time books where we can find them described, and by listening to the remarks made by Physicians and Surgeons in going round with their students? (Take a sly note afterwards, when nobody sees, in order to have a correct remembrance.)

So shall we do everything in our power to become proficient, not only in knowing the symptoms and what is to be done, but in knowing the "Reason Why" of such symptoms, and why such and such a thing is done: and so on, till we can some day train others to know the "reason why."

Many say: "We have no time; the Ward work gives us no time." But it is so easy to degenerate into a mere drudgery about the Wards, when we have goodwill to do it and are fonder of practical work than of giving ourselves the trouble of learning the "reason why.". . . Take ten minutes a day in the Ward to jot down things, and write them out afterwards. . . . It is far better to take these ten minutes to write your cases or to jot down your recollections in the Ward than to give the same ten minutes to bustling about. . . . It is of ourselves and not of others that we must give an account. [496]

Nightingale worked sometimes 20 hours each day. Soon even the most hardened officers noticed the effects of her commanding authority and healing presence. She had an utter disregard of contagion and spent hours over men who were dying of cholera or other fevers. On one occasion, surgeons laid five soldiers aside to die, deeming their condition hopeless. Nightingale and a few nurses got permission to care for these

---

[496] Excerpted from Barbara Montgomery Dossey, *Florence Nightingale, Mystic, Visionary, Healer* (Philadelphia, Pennsylvania: Springhouse Pub. Co., http://lwww.com Lippincott Williams & Wilkins, 2000), p. 305.

men through the night, and by morning they were fit for surgery. When doctors would say, "We can't," her response was "we must." However, some officers continued to show their contempt by calling her "the Bird"; when faced with an unpleasant task, they would excuse themselves by saying, "It's the Bird's duty."

For her part, Nightingale remained self-assured amid the tension and jealousy. To her family she wrote: "Praise, good God! He knows what a situation He had put upon me. For His sake I bear it willingly, but not for the sake of Praise. The cup which my Father hath given me shall I not drink? But how few can sympathize with such a position!"

Within a few weeks, Nightingale had made tremendous progress in obtaining supplies.[497]

She so mastered the situation that soon ladies, orderlies, Turks, Greeks, French, and Italians were coming to her to obtain supplies. When military channels complicated the funding of direly needed expanded facilities, with her own funds she expanded the hospital to accommodate the burgeoning ranks of the wounded. It was her foresight and organization that helped to establish guidelines for hospital operation. And it was her inspiration that led to the eventual legislation in England for the appropriate regulation of hospitals for the poor. "Nightingale's visionary administrative blueprint presaged the structure of modern public health services."[498] Her example was also the inspiration for the founding of the Red Cross and Red Crescent Societies for the administering of medical and nursing aid to all wounded soldiers, regardless of nationality under a banner of neutrality.

Like a fiery comet, Florence Nightingale streaked across the skies of 19th-century England and transformed the world with her passage. She was a towering genius of both intellect and

---

[497] Ibid., p. 129.

[498] Ibid., p. 297.

spirit, and her legacy resonates today as forcefully as during her lifetime.

We know Nightingale best as the founder of modern secular nursing, but that is only one side of her many-faceted life. The source of her strength, vision, and guidance was a deep sense of unity with God, which is the hallmark of the mystical tradition as it is expressed in all the world's great religions. This aspect of her life has been vastly underestimated, yet we cannot understand her legacy without taking it into account.

Evelyn Underhill, one of the most respected authorities on Western mysticism, described Nightingale as "one of the greatest and most balanced contemplatives of the nineteenth century." This conclusion was based on Nightingale's life work of social action, which she considered her way of honoring "God's laws in nature."

Although Nightingale was deeply religious, she was extremely tolerant and honored the beliefs, rituals, and practices of all cultures under the British Empire. Her embrace of cultural diversity was ahead of its time and is particularly apparent in her 40 years of work to improve sanitary conditions in India. She stressed that all the world's great religions should be studied because, as she put it, this gave "unity to the whole—one continuous thread of interest to all these pearls."

Like most of my colleagues in nursing, I gained only a meager and essentially trivialized picture of Nightingale during my professional education. When my interests led me to explore her life more deeply, I was awed by what I found. I realized that her legacy was far more magnificent—and that she, as an individual personality, was much more complex—than I had ever imagined. The further my research took me, the larger Nightingale loomed—not just in nursing but in other fields as well, such as public health, statistics, hospital design, philosophy, and spirituality. By any measure, she is one of the most towering figures in the Victorian age, which her long life spanned. Indeed, it is difficult to find her equal on the entire canvas of

19th-century Western civilization.

As a nurse, my interests have naturally centered on how Nightingale integrated the art and science of nursing. But I am also fascinated by her concept of healing and how one can become an instrument of healing. Nightingale's vision has inspired in me a deeper, richer, and more compassionate view of nursing than I had ever conceived. I believe this awareness is valuable not only for nurses, but for anyone who has ever been drawn to ease the pain and suffering of another.

In today's specialized world, we are often tempted to compartmentalize our lives, assigning our professional interests to one corner and our spiritual lives to another. To Nightingale, such fragmentation would have been unthinkable. As she put it, her work was her "must"—her spiritual vision and her professional identity were seamlessly combined. Nightingale is therefore an icon of wholeness, an emblem of a united, integrated life. By her uncompromising, shining example, she invites each of us to find our meaning and purpose—our own "must"—in our individual journey through life.[499]

---

[499] Excerpted from Barbara Montgomery Dossey, *Florence Nightingale, Mystic, Visionary, Healer* (Philadelphia, Pennsylvania: Springhouse Pub. Co., http://lwww.com Lippincott Williams & Wilkins, 2000), pp. vi-vii.

MARTIN LUTHER KING

> The ultimate measure of a man is not where he stands in moments of comfort and convenience, but where he stands at times of challenge and controversy.
>
> ~ Martin Luther King, Jr.[500]

Martin Luther King, Jr., was born in 1929, in Atlanta, Georgia. The son of a Baptist minister, he was also drawn to the ministry at an early age. At the age of nineteen he was ordained at Ebenezer Baptist Church, Atlanta, Georgia. He later completed a Doctorate of Philosophy in Systematic Theology at Boston University in 1955 and went on to minister to the community of Montgomery, Alabama.

Devoted to the principles of equality of all human beings, Martin Luther King, Jr., became a pivotal figure in the civil rights movement. "His philosophy of nonviolent direct action, and his strategies for rational and non-destructive social change, galvanized the conscience of [the United States] and reordered its priorities." He worked hard to establish equal voting opportunities and equal wage and working conditions and equal access to public transportation and facilities for black people in America.

> [It was] while at seminary [that] King became acquainted with Mohandas Gandhi's philosophy of nonviolent social protest. On a trip to India in 1959 King met with followers of Gandhi. During these discussions he became more convinced than ever that nonviolent resistance was the most potent weapon available to oppressed people in their struggle for freedom.
>
> As a pastor of a Baptist church in Montgomery, Alabama, King lead a black bus boycott. He and ninety others were ar-

[500] Robin Chew, Louisiana State University library website, Selected Reference Resources #218 and Lucidcafe website: Copyright © 1995-2001 Lucid Interactive. Article written January 1996 http://www.lucidcafe.com/library/96jan/king.html.

rested and indicted under the provisions of a law making it illegal to conspire to obstruct the operation of a business. King and several others were found guilty, but appealed their case. As the bus boycott dragged on, King was gaining a national reputation. The ultimate success of the Montgomery bus boycott made King a national hero.[501]

Dr. King's 1963 "Letter from Birmingham Jail" inspired a growing national civil rights movement. In Birmingham, the goal was to completely end the system of segregation in every aspect of public life (stores, no separate bathrooms and drinking fountains, etc.) and in job discrimination. Also in 1963, King led a massive march on Washington DC where he delivered his now famous, "I Have A Dream" speech. King's tactics of active nonviolence (sit-ins, protest marches) had put civil-rights squarely on the national agenda.[502]

"In any nonviolent campaign there are four basic steps: collection of the facts to determine whether injustices exist; negotiation; self-purification; and direct action." ~ Letter from a Birmingham Jail[503]

In 1964, Dr. King's untiring efforts and inspiring leadership were recognized with the Nobel Peace Prize. "At age 35, Dr. King was the youngest man, the second American, and the third black man awarded the Nobel Peace Prize."[504]

On April 4, 1968, King was shot . . . he was only 39 at the time of his death. Dr. King was turning his attention to a nationwide campaign to help the poor at the time of his assasina-

---

[501] Ibid.

[502] Ibid.

[503] Ibid.

[504] Ibid.

tion. He had never waivered in his insistence that nonviolence must remain the central tactic of the civil-rights movement, nor in his faith that everyone in America would someday attain equal justice.[505]

I Have a Dream

The speech delivered by Martin Luther King, Jr., on the steps of the Lincoln Memorial in Washington D.C. on August 28, 1963. [506]

Five score years ago, a great American, in whose symbolic shadow we stand, signed the Emancipation Proclamation. This momentous decree came as a great beacon light of hope to millions of Negro slaves who had been seared in the flames of withering injustice. It came as a joyous daybreak to end the long night of captivity.

But one hundred years later, we must face the tragic fact that the Negro is still not free. One hundred years later, the life of the Negro is still sadly crippled by the manacles of segregation and the chains of discrimination. One hundred years later, the Negro lives on a lonely island of poverty in the midst of a vast ocean of material prosperity. One hundred years later, the Negro is still languishing in the corners of American society and finds himself an exile in his own land. So we have come here today to dramatize an appalling condition.

In a sense we have come to our nation's capital to cash a check. When the architects of our republic wrote the magnificent words of the Constitution and the Declaration of Independence, they were signing a promissory note to which every American was to fall heir. This note was a promise that all men would be guaranteed the inalienable rights of life, liberty, and the pursuit of happiness.

It is obvious today that America has defaulted on this promissory note insofar as her citizens of color are concerned. Instead of honoring this sacred obligation, America has given the Negro people a bad check

---

[505] Ibid.

[506] Martin Luther King, Jr., http://www.mecca.org/~crights/dream.html (accessed Oct. 10, 2003).

which has come back marked "insufficient funds." But we refuse to believe that the bank of justice is bankrupt.

We refuse to believe that there are insufficient funds in the great vaults of opportunity of this nation. So we have come to cash this check—a check that will give us upon demand the riches of freedom and the security of justice. We have also come to this hallowed spot to remind America of the fierce urgency of now. This is no time to engage in the luxury of cooling off or to take the tranquilizing drug of gradualism. Now is the time to rise from the dark and desolate valley of segregation to the sunlit path of racial justice. Now is the time to open the doors of opportunity to all of God's children. Now is the time to lift our nation from the quicksands of racial injustice to the solid rock of brotherhood.

It would be fatal for the nation to overlook the urgency of the moment and to underestimate the determination of the Negro. This sweltering summer of the Negro's legitimate discontent will not pass until there is an invigorating autumn of freedom and equality. Nineteen sixty-three is not an end, but a beginning. Those who hope that the Negro needed to blow off steam and will now be content will have a rude awakening if the nation returns to business as usual. There will be neither rest nor tranquility in America until the Negro is granted his citizenship rights. The whirlwinds of revolt will continue to shake the foundations of our nation until the bright day of justice emerges.

But there is something that I must say to my people who stand on the warm threshold which leads into the palace of justice. In the process of gaining our rightful place we must not be guilty of wrongful deeds. Let us not seek to satisfy our thirst for freedom by drinking from the cup of bitterness and hatred.

We must forever conduct our struggle on the high plane of dignity and discipline. We must not allow our creative protest to degenerate into physical violence. Again and again we must rise to the majestic heights of meeting physical force with soul force. The marvelous new militancy which has engulfed the Negro community must not lead us to distrust of all white people, for many of our white brothers, as evidenced by their presence here today, have come to realize that their destiny is tied up with our destiny and their freedom is inextricably bound to our freedom.

We cannot walk alone.

And as we walk, we must make the pledge that we shall march ahead. We cannot turn back. There are those who are asking the devotees of civil rights, "When will you be satisfied?" We can never be satisfied as long as our bodies, heavy with the fatigue of travel, cannot gain lodging in the motels of the highways and the hotels of the cities. We cannot be satisfied as long as the Negro's basic mobility is from a smaller ghetto to a larger one. We can never be satisfied as long as a Negro in Mississippi cannot vote and a Negro in New York believes he has nothing for which to vote. No, no, we are not satisfied, and we will not be satisfied until justice rolls down like waters and righteousness like a mighty stream.

I am not unmindful that some of you have come here out of great trials and tribulations. Some of you have come fresh from narrow cells. Some of you have come from areas where your quest for freedom left you battered by the storms of persecution and staggered by the winds of police brutality. You have been the veterans of creative suffering. Continue to work with the faith that unearned suffering is redemptive.

Go back to Mississippi, go back to Alabama, go back to Georgia, go back to Louisiana, go back to the slums and ghettos of our northern cities, knowing that somehow this situation can and will be changed. Let us not wallow in the valley of despair.

I say to you today, my friends, that in spite of the difficulties and frustrations of the moment, I still have a dream. It is a dream deeply rooted in the American dream.

I have a dream that one day this nation will rise up and live out the true meaning of its creed: "We hold these truths to be self-evident: that all men are created equal."

I have a dream that one day on the red hills of Georgia the sons of former slaves and the sons of former slave-owners will be able to sit down together at a table of brotherhood.

I have a dream that one day even the state of Mississippi, a desert state, sweltering with the heat of injustice and oppression, will be transformed into an oasis of freedom and justice.

I have a dream that my four children will one day live in a nation where they will not be judged by the color of their skin but by the content of their character.

I have a dream today.

I have a dream that one day the state of Alabama, whose governor's lips are presently dripping with the words of interposition and nullification, will be transformed into a situation where little black boys and black girls will be able to join hands with little white boys and white girls and walk together as sisters and brothers.

I have a dream today.

I have a dream that one day every valley shall be exalted, every hill and mountain shall be made low, the rough places will be made plain, and the crooked places will be made straight, and the glory of the Lord shall be revealed, and all flesh shall see it together.

This is our hope. This is the faith with which I return to the South. With this faith we will be able to hew out of the mountain of despair a stone of hope. With this faith we will be able to transform the jangling discords of our nation into a beautiful symphony of brotherhood. With this faith we will be able to work together, to pray together, to struggle together, to go to jail together, to stand up for freedom together, knowing that we will be free one day.

This will be the day when all of God's children will be able to sing with a new meaning, "My country, 'tis of thee, sweet land of liberty, of thee I sing. Land where my fathers died, land of the pilgrim's pride, from every mountainside, let freedom ring."

And if America is to be a great nation this must become true. So let freedom ring from the prodigious hilltops of New Hampshire. Let freedom ring from the mighty mountains of New York. Let freedom ring from the heightening Alleghenies of Pennsylvania!

Let freedom ring from the snowcapped Rockies of Colorado!

Let freedom ring from the curvaceous peaks of California!

But not only that; let freedom ring from Stone Mountain of Georgia!

Let freedom ring from Lookout Mountain of Tennessee!

Let freedom ring from every hill and every molehill of Mississippi. From every mountainside, let freedom ring.

When we let freedom ring, when we let it ring from every village and every hamlet, from every state and every city, we will be able to speed up that day when all of God's children, black men and white men, Jews and Gentiles, Protestants and Catholics, will be able to join hands and sing in the words of the old Negro spiritual,

"Free at last! Free at last! Thank God Almighty, we are free at last!"

SAMIHA AYVERDI

Samiha Ayverdi (1905-1993) was born of Meliha Hanim and Ismail Hakki Bey in Istanbul, Turkey in 1905. In her early years, she learned much from her grandmother, Halet Hanim, who was a strong role model for her, and also spent many hours listening to her father and his friends engaged in *sohbet* (spiritual conversation). After her standard education, at the age of 16, she began to train herself in history, philosophy, Sufism, and literature, using her family's personal extensive library as a resource. Kenan Rifai became her teacher and spiritual guide, and it was upon his encouragement that she became a writer.

Samiha Ayverdi is no doubt one of the major literary figures of the 20th century in Turkey due to her skill in using the Turkish language and her deep understanding of the Turkish culture. She was the author of thirty-five books of both spirituality and cultural and literary stories of her beloved country. Among the most well-known are *Kenan Rifai and Understanding Islam in the Twentieth Century* (*Kenan Rifai ve 20. Yuzyilin Isiginda Muslumanlik*) which she co-authored with her three female friends, Safiye Erol, Nezihe Araz, and Sofi Huri; *The Friend* (*Dost*),[507] her account of the teachings of Kinan Rifai (1867-1950), and also *Istanbul Nights* (*Istanbul Geceleri*).

For Samiha, the very substance of life was spirituality, and she lived it purely. It was not her intention to be a novelist, storywriter, or historian; for her these were simply a means of communication. In her writing and her teaching she unfolded modern interpretations, expressions, and metaphors from the classical mystical Islamic perspective. On issues related to history, the environment, women, ethics, and education, she never

---

[507] Published by Kubbealti Akademisi Kultur ve San'at Vakfi in 1995. Portions of the above biographical information and the following selections are excerpted from pp. 47, 149-150, 162, 163 of *The Friend*. The Kubbealti Foundation was established by Samiha and her brother and sister-in-law in 1972. It was begun to help ensure the continuation of the Turkish language and culture. Also quite active in social reform, Samiha led the establishment of the Turkish Wives Association in 1966.

hesitated to ply her pen in an attempt to better the relationship of human being with human being, and human being with his or her Creator.

She tells us: "The human being is not, as supposed by many, some mortal being who was arbitrarily tossed on a part of this universe by accident. In the composition of the universe, the human being has a place and a position determined and designed by the Greatest Will. The human being is the creature who in his or her person represents the whole universe and his or her relationship with the Creator is ongoing."

Until the day she passed away, Samiha tried to convey the principles she learned from her mentor, Kenan Rifai, to the students who loved her. She passed away in 1993 and was laid to rest in the Merkez Efendi cemetery. She is survived by one daughter, two grandchildren, and many lively students who all refer to her as *Samiha Anne* (Mother Samiha).

Sharing the Treasure

The human being and the world are in a sense twins. People sometimes fall ill. Why should that not be true also of the world?

That is what we have been seeing for a long time. The world is sick in thought and in feelings. Therefore the world is suffering from nightmares. And so is the individual human being. Because each has committed the blunder of driving away wisdom from his or her life. The body of the human being and his or her soul are no longer in harmony. We have a world in discord, and people who are sick in body and soul.

There are those who diagnose correctly the basic cause of all of this. But diagnosis is not enough. There must also be a cure. And people are as yet unaware of the right cure.

Both the human being and the world are now sunk into a nightmare of thoughtlessness. It is urgently necessary that they wake up from this nightmare.

Who is to awaken the human being? Who is to bring body and soul into harmony? The Friend[508] saw clearly that people have embedded their

~ "Sharing the Treasure" is excerpted from Samiha Ayverdi, *The Friend*, pp. 47, 149-150, 162.

[508] Samiha's beloved teacher, Kenan Rifai.

heads deeply in materialism, and yet are unaware of it. All through his life the Friend tried to awaken people and to bring them to the remedy of Islamic ethics.

For people who can think and eyes that can see, the total union of both the Universe and the human soul is the ultimate coming together to which reliance in God inevitably leads everything. What a pity that lack of proper realization of this truth has led humankind to endless conflict and confusion, like the ceaseless jangling of chains.

All the troubles which afflict the world, all the evils, intrigues, hypocricies and lies which destroy the spiritual peace and happiness of the human being can be traced back to people failing to see the basic Oneness of life, and to being blindly and obstinately tied up in various illusions of multiplicity.

When one reaches a full realization of Oneness in faith in God, one finds not only peace and happiness for oneself, but also a spiritual treasure in human values that can be freely and inexhaustibly given to all creatures. However, the human being who has not reached truthful self-discovery and self-appraisal has no spiritual treasures either for himself or herself, or to give to others. Some heroic natures, born with the capacity to sacrifice themselves for others and for sublime goals, have suffered great pains in life, and have been able to endure such pains and sacrifices through the power they received from their faith in God.

Fourteen centuries ago, Islam brought to humanity a unity of faith, in common moral values, in a sublime moral order, and in the spiritual elevation which this created. However many people diverged from that, entangled their skirts in thorns during the long march, and strayed far afield. From time to time some heroic figures have pierced the enveloping darkness and have tried to make people remember and realize what they have lost. These noble natures, architects of souls, have tried to awaken to nobler goals the masses of people who had abandoned their goals to enemies and to petty purposes. These noble natures often have met with great suffering as a result.

The world is like a wheel that keeps on turning.

It is an insatiable wheel; turning on and on forever; stripping off from people what it gave them; grinding down people as grains of wheat are ground; never being satiated; turning on and on.

It turns on insatiably, mercilessly. . . . Whatever it gave, it wants to take back. Of course it shall. That is the law of nature. Let it do so. Let it take everything away. It is the creditor. We are the debtors.

We are glad to give everything away. For we are under the wing of a great blessing. May God never take that wing from over us, till the end of time!

We are now in the last stage of our passage through the world. Let each do or say as they see fit. But the voice of the Friend, indifferent to praise or blame, keeps calling all to virtue, faith, and love. Tirelessly. Forever.

Why do we not hear? If we hear the sound of the words, why do we not understand? If we understand, why do we not act accordingly?

Bibliography

Abū Ghudda, Shaykh [c]Abdul Fattah. *Islamic Manners.* Translated by Muḥammad Zahid Abū Ghudda and edited by S.M. Ḥasan al-Banna. Swansea, United Kingdom: Awakening Publications, 2001.

Addas, Claude. *Ibn Arabi: The Voyage of No Return.* Translated from the French by David Streight. Cambridge, United Kingdom: Muslim Personalities Series, The Islamic Texts Society, 2000.

Ahmed, Dr. Nazeer. *What Makes Us Human? A Spiritual Perspective.* Concord, California: American Institute of Islamic History and Culture, 2000.

Alīm 6.0: The World's Most Useful Islamic Software. Silver Spring, Maryland: ISL Software Corporation, www.alim.org, © 1986-2002.

Al-[c]Anani, Ḥasan. *Freedom and Responsibility in Qur'anic Perspective (Al-Mas[c]uliya wal-Tanmiyat al-Dhatiya fil Islam).* Translated from the Arabic by M.S. Kayani. Indianapolis, Indiana: American Trust Publishers, Islamic Book Services, 1990.

Armstrong, Lance, with Sally Jenkins. *It's Not About the Bike.* New York, New York: Penguin Putnam, 2000.

Ayverdi, Samiha. *The Friend.* Istanbul, Turkey: Kubbealti Akademisi Kultur ve San'at Vakfi, 1995.

Bancroft, Anne (editor). *The Pocket Buddha Reader.* Boston, Massachusetts: Shambhala Publishing, 2001.

Bashier, Zakaria. *The Makkan Crucible.* Leicestershire, United Kingdom: The Islamic Foundation, 1991.

Bashier, Zakaria. *Sunshine at Madinah.* Leicestershire, United Kingdom:

The Islamic Foundation, 1990.

Boyd, Jean. *The Caliph's Sister, Nana Asmaᶜu 1793-1865, Teacher, Poet, and Islamic Leader.* London, United Kingdom: Frank Cass & Co., 1989, reprinted 1995.

Brown, John Pairman and H.A. Rose (editor). *The Darvishes: Or Oriental Spiritualism.* London, United Kingdom: Frank Cass Publishers, 1968.

Chew, Robin. "*Martin Luther King, Jr., Civil-Rights Leader.*" January 1996. Louisiana State University library website, Selected Reference Resources #218 and Lucidcafe website: http://www.lucidcafe.com/library/96jan/king.html.

Cleary, Thomas. *The Secret of the Golden Flower.* New York, New York: HarperCollins Publishers, Inc., 1991.

Cleary, Thomas (translator). *Living and Dying with Grace: Counsels of Ḥaḍrat ᶜAlī.* Boston, Massachusetts: Shambhala Publications, 1995.

Dossey, Barbara Montgomery. *Florence Nightingale, Mystic, Visionary, Healer.* Philadelphia, Pennsylvania: Springhouse Pub. Co., Lippincott Williams & Wilkins, http://lwww.com, 2000.

Eaton, Charles Le Gai. *Islam and the Destiny of Man.* Albany, New York: State University of New York Press, 1985.

Emerson, Ralph Waldo. *Essays by Ralph Waldo Emerson, First Series.* London, United Kingdom: George G. Harrap & Co., Ltd. 1926.

Ernst, Carl (selection and translation). *Teachings of Sufism.* Boston, Massachusetts: Shambhala Publications, 1999.

Gabrieli, Francesco. *Arab Historians of the Crusades—Selected and Trnaslated from the Arabic Sources.* Edited and translated by E.J. Costello. Andover,

United Kingdom: Routledge and Kegan Paul, Ltd., 1969.

Al-Ghazālī, Abū Hamid. *Al-Ghazālī: On the Duties of Brotherhood.* Translated from the Arabic by Muhtar Holland. Woodstock, New York: Overlook Press, 1979.

Al-Ghazālī, Muḥammad. *Remembrance and Prayer: The Way of the Prophet Muḥammad.* Translated by Yusuf Talal De Lorenzo. Leicester, United Kingdom: The Islamic Foundation, 1986.

Graham, William A. *Divine Word and Prophetic Word in Early Islam: A Reconsideration of the Sources, with Special Reference to the Divine Saying or Ḥadīth Qudsī.* The Hague: Mouton & Co., 1977.

Gulen, M. Fethullah. *Prophet Muhammad, The Infinite Light.* London, United Kingdom: Truestar London, Ltd., 1996. http://www.fgulen.org

Haeri, Shaykh Fadhlalla. *Prophetic Traditions of Islam: On the Authority of the Family of the Prophet.* London, United Kingdom: Zahra Publications, 1999.

Haque, M. Atiqul. *Muslim Heroes of the World.* London, United Kingdom: Ta-Ha Publishers, 1990, 1998.

Hathout, Hassan. *Reading the Muslim Mind.* Plainfield, Indiana: American Trust Publications, Islamic Book Services, 1995.

Helminski, Camille. *Women of Sufism: A Hidden Treasure.* Boston, Massachusetts: Shambhala Publications, 2003.

Herrigel, Eugene. *Zen in the Art of Archery.* New York, New York: Pantheon Books, a division of Random House, 1953, 1981.

Hilmi, Ahmet. *Awakened Dreams.* Translated by Refik Algan and Camille Helminski. Putney, Vermont: Threshold Books, 1993.

Ibn Kathīr, Imām Abū'l-Fidā' Ismā'īl. *The Life of the Prophet Muḥammad (Al-Sīra al-Nabawiyya)*, Vols. I and II. Translated by Prof. Trevor Le Gassick. Reading, United Kingdom: Garnet Publishing Ltd., 1998, 2000.

Ibn Saᶜd, Muḥammad. *The Women of Madina.* Translated by Aisha Bewley. London, United Kingdom: Ta-Ha Publishers, 1995.

Jaspers, Karl. *Socrates, Buddha, Confucius, Jesus.* Harcourt Publishers, Ltd.

Johnston, Anne Fellows. *The Little Colonel in Arizona.* Gretna, Louisiana: Pelican Publishin Co., Inc., 2000.

Karim, Al-Haj Maulana Fazlul (translator). *Mishkāt ul-Maṣābīḥ.* Lahore, Pakistan: The Pakistan Educational Press.

King, Jr., Rev. Martin Luther. *"I Have a Dream."*
http://www.mecca.org/~crights/dream.html (accessed Oct. 10, 2003)

Laozi. *Dao de Jing: The Book of the Way.* Translated and edited by Moss Roberts. Berkeley, California: University of California Press, 2001.

Mack, Beverly and Jean Boyd *One Woman's Jihad.* Bloomington, Indiana: Indiana University, 2000.

Mitchell, Stephen. *A Book of Psalms: Selected and Adapted from the Hebrew.* New York, New York: Harper Collins Publishers, 1993.

al-Murabit, Shaykh ᶜAbdalqadir. *The Hundred Steps.* London, United Kingdom: Madinah Press, 1998.

Murata, Sachiko. *The Tao of Islam: A Sourcebook on Gender Relationships in Islamic Thought.* Albany, New York: State University of New York Press, 1992.

Nurbakhsh, Javad. *Discourses on the Sufi Path.* London, United Kingdom:

Khaniqahi Nimatullahi Publications, 1996.

Nurbakhsh, Javad. *Sufism II: Fear and Hope, Contraction and Expansion, Gathering and Dispersion, Intoxication and Sobriety, Annihilation and Subsistence*. Translated by William Chittick. London and New York: Khaniqahi Nimatullahi Publications, 1982.

Nye, Naomi Shihab. *19 Varities of Gazelle, Poems of the Middle East*. NY, NY: Greenwillow/HarperCollins Publishers, 2002.

Payne, Robert. *The History of Islam* (original title: *The Holy Sword*). New York, New York: Dorset Press, 1959, 1987.

Al-Qushayri. *Principles of Sufism*. Translated from the Arabic by B. R. Von Schlegell. Oneonta, New York: Mizan Press, 1990.

Rafea, Ali, Alia, and Aisha. *Beyond Diversities: Reflections on Revelation*. Cairo, Egypt: Sadek Publishing, 2000.

Ravishankar, Sri Sri. *Hinduism and Islām*. Bangalore, India: Vyakti Vikas Kendra, 2002.

Richards, M. C. *The Crossing Point*. Middletown, Connecticut: Wesleyan University Press, 1973.

Ruiz, Don Miguel. *The Four Agreements*. San Rafael, California: Amber-Allen Publishing, Inc. 1997.

Rūmī, Jalālu'ddin. *The Mathnawī of Jalālu'ddin Rūmī*. Edited and translated from the Persian by Reynold A. Nicholson. London, United Kingdom: Luzac and Company, Ltd., © 1930, reprinted 1982.

Rūmī, Jalālu'ddin. *Open Secret: Versions of Rumi*. Translated by John Moyne and Coleman Barks. Putney, Vermont: Threshold Books, 1984.

Rūmī, Jalālu'ddin. *The Pocket Rumi Reader*. Edited by Kabir Helminski. Boston, Massachusetts: Shambhala Publications, 2001.

Rumi, Jelaluddin. *Love is a Stranger*. Translated by Kabir Edmund Helminski. Brattleboro, Vermont: Threshold Books, 1993.

Rūmī, Mevlāna Jalāluddin. *The Rumi Collection*. Selected and edited by Kabir Helminski. Boston, Massachusetts: Shambhala Publications, 1998.

Sa'ad, Sheikh Tāhā ʿAbdur-Ra'ūf, and Sa'ad Ḥasan Muḥammad ʿAlī, *As-Sayyidah Nafīsa, Nafīsat ul-ʿIlm Karīmat ad-Dārayn*, translated from the Arabic by Mahmoud Mostafa. Cairo, Egypt: Al Safā Library, 2000.

Sabzawārī, Ḥusayn Wāʿiẓ Kāshifī. *The Royal Book of Spiritual Chivalry (Futūwat nāmah-yi sulṭānī)*. Translated by Jay R. Crook, Ph.D. Chicago, Illinois: Great Books of the Islamic World, Inc., Kazi Publications, 2000.

Sharīʿati, ʿAlī. *On the Sociology of Islam: Lectures*. Oneonta, New York: Mizan Press, 2000.

Sheean, Vincent. *Lead, Kindly Light: Gandhi and the Way to Peace*. New York, New York: Random House, 1949.

Ṣiddiqi, Muḥammad Saeed. *The Blessed Women of Islam*. Lahore, Pakistan: Kazi Publications, 1982.

Smith, Margaret. *Rabi'a the Mystic and Her Fellow Saints in Islam.* Cambridge: Cambridge University Press, 1928. San Francisco: Rainbow Bridge, 1977.

Stewart, Dorothy (compiler). *Women of Vision: An Anthology of Spiritual Words from Women Across the Centuries*. Chicago, Illinois: Loyola Press, 2000.

Storm, Hyemeyohsts. *Seven Arrows*. New York, New York: Harper and Row, 1972.

Al-Sulami, Ibn al-Ḥusayn. *The Way of Sufi Chivalry*. An interpretation by

Tosun Bayrak al-Jerrahi. Rochester, Vermont: Inner Traditions International, 1983, 1991. www.InnerTraditions.com.

As-Sulamī, Abū ᶜAbd ar-Raḥmān. *Early Sufi Women: Dhikr an-Niswa al-Mutaᶜabbidāt aṣ-Ṣūfiyyāt.* Edited and translated from the Riyadh manuscript with introduction and notes by Rkia Elaroui Cornell. Louisville, Kentucky: Fons Vitae, 1999.

Ṭabāṭabāʾī, ᶜAllāmah Sayyid Muḥammad Ḥusayn. *Shīᶜite Islam* (*Shīᶜah dar Islām*). Translated from the Persian and edited with an introduction and notes by Seyyed Hossein Nasr. Albany, New York: State University of New York Press, 1980.

Tagore, Rabindranath. *The Religion of Man.* London, United Kingdom: Harper Collins Publishers Ltd., 1931.

Teresa, Mother. Text of her Nobel Peace Prize speech. From the pamphlet published by Missionaries of Charity, 54/A A.J.C. Bose Road, Calcutta 700016 W.B., India.

Upton, Charles. *Doorkeeper of the Heart: Versions of Rābiᶜa.* Putney, Vermont: Threshold Books, 1998.

Walther, Wiebke. *Women in Islam: from Medieval to Modern Times.* Translated from the German by C.S.V. Salt, with an introduction by Guity Nashat. Princeton, New Jersey: Markus Wiener Pub., rev. ed. 1993.

Index

Aaron, 218, 223, 229, 231, 233
ʿAbd al-Muṭṭalib, 22, 27, 38, 59, 84, 86
ablution, 70, 192, 196, 208, 335, 381, 417, 418
Abraham, 2, 12, 14, 15, 27, 36, 47, 169, 178, 219, 220, 221, 223, 235, 236, 312, 383
Abū Bakr, 35, 40, 37–42, 137, 162, 249, 257, 397, 400, 401, 402, 405, 408, 411
Abū Dharr, 175, 182, 356, 382, 383, 393
Abū Jahl, 124, 304
Abū Lahab, 135
Abū Ṭālib, 22, 27, 39, 41, 84, 86, 101, 136, 297, 397
accountability: *iḥtisāb*, 56–60, 207
ādāb: courtesy, 54, 258, 378
Adam, 15, 27, 42, 99, 144, 198, 199, 238, 304, 311, 314, 331, 343, 388
ʿAdl, al-: The Just, 316
Ahl aṣ-Ṣuffah: People of the Bench, 102, 258
Ahl al-Bayt: family of the house of Muḥammad, 421
ʿĀʾishah, 3, 22, 29, 32, 79, 103, 104, 125, 152, 163, 172, 198, 241, 250, 261, 286, 397–403, 408, 411
ʿAlī: (ʿAlī ibn Abī Ṭālib), 3, 9, 27, 35, 36, 39, 41, 52, 53, 63, 71, 86–92, 98, 101, 102, 103, 104, 105, 109, 110, 133, 162, 183, 193, 239, 240, 257, 260, 296, 299, 301, 310, 317, 318, 342, 351, 359, 364, 368, 378, 397, 398, 400, 402, 403, 416
Anṣār, 83, 86, 160
ʿaql: intellect, understanding, 9, 17, 18, 82, 90, 131, 145, 147, 152, 164, 177–90, 192, 208, 211, 212, 213, 214, 215, 216, 223, 225, 226, 241, 242, 243, 245, 246, 251, 285, 286, 289, 290, 300, 303, 322, 329, 330, 358, 365, 373, 402, 432, 434
ʿArafāt, 57, 392
Armstrong, Lance, 126–31
arrogance, 139, 146, 153, 160, 304, 321
astray: (*ḍalāl*) error, going astray, aberration, 13, 15, 30, 66, 68, 108, 168, 199, 209, 221, 233, 241, 243, 392
awareness, 4, 11, 37, 73, 189, 212, 251, 293, 299, 300, 302, 303, 321, 394, 395, 428, 436
awe, 3, 24, 52, 95, 100, 155, 157, 159, 162, 168, 173, 177, 206, 218, 228, 231, 235, 254, 304, 354, 355, 356
āyah: (*āyāt*, pl.) sign, symbol, message, verse, 20, 24, 68, 94, 95, 156, 157, 158, 168, 220, 226, 231, 236, 269, 340, 353, 376
Ayverdi, Samiha, 444–47
balance: mīzān, measure, 227, 309
basṭ: expansion, 124
beauty: *jamāl*, 128, 138, 144, 146, 184, 185, 260, 281, 282–94, 304, 365, 369, 393, 394, 397, 414, 432
bee, 32, 114–20
Being: *al-Wujūd*, 19, 69, 348, 375, 395
Beloved, 370, 395
Bhagavad-Gita, 321
Bible, 23, 26, 63, 65, 66, 97, 186, 227, 239, 298, 356
Bilāl ibn Rabāḥ, 136–37, 163, 409
blessing: *baraka*, 1, 3, 8, 33, 37, 81, 97, 99, 109, 118, 126, 161, 168, 206, 209, 217, 218, 219, 237, 248, 249, 250, 251, 253, 269, 270, 284, 295, 306, 328, 353, 364, 372, 376, 380, 387, 390, 421, 447
blind, 13, 163, 170, 253, 289, 301, 310, 353, 358, 395, 421, 446
Buddha, 36, 213, 215, 242, 287, 344, 345, 393
camel, 4, 31, 32, 84, 112–18, 367, 370, 392, 400
certainty: *yaqīn*, 14, 19, 210, 217, 220, 241, 242, 304
character: *khuluq*, 2, 4, 9, 10, 16, 17, 18, 19, 20, 25, 38, 40, 63, 100, 138, 139, 145, 161, 193, 202, 208, 243,

256, 259, 283, 286, 288, 291, 301, 304, 305, 306, 351, 362, 364, 367, 368, 379, 382, 383, 386–96, 399, 413, 442
charity: *zakāt*, 38, 58, 93–106, 170, 171, 206, 219, 257, 318, 420
chivalry: *futuwwah*, 88, 376–85
Companions, 3, 28, 54, 59, 66, 79, 83, 87, 88, 94, 102, 154, 157, 162, 164, 178, 191, 196, 210, 225, 249, 269, 275, 276, 311, 353, 368, 371, 382, 397, 400, 401, 402, 408, 412
compassion, 19, 43, 46, 68–78, 89, 94, 97, 99, 155, 171, 199, 262, 272, 340, 351, 354, 380, 383, 405, 429
complete man: *al-insān al-kāmil.*, 17
completion, 2, 269, 355
conflict resolution: *iṣlāḥ*, 307–25
Confucius, 137–41, 393
contentment: *qanūʿ*, 19, 109, 192, 328–39
courage: *shujaʿah*, 88, 101, 121, 131, 184, 295–306, 374, 378, 390
courtesy: *ādāb*, 133, 184, 362–75, 390
creativity: *badāʿah*, 37, 212, 282–94, 321, 395
Ḍārr, aḍ-: The Punisher, 52
date-palms, 38, 96, 114, 249, 381
David, 121, 132, 223, 236, 430
Day of Reckoning, 1, 34, 64, 68, 83, 98, 145, 151, 251, 254, 286, 308, 412
denial: *kufr*, 13
deniers, 30, 235
dhikr: remembrance, 9, 66, 109, 125, 131, 132, 146, 158, 168, 171, 172, 178, 179, 183, 196, 206, 209, 281, 328, 354, 356, 357, 371, 388, 391, 433
Dhu'l Nūn al-Miṣrī, 316, 368
dīn: way, religion, 2, 54, 197, 260, 371, 372, 402
discernment: *furqān*, 164, 216–34
discipline, 57, 138, 292, 293, 300, 303, 408, 440
discretion: *ḥusn at-tadbīr*, 149–54, 239, 368
Divine Names: *al-asmāʿ al-ḥusnā*, 16, 20, 385
doubt, 48, 131, 135, 139, 203, 226, 234, 304, 350, 373, 400
duʿāʿ: supplication, prayer, 257, 260, 262, 268, 269, 283, 285, 299, 316, 322, 323, 331, 338, 342, 345, 346, 347, 353, 368, 369, 370, 371, 375, 417, 418, 420, 422
effort, 57, 59, 92, 147, 203, 306
Elias, 223
Elisha, 178, 223
envy, 97, 179, 199, 259, 262, 305, 331, 351, 367, 412
essence, 9, 16, 49, 69, 211, 251, 262, 363, 376, 385, 388, 389, 394
eternity, 10, 19, 46, 161, 243, 290, 395, 430
Eve, 314, 388
Face of God: *wajh*, 193, 297, 303, 310, 328, 395, 417
faith: *īmān*, 4, 8, 19, 20–30, 146, 147, 279, 280, 285, 301
faithful: *muʿmin*, 24, 25, 30, 46, 47, 56, 89, 91, 124, 157, 158, 159, 160, 173, 233, 235, 249, 272, 283, 296, 310, 312, 318, 330, 353, 354, 365, 369, 382, 391, 399, 403, 408, 409, 410
Fāṭimah, 27, 28, 87, 100–106, 124, 397, 399, 416
fasting, 100, 170, 192, 194, 195, 196, 208, 222, 322, 323, 369, 396, 417, 420, 431
fiṭrah: primordial or essential nature, 11, 8–20, 33, 37, 73, 208, 219, 220, 221, 222, 238, 315, 363, 388, 389, 390
forbearance: *ḥilm*, 82, 131–41
forgiveness: *ghufrān*, 24, 25, 53, 58, 61–66, 72, 82, 86, 89, 93, 98, 150, 260, 268, 284, 299, 311, 314, 332
freedom, 11, 14, 207, 208, 212, 220, 236, 237, 287, 293, 321, 323, 358, 374, 379, 394, 395, 412, 413, 437, 440, 441, 442
friendship, 33, 61, 71, 80, 133, 153, 165, 184, 185, 253, 261, 274, 275, 276, 342, 365, 375, 378, 379, 380,

428, 444, 447
Gabriel: *Jibrīl*, 24, 34, 62, 101, 103, 132, 156, 198, 222, 226, 256, 271, 301, 397
Gandhi, 321, 322, 323, 324, 437
garden, 4, 34, 46, 56, 91, 96, 115, 116, 118, 120, 123, 182, 233, 235, 237, 256, 257, 269, 280, 295, 296, 318, 339, 341, 353, 355, 369, 374, 395, 430
generosity, 19, 28, 59, 69, 80, 89, 90, 92, 199, 225, 251, 252, 253–68, 297, 304, 307, 345, 377, 378, 381, 383, 384, 423, 429
Ghaffār, al-: The One Who is Full of Forgiveness, 52
Ghafūr, al-: The All-Forgiving, Ever-Ready to Forgive, 52
Ghanī, al-: The Rich, 19
Ghazālī, al-, 424–27
good word, 97, 177
gratitude: gratefulness, *shukr*, 80, 103, 109, 188, 191, 247–53, 258, 376, 419
grief, 80, 105, 124, 135, 165, 230, 266, 428
guidance, 2, 9, 12, 13, 14, 26, 37, 52, 59, 68, 80, 125, 135, 168, 170, 191, 195, 208, 217, 218, 219, 220, 221, 222, 223, 225, 226, 229, 231, 234, 235, 257, 281, 284, 285, 308, 314, 435
ḥadīth, 15, 32, 35, 79, 83, 97, 99, 126, 133, 151, 152, 156, 162, 173, 179, 191, 193, 207, 240, 241, 262, 274, 283, 285, 310, 311, 342, 371, 384, 388, 401, 422, 424, 428
Ḥafṣah, 408
Ḥakam, al-: The Arbitrator, 320
ḥalāl: permitted, 210
Ḥalīma, 22, 84, 174
happiness, 36, 99, 100, 138, 181, 262, 334, 335, 336, 338, 355, 376, 439, 446
Ḥaqq: Truth, Reality, 2, 10, 11, 12, 13, 15, 18, 23, 26, 33, 36, 39, 41, 47, 51, 55, 59, 63, 68, 69, 86, 87, 95, 123, 128, 138, 158, 159, 160, 170, 174, 177, 184, 185, 186, 188, 189, 195, 206, 207, 218, 219, 221, 222, 224, 226, 230, 231, 241, 235–46, 254, 280, 282, 291, 295, 296, 301, 302, 307, 308, 311, 315, 318, 321, 328, 344, 345, 366, 368, 374, 377, 394, 405, 425, 426, 446
ḥarām: forbidden, 210, 260
Ḥasan: (Ḥasan ibn ʿAlī), 70, 101, 105, 416
Ḥasan al-Baṣrī, 4, 260, 413, 414
hawā: passion, desire for worldly things, 13
heart: *qalb*, 8, 13, 14, 15, 19, 22, 23, 24, 34, 48, 49, 50, 52, 55, 56, 63, 64, 66, 71, 75, 85, 90, 95, 103, 109, 115, 117, 118, 119, 121, 125, 128, 129, 132, 135, 136, 141, 144, 145, 146, 150, 155, 158, 159, 161, 163, 168–76, 180, 192, 194, 196, 197, 200, 206, 207, 211, 220, 221, 226, 229, 232, 235, 236, 238, 239, 242, 243, 244, 246, 249, 250, 251, 253, 256, 257, 260, 262, 266, 282, 283, 285, 286, 288, 296, 297, 298, 299, 301, 302, 303, 305, 321, 325, 328, 329, 333, 341, 344, 345, 346, 347, 349, 350, 351, 352, 354, 356, 362, 368, 369, 372, 373, 375, 376, 380, 382, 383, 387, 393, 397, 409, 414, 424, 428, 430
hijrah, 28, 87, 124, 297, 397
Hilāl, 163–65
Ḥirāʾ, 22, 23, 222
hope, 1, 10, 24, 37, 49, 52, 81, 86, 115, 117, 121, 128, 136, 141, 159, 206, 221, 252, 286, 296, 321, 330, 348, 373, 407, 423, 439, 440, 442
Hū: the pronoun of Divine Presence, the indwelling, unmanifest presence of God, 21, 125, 155, 197, 282, 299
humility: *tawāḍuʿ*, 40, 80, 155, 154–66, 251, 265, 270, 273, 304, 311, 345, 362, 374, 377, 383, 384, 387, 389, 390, 391, 429
Ḥusayn: (Ḥusayn ibn ʿAlī), 70, 100, 101, 105, 329
hypocrisy, 34, 35, 172, 185, 345, 346,

378
Iblīs: Satan, 93, 172, 195, 196, 255, 331, 354
Ibn Umm Maktūm, 51, 310
iḥsān, 285
intention, 35, 48, 69, 147, 188, 206–16, 322, 351, 370, 380, 417
Isaac, 178, 223, 312
Islām, 11, 17, 18, 20, 47, 57, 58, 85, 88, 95, 96, 97, 98, 99, 104, 133, 145, 156, 192, 207, 256, 262, 274, 276, 277, 285, 299, 300, 301, 302, 310, 311, 312, 314, 315, 316, 317, 352, 364, 365, 369, 377, 378, 383, 388, 389, 392, 399, 402, 407, 411, 413, 414, 426, 446
Ismāʿīl: Ishmael, 223, 380
Jacob, 165, 178, 223, 304, 312
Jāmiʿ, al-: The Uniter, 320
Jesus, 2, 12, 36, 63, 66, 75, 104, 171, 223, 226, 242, 312, 393, 430
jihād: struggle, 20, 54, 265, 271, 285, 314, 315, 321, 393
jinns: invisible beings, 180, 336
Job, 125, 223
Jonah, 223
Joseph, 13, 163, 165, 223, 236, 386
justice, 10, 57, 71, 139, 227, 265, 281, 290, 295, 299, 300, 307–25, 344, 369, 373, 379, 381, 390, 400, 405, 422, 439, 440, 441
Kaʿbah, 26, 27, 101, 124, 169, 222, 319
Karīm, al-: The Most Generous, 258
Khadījah, 22, 23, 24, 26, 27, 28, 29, 26–29, 35, 41, 87, 100, 104, 136, 297, 397, 400
khalīfah: representative, vicegerent, 17, 18, 19, 315, 316, 363, 388
kindness: *ṭībah*, 19, 28, 72, 79, 85, 86, 89, 94, 99, 150, 259, 261, 262, 269–78, 297, 341, 345, 373, 377, 378, 383, 384, 387, 399, 405, 423
King, Martin Luther King, Jr., 437–43
knowledge: *ʿilm*, 8, 9, 10, 13, 14, 15, 18, 19, 24, 37, 38, 46, 53, 56, 58, 88, 97, 99, 103, 121, 130, 133, 140, 145, 147, 148, 149, 154, 162, 163, 165, 175, 181, 207, 210, 220, 221, 222, 223, 225, 231, 236, 237, 239, 240, 241, 242, 273, 277, 285, 286, 287, 289, 291, 294, 296, 299, 302, 303, 304, 306, 320, 321, 356, 365, 367, 379, 387, 393, 395, 402, 416, 424, 425, 426, 428
Lao-tzu, 141, 166
light, 2, 5, 10, 12, 18, 25, 90, 91, 100, 144, 161, 168, 170, 175, 208, 211, 212, 213, 215, 216, 218, 221, 224, 226, 228, 229, 266, 269, 284, 289, 293, 301, 303, 316, 318, 321, 323, 343, 349, 353, 357, 380, 382, 386, 413, 417, 430, 439
Lord's Prayer, 66
Lot, 223, 236
love: *hubb*, 2, 4, 15, 17, 27, 29, 34, 47, 61, 71, 73, 74, 75, 76, 77, 79, 82, 91, 92, 96, 97, 99, 104, 105, 133, 135, 136, 144, 145, 146, 151, 155, 158, 173, 185, 186, 187, 188, 190, 192, 208, 219, 221, 226, 227, 230, 239, 243, 252, 253, 254, 259, 261, 264, 271, 273, 274, 283, 285, 286, 289, 290, 300, 304, 312, 314, 328, 330, 339, 340–52, 362, 364, 367, 369, 370, 371, 373, 374, 376, 378, 384, 393, 394, 397, 403, 414, 415, 428, 429, 430, 447
Luqmān, 30, 144, 146, 153, 163, 194, 249, 297, 301, 364
Mary: (mother of Jesus), 104, 293, 295, 328
maturity, 71, 269
Mecca: (Macca, Maccah), 22, 26, 28, 38, 39, 40, 51, 64, 80, 85, 87, 137, 175, 222, 256, 315, 319, 363, 401, 404, 416
Medina, 28, 39, 40, 86, 87, 89, 101, 105, 137, 162, 175, 276, 297, 316, 318, 319, 376, 381, 382, 397, 401, 403, 409, 410, 416, 420
meditation, 183, 212, 216
mercy, 1, 2, 19, 28, 30, 46, 50, 52, 54, 66, 69, 79–92, 94, 95, 99, 126, 133, 134, 145, 157, 160, 163, 208, 217, 218, 227, 238, 242, 250, 258, 259, 283, 304, 310, 311, 314, 315, 330,

342, 353, 356, 357, 371, 379, 405, 417, 429
Mi^c rāj, 35
mihrab, 100
modesty: *ḥayā^c*, 19, 143–49, 163, 304, 373, 378, 381
Moses, 2, 12, 13, 24, 26, 36, 90, 104, 121, 158, 218, 221, 223, 228, 229, 230, 231, 232, 233, 284, 312, 331, 393, 404, 430
Mother Teresa, 73–77, 347
Muḥammad, 2, 3, 4, 11, 12, 13, 15, 17, 18, 20, 22, 24, 26, 27, 28, 31, 32, 35, 36, 38, 39, 40, 41, 51, 52, 53, 54, 57, 58, 59, 60, 62, 64, 65, 69, 70, 71, 72, 79, 80, 84, 85, 86, 87, 88, 94, 99, 100, 101, 102, 103, 104, 108, 124, 132, 133, 134, 136, 137, 146, 161, 162, 163, 170, 171, 172, 173, 176, 179, 182, 194, 195, 208, 209, 211, 219, 222, 223, 225, 235, 237, 241, 242, 249, 253, 255, 256, 257, 258, 264, 266, 272, 273, 283, 286, 297, 299, 301, 311, 313, 319, 320, 342, 362, 366, 371, 386, 389, 392, 397, 398, 399, 400, 401, 402, 403, 404, 406, 418, 421, 424, 449, 451, 452, 454, 455
Muntaqim, al-: The Avenger, 52
nabī: Prophet, 18
Nafisa: (Lady Nafisa), 416–21
nafs al-ammāra: commanding self, 33, 49, 193, 285, 299, 399
neighbor, 74, 76, 98, 208, 226, 227, 271, 274, 275, 314, 316, 330, 369, 378, 399
Nightingale, Florence, 431–36
Noah, 12, 36, 223, 236
noble character: *akhlāq*, 386–96
Old Testament, 25
olive, 8, 96
patience: *sabr*, 3, 19, 42, 43, 91, 94, 108–22, 123, 124, 125, 126, 132, 150, 197, 201, 251, 253, 291, 297, 306, 309, 330, 354, 377
peace: *salām*, 1, 3, 10, 34, 73, 76, 102, 172, 177, 184, 190, 208, 231, 238, 251, 268, 286, 300, 310, 312, 322, 323, 329, 331, 341, 342, 345, 346, 347, 353, 354, 357, 359, 372, 377, 381, 420, 446
perseverance: *thabāt*, 3, 48, 123–31, 138, 144, 353
Pharoah, 104
pilgrimage: *ḥajj* or *^c umrah*, 57, 58, 208, 302, 401, 412, 420, 421
pomegranate, 96
prayer, 22, 24, 27, 43, 46, 47, 58, 64, 65, 66, 69, 70, 75, 81, 82, 91, 93, 95, 97, 98, 100, 108, 109, 124, 126, 136, 137, 144, 150, 155, 169, 172, 173, 183, 191, 192, 194, 196, 197, 206, 211, 219, 225, 229, 240, 250, 252, 254, 260, 262, 273, 276, 277, 280, 281, 283, 285, 287, 298, 302, 316, 322, 335, 339, 343, 347, 364, 369, 375, 402, 403, 409, 412, 413, 416, 417, 418, 419, 421, 422, 428, 442
Presence, 18, 21, 217, 220, 241, 283, 328, 348, 354, 375, 385, 387, 429
prostration, 69, 108, 155, 182, 273, 331, 354, 395, 403
purity: *ṭahārah*, 18, 28, 51, 62, 69, 82, 144, 168–205, 207, 233, 255, 304, 318, 335, 388
qabḍ: cntraction, 124
Qaṣwā^ɔ: Muḥammad's camel, 80
Qayyūm, al-: The Self-Subsisting, 19
Qur^ɔān, 2, 3, 5, 11, 12, 13, 14, 18, 19, 22, 27, 32, 37, 38, 51, 57, 69, 79, 80, 88, 93, 95, 100, 102, 108, 133, 154, 157, 160, 170, 173, 179, 193, 195, 218, 219, 220, 221, 226, 228, 235, 236, 237, 238, 241, 264, 265, 267, 281, 283, 285, 286, 297, 310, 311, 312, 313, 314, 339, 343, 388, 392, 400, 401, 408, 416, 420, 424, 427, 428
Quraysh, 38, 80, 256, 319, 320
Ra^c ūf, ar-: The Most Kind, 52
Raḥīm, ar-: The Infinitely Merciful, 69, 79–92, 343
Raḥmān, ar-: The Infinitely Compassionate, 69, 68–78, 343
Rābi^c a al-^c Adawiyyah, 347, 412–15

Ramaḍān, 22, 27, 58, 161, 192, 302, 416, 417, 419
rasūl: (Messenger), 18
reflection, 90, 126, 138, 173, 181, 182, 183, 194, 203, 284
remorse, 47, 48, 50, 52, 64, 235, 289
repentance: *tawbah*, 46–55, 64, 94, 178, 222, 230, 253, 322, 353, 403
responsibility: *masʿūliyyah*, 1, 10, 27, 56–60, 84, 98, 130, 138, 141, 188, 218, 259, 275, 303, 363, 432
revelation, 2, 11, 18, 20, 22, 25, 27, 32, 36, 57, 69, 87, 108, 124, 134, 158, 195, 217, 219, 222, 223, 226, 228, 235, 283, 309, 312, 392, 399, 404
right action: *ʿamal uṣ-ṣāliḥāt*, righteous deeds, 8, 30, 33, 109, 123, 138, 146, 161, 169, 191, 192, 207, 208, 210, 233, 234, 237, 238, 260, 265, 269, 276, 280–81, 285, 286, 288, 297, 304, 314, 328, 331, 340, 351, 355, 364, 365, 370, 377
rose, 182, 386, 395, 430
Rūmī: Jalālu'ddin, 36, 286, 316, 428–30
Ruqayyah, 28
Ṣādiq, aṣ-: (Imām Jaʿfar aṣ-Ṣādiq), 4, 63, 225, 259, 261, 271, 272, 329, 362, 416
sakīnah: inner peacefulness, 19, 174, 358, 353–59
Saladin: (Ṣalāh ad-Dīn), 422–23
secret, 34, 100, 121, 212, 218, 227, 228, 232, 257, 289, 296, 315, 335, 363, 368, 415
servant: *ʿabd*, 16, 17, 19, 47, 48, 53, 63, 65, 70, 132, 146, 160, 163, 173, 198, 217, 225, 226, 249, 250, 284, 302, 333, 365, 379, 384, 385, 389, 394, 414
service, 74, 77, 100, 115, 116, 117, 124, 166, 199, 200, 230, 250, 298, 299, 319, 365, 380, 384, 410, 419, 430, 431
sharīʿah: sacred law, 80, 157, 192, 210, 219, 222, 223, 238, 289, 300, 306, 307, 320, 350, 382, 422, 424, 428
Shifa Clinic, 77–78
shirk: *attributing partners to God*, 14, 15, 172, 209, 221, 238, 282
Shuʿayb, 66
sin, 47, 49, 178, 187, 188, 197, 233, 309, 314, 331
sincerity: *ikhlāṣ*, 7, 19, 33, 34, 37, 30–44, 49, 103, 184, 185, 284, 363, 404
smile, 60, 74, 75, 77, 99, 102, 104, 105, 111, 140, 153, 272, 324, 333, 368, 432
Solomon, 50, 223, 236, 238, 249
spider, 40
spirit: *rūḥ*, 11, 12, 19, 25, 28, 37, 69, 131, 159, 164, 192, 200, 211, 212, 213, 214, 215, 216, 238, 252, 284, 285, 320, 330, 351, 394, 395, 396, 426, 431, 435
St. Francis, 72–73
strength: *quwwah*, 29, 37, 40, 132, 162, 178, 194, 197, 200, 201, 202, 203, 206, 225, 229, 253, 262, 281, 283, 295–306, 323, 330, 379, 387, 393, 406, 411, 435
submission, 11, 17, 18, 19, 57, 156, 157, 195, 208, 237, 250, 285, 288, 312, 315, 320, 330, 393
Sufyan at-Thawri, 380
sunnah: the example of the Prophet Muḥammad, 47, 83, 134, 264, 265, 310, 378
surrender, 1, 8, 11, 12, 62, 155, 168, 180, 269, 280, 299, 344, 386
Sustainer: *Rabb*, Lord, Educator, 1, 8, 21, 24, 25, 28, 31, 37, 46, 47, 54, 56, 58, 61, 62, 64, 66, 68, 80, 95, 108, 123, 124, 125, 132, 155, 168, 174, 177, 180, 196, 197, 206, 209, 217, 218, 219, 231, 235, 238, 248, 249, 255, 269, 270, 280, 281, 283, 295, 296, 308, 309, 328, 340, 353, 354, 355, 370, 387, 402, 417, 428
Ṭalḥa, 38, 39
taṣawwuf: mysticism, 426
taqwā: vigilant awareness, God-consciousness, 4, 295–306, 370, 387
Ten Commandments, 26, 226, 227
Throne: *ʿarsh*, 79, 340
Torah, 26, 69, 218

trust: *tawwakul*, 19, 24, 30–44, 47, 58, 64, 73, 81, 82, 123, 132, 140, 183, 209, 224, 238, 244, 245, 291, 330, 332, 340, 363, 388, 391, 393, 394
trustworthiness: *amānah*, 7, 27, 30–44, 297, 319
truthfulness: *ṣidq*, 3, 7, 10, 11, 12, 19, 25, 33, 30–44, 71, 138, 170, 182, 183, 184, 195, 197, 222, 236, 237, 363, 368, 378, 381, 399, 446
Uḥud, 64, 88
ᶜUmar, 32, 40, 41, 59, 60, 159, 160, 272, 350, 381, 382, 400, 401, 402, 403, 397–411
Umm Kulthūm: daughter of Muḥammad and wife of ᶜUmar, 28, 101, 410
ummah: community, 2, 28, 57, 82, 100, 101, 124, 125, 137, 138, 141, 198, 258, 264, 266, 283, 307, 319, 376, 397, 399, 401, 405, 406, 407, 413, 428, 437, 440
unity: *tawḥīd*, oneness, 18, 25, 58, 69, 179, 243, 283, 286, 288, 319, 320, 321, 358, 372, 429, 435, 446
unseen: *ghayb*, 14, 219
ᶜUthmān, 38, 251, 303, 400, 402
virtue, 19, 20, 33, 84, 88, 101, 155, 156, 193, 241, 284, 285, 287, 288, 289, 296, 298, 299, 310, 311, 330, 337, 339, 344, 362, 369, 374, 377, 378, 381, 382, 383, 384, 389, 394, 411, 447
Waraqa, 23, 24, 28
will: *irāda*, 9, 17, 49, 52, 66, 81, 138, 192, 207, 222, 236, 248, 285, 286, 289, 312, 316, 320, 344, 346, 359, 367, 377, 385, 393, 394, 395, 412, 419, 445
wisdom: *ḥikmah*, 1, 10, 19, 25, 28, 59, 85, 93, 103, 132, 138, 140, 145, 158, 170, 173, 175, 176, 181, 194, 217, 227, 235, 239, 243, 249, 282, 283, 285, 288, 289, 304, 306, 308, 344, 346, 358, 394, 445
witness, 8, 16, 22, 26, 33, 48, 58, 68, 73, 81, 94, 102, 135, 144, 158, 161, 165, 171, 180, 206, 226, 227, 238, 241, 249, 250, 255, 273, 295, 296, 299, 308, 312, 313, 318, 353, 354, 373, 381, 391, 420, 426
worship: *ᶜibādah*, 1, 8, 13, 21, 37, 68, 88, 93, 100, 155, 157, 162, 173, 193, 194, 208, 219, 238, 269, 284, 285, 288, 291, 297, 302, 303, 323, 342, 349, 413, 414, 416, 417, 426
wrath: stringency, 40, 43, 68, 69, 79, 84, 94, 191, 234, 405
yearning, 157
Zakariya, 223
zakāt: (also see charity), 58, 109, 170, 197, 302
zamzam, 175
Zayd b. Saᶜya, 59, 60
Zaynab, 28, 101, 273, 418, 421
Zubayr, az-: (Az-Zubayr b. al-ᶜAwwām), 38, 84
Zul-Kifl, 178

At **The Book Foundation** our goal is to express the highest ideals of Islam and the Qur'an through publications, curricula, and other learning resources, suitable for schools, parents, and individuals, whether non-Muslims seeking to understand the Islamic perspective, or Muslims wanting to deepen their understanding of their own faith. Please visit our website: **thebook.org**

The Book of Revelations

A Sourcebook of Themes from the Holy Qur'an,

Edited by Kabir Helminski

$33 £16.95 6 x 9" 508pp

1-904510-12-4

This book invites us to recognize and reflect upon the essential spiritual themes of the Qur'an. It offers 265 titled selections of ayats, presented in a fresh contemporary translation of high literary quality, with accompanying interpretations by Muhammad Asad, Yusuf Ali, and others. It is an essential sourcebook for Muslims and non-Muslims alike.

The Book of Character

An Anthology of Writings on Virtue from Islamic and Other Sources

Edited by Camille Helminski

$33 £16.95 6 x 9" 484pp

1-904510-09-4

A collection of writings dealing with the qualities of our essential Human Nature: Faith and Trust; Repentance and Forgiveness; Compassion and Mercy; Patience and Forbearance; Modesty, Humility, and Discretion; Purity; Intention and Discernment; Generosity and Gratitude; Courage, Justice, and Right Action; Contentment and Inner Peace; Courtesy and Chivalry. From the Prophets Abraham and Moses, to the sages Confucius and Buddha, to the Prophet Muhammad, his wife, Khadija, and his companions Abu Bakr and 'Ali, through great saints like Rumi, and humanitarians like Florence Nightingale, Mother Theresa, and Martin Luther King, and even in the personal story of the bicyclist Lance Armstrong, we find stories and wisdom that will help us toward spiritual well-being.

The Book Foundation *has embarked on an important effort to develop books and teaching tools that are approachable and relevant to Muslims and non-Muslims.* ~**Shabbir Mansuri**, *Founding Director, Council on Islamic Education (CIE)*

The Book of Essential Islam

The Spiritual Training System of Islam

Ali Rafea,
with Aisha and Aliaa Rafea

$21 £10.95 6 x 9" 276 pp

1-904510-13-2

This book examines the main teachings and practices of Islam with lucidity and depth. It is a corrective to the distortions and misconceptions of Islam that abound. It can serve equally well to introduce non-Muslims to Islam, as well as to enhance Muslims understanding of their own faith. This book presents Islam as a spiritual training system that supports us in harmonizing ourselves with the Divine Order and thus with each other and our environment. It reveals the intent and inner significance of practices like ablution, ritual prayer, fasting, and pilgrimage.

The Fragrance of Faith

The Enlightened Heart of Islam

Jamal Rahman

$15.95 £9.95 6 x 9" 176pp

1-904510-08-6

The Fragrance of Faith reveals the inner Islam that has been passed down through the generations. Jamal is a link in this chain, passing along the message, just as he received it from his grandfather, a village wiseman in Bangladesh. We need reminders of this "enlightened heart of Islam" in our lives, our homes, and our schools. In Jamal Rahman's book Islam is alive and well. ~**Imam Feisal Abdul Rauf**, Author *Islam: A Sacred Law* and *What's Right With Islam*.

This heartfelt book is perfect for the classroom, whether in a Muslim context, or outside of it. It conveys a tradition of compassion and humor passed through one family that represents the best Islam has to offer. And Mr. Rahman is highly entertaining. ~**Michael Wolfe**, *The Hadj: An American's Pilgrimage to Mecca*, Producer of the PBS Documentary: *Muhammad: The Legacy of a Prophet.*

Printed in the United States
R2462000001B/R24620PG55575LVSX00001B/2}